The Guru Guide™
to Entrepreneurship

The Guru Guide™
to Entrepreneurship

A Concise Guide
to the Best Ideas
from the
World's Top Entrepreneurs

Joseph H. Boyett
and
Jimmie T. Boyett

John Wiley & Sons, Inc.
New York • Chichester • Weinheim • Brisbane • Singapore • Toronto

This book is printed on acid-free paper. ∞

Published by John Wiley & Sons, Inc.
Published simultaneously in Canada.

This publication is designed to provide accurate and authoritative information in regard to the subject
matter covered. It is sold with the understanding that the publisher is not engaged in rendering legal,
accounting, or other professional services. If legal advice or other expert assistance is required, the
services of a competent professional person should be sought.

Library of Congress Cataloging-in-Publication Data

Boyett, Joseph H.
    The guru guide to entrepreneurship: a concise guide to the best ideas from the world's
top entrepreneurs / Joseph Boyett & Jimmie Boyett.
        p. cm.
    Includes bibliographical references and index.
    ISBN 0-471-39084-4 (cloth : alk. paper)
        1. Entrepreneurship. 2. Businesspeople. 3. New business enterprises–Management.
    I. Boyett, Jimmie T. II. Title.

HB615 .B685 2000
658.4'21–dc21

                                                                        00-042886

Printed in the United States of America.

10 9 8 7 6 5 4 3 2 1

To our grandson,

Tobias Joseph Luongo,

the newest branch on our family tree.

Contents

Introduction

This book answers a very simple question: If you had all the time you needed to acquire and read all of the books and articles that you could find written by and about the world's greatest entrepreneurs—people like Bill Gates, Richard Branson, Michael Dell, and Sam Walton—what would you learn about starting and running a successful business? "Nice idea," you say, "but I don't have the time to do something like that. I've got a day job, and the kids have to be fed." Well, research is our day job and our kids are all grown now and feeding kids of their own, so we took the time to do what you might like to do yourself but can't. This book is the result of that effort. Here you will find the wisdom of 70 of the world's greatest entrepreneurs carefully extracted from more than two hundred fifty books and over two thousand articles about their ideas and exploits. *The Guru Guide™ to Entrepreneurship* is your synthesis and digest of the best thinking about what it takes to succeed on your own from the people who have been there and done it—the world's greatest entrepreneurs.

The Guru Guide™ to Entrepreneurship is a clear, concise, and informative guide to the wisdom of some of the world's most-successful entrepreneurs. You hold in your hand a digest of the best thinking about what it takes to start your own business and succeed, but we have designed this book to be more than just a digest. It also provides you with a much-needed cross-reference to the best thinking about the key issues involved in starting and running a business. The ideas of each entrepreneur are linked with those of others who agree or disagree. We identify the ideas and concepts that fit together and those that conflict. We provide you with an easy-to-follow guide to exploring the secrets of these entrepreneurs. We report on methods and results. Finally, we provide you with an evaluation of their strengths and weaknesses.

OUR GURUS

You may wonder how we decided whose ideas to include and which topics to cover. We started by making a list of the kinds of questions we would want answered if we were starting our own business. What does it take to succeed as an entrepreneur? How does a person know if he or she has the right stuff? Where do entrepreneurs get their ideas? Are some business ideas better than others? How do you pick the right business? How do you get financing? How do successful entrepreneurs find and keep customers? How do they manage money? And, finally, how do they manage people?

Once we had a list of topics, we began making a list of entrepreneurs. Some came readily to mind—Bill Gates, the cofounder of Microsoft; Sam Walton, the founder of Wal-Mart; and Ray Kroc, the founder of McDonald's Corporation. In other cases, we knew the companies but did not know much about their founders or in some cases, even who their founders were. White Castle, Netscape Communications, Home Depot, Boston Beer, TCBY, and Southwest Airlines are all examples. We ultimately developed a list of over a hundred entrepreneurs and companies. Our list covered just about every industry and type of business. We then went searching for everything we could find about them. What had been written by and about the founders of these companies that would shed light on how they answered the questions we had posed? The thoughts and ideas of some of our entrepreneur gurus were easy to find. People like Bill Gates, Sam Walton, and Michael Dell have all written books or articles outlining their management strategies and offering their advice about starting a business. The ideas of other entrepreneur gurus were harder to locate because little had been written about them or they had been so busy building their companies that they hadn't stopped to tell their stories. Still, we kept digging. We ultimately compiled data covering the thoughts and ideas of 70 entrepreneurs who became the gurus for this book. Here are the entrepreneur gurus that we selected, listed in alphabetical order. Their biographies can be found in the appendix.

Paul Allen, cofounder of Microsoft Corporation

J. Walter (Walt) Anderson, cofounder of White Castle

Marc Andreessen, cofounder of Netscape Communications

Mary Kay Ash, founder of Mary Kay Cosmetics

James L. (Jim) Barksdale, cofounder of Netscape Communications

Phineas Taylor (P.T.) Barnum, founder of "The Greatest Show on Earth"

Jeffrey P. Bezos, founder and chief executive officer (CEO) of Amazon.com°

Arthur Blank, cofounder of Home Depot

Richard Branson, founder of the Virgin Group

Charles M. Brewer, founder of MindSpring Enterprises

Warren Buffett, founder of numerous investment companies and chairman of Berkshire Hathaway, Inc.

Washington Atlee Burpee, founder of Burpee Seed Company

Tom Chappell, cofounder of Tom's of Maine, Inc.

Jim Clark, founder of Silicon Graphics and cofounder of Netscape Communications

Ben Cohen, cofounder of Ben & Jerry's Ice Cream

Finis Conner, founder of Conner Peripherals

Joshua Lionel Cowen, cofounder of Lionel Manufacturing Company

Cecil B. Day, cofounder of Days Inn of America, Inc.

Michael Dell, founder of Dell Computer Corporation

Anthony Desio, founder of Mail Boxes Etc.

Roy Disney, cofounder of Disney Brothers Studio (later Walt Disney Productions, Ltd.)

Walt Disney, cofounder of Disney Brothers Studio (later Walt Disney Productions, Ltd.)

Charles Ferguson, cofounder of Vermeer Technologies, Inc.

Debbi Fields, founder of Mrs. Fields Cookies, Inc.

Bill Gates, cofounder of Microsoft Corporation

Earl Graves, founder, publisher, and editor of *Black Enterprise*

Robert Greenberg, cofounder of L.A. Gear

Jerry Greenfield, cofounder of Ben & Jerry's Ice Cream

Bud Hadfield, founder of Kwik Kopy

Wilson Harrell, founder of over one hundred companies, columnist for *Success Magazine,* and former publisher of *Inc. Magazine*

Frank Hickingbotham, founder of TCBY (This Can't Be Yogurt)

Soichiro Honda, cofounder of Honda Motor Company, Ltd.

Wayne Huizenga, founder of Waste Management, Inc.

Masaru Ibuka, cofounder of Sony Corporation

Edgar Waldo (Billy) Ingram, cofounder of White Castle

Ken Iverson, former president, chairman, and CEO of Nucor Corporation

Steven Jobs, cofounder of Apple Computer, Inc., and cofounder of NeXT

Howard Johnson, founder of Howard Johnson Company

Herb Kelleher, founder of Southwest Airlines

Phil Knight, cofounder of Nike, Inc.

C. James (Jim) Koch, founder of Boston Beer Company

Ray Kroc, founder of McDonald's Corporation

Edwin Land, founder of Polaroid Corporation

Chris Larsen, cofounder of E-Loan

Charles Lazarus, founder of Toys "R" Us

Bill Lear, founder of Lear Jet Corporation

Bernie Marcus, cofounder of Home Depot

Konosuke Matsushita, founder of Matsushita Electric Industrial Company

James W. (Jim) McLamore, cofounder of Burger King

Edward Miller, cofounder of Spic and Span, Inc.

Tom Monaghan, founder of Domino's Pizza

Robert Mondavi, founder of Robert Mondavi Winery

Akio Morita, cofounder of Sony Corporation

David Packard, cofounder of Hewlett-Packard

Ross Perot, founder of Electronic Data Systems (EDS) and of Perot Systems Corporation

Stephen M. Pollan, financial consultant and writer

Anita Roddick, founder of The Body Shop

Bill Rosenberg, founder of Dunkin' Donuts

Pleasant Rowland, founder of Pleasant Company

Colonel Harland Sanders, founder of Kentucky Fried Chicken (KFC)

Howard Schultz, founder of Starbucks Coffee Company

Ricardo Semler, president and CEO of Semco, S.A.

Fred Smith, founder of Federal Express

Thomas Stemberg, cofounder of Staples, Inc.

R. David (Dave) Thomas, founder of Wendy's International, Inc.

Ted Turner, founder of Turner Broadcasting System, Cable News Network (CNN), and Turner Network Television (TNT)

Jay Van Andel, cofounder of Amway Corporation

Lillian Vernon, founder of Lillian Vernon Corporation

Sam Walton, founder of Wal-Mart Stores, Inc.

An Wang, founder of Wang Laboratories, Inc.

HOW WE SELECTED OUR GURUS

As you peruse our list of entrepreneur gurus, you may question some of our selections. Wait a minute, you may be saying, isn't an entrepreneur someone who starts a business? If so, then what is Ray Kroc doing on the list? Weren't the McDonald brothers the founders of McDonald's? Ray Kroc acquired franchising rights from them, but he didn't invent McDonald's, did he? We have to admit, you are right about that. And, you might be asking, how did Ricardo Semler get on the list? He didn't found Semco; he inherited it. Again, we have to admit you are right. Technically neither Kroc nor Semler founded the businesses they are so famous for running, but does that make them any less entrepreneurial than someone like Bill Gates, who cofounded Microsoft? It does if you accept only a narrow dictionary definition of the term *entrepreneur.*

We prefer something broader like that proposed by Lloyd Shefsky, author of *Entrepreneurs Are Made Not Born.* Shefsky defines the word *entrepreneur* by looking at the word in its three parts—*entre, pre,* and *neur*—and tracing them to their Latin roots. *Entre* means "enter," *pre* means "before," and *neur* means "nerve center." Thus, concludes Shefsky, an entrepreneur is someone who enters a business—any business—in time to form or change substantially that business's nerve center. Shefsky notes that entrepreneurship isn't concerned with whether people start, buy, or inherit the business they run but with what they do to develop or change the nerve center of the business itself. Kroc, Semler, and indeed all of our entrepreneur gurus certainly did that. In that respect, they are all entrepreneurs.

ORGANIZATION OF THIS BOOK

We have organized our gurus' ideas into six chapters. Each chapter covers an important issue about starting and running a business and summarizes the ideas of our panel of gurus on that issue.

Chapter 1, Should You Do It? answers the most basic of questions: What does it take to be an entrepreneur? What attributes or characteristics are essential for success? How do you know if you have what it takes to become the next Bill Gates or Sam Walton? In this chapter we provide three self-tests for entrepreneurial potential offered by our gurus. We then discuss five constants of experience and opinion that our gurus believe successful entrepreneurs share.

In **Chapter 2, The Perfect Idea,** we examine where our gurus get their ideas for businesses, how they conduct their search, and what they have learned about the necessary ingredients for a foolproof business. We outline what our gurus say are six near-perfect foundations for businesses and seven suggestions our gurus offer for sharpening any business idea to the point of perfection.

Chapter 3, Money Matters, deals with one of the activities entrepreneurs say they hate most—raising money. In this chapter we discuss our gurus' recommendations for deriving your estimate of start-up costs, raising initial capital, working with bankers and venture capitalists, managing your finances, and weighing the pros and cons of going public.

In **Chapter 4, Getting Customers,** we reveal our gurus' tricks, tips, and techniques for attracting customers. We show you how they use promotions and gimmicks to get attention, how they court the press to garner free publicity, how they conduct market research, and how they develop and use advertising.

Of course, once you attract customers, you want to keep them, which is what **Chapter 5, Keeping Customers,** is all about. We show you how our gurus calculate the value of a customer and describe nine things that our gurus consider key to keeping customers for life. Among other things, we outline our gurus' secrets for providing world-class quality and service and for listening and responding effectively to customer complaints, ideas, and suggestions.

In our concluding chapter, **Chapter 6, Managing People,** we discuss how our gurus hire, inspire, motivate, reward, and when necessary, fire the people who work for them. We explain in this chapter why our gurus feel it is a mistake to try to hire people for specific jobs and why it is good to be a tough boss. We reveal our gurus' secrets for developing team spirit and how they empower people to do what is right to exceed customer expectations all the time.

SOME GUIDANCE FOR WHAT FOLLOWS: HOW THE CHAPTERS ARE ORGANIZED

Throughout *The Guru Guide™ to Entrepreneurship,* we have tried to summarize as clearly, succinctly, and objectively as possible our gurus' key ideas. Our personal opinions are expressed in sections entitled "Our View" and preceded by the following icon:

OUR VIEW

At the beginning of each chapter, we use the following icon to identify the gurus whose ideas are covered in that chapter. For example, the chapter on managing people begins as follows:

MANAGING PEOPLE—The Gurus

At the end of each chapter, we provide a summary of the key ideas presented in that chapter. Key ideas are identified by the following icon:

KEY POINTS

You can read this book straight through, from beginning to end, covering the topics in the order we present them, or you can go directly to a topic that interests you. You can read the chapters in any order you wish, because each chapter has been designed to stand on its own. We therefore encourage you to start with whatever topic is of most interest to you at the moment. If you are interested in specific gurus, check the index or the guru lists at the beginning of each chapter to find out where they appear in the book and proceed accordingly. You are in control of how you read this book. In fact, this advice is a good summary of the message contained herein. You are in control, or at least you had better be.

So here it is—an unbiased but highly opinionated look at the best advice the world's greatest entrepreneurs have to offer about starting and running your own business or making the business you now run even better. We wish you good reading and success in all your entrepreneurial endeavors. If you have comments about *The Guru Guide™ to Entrepreneurship* or would like to learn about other *Guru Guides™* as they become available, please visit our Web site at http://www.jboyett.com or e-mail us at Boyett@jboyett.com.

Joseph H. Boyett
Jimmie T. Boyett

Marc Andreessen, cofounder of Netscape Communications

Mary Kay Ash, founder of Mary Kay Cosmetics

Richard Branson, founder of the Virgin Group

Ben Cohen, cofounder of Ben & Jerry's Ice Cream

Walt Disney, cofounder of Disney Brothers Studio (later Walt Disney Productions, Ltd.)

Debbi Fields, founder of Mrs. Fields Cookies, Inc.

Bill Gates, cofounder of Microsoft Corporation

Earl Graves, founder, publisher, and editor of *Black Enterprise*

Jerry Greenfield, cofounder of Ben & Jerry's Ice Cream

Bud Hadfield, founder of Kwik Kopy

Wilson Harrell, founder of over one hundred companies, columnist for *Success Magazine,* and former publisher of *Inc. Magazine*

Soichiro Honda, cofounder of Honda Motor Company, Ltd.

Wayne Huizenga, founder of Waste Management, Inc.

Masaru Ibuka, cofounder of Sony Corporation

Howard Johnson, founder of Howard Johnson Company

Ray Kroc, founder of McDonald's Corporation

Edwin Land, founder of Polaroid Corporation

Bill Lear, founder of Lear Jet Corporation

James W. (Jim) McLamore, cofounder of Burger King

Tom Monaghan, founder of Domino's Pizza

Robert Mondavi, founder of Robert Mondavi Winery

Akio Morita, cofounder of Sony Corporation

Anita Roddick, founder of The Body Shop

Pleasant Rowland, founder of Pleasant Company

Howard Schultz, founder of Starbucks Coffee Company

Fred Smith, founder of Federal Express

Thomas Stemberg, cofounder of Staples, Inc.

R. David (Dave) Thomas, founder of Wendy's International, Inc.

Ted Turner, founder of Turner Broadcasting System, Cable News Network (CNN), and Turner Network Television (TNT)

Jay Van Andel, cofounder of Amway Corporation

Lillian Vernon, founder of Lillian Vernon Corporation

Sam Walton, founder of Wal-Mart Stores, Inc.

An Wang, founder of Wang Laboratories, Inc.

Should You Do It?

We start this book about entrepreneurship seeking answers to the most basic of questions: What does it take to be an entrepreneur? What attributes or characteristics are essential for success? How do you know if you have what it takes to become the next Bill Gates or Sam Walton? What questions should you ask yourself before you quit Father Corporation and Mama Employer and strike out on your own?

Being entrepreneurs themselves, our gurus have grappled with such questions. Their answers are scattered throughout their writings, and we have harvested as many of those answers as we could find. Some entrepreneurs made it easy for us. They have posed questions they think you should ask yourself to gauge your mettle. We begin our quest for answers with the questions these entrepreneur gurus pose. Then we turn to an examination of some recurring themes, warnings, and admonitions that populate the writings and interviews of our other gurus. What does it take to succeed as an entrepreneur today? Quite a lot, it turns out.

DO YOU HAVE WHAT IT TAKES? SOME BASIC SELF-TESTS

Let's start with questions posed by three of our gurus. We invite you to score your entrepreneurial potential by checking off those questions to which you can answer positively. The more questions you can truthfully check off, the greater the likelihood you have what it takes.

You may know the first guru, Lillian Katz, better by the name Lillian Vernon. She is the founder of the $258 million direct-marketing company Lillian Vernon Corporation. Exhibit 1.1 contains 10 questions Vernon thinks you should ask yourself before you attempt to start your own business.

EXHIBIT 1.1. **Lillian Vernon's Questions to Determine If You Are an Entrepreneur**

✓	QUESTION	LILLIAN VERNON'S COMMENTS
❏	1. Do you have the necessary commitment?	To succeed, you must feel passionate about the work you have chosen. Lukewarm enthusiasm will not sustain you through the challenges you will face in a start-up business.
❏	2. Are you prepared to work extremely hard?	Launching your own business demands long hours of labor. Are you sure you want to give up a good part of your social life: your weekends, golf games, and vacations? For your developing business to succeed, you will need to focus all your energies on it.
❏	3. Do you have the mental stamina and concentration to meet the demands your project will impose on you?	If your attention flags, you may jeopardize your venture.
❏	4. Do you: a. Accept new ideas easily? b. Treat other people's ideas with respect? c. Make decisions right away?	An entrepreneur must be open-minded, flexible, and able to respond to new ideas.
❏	5. Are you prepared to spend time analyzing a problem and finding a solution?	No matter how carefully you plan, you are bound to run into an unforeseen problem now and then. Be prepared to cope with such a situation.
❏	6. Are you ready to commit to the long term?	A company's success is never an overnight miracle. That is one reason you must be absolutely certain that you love your work—there will be a lot of it.

(continued)

EXHIBIT 1.1. **(continued)**

✓	QUESTION	LILLIAN VERNON'S COMMENTS
☐	7. Do you have adequate backup resources?	Banks and other financial institutions seldom lend money to start-up businesses. Will family members or friends invest in your company or tide you over during a rough patch?
☐	8. Are you good at concentrating on detail?	Often, no one but you will be able to take care of small items. An entrepreneur's life is not one of ideas alone.
☐	9. Are you ready to sit down and write a careful analysis of your business prospects?	Without a best-case/worst-case scenario to guide you through the first years, you may be in for an unpleasant surprise or two. Be aware and be prepared.
☐	10. Are you an optimist by nature?	Mistakes and setbacks are bound to occur. Can you learn from your mistakes without getting derailed or discouraged?

Source: Adapted from Lillian Vernon, An Eye for Winners: How I Built One of America's Greatest Direct-Mail Businesses (New York: HarperCollins, 1996), pp. 204–205.

Next, we turn to a series of questions posed by Earl Graves, the founder, publisher, and editor of *Black Enterprise,* in his book *How to Succeed in Business without Being White* (see Exhibit 1.2). Graves addresses his questions specifically to African-American entrepreneurs, but we think these questions are good ones to answer regardless of your race or gender. He warns that entrepreneurship is not an easy road, and his questions bear that out.

EXHIBIT 1.2. **Earl Graves's Questions concerning What It Takes to Be an African-American Entrepreneur**

✓	QUESTION	EARL GRAVES'S COMMENTS
☐	1. Do you have a junkyard-dog mentality?	If you don't know what that means, you've never climbed a junkyard fence and encountered a guard dog trained to get a grip on you and not let go. True entrepreneurs don't let go. If one venture fails, they try another. If one product doesn't sell, they look for a better idea. If one company official isn't buying, they look for another who is. Like the junkyard dog, they hang on no matter how much they are shaken, cursed, beaten and kicked because they stay focused on the task at hand.

(continued)

EXHIBIT 1.2. **(continued)**

✓	QUESTION	EARL GRAVES'S COMMENTS
❏	2. Are you willing to take a risky leap, but only after a good look?	Successful entrepreneurs are not afraid to make leaps, but they look first. They don't have a death wish, but they are willing to take a risk to accomplish their goals. The really good ones take a risk only after they've established a Plan B and even a Plan C and Plan D to fall back on. They know what they are getting into and how they can get out.
❏	3. Do you have a talent for focusing on solutions rather than problems?	Entrepreneurs are usually natural leaders, and while the people around them are busy pointing at problems and pitfalls, entrepreneurs are usually engaged in finding solutions and bridges over the trouble spots. I have no patience with people who want to tell me what's wrong. I only want to hear from the person who first tells me the solution and then fills me in on the problem. I don't want to hear that your basement is flooded. I want to hear that you've found the phone number of the cleanup company. Then tell me why you're calling them.
❏	4. Do you have a high level of energy?	If you are doing business with me, chances are you can expect a call anywhere from six in the morning until, well, nearly six the next morning. And it might come while I'm on my exercise bike, in the car, riding a train or on an airplane. A real entrepreneur never rests. If you're the kind of person who likes to go home on Friday night and hit the hammock or stay on the golf course for the entire weekend, you won't cut it as an entrepreneur.
❏	5. Do you have a drive to make money so that you can make more money?	Other people might set a goal of making money so that they can buy a fancy house, send their kids to private schools or pay off debts. Entrepreneurs will do those things, but most are driven to make money so that they can use it to make even more. They never say, "I've got enough money." They are capitalists to the bone, and the product is not as important as the return on investment. If there is an opportunity to make more, they'll generally pursue it.

(continued)

EXHIBIT 1.2. **(continued)**		
✓	QUESTION	EARL GRAVES'S COMMENTS
❏	6. Do you have a talent for starting companies, but not necessarily managing them?	Like most entrepreneurs, I get my biggest kick out of finding and developing new companies and new products, though I no longer have a great deal of interest in micromanaging my businesses. I keep a close eye on my managers, mind you, but I prefer to focus on the long-range plans and opportunities. That is typical of most entrepreneurs, and it is also a reason why many of them have problems running the businesses they have launched.
❏	7. Are you flexible?	The only thing that owning a soft drink bottling franchise and publishing a magazine have in common is that both are businesses that if run right will make money. Good entrepreneurs are flexible and adaptable. They can learn what they need to learn about an industry in order to make money in it. They leave the technical stuff to the hired experts. Entrepreneurs are focused on the profit potential, not the ingredients or chemical composition of the product.
❏	8. Do you have an abundance of courage?	Of all the qualities typically cited as crucial to the makeup of a successful entrepreneur, none is more taken for granted than pure courage. Countless would-be entrepreneurs armed with Ivy League MBAs, the latest management theories and fail-safe concepts fall by the wayside because they don't have the guts for it. On the other hand, many entrepreneurs armed only with dedication and intestinal fortitude thrive.

Source: Adapted from Earl Graves and Robert L. Crandall, How to Succeed in Business without Being White: Straight Talk on Making It in America (New York: HarperBusiness, 1997), pp. 123–126.

Finally, listed in Exhibit 1.3 are 10 questions posed by Dave Thomas, the founder and spokesperson for Wendy's fast-food chain. Thomas believes that you should not even think about a business you might open until you have first taken a close look at "what makes you click." He suggests that you think of your answers to the questions he raises as a kind of personal inventory that will help you decide if you have the personality to be an entrepreneur.

EXHIBIT 1.3. **Dave Thomas's Ten Questions to Ask Yourself before Starting Your Own Business**

✓	QUESTION	DAVE THOMAS'S COMMENTS
❏	1. After you achieve something, do you like to go ahead and do something new?	Do you like to sit back and savor [your achievements], or is the success quickly yesterday's news as far as you're concerned? I'm not saying that sitting back is wrong. I often wish that I could, but achieving the last challenge doesn't stick with me long. It's never enough. When I [succeed at something] I [want] to move on to do new things. Most entrepreneurs are like this.
❏	2. Are you willing to commit all of your time and energy to an idea?	You'd better know if you're prepared to be single-minded about something. The best way to find out is to look at your past. Have you done it before? Did you like doing it?
❏	3. Do you have self-confidence?	A person can do anything he or she wants to do [but cannot] do something if they don't want to. It's a matter of personal choice. It helps if you have self-confidence, if you believe in yourself, and have family and friends who believe in you, too. Self-confidence is something most of us have to work at constantly. We have to think positive thoughts, and take care not to let the jerks of this world get us down. Some of the most unlikely people will try to shake your confidence by throwing their education, their money, or their social position in your face. They try to make themselves feel big by making you feel small.
❏	4. Do you like to work with people?	There is nothing I ever achieved that didn't involve plenty of other people. You can't do it alone, that's for sure. And, remember: Who's going to run the business and keep it going if you decide you want to move on and do something else?
❏	5. Are you willing to slice the pie?	Along with liking to work with other people, you have to be able to share the successes—to give others an ownership stake and part of the rewards. People who are focused on themselves and don't enjoy sharing usually don't make good entrepreneurs.

(continued)

EXHIBIT 1.3. **(continued)**

✓	QUESTION	DAVE THOMAS'S COMMENTS
❑	6. Do you want to be an innovator or a creator?	In my mind, the difference between being innovative and being creative is that creators invent things, while innovators use inventions in new ways. We've done a lot of innovative things at Wendy's—the Pick-Up Window and the square hamburger are two. We didn't invent the salad bar or the stuffed baked potato, but we were the first ones to put them into a national chain of quick-service restaurants. Creators like to perfect things, innovators want to apply them. Entrepreneurs are mostly innovators.
❑	7. Even when things are going well, are you always trying to fix problems?	Back in 1975, when the Wendy's business had been opened only six years, I used to keep a list of all the stores in the bottom 10% of sales. Whenever a store hit that group, we would throw in extra promotions, more advertising, and coupons. It was a simple program, but it worked, and it saved a lot of stores that proved later to be winners from being closed in the early days. Some people like to polish the best of what they do better; I'm more concerned with getting everything up to the same high standard.
❑	8. Are you always trying to learn from others?	Keep thinking, "How can I improve myself and do better?" One way is to learn from other people and not resent them for their success. I never resented anyone for owning anything. I just wanted to figure out how I could own something myself. Too many people spend all of their energy being resentful and jealous, instead of using that energy to benefit themselves. The bottom line is to find out how someone became successful, learn from that, and then go out and do it.
❑	9. Do you think there's a solution to every problem?	No problem is too small because small problems can grow into big ones. For example, every now and then, I get claustrophobic. It makes me nervous to ride in elevators and in the backseat of cars. One time I was riding in the backseat of a limousine with President Gerald Ford and I started feeling closed in. Instead of going into a panic and spoiling the day for myself, I looked out the window and stared outside. When I am on an elevator that is crowded, I get off at the next floor and wait for one that is not so full. But I don't stop riding elevators. Just don't ever stop looking for solutions.

(continued)

✓	QUESTION	DAVE THOMAS'S COMMENTS

EXHIBIT 1.3. **(continued)**

❏ 10. Can you rely on your business intuition?

Can you live with the downside—really live with it? Can your family live with it, and do they understand it as well as they should? Lots of people will bravely say, "Let's go for it. It doesn't matter if we're broke tomorrow." But they don't try to imagine what they would have to sacrifice if they only had half of their current income and none of their benefits for a few months.

On the other hand, if you need lots of studies and information to make decisions, it's risky to be on your own in business. You can't afford that kind of comfort. Had I said, "Let's go research this Wendy's idea and see how we make a niche for ourselves," the first Wendy's would never have been built.

Source: Adapted from R. David Thomas, Dave's Way (New York: Berkley Books, 1992), pp. 214–218.

Well, how did you do? Do you have what it takes, or did the questions and comments raise a few hairs on the back of your neck? If you are like most people, you probably have at least one or two hairs reaching for the stars.

Vernon, Graves, and Thomas cover a lot of ground, and you might ask: Are these just their ideas or do they reflect the thinking of most successful entrepreneurs? To be honest, we may not be able to answer that question fully. We examined the ideas of over a hundred entrepreneurs in conducting the research for this book, but of course, there are many more successful entrepreneurs. What we can say, however, is that many of the characteristics that Vernon, Graves, and Thomas mention—such as commitment, willingness to work hard, self-confidence, high energy level, and so on—are also mentioned by most of the other gurus we examined. They tend to discuss them, however, in response to one common characteristic shared by all entrepreneurs. This universal entrepreneurial characteristic is the explicit or implicit topic of much of our gurus' musings about the necessary ingredients for successful entrepreneurship. It has to do with membership in a very special club. Successful entrepreneurs pay dues to join this club. Unsuccessful entrepreneurs, and the rest of us, never join the club—or if we do, we resign quickly. What club is this? Wilson Harrell, the entrepreneur extraordinaire and columnist for *Success Magazine,* called it simply "Club

Terror."[1] According to Harrell, admission to this exclusive club is automatic for all entrepreneurs, permission to join is neither needed nor sought, and tenure is indefinite. We will spend the remainder of this chapter discussing Club Terror because if you believe our gurus, the ability to pay the dues of this club is *the* defining characteristic of all entrepreneurs. We will share with you what we learned about the severity of the dues and how our gurus found the resources to pay the price of membership.

WELCOME TO CLUB TERROR

When you become an entrepreneur, writes Wilson Harrell, you "no longer . . . have to be bothered with such ordinary feelings as concern, frustration, or even fear. Those genteel things are the least of your troubles now. You can put them away as a child puts away toys. From now on, you will be in the grip of a human emotion that the good Lord, or more likely His nemesis, created just for entrepreneurs."[2] For Harrell, true terror isn't fear like the sudden rush of adrenaline that you feel when you are almost hit by a drunk driver. It isn't accidental, unexpected, or short-lived. It is, instead, "a private world filled with monsters sucking at every morsel of your being . . . [where] there can be no sleep . . . just wide-awake nightmares."[3] He compares Club Terror to an experience of his during World War II:

> As a fighter pilot during World War II, . . . I was shot down behind enemy lines. There, badly burned, I was picked up by members of the French Underground, who devised a unique and cynical way to hide me from the Germans: They buried me in a cornfield with a hose stuck in my mouth so I could breathe. The first time they buried me, I lay there for four hours—time enough to consider all the bleak possibilities. I figured the Germans would 1) stick a bayonet through the dirt and into me; 2) riddle the hole with bullets; 3) accidentally kick the hose; or, worst of all, 4) turn on the faucet. For 11 days in succession, I was buried. For 11 days I lived with a new and unwanted friend—stark, raving fear.[4]

Harrell remarks that his experience in the war may have been the ultimate in fear but that his experience as an entrepreneur has been almost as grueling. When asked why anyone would want to voluntarily put themselves through such torture, he continues his war story. Along with the terror, notes Harrell, he was amazed to discover that he felt a kind of exhilaration that he had never felt before: "Each time the French partisans dug me up, I was amazed at how high I felt. I was elated. I had conquered fear and I knew it. Of course, it helped quite a bit that I was still alive."[5]

To conquer fear and know it. To be elated. To feel *alive.* To have survived in the face of impossible odds. It seems that, in addition to the "monsters sucking at your being," Club Terror offers something else—a high that people who have what it takes to be entrepreneurs find irresistible. For most of us, the emotional high promised by Club Terror carries too great a price tag. We just can't summon what it takes to sustain our membership, so we never join or we drop out quickly. Consequently, we never experience either the terror or the high. Successful entrepreneurs summon the resources to pay their Club Terror dues, and this is how they do it.

PAYING CLUB TERROR DUES

As we read the biographies, autobiographies, and interviews of successful entrepreneurs, we were struck by several recurring themes—constants of experience and opinion that our gurus share. Think of them as a few basic requirements for entrepreneurship. If you want to be a successful entrepreneur, insist our gurus, you must do the following:

- Embrace failure.
- Reject money as your goal.
- Exhibit a dogged determination.
- Sacrifice your personal life.
- Believe passionately in your vision.

We expand on each of these requirements in the following sections.

Requirement #1: Embrace Failure

The terror in Club Terror often comes from a fear of failure. When starting out, entrepreneurs frequently risk their entire life savings and substantial portions of the life savings of friends and relatives. Mary Kay Ash, founder of Mary Kay Cosmetics, describes what it was like when she started her business:

> When we started our business [in 1963], we were well aware of the risks. Every single penny I had went into the investment. My son Richard, a life insurance agent, quit his $480-a-month job to work with his mother on her "crazy idea" at $250 a month. A few months later my son Ben gave up a $750-a-month job in Houston and moved his family to Dallas to join us—for the same pay as his younger brother's!
>
> Richard and Ben took substantial reductions in salary, and my lifetime savings of $5,000 was on the line. I desperately wanted to start my own business—it was my only chance to be self-employed. All bridges were burned behind us.[6]

Ash's experience is common to many entrepreneurs. It is only natural in such a situation to feel fear, even terror; yet, successful entrepreneurs persevere. They do the following in response to their fears:

- Take the risk out of the risks.
- Persevere through their failures.
- Learn from their failures.

Taking the Risk out of Risk

Randy Fields, husband of Debbi Fields, the founder of Mrs. Fields Cookies, writes that his experience with his wife and other entrepreneurs has convinced him that entrepreneurs are not risk takers in their own minds. "Ask an entrepreneur if his idea is going to work," says Fields, "and [the entrepreneur will reply], 'Of course, it will.'"[7] Fields jokes that he believes this inability on his wife's part, and on the part of other entrepreneurs, to perceive and be intimidated by the possibility of failure is a "mental defect."[8] Defect or not, Wilson Harrell asserts that this ability to convince oneself that risky ideas aren't so risky is essential to an entrepreneur's success.

It is no achievement to walk a tightrope laid flat on the floor. Where there is no risk, there can be no pride in achievement and, consequently, no happiness.

Ray Kroc[9]

One of the ways entrepreneurs convince themselves that their idea is going to work is to weigh the risks and find them acceptable. For example, Richard Branson, founder of Virgin Airlines and the rest of the Virgin Group, examines the downside in everything he does and prepares for the worst. When he started Virgin Airlines, Branson bought just one plane, later explaining, "I had an agreement with Boeing to take it back if things didn't work out."[10] Upon weighing the consequences if her company were to fail, Debbi Fields reasoned, "Gosh, is that the worst thing that can happen? I'm going to go into the cookie business and lose the $50,000. I'd have to figure out a way to pay it back. I'm willing to do that."[11]

> I look at it this way: I've been broke five times in my life. One more time won't hurt.
>
> *Walt Disney*[12]

Persevering through Failure

Although Fields didn't fail, others did—some of them multiple times. For example, Bud Hadfield, who founded Kwik Kopy, recalls that his early entrepreneurial career was quite a struggle: "In a fairly short period of time, I rang up an impressive record of failed businesses. There was my half-interest in a pig farm; the pigs ate so much I virtually gave my half away. I went broke with an ice cream parlor, a gas station, a frozen food business, a fireworks stand and a personnel agency."[13]

Finally, in 1966 Hadfield ran out of reasons to fail and succeeded for a while with a printing company he called Instant Print. That same year Hadfield got a letter from a lawyer in Chicago threatening legal action. "The letter said if we continued to use that name, they would sue us, throw us in jail, take away our children—the usual threats." As a result, Hadfield was forced to find a new name for his business. His wife suggested "Quick Copy" with a "K" (Kwik Kopy). For your logo, she continued, "you could have one K chasing another K."[14]

> My attitude toward mistakes in business is somewhat similar to my attitude toward failed experiments in technology. Both are inevitable and provide valuable feedback that can direct you to the right path.
>
> *An Wang*[15]

Hadfield's story is typical of many successful entrepreneurs. Their history is one of failure after failure until one day they hit upon the right idea or right circumstances and finally succeed. Entrepreneurs know, remarks Debbi Fields, that they only truly fail when they stop trying, because it is only then that failure becomes official. They view failures as hurdles that may hurt their shins but don't prevent them from chugging along. And, says Fields, failures can also be blessings in disguise, "signs of your destiny correcting itself. . . . Failures can lead you in a new and better direction [whereas] successes can sometimes be diversions, because they let you think you had everything solved when that turns out not to be true."[16]

Learning from Failure

Edwin Land, founder of Polaroid Corporation, compares the entrepreneurial experience to scientific research, where "you fail and fail and fail, and when you succeed you stop."[17] Mary Kay Ash calls this pattern "failing forward to success" and says that it has been the pattern of her business life:

> I failed miserably at my very first Mary Kay beauty show. I was anxious to prove that our skin-care products could be sold to small groups of women, and I wanted to make my first show a huge success. But that evening I sold a grand total of $1.50. When I left, I drove around the corner, put my head on the steering wheel, and cried. "What's wrong with those people?" I asked myself. "Why didn't they buy this fantastic product?" Bursts of fear flashed through my mind. My initial reaction was to doubt my new business venture. I became worried because my lifetime savings were tied up in the company. I looked in the mirror and asked myself, "What did you do wrong, Mary Kay?" Then it hit, I had never even bothered to ask anyone for an order. I had forgotten to pass out order cards and had just expected those women to buy automatically! You can bet I didn't make the same mistake at the next beauty show.
>
> Yes, I failed—and for a few brief moments I was fearful. But after analyzing what had happened, I learned from that failure.[18]

Even Sam Walton, founder of Wal-Mart, experienced failures and setbacks, but he prided himself in learning from those experiences. Walton purchased a Ben Franklin variety store in Newport, Arkansas, in 1945. He set as his personal five-year goal the task of making his store the most profitable variety store in the region. At the end of that time, Walton thought he had succeeded, but an innocuous legal oversight cost him his success. Here is how he described what he learned from that experience:

My five years in Newport were about up, and I had met my goal. That little Ben Franklin store was doing $250,000 in sales a year, and turning $30,000 to $40,000 a year in profit. It was the number-one Ben Franklin store—for sales or profit—not only in Arkansas, but in the whole six-state region. It was the largest variety store of any sort in Arkansas, and I don't believe there was a bigger one in the three or four neighboring states.

Every crazy thing we tried hadn't turned out . . . well, . . . of course, but we hadn't made any mistakes we couldn't correct quickly, none so big that they threatened the business. Except, it turned out, for one little legal error we made right at the beginning. In all my excitement at becoming Sam Walton, merchant, I had neglected to include a clause in my lease which gave me an option to renew after the first five years.

And our success, it turned out, had attracted a lot of attention. My landlord, the department store owner, was so impressed with our Ben Franklin's success that he decided not to renew our lease at any price—knowing full well that we had nowhere else in town to move the store. He did offer to buy the franchise, fixtures, and inventory at a fair price; he wanted to give the store to his son. I had no alternative but to give it up. . . .

It was the low point of my business life. I felt sick to my stomach. I couldn't believe it was happening to me. It really was like a nightmare. I had built the best variety store in the whole region and worked hard in the community, done everything right—and now I was being kicked out of town. It didn't seem fair. I blamed myself for ever getting suckered into such an awful lease, and I was furious at the landlord. Helen [Walton's wife], just settling in with a brand-new family of four, was heartsick at the prospect of leaving Newport. But that's what we were going to do.

I've never been one to dwell on reverses, and I didn't do so then. It's not just a corny saying that you can make a positive out of most any negative if you work at it hard enough. I've always thought of problems as challenges, and this one wasn't any different. I don't know if that experience changed me or not. I know I read my leases a lot more carefully after that, and maybe I became a little more wary of just how tough the world can be. Also, it may have been about then that I began encouraging our oldest boy—six-year-old Bob—to become a lawyer. But I didn't dwell on my disappointment. The challenge at hand was simple enough to figure out. I had to pick myself up and get on with it, do it all over again, only even better this time.[19]

Later, Walton was to call his Newport experience a blessing in disguise. He had a chance for a brand-new start. So, he started over and did it again—only even better. It was a typical entrepreneurial response to failure—pick yourself up, ask what you can learn from the experience, and try again, even better this time.

Requirement #2: Reject Money as a Goal

As Wilson Harrell roamed around the country making speeches to budding entrepreneurs, he would always ask his audience the same questions:

"What's your motivation?"
"What are you after?"
"What, in your mind, constitutes success?"

Predictably, the answers he received often revolved around money, power, influence, or something specific such as big homes, yachts, and private planes. Harrell would give members of his audience with those kinds of answers the following advice:

If you've got a job, keep it. If you haven't, go try and get one, because I don't think you're going to make it as an entrepreneur. . . . Most entrepreneurs fail because they're not entrepreneurs in the first place. Entrepreneurs are a special breed, with the gate to their kingdom well-guarded against the greedy and get-rich-quick. Many knock, few are admitted. Entrepreneurship is about more than money, power or influence.[20]

Our gurus repeatedly maintain that they are not and were not motivated by money. In fact, Richard Branson recalls that the great fortune he made was often bittersweet. After he sold Virgin Records, he was enormously rich but grieving. "I remember walking down the street [after the sale was completed]. I was crying," he writes. "Tears . . . [were] streaming down my face. And there I was holding a check for a billion dollars. . . . If you'd seen me, you would have thought I was loony. A billion dollars."[21] Still Branson wasn't happy. It wasn't the money that mattered.

> [Money] is not the motivator or even the measure of my success.
>
> Marc Andreessen[22]

Some gurus become almost indignant when asked about money. They can't understand the obsession some people seem to have with it. As a case in point, consider Bill Gates's response to an insistent reporter's questioning in a December 1990 interview:

Q: What does all the money you have mean to you?

Gates: I don't have any money. I have stock. I own about 35 percent of the shares of Microsoft, and I take a salary of $175,000 a year.

Q: Yes, but you sold about $30 million worth of Microsoft stock, didn't you?

Gates: About a year ago.

Q: Most people still consider that "money." Don't you?

Gates: Yes, that's money, . . . that's money.

Q: Now that we've established that you do have money, what does it mean to you?[23]

After this exchange, Gates went on to argue that all money really meant to him was that he didn't have to worry about the price of a meal in a restaurant and that he would be able to have a nice house overlooking Lake Washington. He declared that his primary concern wasn't the money; it was selling software.

Sam Walton and Ted Turner (founder of Turner Broadcasting System) have expressed similar disdain for their accumulated wealth (see Exhibits 1.4 and 1.5).

One reason for not having money as your primary goal, say our gurus, is that the single-minded pursuit of personal wealth will very likely make it impossible for you ever to gain real wealth. If you chase money, declares Debbi Fields, you'll never catch it. Ted Turner explains why: "If you think money is a real big deal, . . . you'll be too scared of losing it to get it."[24]

In short, if you are afraid of losing money, you won't take the prudent risks that all entrepreneurs must take to succeed. The money-stealing monsters of Club Terror will win.

EXHIBIT 1.4. **Sam Walton on What Money Meant to Him**

In his 1993 book *Sam Walton: Made in America, My Story*, Walton discussed his attitude about his wealth:

> Here's the thing: money never has meant that much to me. . . . If we had enough groceries, and a nice place to live, plenty of room to keep and feed my bird dogs, a place to hunt, a place to play tennis, and the means to get the kids good educations—that's rich. . . .
>
> We're not ashamed of having money, but I just don't believe a big showy lifestyle is appropriate for anywhere, least of all here in Bentonville where folks work hard for their money and where we all know that everyone puts on their trousers one leg at a time. . . . I still can't believe it was news that I get my hair cut at the barbershop. Where else would I get it cut? Why do I drive a pickup truck? What am I supposed to haul my dogs around in, a Rolls-Royce?

Sam Walton

Source: Sam Walton and John Huey, Sam Walton: Made in America, My Story (New York: Bantam Books, 1993), pp. 9–10.

EXHIBIT 1.5. **Ted Turner on the Importance of Money**

Ted Turner, founder of CNN, lays it right on the line in his own inimitable fashion. Don't worry about the money, he says, other things are more important.

> Years ago, there was a time when my stock had been rising quickly. I knew how many shares of stock I had. (I only had one stock; I've only had one stock. I've never had time to play the market.) So I figured out that if the stock hit a certain point, I was going to be a billionaire, and I'm still in the tiny office where I was when I was only worth a few million. I couldn't tell anyone at the office. All of my friends were working at the company; the highest-paid person was making $100,000. I was so much richer than my other friends in Atlanta that I couldn't tell them—they'd think I was bragging. I did go home and tell my wife, and she said, "I don't care. I've got to help the kids with their homework." No one even cared. I thought bells and whistles would go off. Nothing happened at all. Ever since then, having great wealth is one of the most disappointing things. It's overrated, I can tell you that. It's not as good as average sex. Average sex is better that being a billionaire. It's good to know so you don't have to worry about it too much.

Ted Turner

Source: "The Wit and Wisdom of Ted Turner," Across the Board, July–August 1997, p. 13.

◉ OUR VIEW

Although our gurus maintain that they are not motivated by money and would do their jobs even if they were not compensated, that is not to say that they would volunteer to give up their stock options or ask their boards to take them off the payroll.

Of course, our gurus aren't saying that money doesn't matter. In fact, Chapter 3 is devoted to this topic. What the gurus are saying is that money is not their primary objective. Money may be a way of keeping score, and it is always necessary for financing the pursuit of a dream, but rarely, if ever, should it be considered an end in itself. Instead, they recommend doing something you were born to do and having fun making money while you do it.

> Success should not be measured in dollars. It's about how you conduct the journey, and how big your heart is at the end of it.
>
> *Howard Schultz*[25]

Do What You Love and Get Paid for It

First and foremost, say our gurus, success means doing something you find to be fun. Richard Branson recalls that 1993 was a watershed year for his company. Virgin was making money and finally had become a strong brand name that could be used to launch a wide variety of businesses. "At this point," he notes, "I could have retired and concentrated my energies on learning how to paint watercolors or how to beat my mum at golf. It wasn't in my nature to do so. People asked me, 'Why don't you have some fun now?' but they were missing the point. As far as I was concerned, this was fun."[26]

> Life is too precious to be wasted in doing work you don't love.
>
> *Tom Monaghan*[27]

Our gurus add that it is also important to do something that you believe is worthwhile—something for which you would like to be remembered.

EXHIBIT 1.6. **Ben & Jerry's Mission Statement**

We're in business to make and serve the best all natural ice cream, frozen yogurt, and sorbet, to provide fair economic return to our staff and our shareholders, and to include an active concern for the community in our day-to-day decisions. As a company

- we have a progressive, nonpartisan social agenda;
- we seek peace by supporting nonviolent ways to resolve conflict;
- we will look for ways to create economic opportunities for the disenfranchised;
- we are committed to practicing caring capitalism;
- we seek to minimize our negative impact on the environment;
- we support sustainable methods of food production and family farming.

There will always be differences of opinion about how we actualize our mission, but a commitment to the intent of our mission is an essential part of membership at Ben & Jerry's. No amount of expertise can compensate for a lack of commitment to our mission and to our aspirations. In calling these "Our Aspirations" we are mindful that we will constantly be striving to reach these ideals.

Source: Ben Cohen, Jerry Greenfield, and Meredith Maran, Ben & Jerry's Double-Dip: How to Run a Values-Led Business and Make Money Too (New York: Simon & Schuster, 1997), p. 173.

Pleasant Rowland, founder of Pleasant Company (manufacturer of the American Girl doll) quotes Yeats: "Look up in the sun's eye and see what the exultant heart calls good, that some new day may breed the best because we gave, not what they would, but the right twigs for an eagle's nest."[28]

Many of our gurus began with a mission or a vision of doing something worthwhile. For example, Ben Cohen and Jerry Greenfield, cofounders of Ben & Jerry's Ice Cream, wanted to do more than just sell ice cream. They wanted to create a company that was employee friendly, was environmentally sensitive, and generated a fair return to investors (see Exhibit 1.6).

Our gurus argue that you will not have the courage to endure Club Terror over the long term if you are not having fun doing something you feel is worthwhile.

OUR VIEW

We applaud the gurus' invocation to pursue worthwhile ventures. Nonetheless, we caution novice entrepreneurs not to lose site of fundamental business practices. Many of the successful entrepreneurs discussed in this book, including Ben Cohen and Jerry Greenfield, Tom Chappell, cofounder of Tom's of Maine, and Anita Roddick, founder of The Body Shop, had to be rescued by business practitioners who did not necessarily share their high ideals and values or, in the words of Yeats, the desire to build an eagle's nest.

Requirement #3: Junkyard-Dogged Determination

In Exhibit 1.2 we listed eight questions posed by Earl Graves for determining if you have what it takes to become a successful entrepreneur. Graves's first question was, "Do you have a junkyard-dog mentality?" For him, this means that "True entrepreneurs don't let go."[29] A dogged determination to succeed in the face of what seems like impossible odds is the defining characteristic of entrepreneurs cited by all of our gurus. For example, Howard Johnson, founder of Howard Johnson Company, explains, "Most projects that fail do so simply because their initiators just do not keep doggedly at them—and all too often they give up just short of the goal."[30]

Porter Bibb, author of *It Ain't as Easy as It Looks*, an unauthorized biography of Ted Turner, credits Turner's persistence as one of his defining traits. "Stack the odds against Turner," writes Bibb, "and he will usually prevail, not because he is necessarily the biggest, bravest, strongest, or smartest, but because he simply will not give up. Ted Turner does not know how to quit and will keep fighting until the tide has turned and the battle is won."[31] Turner himself agrees: "I never quit. I've got a bunch of flags on my boat, but there ain't no white flags. I don't surrender. That's the story of my life."[32] And it is the story of most entrepreneurs' lives. Richard Branson is a good example.

Branson beat the odds repeatedly, not because he was, as Bibb described Turner, bigger, braver, stronger, or smarter, but largely because he was doggedly determined. Take Branson's experience somewhere over the Pacific in the early 1990s. He and his partner had accidentally jettisoned the fuel for their hot-air balloon. They were literally out of gas, suspended above rough seas. Everyone expected them to crash. Branson and his partner had two options, neither of which offered much hope. They could bail out with slim hope of being rescued, or they could stay aloft in 200-mile-per-hour winds and hope their balloon could withstand the strain, catch the jet stream, and miraculously make it to land. In characteristic junkyard-dog fashion, Branson hung on and eventually crash-landed the remnants of his balloon on a frozen lake in Canada. Not only had he and his partner survived, but they had broken the world balloon-travel speed record. Branson considered the adventure one of the great moments in his life and a metaphor for what it takes to succeed as an entrepreneur. "When we lost our fuel, all that mattered was keeping the balloon moving in the jet stream; it wasn't a matter of giving up," he said after his safe landing. "The same applies in business. If things are not looking good, you don't just give up. You try to keep going."[33]

> "Quitters never win and winners never quit." Be guided by that. You can still do a lot of dumb things, make a lot of mistakes, and get discouraged, but usually there is a solution out there somewhere.
>
> Jim McLamore[34]

And keep going they do. Successful entrepreneurs find a way to win—somehow. David Cook, cofounder of Blockbuster, describes Wayne Huizenga's "keep-going" style this way: "It's like he's got a goal and he tries to run around this way to it and if that doesn't work, he runs around the other way and he finally finds a way through, but as long as he reaches his goal who the hell cares how he got there. But he always gets his goal."[35]

To Debbi Fields, it is just a matter of the word *No* being an unacceptable answer. She knows what she wants to accomplish, and she is determined to accomplish it, even if the "it" is only a minor travel irritant, such as not getting room service when she wants it.

> "I call up room service . . . and I say, 'I know that it says room service isn't available until 7 o'clock, however I need to have coffee at 6. Is that a possibility?'" When the answer is no, as it usually is, Fields then calls the assistant manager, or if necessary, the general manager. "Hi Manager," she says, "I'm only the customer and I want to know what possibilities exist to have you deliver coffee to my room at 6 o'clock, since your room service isn't available until 7?"
>
> She has not yet failed, Fields says triumphantly, to get coffee before 7. "You need to explore the possibilities," she says, "and find out what kind of negotiations will work—to *not take no for an answer*."[36]

> When I climbed the hills, I saw the mountains. Then I started climbing the mountains.
>
> *Ted Turner*[37]

According to our gurus, dogged determination is a requirement for successful entrepreneurship that must be exhibited over and over. Rarely, it seems, can an entrepreneur start a new business without having to overcome obstacle after obstacle. The early entrepreneurial experiences of Jay Van Andel, cofounder of Amway, are good illustrations of this type of determination. Van Andel's story begins at the end of World War II. There was a kind of airplane craze after the war, so Van Andel and two friends decided to get in on the action.

> We bought a two-seat Piper Cub in Detroit for a down payment of $700. We didn't know the first thing about flying, so we had to hire a pilot to fly it from Detroit to Grand Rapids. . . . The next difficulty was making enough money to pay off and fly the airplane we just bought.
>
> The solution to that problem was to open a flying service. We named it Wolverine Air Service, which wasn't too original in the Wolverine State, but we didn't care. Flying instruction was our mainstay, but we also offered passenger rides, group transportation, and sales and rentals of airplanes. We still didn't know how to fly, so we hired two veteran pilots to do that job while we did the legwork on the ground. . . .
>
> We were counting on being able to use the new Grand River Air Park in Comstock Park, which was under construction when we started. When the airport project ran out of money, we attached pontoons to the bottom of our airplane and used the Grand River for our airstrip. This was a lesson to us in improvisation, and we learned a few more like it during our air service days. . . . [We] employed the services of an old chicken coop for an office. . . .
>
> While on a trip to Florida to deliver a plane, the idea occurred to us to open a drive-in restaurant, like ones we had seen elsewhere. We had $300 to invest, so on May 20, 1947, we opened the "Riverside Drive-Inn Restaurant," which was the very first of its kind in the area. We knew just about as much about running a restaurant as we had known about flying when we started, but we didn't let that stop us. [We] built a diminutive wooden

structure there at the air park, laying the foundation and nailing the clapboards ourselves. It took several months to get electricity hooked up properly, so we bought a generator. We also had no water for some time, so every evening we would fill up jugs at the nearest place that had plumbing and carry them to the restaurant.

From five o'clock in the afternoon until midnight we kept the restaurant open, [trading off jobs]....A good entrepreneur never rests, so we were always trying to think of something else that we could provide the customers at the air park. At one point, we started offering canoe rides down the Grand River....We also began offering fishing excursions on that lake. After just two years in business, we were operating a flight school, charter service, repair service, and aircraft and gasoline sales organization, as well as the boat rental and charter business, and the restaurant....

We learned a lot of lessons about business during these several years.... Lesson number one was that running a business is a matter of pressing on in spite of an unending series of unexpected problems....The problems we ran into were never ending, but we persisted. When the air park didn't open on time, when the electricity and water weren't hooked up for our restaurant on time, when several of our airplane engines were destroyed after we used the wrong lubricating oil, when hail and wind seriously damaged several of our airplanes, we didn't give up. Winter snows forced us to put skis on all the airplanes, but it seemed that as soon as the skis were on, the snow would melt, and as soon as we removed them, the snow would fly. But the first year, we flew two million passenger miles and earned $50,000.[38]

Van Andel and his partners overcame the obstacles. Faced with a Club Terror monster, they found a solution. They fought back again and again:

No landing strip? We'll use the river.
No office? We'll use that chicken coop.
No electricity? Find a generator.
No water? Haul some in.
Snow on the ground? Put skis on the plane.

Every guru tells the same kind of story. They survived because they refused not to survive. The monsters weren't going to kick them out of Club Terror. Like Debbi Fields, they just wouldn't take "no" for an answer.

Don't tell me it can't be done.

Bill Lear[39]

Requirement #4: Sacrifice Your Personal Life

Someone once said that at some point everything must degenerate to work. Entrepreneurs know this better than anyone because if there is one thing entrepreneurs do, it is work. Reflecting on his life, Howard Johnson recalled that he had no interest or time for anything but building his business. "I think that [building the business] was my only form of recreation. I never played golf. I never played tennis. I never did anything athletic after I left school. I ate, slept and thought of nothing but the business. If I went to a party or anywhere, I would always end up talking business."[40]

Our gurus describe their lives as consisting mostly of work, particularly during the early years of starting their business. Wayne Huizenga claims to have worked 20 hours a day, bar none. When asked about the hours he put in, Bill Gates said that rumors of his still working until 4:00 A.M. were exaggerated. "I generally work until midnight, with a break for dinner with someone from work," said Gates in *Playboy* interview. "Then I go home and read a book or the *Economist* for an hour or so. Generally, I'm back in the office by nine the next morning."[41] By the time he was 37, Gates claimed to have slowed his pace to just 72 hours a week. "I mean, I assume you don't count reading business magazines, the *Journal,* or the *Economist,*" he quipped.[42]

The only place where luck comes before work is in the dictionary.

Anita Roddick[43]

Of course, some of this may just be bravado, the equivalent of working-hour tall tales. Still, most gurus report that the early years of their business ventures are quite demanding. Fred Lager, author of *Ben & Jerry's: The Inside Scoop,* describes some of Ben Cohen and Jerry Greenfield's experiences as they tried to turn a ramshackled 1940s vintage gas station into an ice-cream parlor. It was February 1978, winter in Vermont:

They worked incredibly long days on the renovations, starting first thing in the morning, and going long into the night. When they couldn't stand the cold anymore, they took a break at the bus station down the street, where they'd warm up and use the bathrooms. They were trying to conserve all their cash, living on saltine crackers and tins of sardines that they got at Woolworth's, three for a buck.

By the time they got home, they would fall into bed, only to wake up exhausted in a freezing cold house. The house, which was really a summer cottage, wasn't insulated, and the wind would whip up off the lake and blow right through the walls. Eventually they stopped driving home at night and started sleeping in the gas station. Ben slept on top of the chest freezer in the back room; Jerry was out front on a cot that he'd bought at the army-navy store. . . .

[By the spring, Ben and Jerry had their business up and running at last, but the work got even harder.] As the summer ended, the exhilaration of being in business gave way to exhaustion from working endless hours, seven days a week. One night Jerry was so tired when he left the store, that he dropped the night deposit bag into the mailbox on the corner by mistake. Another night, Ben went outside while Jerry did the final mopping, and fell asleep in the gravel parking lot.[44]

Most gurus report similar experiences. They started early, worked late, got only a few hours sleep, and started all over the next day.

Why do entrepreneurs work so hard? Because they have to. During the first years, in particular, there's no one else to do all of the things that have to be done. Ben Cohen recalls that reality:

In the beginning there was Ben and there was Jerry, and we did it all: made all the ice cream and all the decisions, borrowed all the money, patched together all the broken-down equipment. That's one thing about starting a business: when you're an employee you can blame the boss for buying the wrong machine or making you work long hours. But when you're the boss, you have no one to blame but yourself. Darn—I bought the wrong equipment. Now I'll have to work all night. Again.

Another thing about starting a business: you get plenty of on-the-job training. Between us, over the years, we've been dilapidated-gas-station renovators; ice-cream-flavor inventors; short-order crepe chefs; hot fudge makers; ice cream scoopers; delivery persons; line workers; manufacturing overseers; vehicle, equipment, and facility procurers; circus-bus outfitters; ice cream distributors; and communications specialists. (Until about 1982, Jerry wrote a personal response to every person who sent a letter to the company.) And that just covers the first few years.[45]

Tom Monaghan, founder of Domino's Pizza, recalls that his experience as jack-of-all-trades during his first years in the pizza business was similar to Ben and Jerry's.

Although I didn't open until five o'clock in the afternoon, there was a lot of what I call backroom work to be done first. I made the sauce and the pizza dough fresh every day. Then the meat and vegetable toppings had to be pre-pared and sliced. The most tedious and time-consuming job was dicing the cheese. I vowed I would find a way to do that mechanically, but there was nothing suitable in the restaurant equipment catalogues I pored over. There were always errands to be run: supplies to pick up, bills to be paid. And any extra time I had went into making improvements in the store. My chief concern was with the layout of the oven and counters. I kept rearranging them, trying to cut a few steps and shave fractions of seconds off the time it took to make pizzas. Given the oven I had, there was nothing I could do to reduce cooking time. But I could control the assembly of raw materials, and I was obsessed with finding ways to speed up this end of the process. I was constantly on the run.

I wouldn't have been able to function if it hadn't been for . . . [two early associates] making deliveries. A few times when they weren't around, I'd take an order on the phone, make the pizza, then lock the door and do the delivery myself. It was a crazy situation.

If I ran out of something, I would take money out of the till and run to the grocery store next door. The couple who owned it felt sorry for me, and they'd sell me stale fruit pies for a dime. I'd go back to my kitchen and eat a whole darned pie. I was always hungry. Much as I loved pizza, I couldn't afford to eat my own product, unless it was a burned one or an order someone hadn't picked up.[46]

Of course, the long hours eventually take a toll, and the price is usually borne by the entrepreneur's family. He or she simply isn't around much of the time. That absence is inevitably the source of regrets. Wayne Huizenga recalls the lyrics of the Harry Chapin song "Cats Cradle"—"we're going to have a good time, Dad." "That hits me every time I hear that song because that's me right to the T," says Huizenga. "That comes back and hits you real hard and I wish I'd have spent more time with them. I never saw my kids play Little League ball. I never went to a PTA meeting, Marti [Huizenga's wife] did all that stuff. The only play I ever saw was when our daughter Pam one time was in a play. I missed all that stuff with all the kids. That's not good and I wouldn't advise anyone to put that much into it."[47] Huizenga might not advise it, but he did it. Most successful entrepreneurs do. It's part of the dues of Club Terror.

Requirement #5: Be Passionate about Your Vision

Why is it that successful entrepreneurs can make such sacrifices, even sacrifices that they know they may regret later? Is it just the thrill of it all, as Wilson Harrell suggests, or is there something more? Our gurus say there is something more—one last characteristic that separates the genuine entrepreneur from the rest of us—and this may be the ultimate defining characteristic of the successful entrepreneur. It is an unbridled, unconditional belief in their idea, despite overwhelming opposition.

> The biggest risk that an entrepreneur has to face is internal. They have to decide that this is the thing that they want to do with their time and their life more than any other thing.
>
> *Fred Smith*[48]

So, you want to sell cookies, start a package delivery service to compete with the U.S. Postal Service, or maybe just launch something simple like a 24-hour, seven-day-a-week cable news channel. You mention your idea to a few friends, relatives, and business associates, and they all respond with the same three little words—Are you crazy? Let's look at one entrepreneur's idea and examine her commitment to that idea, in the face of such opposition.

Debbi Fields remembers that everyone she consulted about starting a cookie business thought it was a bad idea.

To me, selling cookies in a store was a good idea.

Wrong!

A terrible idea!

At least, that's what everyone said.

Everyone.

First of all, there were the surveys. Randy [Fields' husband], a good, tough business head, pointed me in the direction of market analyses and I became an eager reader of such reports. They all said the same thing: America loves crispy cookies. . . .

I had some good evidence to the contrary, however. Randy's clients really liked the cookies the way I fixed them—[lusciously soft]. After two or three visits to the house, they took to telephoning before they flew in to consult with Randy . . . wondering out loud if Randy's wife wasn't planning to bake some of those terrific cookies. . . .

We're talking about executives here, important people, hardheaded decision makers. They're flying thousands of miles to consult with this financial wizard who does magic with numbers . . . and all they can think about is whether or not they're going to get a cookie.

Who better to ask? So I said to them, "What would you think about my starting a business to sell these cookies to the public?"

"Bad idea," they said, their mouths full of cookies, what had been a plateful only minutes earlier now reduced to crumbs that they were artfully dabbing up with genteel thumbs. "Never work," they said. "Forget it."

I went to one fellow, a marketing specialist who had been a successful executive with one of the most aggressive—and market-sensitive corporations in the world, and I said to him, "You've always loved my cookies. Well, now I want to go into the cookie business. What do you think? How should I go about selling them?"

He said, "Debbi, it's never going to work. Nobody's going to buy your cookies."

All the professionals were negative and it made me crazy. I couldn't understand it. I knew I wasn't sophisticated but I had eyes to see with. It was like they were telling me one thing yet showing me something completely opposite. It didn't make any sense at all.

So I tried my family—they'd loved my cookies for years.

My mom said, "Debbi, I cannot believe you're going to waste your life standing over a hot oven."

I tried Randy's parents.

"Debbi," Randy's mom said, "it'll never work." She and Randy's dad were very disappointed. I think they feared for both of us, believing that we would ensnarl ourselves in something that wouldn't work out and wind up broke and miserable and unhappy with each other.

At last, I went to my friends at the junior college and told them what I had in mind. No luck there, either. Everybody was singing in the same key: the idea seemed strange, the concept didn't exist. I'd go on and on about my cookies, the little store, the fresh-baked treat served hot in a napkin. It seemed to make people hungry, but they still didn't think my idea would work.

Finally, in desperation, I phoned up [my friend,] good, old, dependable Wendy Marks and told her what I had in mind. At this point I would have been satisfied with even hesitant support.

She couldn't believe it. "Debbi, I can't imagine it ever working."[49]

Far from being unique, Fields' experience is typical. All of our gurus report similar opposition to their ideas. Howard Schultz warns that you should expect it. "People will shut you out. They'll regard you with suspicion. They'll undermine your self-confidence. They'll offer you every reason imaginable why your idea simply won't work."[50] In short, says Schultz, you'll find yourself very much the underdog.

Given so much "grumpy negativism," as Debbi Fields calls it, most of us would just give up. Characteristically, entrepreneurs respond in just the opposite way. Schultz says that he found the opposition to his idea invigorating. "Part of me relished the fact that so many people said my plan couldn't be done."[51] Robert Mondavi, founder of Robert Mondavi Winery, recalls being energized by his decision to launch out on his own. "I felt totally reborn," he writes. "I was like a kid again, bursting with energy, ready to climb the mountain, conquer the world, go for the gold. Yes, at the unlikely age of fifty-two, the great adventure of my life had finally begun."[52]

Entrepreneurs respond to the negativism they meet by becoming even more committed to their idea—more convinced that they are right. Their idea becomes their life dream, the opportunity to control their own destiny, and the opportunity to do something that others may think is impossible but that they think is unique, worthwhile, and immanently doable. They become stubborn.

And their stubbornness becomes infectious. Even those who have the gravest doubts begin to wonder if the idea might work after all. George

Babick of CNN's New York office said of Ted Turner: "If Ted predicted the sun will come up in the west tomorrow morning, you'd laugh and say he's full of it. But you'd still set the alarm. You wouldn't want to miss the miracle."[53]

So, where does this unbridled confidence come from? Two sources, say our gurus—ignorance and optimism. Entrepreneurs have a heavy dose of both.

Ignorance Can Be Bliss

If you don't know that something can't be done, then you don't know you can't do it. Ted Turner didn't know anything about television. In fact, he said he didn't even watch television, so he created the superstation. He didn't know anything about news. In fact, he had made jokes about the news on his superstations, so he created CNN. He didn't know he couldn't do these things, so he just went out and did them.

Masaru Ibuka, cofounder of Sony, credits ignorance for some of his greatest accomplishments, as well as for those of Soichiro Honda, cofounder of Honda Motor Company.

We had been working on making the tape recorder for the first time in Japan. We then decided to go with the transistor radio, so we started product development, but the yield rate of the main transistor was awfully low. At best, only four or five would be any good. American companies were also trying to make successful transistor radios, but they too were not getting anywhere with development. . . .

Nobody had the experience of developing transistor manufacturing techniques, so no one really knew how difficult it was, and besides, there were no experts in the field. Today, there are experts whom we can get advice from, and usually after getting the advice we are supposed to give up on a new innovation. Those days, there weren't any experts to get advice from. So, I had to decide by myself.

Both Honda and I in that sense were amateurs at technology. Using myself as an example, we also started on development of the transistor television much earlier than other companies. We didn't know anything about electric circuits for television, so we weren't aware of the complexities involved. If we had known about the complexity of those circuits from the beginning, we probably would have stayed away from them.[54]

Time and again, entrepreneurs succeed when others won't even try. The entrepreneurs try because they don't know enough to know that what they want to do can't be done. It's a good idea, they reason, so everything will turn out right.

A Little Optimism Can't Hurt

Successful entrepreneurs are the eternal optimists. Thomas Stemberg, co-founder of Staples, says that his defining bias is his ability to see opportunity in every setback. He likes to retell a joke that he attributes to Bryant Gumble, the host of *The Early Show*:

> It's Christmas morning and two kids—one a pessimist, the other an optimist—open their presents. The pessimist gets a brand-new bike decked out with decals and accessories in the latest style. "It looks great," he says. "But it'll probably break soon." The second kid, an optimist, opens up a huge package, finds it filled with horse manure and jumps with glee, exclaiming, "There must be a pony in there somewhere!"[55]

Randy Fields sees that same type of optimism in his wife, Debbi:

> [She] is the kind of person that on Christmas Eve would go shopping at the shopping center and instead of taking the first [parking] space that she finds, which is what I think most people would do, which is way in the back of the parking lot, she says, "Oh no, there'll be one right in front of the door." And she'll go get the one right in front of the door. It's irrational to imagine there is one right in front of the door . . . but it's always there.[56]

Of course it's there. Debbi Fields couldn't believe it wouldn't be. David Gardner, one of the on-line personal finance advisors known as the Motley Fool, believes that Fields's kind of effusive optimism is a defining characteristic of entrepreneurs:

> There are people in the world who can't see how anything will ever work out, or just think it will be too much of a pain . . . to do it. And then there are the people who think all of life is wonderful and work so hard because of those feelings that they have. Ultimately, it's not a value judgment. I mean, maybe optimism is just a flight of fancy and we'd all be better off if we were

pessimists. But when you're talking about starting your own business, you have to be one of those people who believes you can do anything if you set your mind to it.[57]

We close this chapter with one final story. It's a favorite of Akio Morita, cofounder of Sony Corporation.

Two shoe salesmen . . . find themselves in a rustic backward part of Africa. The first salesman wires back to his head office: "There is no prospect of sales. Natives do not wear shoes!" The other salesman wires: "No one wears shoes here. We can dominate the market. Send all possible stock."[58]

Now that's the response of a true entrepreneur!

KEY POINTS

- The universal characteristic that all entrepreneurs possess is a willingness—even eagerness—to live with the fear of failure, what Wilson Harrell calls Club Terror.

- Conquering Club Terror makes entrepreneurs feel elated and alive. Rather than being intimidated, they are stimulated by the risks involved in entrepreneurship.

- Entrepreneurs don't consider themselves to be risk takers. They have weighed the pros and cons and convinced themselves that their so-called risky idea isn't that risky after all.

- Entrepreneurs accept occasional or even repeated failure as the price they must pay to succeed eventually. In the words of Mary Kay Ash, they see themselves as "failing forward to success."

- One of the reasons entrepreneurs can tolerate failure is that they see it as the source of real learning. When knocked down, successful entrepreneurs pick themselves up and figure out what they can learn from the experience.

- Money is almost never the primary motivation for a successful entrepreneur. In fact, most successful entrepreneurs argue that no one can acquire real wealth by pursuing money exclusively since they will be unwilling to take the financial risks from which real wealth flows.

- The real goal of most successful entrepreneurs is to have fun while accomplishing something worthwhile.

- True entrepreneurs have a junkyard-dog mentality. They are determined to make their endeavor a success. They take on any job, no matter how menial, and work as many hours as necessary to succeed. Most end up paying a high personal price for their devotion to their business.

- Finally, successful entrepreneurs believe passionately in what they are doing. The negativism of others only strengthens their resolve. Their confidence in their ultimate success is further strengthened by their ignorance—they don't know that what they are trying to do can't be done—and by their optimism: At heart, they believe that things will just turn out right in the end.

J. Walter (Walt) Anderson, cofounder of White Castle

Mary Kay Ash, founder of Mary Kay Cosmetics

James L. (Jim) Barksdale, cofounder of Netscape Communications

Phineas Taylor (P.T.) Barnum, founder of "The Greatest Show on Earth"

Jeffrey P. Bezos, founder and CEO of Amazon.com

Arthur Blank, cofounder of Home Depot

Richard Branson, founder of the Virgin Group

Warren Buffett, founder of numerous investment companies and chairman of Berkshire Hathaway, Inc.

Washington Atlee Burpee, founder of Burpee Seed Company

Tom Chappell, cofounder of Tom's of Maine, Inc.

Ben Cohen, cofounder of Ben & Jerry's Ice Cream

Finis Conner, founder of Conner Peripherals

Joshua Lionel Cowen, cofounder of Lionel Manufacturing Company

Michael Dell, founder of Dell Computer Corporation

Anthony Desio, founder of Mail Boxes Etc.

Bill Gates, cofounder of Microsoft Corporation

Earl Graves, founder, publisher, and editor of *Black Enterprise*

Robert Greenberg, founder of LA Gear

Jerry Greenfield, cofounder of Ben & Jerry's Ice Cream

Wilson Harrell, founder of over one hundred companies, columnist for *Success Magazine,* and former publisher of *Inc. Magazine*

Frank Hickingbotham, founder of TCBY (This Can't Be Yogurt)

Wayne Huizenga, founder of Waste Management, Inc.

Edgar Waldo (Billy) Ingram, cofounder of White Castle

C. James (Jim) Koch, founder of Boston Beer Company

Ray Kroc, founder of McDonald's Corporation

Edwin Land, founder of Polaroid Corporation

Bill Lear, founder of Lear Jet Corporation

Bernie Marcus, cofounder of Home Depot

Konosuke Matsushita, founder of Matsushita Electric Industrial Company

Robert Mondavi, founder of Robert Mondavi Winery

David Packard, cofounder of Hewlett-Packard

Anita Roddick, founder of The Body Shop

Pleasant Rowland, founder of Pleasant Company

Howard Schultz, founder of Starbucks Coffee Company

Fred Smith, founder of Federal Express

Thomas Stemberg, cofounder of Staples, Inc.

R. David (Dave) Thomas, founder of Wendy's International, Inc.

Ted Turner, founder of Turner Broadcasting System, Cable News Network (CNN), and Turner Network Television (TNT)

Lillian Vernon, founder of Lillian Vernon Corporation

Sam Walton, founder of Wal-Mart Stores, Inc.

2

The Perfect Idea

We call this chapter "The Perfect Idea," but of course there is no such thing. Every idea for a new business is flawed in some way. However, that doesn't keep entrepreneurs from searching for the foolproof business proposition. In this chapter, we examine where our gurus get their ideas for businesses, how they conduct their search, and what they have learned about the necessary ingredients for the perfect business.

FINDING THE PERFECT IDEA

Let's start with the basic question: Where do entrepreneurs look for their ideas? According to our gurus, the answer is simply anywhere and everywhere. Their first piece of advice about finding the perfect idea is to be open to them all the time. Watch, look, and listen, say our gurus. There are plenty of ideas around if you are just paying attention. All the best ideas have not been taken. Our gurus are confident that many remain. After all, they pick up ideas for new businesses every day, and you can, too, if you know how. Here are some suggestions.

Constantly Gather Ideas

Lillian Vernon suggest that you "gather ideas as you work, chat with friends, garden, watch children play, drive, watch television, and, shop." "It is a good investment of your time," she continues, "to browse through shops, street fairs, and offbeat little boutiques. Wherever you find yourself and whatever you are doing, keep your mind open to ideas for products or services that might satisfy needs. Also watch for ways to improve what is already on the market."[1] That last one was the source of Vernon's first idea.

Vernon notes that her emphasis has always been on the words *special* and *exclusive.* It is not surprising, therefore, that her first idea for a product came to her when she noticed that, although there were plenty of belts and bags on the market for teenagers to choose from, they weren't distinctive. Nothing made them special or exclusive. Vernon decided to offer bags and belts that would be personalized with the owner's initials, and it worked. On the basis of a single ad in the September 1951 issue of *Seventeen,* Vernon launched a mail-order business with orders for over sixty-four hundred bags and belts in the first four months, a response that she terms no less than astounding. From the kernel of that simple idea, Vernon has built a business that in 1998 had revenues of $258 million.

Richard Branson has a similar penchant for shamelessly picking up suggestions and ideas as he goes about his daily business. He even carries around a black notebook to record his notes on conversations, observations, and ideas that he thinks he can put to use. Members of the senior staff in Branson's various Virgin Companies carry the same black notebooks, and they put them to similar use. Branson attributes this openness to ideas, regardless of source, as a key to his success.

Today's booming economy offers particularly good opportunities both in new and in traditional industries. Exhibit 2.1 contains a list of hot entrepreneurial opportunities.

Our gurus preach caution when exploring ideas for businesses. There are many ideas—some good, some bad, some based in the hard reality of the marketplace, some just impossible schemes. The gurus warn you not to let the excitement you feel at hearing about a great new business opportunity blind you to the truth. Warren Buffett, investor extraordinaire, tells the following story to make this point:

[An] oil prospector . . . met St. Peter at the Pearly Gates. When told his occupation, St. Peter said, "Oh, I'm really sorry. You seem to meet all the tests to get into heaven. But we've got a terrible problem. See that pen over there? That's where we keep the oil prospectors waiting to get into heaven.

EXHIBIT 2.1. **Hot Entrepreneurial Opportunities**

Biotechnology

- Blood screening tests.
- Genetic engineering.
- Alternative medicines.
- Bionic parts and artificial organs.
- Bioelectronic products.
- Animal drugs.
- Inoculated eggs.
- Implantable animal microchips.
- Grass that doesn't need cutting.

Internet

- Designing Web sites.
- Internet marketing services.
- Office supplies.
- Small-business equipment.
- Health supplements.
- Specialty foods.
- Gaming and add-on products.
- Travel and leisure products.
- Video games and multimedia.
- Books and magazines.

Training and Professional Development

- Customized on-site computer training.
- Computer-training centers.
- Image consultants and executive coaches.
- Professional organizers.
- On-line and multimedia content consultants.
- Videoconferencing organizers.
- Programming consultants.
- Electronic data interchange consultants.

Fitness and Health

- Healthier foods.
- Door-to-door wellness services.
- Low-tech healing specialists versus traditional doctors for remedies.
- Holistic healing.
- Ancient remedies.
- Spas and cosmetic-surgery centers.
- Holistic health clubs and fitness services.
- Exercise machines.

Indulgence Goods

- Gourmet food in small servings.
- Ice cream and other sinful desserts.
- Natural goods and organic produce.
- Energy-producing products and vitamin supplements.
- Specialty coffee, tea, wine shops.
- Natural water products.
- Healthy frozen foods.
- Brew pubs and customized beers.
- Flowers.
- Specialty breads, soft pretzels, and bagel outlets.
- Exotic meats such as buffalo, elk, venison, ostrich.
- Quaint hotels and boutiques with specialty services.
- Adult toys (laptops, CD players).
- Designer baby clothes.
- Aromatherapy (scented candles, bath oils, and lotions).

Child Care and Elder Care

- Child-care centers and camps.
- Rent-a-grandmother services.
- Products and services for the homebound.
- Elder-care consulting services.
- Day-care centers and activities for the elderly.
- Senior travel clubs.
- Independent-living centers.
- Assisted-living centers.

(continued)

EXHIBIT 2.1. (continued)

Home Health Services

- Home health-care providers.
- Door-to-door medical transportation services.
- Homemaking services.
- Elderly relative services.

Children's Products and Services

- Juvenile safety products.
- Infant and children's organic food products.
- Children's fitness centers.
- Kiddie golf.
- Nursery design and furniture.
- Home health care for newborns.
- Children's educational software for math, reading, science, etc.
- Multimedia computers.
- CD-ROM encyclopedias.
- Educational toys, games, and puzzles.
- Children's learning centers and camps.
- Centers for children with learning disabilities.
- Children's bookstores.

Ethnic Products

- Specialty lines of cosmetics.
- Hair-care products and salons.
- Ethnic grocery stores and cookbooks.
- Ethnic food mail-order catalogs.
- Ethnic cafes, restaurants, and food courts.
- Vitamins and dietary products.

Home-Office Products and Services

- Home decorating and furnishings.
- Home-safety devices.
- Home-office furniture and technical equipment.
- On-site repair services for home offices.

- Auto safety alarms and sound systems.
- Personal-safety items while traveling.
- Home-delivery services for computers, printers, etc.

Smart Appliances

- Digital cellular phone, radios, and interactive television.
- Digital-imaging products.
- Electronic notepads.
- Multisensory robotics.
- Smart homes and appliances.
- Voice-recognition products.
- Electronic film cameras.

Pet Pampering

- Pet hotels.
- Pet grooming and traveling vans.
- Pet home-care visits.
- Pet emergency clinics.
- Old-age homes for pets.
- Pet television and radio shows.
- Doggie day care.
- Doggie bakeries.
- Cat furniture and clothing stores.
- Seat belts for pets.

One-of-a-Kind Retail Boutiques

- Clothing.
- Jewelry.
- CD stores.
- Delicatessens.
- Bakery cafes.
- Travel-related outlets.
- Paint-your-own pottery stores.
- Customized breweries.
- Specialty shoe stores.

(continued)

EXHIBIT 2.1.   **(continued)**

Personal Shopping and Errand Services

- Wardrobe consultants.
- On-site customer apparel shoppers.
- Gift services.
- Corporate pickup and delivery services.

- Messenger services.
- Rent-a-butler.
- Rent-a-chef.
- Rent-a-driver.
- Publicity escort services.

Source: Adapted from Courtney Price and Kathleen Allen, Tips and Traps for Entrepreneurs *(New York: McGraw-Hill, 1998), pp. 12–25.*

And it's filled—we haven't got room for even one more." The oil prospector thought for a minute and said, "Would you mind if I just said four words to those folks?" "I can't see any harm in that," said St. Pete. So the old-timer cupped his hands and yelled out, "Oil discovered in hell!" Immediately, the oil prospectors wrenched the lock off the door of the pen and out they flew, flapping their wings as hard as they could for the lower regions. "You know, that's a pretty good trick," St. Pete said. "Move in. The place is yours. You've got plenty of room." The old fellow scratched his head and said, "No. If you don't mind, I think I'll go along with the rest of 'em. There may be some truth to that rumor after all."[2]

Buffett's point is that the mass exodus to hell is unfortunately what happens with too many business investments. "People know better," writes Buffett, "but when they hear a rumor—particularly when they hear it from a high place—they just can't resist the temptation to go along. It happens on Wall Street periodically, where you get what are, in effect, manias. Looking back no one can quite understand how everyone could have gotten so swept up in the moment. A group of lemmings looks like a pack of individualists compared with Wall Street when it gets a concept in its teeth."[3] The same can be said for entrepreneurs.

Check Out the Competition

While you are out there doing some cautious looking and listening, suggest our gurus, be sure that you are spending at least some of your time looking at and listening to your would-be competition. All good entrepreneurs are snoops. It's part of the trade. Sam Walton relished the time he could spend prowling the competition, stealing ideas. He even recalled one experience when he got caught:

> I was in the big Price Club on Marino Avenue in San Diego, and I had my lit-tle tape recorder with me—like I always do and I was making notes to my-self about prices and merchandising ideas. This guy, a big guy, comes up to me and says, "I'm sorry but I'll have to take your tape recorder and erase the material you've got on it. We have a policy against people using them in the stores." Well, we have the same policy, and I knew I was caught. So I said, "I respect that. But I've got things on here from other stores that I don't want to lose, so let me write a note to Robert Price"—that's Sol's son. So I wrote: "Robert, your guy is just too good. I was trying to get some information on this recorder about some of the items you were carrying and some of my impressions of your store, and he caught me. So here's the tape. If you want to listen to it, you certainly have that privilege, but I have some other material on here I would like very much to have back." So in about four days I got a nice note back from Robert, with the tape, and none of it had been blurred or scratched out. He probably treated me better than I deserved.[4]

Entrepreneurs can be very inventive with their snooping. Thomas Stem-berg recalls employing both his mother-in-law and his wife as amateur sleuths for his office-supply company, Staples:

> I used to shop with my mother-in-law. She had an apartment in Fort Lau-derdale, and together we put the nearest Office Depot store through its paces. She'd order paper clips, pens, and paper to be delivered to her apart-ment, and then call to complain and ask that the stuff be picked up and re-turned to the store. I really wanted to learn how they did everything: what their systems were like, what they had in stock, and what they couldn't do. I visited stores constantly.
>
> On another occasion, I had my wife, Dola, apply for a job at Office Depot's Atlanta delivery-order center. She said she had experience in tele-marketing and, in a soft, Southern accent, explained that she was anxious to move back "home." Staples did not offer delivery service at the time, so I wanted to investigate how Office Depot's delivery system worked, how many people were in the operation, and how it trained employees. Dola

stopped the application process before the company even offered her a job interview, but we still got the information.[5]

Occasionally, writes Stemberg, his snooping and that of his team has gotten almost silly—more Laurel and Hardy than James Bond. He vividly recalls one particular two-reeler played out in Florida:

During a visit to Florida, five executives, including Krasnow [Staples' executive vice president for sales and marketing], visited Office Depot's North Miami Beach store. While scouring the facility for information, Krasnow noticed the employee schedule posted on a bulletin board and quickly made a mental note of all the pertinent numbers. Fifteen minutes later, the Staples executives were preparing to leave when they heard a commotion. One of the Staples executives was racing down an aisle, waving a piece of paper in his hand and crying, "I got the schedule! I got the schedule!" Behind him, a half-dozen Office Depot associates were in hot pursuit. "It was the same report that I saw," says Krasnow. "We all bolted out of the store and ran to the parking lot."[6]

OUR VIEW

A little stealth can be a lot of fun. Just don't get caught up in your spy capers and do something you shouldn't do. Use some discretion. Don't do anything illegal. Play fair with the competition. Keep your sense of humor, and most of all, don't forget why you are doing it. You're not just interested in finding out what your competition is doing wrong. You also need to be looking at what your competition is doing right.

Stemberg recalls sending a team to Florida in 1987 to check out Office Depot's first four stores. The team's report was highly encouraging for Staples. In part, it read as follows:

They make very little effort in the areas of customer service. We asked a number of questions of various employees [to] which we received fair to poor responses. They appeared indifferent and basically uninformed. In the area of service to the consumer, it simply came down to our having consultants, management, and employees in general trained and available to assist the customer where Office Depot had a work force designed to strickly [*sic*] deal with product packout and display at all locations. Many items out of stock, shelves not straightened, and shelf tags that were missing, out dated, and in wrong locations. . . .We personally felt much better about our operation and were not impressed by their lack of standards and personnel. If we were to put a store up against them there's no doubt we would be much superior.[7]

The Staples team was confident that Office Depot would never make it. In reality, Office Depot not only made it, but by 1995 it had outstripped Staples to become the largest office-supply retailer in the country. What had the Staples team missed? Krasnow explained, "In hindsight, what the ripped boxes and messy stores reflected was that their prices were really, really good. . . . Customers were snapping up merchandise. Office Depot had challenges that needed to be overcome, but the basic demand was there. And it obviously became very, very successful."[8]

Michael Dell, founder of Dell Computer Corporation, believes that one of the biggest mistakes entrepreneurs make is failing to fully understand the fundamental economics of the industry they are in. By this he means understanding where the leaders in the industry really make their money. "Understanding the profit pool of your industry," advises Dell, "can open your eyes to new opportunities." Dell explains that you should "think of a competitor that has high market share and is very profitable in a specific part of the market. Then think about how compelling it would be to exploit that strength as a weakness. Your competitor will most likely not be able to respond to an aggressive attack without significantly reducing its profit."[9] Case in point, in the mid-1990s Dell recognized that the major strength of some of his competitors (Compaq, IBM, and Hewlett-Packard) was their position in the market for servers. Although the competitors' servers were good, Dell felt they were priced unjustifiably high. Instead of passing savings along to their customers, Dell's competitors used their excess profits in servers to subsidize other parts of their businesses, such as entries into the markets for notebook and desktop computers. Dell decided he could exploit his competitors' strength by introducing a line of Dell servers at much lower prices. Dell Computer eventually took 20 percent of the market for servers and drained its competitors' profit pools, thus making it difficult for the competitors to compete in the market for notebook and desktop computers. Dell saw a competitor's strength and exploited it as a weakness.[10]

Recognize Opportunities

Of course, the key to gathering ideas from daily contacts or from the competition is to recognize business opportunities when you hear or see them. Many people would never have seen the profit potential in a competitor's strength like Michael Dell did. The knack for spotting business opportunities that others of us miss is a specialty of entrepreneurs. Successful entrepreneurs have well-tuned opportunity antennae. Wilson Harrell is a good example. Here is a story about the way a surefire money-making idea came to him one day. See if you figure out the exciting business opportunity Harrell spotted.

One day I found myself in Baghdad, Iraq, in the office of a man named Ahmed, who befriended me and let me stay at his house for a few days. He held a cocktail party, which of course was illegal, since liquor is a no-no in Moslem countries. I have found that rich people all over the world don't pay much attention to religious laws if they interfere with having fun. Sure enough, I met the son of the prime minister there. He invited me to go on a wild boar hunt the next day, which sounded like a lot of fun. I had killed a lot of hogs in my youth on our Georgia farm. The next day at daybreak, I arrived with my host at a palace in the middle of nowhere with a humongous hangover. A guy in a white sheet presented me with a 12-foot spear and a horse. It gradually sank into my still-inebriated brain that these would be our only weapons against the boars. Back where I came from, you hunt wild hogs from a platform in a very high tree with a 30-30 rifle. Nobody in his right mind ever got any closer to a mad Georgia hog than that. These were wild boars with tusks about a foot long. With nothing between me and death or dismemberment but a pointed stick, I mounted my trusty Arabian steed.

Everybody yelled and charged around. I got into the spirit of things, and somehow a hog ran into my spear. What happened next set off entrepreneurial bells in my head: All the killers were presented with a certificate good for a bounty of one pound sterling—about $4—from the government. You see, in Iraq, wild hogs roamed the country rooting up crops—a menace to farmers. Since Moslems aren't allowed to eat pork, wild hogs had no natural enemies, except a bunch of guys on horses with spears, having fun.[11]

Well, how did you do? Did you spot the opportunity, or are you mystified as to how Harrell planned to turn wild hogs in Iraq into a money-making proposition? We couldn't see much of a market for wild boar hunting when we first read this story; then we read on:

> I had spotted a deal. There I was in a country with 10 million hogs. I cornered the son of the prime minister and asked him if his daddy would give me the exclusive rights to commercially rid his nation of wild hogs. He thought I was crazy. I explained that we could use about 100 jeeps with mounted machine guns. It wasn't just the $4 that interested me, but the hog meat. I reckoned that we could put up a processing plant and supply the world's cheapest dog food to American supermarkets. How could we miss?
>
> By the time the son of the prime minister had stopped laughing and telling the story, all his friends wanted to invest. I was about to become king of the dog-food business. Armed with the exclusive franchise to establish a processing operation in Iraq, along with a lot of investors' money, I grabbed a plane to America in search of equipment for processing and canning dog food. I met with food brokers and supermarket buyers. Everybody was excited. My price for 100 percent pork was about half the going rate for the slop they were calling dog food. I was on a roll. Every day was more exciting than yesterday.[12]

Unfortunately for Harrell, he never became the king of dog food. Before he could get his venture off the ground, Communists overthrew the Iraqi government and exiled, killed, or jailed all the capitalists. Harrell lost the chance to make a fortune, Iraq remained stuck with its wild boars, and pet lovers in the United States never got to feed their animals gourmet 100 percent wild boar pet food.

Find an Irritant

The genesis of Harrell's idea was an irritant. The wild boars were a menace to farmers. The opportunity Harrell spotted was a creative way to remove the irritant and create value for himself and others—in this case both the Iraq farmers and U.S. pet lovers. Anita Roddick notes that one of the mistakes would-be entrepreneurs make is not trusting their gut instincts enough, especially when it comes to things that irritate them. (Exhibit 2.2 lists four million-dollar ideas that originated from little irritants.)

EXHIBIT 2.2. **Four Million-Dollar Ideas**

S.C.R.U.B.S. is the brainchild of a nurse, Sue Callaway, who was bored with the drab medical scrubwear she had to wear to work. She turned her own colorful, fashionable designs into an estimated $23 million company.

Perfect Curve Inc. was created when Gregg Levin noticed that his friends went to a lot of trouble to make the brims of their baseball caps curve just the right way when they wore them backwards. Levin developed a little piece of plastic that bends the brims perfectly and has grossed in excess of $1 million from it.

FUBU (For Us, By Us) is the creation of Queens, New York, friends Daymond John, J. Alexander Martin, Keith Perrin, and Carl Brown, who found that they could not buy the urban fashions that they wanted in their neighborhood retail stores. The FUBU line of clothing is now worth in excess of $200 million.

Direct Root Water Spikes were developed after their inventor, Andrew Rose, attempted to get a six-foot plant into a sink so he could water its roots—the way his mother had told him he should water all plants. Rose lost the behemoth plant, but his simple plastic spike that waters plant roots efficiently has generated more than $1 million in revenues.

Source: Debra Phillips, G. David Doran, Elaine W. Teague, and Laura Tiffany, "Young Millionaires: Thirty Entrepreneurial Superstars Under 40 Reveal How They Made It to the Million-Dollar Club," Entrepreneur, November 1998, pp. 118–126.

"The fact is," Roddick writes, "that if something irritates you it is a pretty good indication that there are other people who feel the same. Irritation is a great source of energy and creativity. It leads to dissatisfaction and should prompt you to begin asking yourself the types of questions that can lead to a good business idea."[13] Roddick explains that her idea for The Body Shop came from just such an irritant. "It seemed ridiculous to me that you go into a sweet shop, and ask for an ounce of jelly babies and you can go into the grocers' and ask for two ounces of cheese, but when you wanted to buy a body lotion you had to go into Boots and lay out five quid for a bloody great bottle of the stuff. Then, if you didn't like it, you were stuck with it."[14]

Roddick's observation led her to ask herself a series of questions:

Why couldn't I buy cosmetics by weight or bulk, like I could if I wanted groceries or vegetables? Why couldn't I buy a small size of a cream or lotion, so I could try it out before buying a big bottle? These were simple enough questions, but at the time there were no sensible answers, although it did not take a brilliant business brain to work out that bigger profits accrued from selling bigger bottles.[15]

Roddick had her idea, and The Body Shop was born. Similar experiences have led our other gurus to their "perfect idea." For example, Fred Smith explains that he developed the idea for Federal Express because of his poor experience in getting spare parts delivered for his first business venture, a jet-aircraft sales company called Arkansas Aviation that he had started after his return from Vietnam. "I became infuriated," writes Smith, "that I could not receive on any timely and reliable basis air freight shipments from places around the United States."[16] Federal Express was Smith's way of removing an irritant to himself and others.

Similarly, Thomas Stemberg says his idea for Staples came at least partially from the frustration he felt late one afternoon when he could find no office-supply store that stocked the type of ribbon he needed for his printer.[17] And Anthony Desio credits his idea for Mail Boxes Etc. to his impatience with the U.S. Postal Service's long lines, short hours, and limited services. "I saw that companies like Federal Express and DHL had become successful by offering alternatives to the post office," he writes, "and I thought the same alternatives could work for retail services."[18]

ARE YOU CRAZY?

Okay, you have kept your eyes and ears open, checked out the competition, tuned your opportunity antenna on multiple wild boar hunts, and made a laundry list of all those day-to-day irritants that make you so mad that you're just not going to take them anymore. You've come up with what you think just might be the perfect idea. This, you think, just can't miss. So, you start chatting up your idea with your friends, relatives, business associates—anyone and everyone you can corner. Regardless of how good you may think your idea is, though, the reaction of almost everyone you talk to about it is the same. Remember the three little words we mentioned in the last chapter? That's right—*"Are you crazy?"*

As we said before, no matter how good your idea may be, the people you trust most are going to reject it out of hand. Practically every guru tells the same story. You will recall that Debbi Fields met with what she called "grumpy negativism" from everyone. Our other gurus had similar experiences.

Arthur Blank:

Building Home Depot was a tough, uphill battle from the day we started in a Los Angeles coffee shop.... No one believed we could do it, and very few people trusted our judgment. Or they trusted our judgment, but just didn't think the concept of a home improvement warehouse with the lowest prices, best selection, and best service was going to work.[19]

Mary Kay Ash:

When I began Mary Kay, my accountant looked at my proposed commission structure and said, "There's no way, Mary Kay. You can't pay this many cents out of a dollar and still operate. It just won't work." Many well-intentioned people, including my attorney, assured me it would fail. After all, who ever *heard* of a company based on the golden rule? My attorney went so far as to send to Washington for a pamphlet that showed how many cosmetics companies went broke every year. "Listen," people said, "you're *dreaming.*"[20]

Robert Mondavi:

Everyone thought I was crazy, of course. As soon as word spread of my plan to build my own winery—the first new winery in the Napa Valley since the late 1930s—I began to get skeptical looks and comments. Start a new winery? Make wine that would stand beside the greatest wines in the world? Set out to transform the eating and drinking habits of an entire nation? What arrogance! What folly! Bob Mondavi has a screw loose. He's spent too much time with his head in his barrels. . . . I could hear the guffaws up and down the Napa Valley.[21]

Every entrepreneur hears the guffaws. You will too. As Thomas Stemberg notes: "There is no shortage of forces that conspire to minimize your dream, to suggest that failure is the probable outcome. Like Darth Vader luring Luke Skywalker over to 'the dark side,' new competitors, experienced experts, even the status quo conspire against someone who is trying to do something new."[22] As Mary Kay Ash explains, all of these naysayers are well-intentioned people. They aren't out to rain on your parade. They are trying to save you from making a terrible mistake. They genuinely do not believe that the idea you are proposing will work. But why?

Business is full of lawyers and advisers, and you've got to remember, whatever you're doing, that these guys are trying to keep you from getting burned. That's their job. So if you get a new idea, don't expect everybody to say, "Let's go." You're the one who says that.

Ted Turner[23]

If It's Really New, There Can't Be Market for It

Think about what makes a good idea such a jewel in the first place. As Tom Chappell, cofounder of Tom's of Maine, explains, "entrepreneurship by definition is creating something new, discovering markets that no one thought were there, markets that will not be counted until the entrepreneur announces they are there."[24] "If you look at the history of most entrepreneurial ideas," notes Fred Smith, "there's that common denominator that somebody had a different perspective or slightly different view of something than the traditional wisdom or the traditional thinking was at the time."[25] When Frank Hickingbotham proposed selling a creamy, sweet, dessertlike frozen yogurt and positioning his company, TCBY, as an ice-cream parlor, most analysts said it couldn't be done and that his company would never survive the winter. The conventional wisdom at the time was that yogurt was a product that could only be sold as a side order in pizza, barbecue, or sandwich shops or as a health food in a health-food store.[26]

Suppose you were approached by an enterprising young man in the early 1980s who said he wanted you to invest your hard-earned money to help him build a chain of coffee bars in the United States patterned after the kind he had seen in Italy, where fine coffee would be served and, as he put it, "the social aspect of coffee drinking would be a conduit to conversation." Now, suppose also that you were familiar with the coffee trade in the United States. For example, you knew that coffee was the world's most widely traded commodity, after oil; that it was mostly sold in bulk; that the consumption of coffee by Americans had been declining since the 1960s; that coffee shops were nothing new, and those that made money did so on food and not coffee; that specialty coffee drinks, like espresso, were sold primarily in restaurants as an after-dinner drink. And suppose you knew that, like you, most Americans gave little thought to their cup of coffee beyond choosing between regular and decaf. Would you loan this young man the money he wanted, or would you tell him the same thing most people told Howard Schultz: "Wake up and smell the coffee, son, this is America, not Italy. Go get a serious job and support your family?"[27] Our guess is you would have thought the kid was nuts.

> The best ideas are those that create a new mind-set or sense a need before others do, and it takes an astute investor to recognize an idea that not only is ahead of its time but also has long-term prospects.
>
> *Howard Schultz*[28]

So, what do you do when you run up against this wall of opposition? Do you give up and go back to your day job? Not if you're an entrepreneur. As Robert Mondavi maintains, "if you want to succeed, you have to listen to yourself, to your own heart, and you have to have the courage to go your own way."[29] But of course, you also know enough not to proceed without giving your idea another look just to see if by chance you missed something. Our gurus call this necessary step toward the perfect idea "sharpening."

> An invention that is quickly accepted will turn out to be a rather trivial alteration of something that has already existed.
>
> *Edwin Land*[30]

SHARPENING YOUR IDEA

Throughout their writings, our gurus offer a number of suggestions concerning how you can "reality check" your idea, sharpen it, and make it better. Although it is unlikely that you will win over all, or even the majority, of your naysayers by following these suggestions, they should help you either gain confidence in your idea or redirect your thinking toward a more workable one. These suggestions are summarized in the form of questions in Exhibit 2.3. We give a more complete discussion of each suggestion in the following sections.

EXHIBIT 2.3. **Sharpening Your Idea**

✓	Question
❑	1. Does your idea meet a genuine need in the marketplace?
❑	2. Has you idea been refined with real input from customers?
❑	3. Is your idea unique, or does it represent a real enhancement to an existing business model?
❑	4. Does your idea focus on a specific market niche?
❑	5. Can the success of you idea be improved by linking it to another business venture?
❑	6. Is there a way to minimize your downside risk through creative financing and/or a joint venture?
❑	7. Are you being realistic? Are you prepared to admit that the idea isn't workable if the facts tend to bear that out?

Suggestion #1: Make Sure Your Idea Meets a Need

There has to be a need. Mary Kay Ash makes this point beautifully:

> Only a small percentage of new businesses do succeed. I think one reason for that is that people go into a business simply because they want to be in that business. That's not a good enough reason. A woman may love decorating her own home, so she thinks, "Gee, I want to be an interior decorator." The community probably already has skilled, well-established decorators. Many women want to go into the glamour professions, like fashion, without any real training or experience. It is not wise to start a business unless you have something new or different or better to offer than is presently being offered.
>
> The best reason to start a new company is that there is a need for what you have to offer, or that you're better than what is being offered. When we began, no cosmetic company was actually teaching skin care. All of them were just selling rouge or lipstick or new eye colors. No company was teaching women how to care for their skin. So we came into a market where there was a real need—and we filled it. Oddly enough, it's still true today that women are not knowledgeable about skin care, despite all the information on television, in magazines, and in newspapers. They buy a product here, there, and everywhere, but they don't have a coordinated program. We fill a void by helping women understand how to take care of

their skin. So, if you want to start a successful business, you must offer something different or something better than what is available.[31]

You first have to meet a need.

Every man's occupation should be beneficial to his fellow-man as well as profitable to himself. All else is vanity and folly.

P.T. Barnum[32]

David Packard, cofounder of Hewlett-Packard (HP), argues that, for an idea to be worth pursuing, it must be both practical (workable) and useful. It must not only fill a need, it must do so economically and efficiently. He recalls that, in the early days of HP, he and Bill Hewlett had a built-in method of determining if an idea met the needs test. "When HP was making primarily test and measuring instruments for engineers, we had a built-in method for helping us determine what customers might need in the way of innovative new instruments. We called it the "next bench" syndrome. If the idea for a new instrument appealed to the HP engineer working at the next bench, it would very likely appeal to our customers as well."[33]

As HP's business and product line expanded, HP expanded its listening to include nonengineering customers. That's the second suggestion.

Suggestion #2: Let Your Customers Be Your Guide

We will say more about listening to customers in Chapters 4 and 5. For now, we will only note that our gurus believe the key to listening to customers involves the following:

- Getting out into the marketplace.
- Talking to customers.
- Observing them.
- Showing them your product.
- Explaining your service.
- Asking them what they think.

In the early years at Home Depot, cofounders Bernie Marcus and Arthur Blank donned orange aprons and worked in their stores waiting on customers and listening to complaints. Marcus explains that the personal experiences he and Blank had in the stores was a key to their success. "We found out by talking to customers what we were doing right, and what we needed to do to make the company better, and the things we were doing wrong."[34]

> My grandmother always said that God gave you two ears and one mouth for a reason.
>
> *Finis Conner[35]*

Entrepreneurs who listen to customers—and we mean really listen—often find themselves changing their idea for a business, sometimes in very dramatic ways. Robert Greenberg, founder of LA Gear, originally opened a retail store on Melrose Avenue in Los Angeles to sell his own line of apparel, jeans, and footwear. Greenberg said that he wasn't sure at the start which part of the business would catch on, but he hoped that at least one would. When he observed that customers were buying a lot more shoes than they were apparel and jeans, he sold off the apparel business and announced that from then on he was in the shoe business.[36]

Other successful entrepreneurs have listened to their customers and found themselves totally rethinking their ideas. For example, Joshua Lionel Cowen originally marketed his Lionel train as a store window novelty meant to be used to display merchandise and attract customers. It was only when the customers began insisting on buying the trains themselves that Cowen got the idea to market his device, not as a store display, but as a toy.[37] Washington Atlee Burpee, founder of Burpee Seed, had a similar experience. He set out originally to sell purebred livestock and fowl by mail order. As an additional service, he began including several varieties of seeds to provide purchasers of his livestock and fowl with the proper feed for their animals. It wasn't until he noticed that his seeds were outselling his animals that Burpee came to the conclusion that he was in the seed business, not the animal business.[38]

> Companies that are successful today—and, perhaps more importantly, companies that will be successful tomorrow—are those that can get closest to their customers' needs.
>
> *Michael Dell[39]*

Suggestion #3: Be Unique, or At Least Be Better

Let's say your idea passes the needs test and you have checked it out with your potential customer and found them responsive. The next question to ask yourself, say our gurus, is, Is your idea unique? Imitation may be the sincerest form of flattery, but in the entrepreneurial business, it is more often a ticket to failure than to success. "Make sure you are offering something different from the rest," advises Lillian Vernon. "Is your product unique or sufficiently unusual to fill a neglected niche in the market?"[40]

You may be saying, "Wait a minute. I know successful businesses that are really no more than clones of other successful businesses." You're right. Cloning is a great entrepreneurial pastime. How many fast-food hamburger chains owe their inspiration to Billy Ingram and Walt Anderson and their famous White Castle system? McDonald's, for one. Earlier in this chapter we discussed Staples and one of its clones, Office Depot. So, what gives? The difference, according to our gurus, is that there are clones and then there are clones plus. The successful clones add better execution or a unique twist to set themselves apart, if only temporarily. Office Depot, you will recall, was beating Staples on price, and to gain an edge, McDonald's invented a number of enhancements to the White Castle fast-food system. For example, McDonald's was the first to premake hamburgers and keep them warm under infrared lamps, thus making the quick service White Castle was known for even speedier.[41] Lesson: You can clone and succeed if you clone and enhance.

What Makes the Pleasant Company Successful

We are not the first doll company. There have always been dolls out there for girls. We are not the first publishing company that publishes for children or girls. There are lots of children's book publishers. We're not the first people to publish historical fiction for girls. There is lots of historical fiction out there. We are not the only catalog company that sells children's products. We are unique for one thing. We have targeted little girls as intelligent, important people, and we talk to them that way. And their parents appreciate that. And that's what matters here. And that's why we're successful.

Pleasant Rowland[42]

Suggestion #4: Focus on a Single Market or Type of Product or Service

You will increase your chance of success, say our gurus, if you find a market niche and keep to it. Lillian Vernon quotes Peter Drucker, the famous management consultant: "Concentration is the key to economic results." "That's advice every entrepreneur should heed," writes Vernon. "Concentrate on the products you know how to sell and on the market with which you are familiar. Stay in the business you know."[43] The risk of straying from your niche, warns Jim Barksdale, cofounder of Netscape, is that your resources will be spread too thin and you will become distracted from your main goal. P.T. Barnum put his advice this way: "Engage in one kind of business only, and stick to it faithfully until you succeed, or until you conclude to abandon it. A constant hammering on one nail will generally drive it home at last, so that it can be clinched."[44]

Suggestion #5: Leverage Your New Idea by Linking It to Your Other Business Ventures

One way to increase the odds of success for your new business venture, argue our gurus, is to link it to other businesses you own. In short, you use one established business to help another get on its feet. This assumes, of course, that like most entrepreneurs you will start a number of different businesses in your lifetime. Richard Branson and Ted Turner are masters at pulling off such leverage. Here is how Branson explains the symbiotic relationships between the jigsaw of companies he has founded under the Virgin Group umbrella. Notice that Branson appears to violate the "stay focused" rule by branching into seemingly unrelated businesses.

> My vision for Virgin was ultimately summed up by [the musician] Peter Gabriel, who once said to me on a ski lift: "It's outrageous! Virgin is becoming everything. You wake up in the morning to Virgin Radio; you put on your Virgin jeans; you go to the Virgin Megastore; you drink Virgin Cola; you fly to America on Virgin Atlantic. Soon you'll be offering Virgin births, Virgin marriages, Virgin funerals. I think you should rename Virgin the 'In and Out Company.' Virgin will be there at the beginning and there at the end."
>
> As ever, Peter, an astute businessman as well as a gifted musician, was close to the truth. He had no idea at the time that we had two hundred

people down in Eastbourne working on a range of Virgin cosmetics, another designing a range of Virgin clothes, or that we were just about to bid for two British Rail franchises, which would make us the largest train operator in Britain. I doubt that we'll ever go into Virgin Funerals, but Virgin Births has certain ring to it. If there's a good business plan that offers good value, limited downside, good people, a good product, we'll go for it. . . .

This partly explains the jigsaw of companies we have. As well as protecting each other, they have symbiotic relationships. When Virgin Atlantic opens a flight to South Africa, I find that we can launch Virgin Radio and Virgin Cola there. We can use our experience in the airline industry to make buying train tickets easier and cheaper. We can draw on our experience of entertaining people on planes to entertain people on trains; we can use enormous stock of entertainment at the Virgin Megastores to make trips to Virgin Cinemas more fun. We can use the cinemas to have people sample our Virgin Cola. A trip to the cinema used to involve queuing up in the rain to buy your ticket from a man behind thick plate glass, watching the movie with one cup of popcorn, and then blundering out through a fire escape into some back street piled high with litter. Not anymore it doesn't—and that's because we have put all the Virgin experience together across retailing, entertainment, food, music, and travel to make it an easy-to-organize and enjoyable night.[45]

Ted Turner describes how he linked his billboard company and his radio stations to their mutual benefit this way:

One reason I wanted the [radio] station in Chattanooga so much was that I also owned the billboards there. See, I could take my vacant signs and promote my radio station. One of the things that was wrong with the billboard business was that although we had a 25 percent profit, we would also have 25 percent of our signs not being used. It seemed like an awful waste to have any unsold signs, because you have to do the upkeep on them anyway. It's not like a newspaper, where if you don't get ads you can cut the number of pages. So I would put up my own radio ads on the open billboards, and use them that way. It doesn't sound too brilliant, but it worked.[46]

Suggestion #6: Limit the Downside Risk

One of the reasons Branson likes his symbiotic relationships and Ted Turner seeks synergy is that they both are seeking to reduce the risk of a new venture. Here are three more ways Branson advises in order to reduce the downside:

1. *Arrange financing in such a way that any borrowing or liabilities are without resource to your other funds.* Branson cites the financing of Virgin Airlines as a good example. "There, we [had] the banks lending on the basis of the airline's performance and the value of the aircraft themselves. The Group's [parent company] only obligation to the banks [was] to provide leadership and management to the team at the airline."[47]

2. *Develop the business as a joint venture with someone else.* Branson developed Music Box, a pan-European television venture based on the MTV network in the United States, as a joint venture with Thorn EMI and Yorkshire Television.

3. *Have a way out.* Again Branson cites his airline as a good example. "We went into the airline business on the basis that we could get out after a year or two or so, (using the 'walk away' rule) we said to Boeing that we were not going ahead unless they gave a commitment to buy back the 747 during the first three years of its life at a fixed price. They agreed, so we were able to embark on the airline business, knowing that the downside was very limited."[48]

Suggestion #7: Suspend Disbelief, but Not Forever

The main reason to limit the downside is to make it easy for you to get out of an investment should your perfect idea turn out to be not so perfect after all. One of the tricky things about being an entrepreneur, say our gurus, is that you have to have a stubborn belief in your idea to succeed. You have to be willing to stand up to the naysayers and often go against the prevailing opinion. You have to insist that you are right when almost everyone else thinks you are not only wrong, but you're crazy. As Bill Gates puts it, to a certain extent, you have to suspend disbelief and say, "Hey, we're going to go for this new business," regardless of what anyone else thinks.[49] On the other hand, warn our gurus, your stubbornness can be a death trap. You can become so psychologically committed to the idea that you stay with it long past the time when you should have let it go. According to our gurus, the real key to sharpening your idea and reducing risk in a new investment is to be prepared to walk away from the idea if you have sharpened it all you can and it still seems dull. "If an idea is a clunker," advises Branson, "admit it. There's no glory in prolonging a failure. . . . Don't let ego get in the way."[50]

> Deals are like London buses—there is always one coming. And it is surprising how often the next deal is better than the one you have, with great reluctance, had to give up.
>
> *Richard Branson*[51]

SIX NEAR-PERFECT FOUNDATIONS FOR A SUCCESSFUL BUSINESS

We said at the beginning of this chapter that there was no perfect business idea, and there isn't. You can do all sorts of sleuthing to find irritants or competitor weaknesses. You can follow all of our gurus' suggestions for putting a razor-sharp edge on your proposal. And you may still have to admit that what you first thought was perfect just isn't. No one can give you a surefire plan for finding the idea that makes you the next Bill Gates. However, our gurus do offer a variety of suggestions for what you should be looking for as you sort through the various business ideas that come to your attention. Exhibit 2.4 summarizes what we call "near-perfect" foundations for businesses. The sections that follow provide a more complete discussion of each foundation. Although they can't guarantee your success, our gurus say they sure don't hurt.

Foundation #1: Have a Proprietary Idea or Technology

Having a proprietary idea or technology may be the best foundation of all, but it is also the hardest to find. You have such an idea or technology if you have something like Apple's Macintosh operating system. Obviously, your exclusive idea or technology, particularly if you own the patent, gives you an advantage. "It's less risky," explains Howard Schultz, "if you can erect some barrier to entry, to prevent a dozen competitors from popping up and grabbing your market away from you before you can establish yourself."[52] Where are you most likely to find a proprietary idea or technology today?

EXHIBIT 2.4. **Six Near-Perfect Foundations for a Successful Business**

1. A proprietary idea or technology.
2. Significantly better execution and/or commitment to perfection.
3. Being first to market, skating ahead of the competition.
4. Playing the underdog—using agility to fight an established, larger competitor while simultaneously avoiding head-to-head combat.
5. Turning a presumed disadvantage into an advantage.
6. Serving others—being values led.

Schultz suggests you look in the fields of biotechnology, software, or telecommunications. Notice that he does not mention coffee bars.

Foundation #2: Execute Better

Jim Koch, cofounder of the Boston Beer Company, which makes Samuel Adams beer, is fond of telling about his meeting with a group of Harvard Business School students. Koch had been asked to appear before the students and give a presentation about his experiences as an entrepreneur. In the course of the presentation, Koch asked the future MBAs what they felt he should have focused on when starting his company. The students offered typical business school responses:

"Do good market research."
"Hire an ad agency."
"Find a good PR firm."

One student suggested that none of his fellow students had it right. The most important thing for Koch to do, advised this future business leader, was to "locate the hot buttons on the quality vector." Koch recalled that he could only respond with, "What the hell is that supposed to mean?" Koch says that he was amazed that in all of the suggestions no student mentioned the one thing he thought was both obvious and critical—brew a better beer.[53]

> When asked to what he attributed the success of McDonald's, Ray Kroc responded simply; "We take the hamburger business more seriously than anyone else." He added: "The French fry has become almost sacrosanct for me. . . . Its preparation is a ritual to be followed religiously."
>
> *Ray Kroc*[54]

If you don't have a proprietary idea or technology—or even if you do—our gurus argue that you can win if you just execute better. In fact, Michael Dell says that, while some businesses are founded on one silver-bullet idea—one product or patent that is guarded 24 hours a day—that's not where growth in tomorrow's economy will come from. Real growth, argues Dell, will come from companies that execute better than their competition:

> The key is not so much one great idea or patent as it is the execution and implementation of a great strategy.
>
> Look at Disney or Wal-Mart or Coke. You can understand their strategy—it's really not that complicated. But it's genius! It's completely comprehensible, yet few companies can really replicate their success.
>
> Why? It's all about knowledge and execution. . . .
>
> Besides Dell, there are countless successful companies that are thriving now despite the fact that they started with little more than passion and a good idea. There are also many that failed, for the very same reason. The difference is that the thriving companies gathered the knowledge that gave them a substantial edge over their competition, which they then used to improve their execution, whatever their product or service. Those that didn't simply didn't make it.[55]

Moreover, execution isn't just about getting the big things right. You have to pay attention to the little things as well. Dell says he learned that from weekly customer advocate meetings that Dell Computer held in its early days.

> In these meetings, salespeople served as "advocates" for their customers who had issues with Dell by sharing the issues with a larger group of employees from many different functions within the company. Actions were assigned on the spot to correct any processes that might be affecting customer satisfaction.

If you attended this meeting regularly, you soon noticed a pattern: Almost all the complaints were about what the industry deems "little things," like whether the power cord was in the box, whether the box was designed for easy access, or whether it was delivered when we said it would be. We began to realize that customers were less focused on what the industry calls "big things"—such as product features or hot technology— probably because those needs had been largely satisfied. We were fascinated to learn how the "little things" became "big things" to the people who really mattered.[56]

> Ideas are easy. It's execution that's hard.
>
> *Jeff Bezos*[57]

The key to execution, declares Dell, is expectation. You have to set tough goals for yourself and your people. "In coming up with strategies to beat your competition, consider your core strengths," writes Dell, "and then dial it up a few notches."[58]

> If you can't do something first class, don't do it at all.
>
> *Ted Turner*[59]

Robert Mondavi states that, when he created Robert Mondavi Winery, he set forth one guiding ethic—the pursuit of excellence regardless of the cost, work, or personal sacrifice. "I was going to work like a fanatic, and I'd probably drive everyone around me like a fanatic."[60] But, reasoned Mondavi, wasn't that what it would take to be the best? He recalls thinking of the way great artists approached their work:

> Great artists are always fanatics. The painting or the poem or the symphony is not finished until every brushstroke, every syllable, every note, is finally perfect. And in perfect harmony with the rest of the creation. If we wanted to enter the ranks of The Best, if we wanted our wines to stand beside the great wines of Bordeaux and Burgundy, we had to hold ourselves to just as rigorous a standard. If we wanted to enter the kingdom of high art, I knew

we had to go beyond the pursuit of excellence and cultivate a passion for perfection.

Nothing less would do.[61]

> I really don't think that we do anything different. I don't think we're unique, we're certainly not smarter than the next guy. So the only thing that I can think of that we might do a little differently than some people is we work harder and when we focus in on something we are consumed by it. It becomes a passion.
>
> *Wayne Huizenga*[62]

If you intend to build your business on a foundation of excellence, your goal, advises Howard Schultz, should not be to just give your customers what they ask for. You should be trying to offer them much more. Don't just get the big things right. Get the little things right also. Strive for the perfection of the great artists. Then offer your customers even more—excellence that is way beyond what they have known before. "If you offer something [your customers] are not accustomed to, something so far superior that it takes a while to develop their palates," argues Schultz, "you can create a sense of discovery and excitement and loyalty that will bond them to you."[63]

A Fable about the Value of Excellence in Execution

IN EARLY 1994 two men, an American and a Briton, independently had the same inspired thought about the Internet. At a time when many retailers were setting up on-line malls for existing stores, these two men realised that the Internet could do something traditional retailing could not. Without the constraints of shelf space and physical locations, on-line stores could be infinitely big, dwarfing their physical-world competition. Both turned towards bookselling as the area to prove this because of their wives—the American's wife was an aspiring novelist, the Briton's works in publishing.

In a few months, the two men, who were in their early 30s, had both set up what they each claimed was the world's biggest on-line bookstore, one based in Oxford, the other Seattle. Both listed around 1m [one million] books, both were equally accessible from anywhere in the world, and both offered similar services for customers, such as e-mail notification when a new book by a favourite author had arrived. . . .

In May [1997], Jeff Bezos, the American, took his bookstore, Amazon.com, public at a valuation of nearly $500 m[illion]. Mr. Bezos himself is now worth nearly $500 m[illion]. Two months earlier, Darryl Mattocks, the Briton, had listed his bookstore, the Internet Bookshop, on Britain's Ofex, a small pseudo-market that matches traders' orders. It is now worth about $10 m[illion], and his stake is worth about $3 m[illion]. . . .

Whilst $3 m[illion] is hardly something to be sneezed at—and the amiable Mr. Mattocks seems anything but an unhappy soul why has the Briton fared less well? The chief reason is that Amazon is the better bookshop.[64]

Foundation #3: Be First—Skate Ahead of the Competition

Wayne Gretzky, the great hockey star, once said that his success came not from his ability to skate where the puck was but rather from his ability to skate where the puck was going to be. If you can do that with your business idea, say our gurus, then you have a strong foundation for your business. How do you anticipate where the business puck is going to be? Michael Dell suggests that you think about "changes in customers' buying behavior, in technology, in the existing competition, in potential competition, and the most fundamental change of all, in what your business is doing [or your competitors are doing] that could be done in a different way."[65]

Foundation #4: Be the Underdog

At first blush, playing the underdog doesn't sound like a very good strategy. Intentionally going after the Goliath of your industry seems more like a recipe for disaster. And yet Federal Express did it (versus UPS and Airborne), Netscape did it (against Microsoft), Ted Turner did it (against the networks), and Richard Branson did it (against British Airways and Coca Cola, among others.) The advantage of going after a big established player like Coca Cola, for example, Branson explains, is that they often have gotten fat and have very vulnerable skin.[66] You can actually exploit both their weaknesses and their strengths. Jim Barksdale says he learned while he was at Federal Express that there were certain advantages to being a small company competing against bigger, more established, longer-term companies. He discovered, for example, that "the larger company typically has more difficulty in moving rapidly. Their people are not as fresh and ready to do battle. [And] they tend to have many irons in the fire that they have to worry about."[67]

There are two secrets to competing against the Goliaths, say our gurus. First, take advantage of your small size to be agile and nimble. "Lightning strokes, sneak attacks, hit them before they know what's happening, don't give them a chance to regroup," says Ted Turner. "That's the only way it will work, that's the only way a little guy can beat a big guy. No holds barred. Don't stop just because you're little and you're afraid and it looks like you haven't got a chance. The rabbit can get away from the fox, but he better get on his hind legs and hop."[68]

Second, say our gurus, avoid head-to-head combat. Your strategy should be to fight the entrenched big companies on your ground, not theirs. As Jim Barksdale puts it, the lesson to be learned is that, "in the fight between the bear and the alligator, the outcome is determined by the terrain."[69] For example, if you are a small-town retailer up against a giant Wal-Mart, you certainly aren't going to be able to compete head-on against America's number-one retailer. Your best bet, say our gurus, is to change the terrain. How do you do that? Here is a lesson on competing against a big company like Wal-Mart from a real expert—Sam Walton himself.

Unless small merchants are already doing a great job, they'll probably have to rethink their merchandising and advertising and promotional programs once a discounter arrives on the scene. They need to avoid coming at us head-on, and do their own thing better than we do ours. It doesn't make any sense to try to underprice Wal-Mart on something like toothpaste. That's not what the customer is looking to a small store for anyway. Most independents are best off, I think, doing what I prided myself on doing for so many years as a storekeeper: getting out on the floor and meeting every one of the customers. Let them know how much you appreciate them, and ring that cash register yourself. That little personal touch is so important for an independent merchant because no matter how hard Wal-Mart tries to duplicate it—and we try awfully hard—we can't really do it.

I think in the case of variety stores, they have to completely reposition themselves, something like the way Don Soderquist did when he was president of Ben Franklin. He saw that there just wasn't any future in competing with Wal-Mart and Kmart so he started converting a lot of their variety stores into craft stores. They offered a much bigger assortment of craft merchandise than any Wal-Mart could, and they held classes in things like pottery and flower arranging, services we could never think about providing. It worked. They stayed in business in the small towns and have been quite successful with many of those stores. The same thing can be done with fabrics: offer higher quality material and throw in some sewing classes. Or ladies' apparel. I don't care how many Wal-Marts come to town, there are always niches that we can't reach.[70]

Foundation #5: Turn a Disadvantage into Profits

A variation on the theme of avoiding head-to-head combat that our gurus suggest is taking a disadvantage and turning it into an advantage. Michael Dell explains how Dell Computer used such a tactic in the mid-1980s:

> Back in the 1980s, when PC sales really began taking off, getting your computer serviced was about as enticing—and involved—as having a root canal. If you bought the machine at a computer dealer, you had to put it into the car and drive it over to the service center, where you would wait in line to drop it off and come back days, maybe weeks later.
>
> And then there was no guarantee it could—or would—actually be fixed.
>
> When I first founded Dell, prospective customers initially had a hard time imagining buying a computer over the phone because they assumed that servicing it would be impossible. Without a store to drive it to, they figured they'd have to box it up, mail it in, and then wait even longer to get it back. Then of course there was the fear that, because a computer was an expensive proposition to begin with, sending it in the mail would pose an even greater opportunity for damage (not to mention the shipping cost).
>
> Competitors also assumed that because Dell sold direct to customers, we would not be able to create an advantage in service. With the added "benefit" of resellers and physical stores, they assumed they would always have an advantage in service, however bad theirs might be.
>
> They were clearly wrong.
>
> From the very beginning, we saw a huge opportunity to provide extraordinary service where our competitors saw none—and designated it one of the company's early objectives. In 1986, we offered the very first program in our industry for on-site service—a kind of "house call" service for sick computers. If your computer had a problem, you didn't have to go anywhere; we came to you—to your business, house, or hotel room. And we

would come by the very next business day or on the same day. [Later Dell offered four-hour and even two-hour on-site service.]

Suddenly, our competitors' service centers looked a little old-fashioned—and really slow. Even today, if you take your computer to be serviced at a retail service center, the repair time can be as much as two weeks, a far cry from the next business day. And there's still no guarantee that it will be fixed. What the competition initially assumed would be a disadvantage for us turned out to be a massive advantage.[71]

Foundation #6: Be Values Led

The final foundation for a business—being values led—may sound a little strange, but it is strongly advocated by a select group of our gurus, including Mary Kay Ash, Tom Chappell, Ben Cohen, Konosuke Matsushita (founder of Matsushita Electric Industrial Company), Anita Roddick, and Jay Van Andel. Each of these gurus expresses the concept differently, but essentially it is this: Service to others is the best and strongest foundation for any business.

> Possessing material comforts in no way guarantees happiness. Only spiritual wealth can bring true happiness. If that is correct, should business be concerned only with the material aspect of life and leave the care of the human spirit to religion or ethics? I do not think so. Businessmen too should be able to share in creating a society that is spiritually rich and materially affluent.
>
> *Konosuke Matsushita*[72]

Mary Kay Ash states that service to others is the most important justification for being in business and that "every new business must be built upon this premise, since wanting to make money or desiring to 'dabble' in a favorite pastime are not enough to sustain such a venture."[73] She cites the Bible passage Matthew 25:14–30, the parable of the talents, which teaches that you should use and increase whatever God has given to you, and that when you do, the good you do will come back to you. Ash says that in her case she wanted to help women: "I wanted to provide opportunities for them to create better lives. I saw Mary Kay Cosmetics as a vehicle for women to realize their dreams. Our organization would supply the quality products, education, encouragement, and motivation women need to succeed."[74] "Then and now," adds Ash, "everything anyone in our sales organization does to succeed is based upon helping others. As beauty consultants we must help customers; and as sales directors we must help our people to succeed. The company structure requires each person to help others in order to climb the ladder of success. The individual who thinks only 'What's in it for me?' will never make it in our company. We truly believe that if you help enough other people get what they want you will get what you want! The people who are the most successful in our company are those who have helped the most people grow."[75]

Ash admits that some people may find such altruism strange and in conflict with the profit motive, but, she argues, in reality there is no conflict at all. "Actually," she writes, "the two are harmonious, because when your employees do well, they become content, enthusiastic, and loyal, resulting in a healthy bottom line."[76]

> One of the greatest responsibilities of an entrepreneur is to imprint his or her values on the organization.
>
> *Howard Schultz*[77]

Ben Cohen says the experiences of a wide range of companies—Patagonia, Inc. (clothing), Odwalla, Inc. (juice), Tom's of Maine, Inc. (personal-care products), The Body Shop International PLC (body-care products), Blue Fish Clothing, Frontier Cooperative Herbs, Working Assets Funding Service (credit cards and long-distance phone service), Rhino Entertainment (music), Tommy Boy (music), Whole Foods Market, Just Desserts, Stonyfield Farm Yogurt, Aveda Corporation (personal-care products), and many more—prove his contention that serving others, or as he terms it, "being values led," is good for business.[78] Cohen cites the following results of a 1994 Cone Communications and Roper Research survey to back up his contention.

- Seventy-eight percent of adults said they were more likely to buy a product associated with a cause they care about.

- Sixty-six percent of adults said they'd be likely to switch brands to support a cause they care about.
- Fifty-four percent of adults said they'd pay more for a product that supports a cause they care about.
- After price and quality, 33 percent of Americans consider a company's responsible business practices the most important factor in deciding whether to buy a brand.[79]

Still not convinced? Well, say our gurus, there is one other thing to think about. Maybe, just maybe, it is immoral not to take your values, service to others, and so on in consideration as you are laying the foundation for your business. That's what Anita Roddick thinks. In her 1991 book *Body and Soul,* Roddick explains her beliefs this way:

> I believe this to be immoral. It is immoral to trade on fear. It is immoral constantly to make women feel dissatisfied with their bodies. It is immoral to deceive a customer by making miracle claims for a product. It is immoral to use a photograph of a glowing sixteen-year-old to sell a cream aimed at preventing wrinkles in a forty-year-old.
>
> It is immoral, but it slots perfectly well into the context of a general business environment in which greed has become respectable and worth is measured by what you accumulate rather than what you contribute; into an environment of insider trading and backhanders; into an environment in which bosses award themselves exorbitant pay rises while they are sacking hundreds of their employees. . . .
>
> I am mystified by the fact that the business world is apparently proud to be seen as hard and uncaring and detached from human values. Why is altruism in business seen as alien to the point where anyone claiming to be motivated by it is considered suspect? I personally don't know how the hell anybody can survive running a successful business . . . without caring. I don't know how they keep their role within the community. I don't know how they keep their soul intact.[80]

👁 OUR VIEW

We don't either. If you agree and want to put a little soul into your business proposal, take a look at Tom Chappell's suggestions for incorporating your values into your business strategy, as summarized in Exhibit 2.5.

EXHIBIT 2.5. **Tom Chappell's Key Steps for Incorporating Your Values into Corporate Strategy**

Step	Activity	Description
1.	Identify your personal and professional values.	The simplest way to articulate your values, says Chappell, is to write out your "I believe" statements. For example: ■ "I believe that profit is essential to a healthy business." ■ "I believe that people are worthy of respect." ■ "I believe our business should benefit this community."
2.	Ask yourself the big questions.	Chappell advises you to raise the questions that will provoke answers about beliefs and values and force them to the surface. You shouldn't be afraid to be too general or philosophical. He explains, "You are questioning the nature of your business, its essence, and that, after all, is what philosophy is all about." Chappell suggests you ask yourself questions such as the following: ■ Is business only quantitative—about the numbers? ■ Is it qualitative—about values? ■ Is it about both? ■ Do I want my business plans to include what I value? ■ Should there be some coherence between what I value in business and what I value in my life outside the office?
3.	Read material that raises ethical issues.	Chappell suggests the following as a good starting point for your reading list: ■ *Leadership and the Quest for Integrity*, by Joseph L. Badaracco Jr. and Richard R. Ellsworth ■ *Corporate Ethics and Strategic Planning*, by R. Edward Freeman and Daniel R. Gilbert Jr. ■ "On Enlightenment," in Immanuel Kant's *On History* ■ *I and Thou*, by Martin Buber ■ *Essay on the Mind*, by Jonathan Edwards ■ I Corinthians, in the New Testament

(continued)

EXHIBIT 2.5. **(continued)**

STEP	ACTIVITY	DESCRIPTION
4.	**Answer the following questions:** ■ **Who are we?** ■ **What are we about?**	Chappell advises you to write down your answers to these questions, edit them, and invite comments from others.
5.	**Implement your beliefs.**	Remember, says Chappell, nothing is written in stone. Your first attempt may not work. If it doesn't, try again.

Source: Adapted from Tom Chappell, The Soul of a Business (New York: Bantam Trade Paperbook, 1994), pp. 35–37.

THE BUSINESS PLAN

If you have followed our gurus' suggestions in this chapter, by now you have gathered ideas for a business, checked out your potential competition, sharpened your idea, and picked a foundation that you think will serve your company well as it grows. You may have even clarified some of your personal values and decided how you would incorporate them into your business. You are now ready to write your business plan.

Exhibit 2.6 presents a brief summary of a standard business plan as described by Earl Graves. Graves suggests that you keep your plan to a length of about twenty-five to fifty pages. It should contain four major sections: the executive summary, market analysis, management summary, and financial analysis. Also see Exhibit 2.7 for a list of books, software, and Web sites that offer advice on preparing a business plan.

EXHIBIT 2.6. **The Standard Business Plan**

Section	Description
Executive summary	This is a two- to three-page overview intended to convince readers to read your plan in its entity. Graves explains that it is important for you to convey your passion for the project in this summary. Briefly describe your product, market, customers, and suppliers. Explain what makes your company unique, how much start-up capital you feel you require, and what you expect the returns on investment to be over what time period.
Market analysis	Who are your customers? Why will they be attracted to your business? What are the industry trends? Who are your existing and potential competitors? What are your strengths and weaknesses compared to them? Graves suggests that you consult *The Encyclopedia of Associations* for trade associations for your industry. You should contact them for information you will need to complete this section of your plan. Other potential resources include the World Wide Web, *Thomas Register of Manufacturers,* and the *Rand McNally Commercial Atlas and Commercial Guide.*
Management summary	Who will run the company? Include biographies of yourself and any other managers. Investors want to know about relevant skills you and your other managers bring to the business, your prior experience, and any degrees or training you might have that will be of benefit to the company. Explain what role each manager will play in the business. Graves suggests that you include an organization chart if you have more than five managers.
Financial analysis	This section should provide your financial projections over the first three to five years. How will you generate the money to operate the business? What do you expect the cash flow to be like during the start-up years? How much money will you need to borrow? What assets and liabilities will the company have over the time period covered by the financial analysis? How long will it take for the company to break even (e.g., sales revenues equal total cost)? (See Chapter 3 for more information on how to calculate start-up costs.)

Source: Earl G. Graves and Robert L. Crandall, How to Succeed in Business without Being White: Straight Talk on Making It in America (New York: HarperBusiness, 1997), pp. 141–148.

EXHIBIT 2.7. **Business-Plan Resources**

Books

- *Anatomy of a Business Plan: A Step-by-Step Guide to Starting Smart, Building the Business, and Securing Your Company's Future,* 4th edition, by Linda Pinson and Jerry Jinnett (Chicago: Dearborn Trade, 1999). Award-winning best-seller.
- *The Business Planning Guide: Creating a Plan for Success in Your Own Business,* 8th edition, by David H. Bangs (Chicago: Upstart Publishing, 1998). Named by *Forbes* as its favorite, most useful small-business book.
- *The Complete Book of Business Plans: Simple Steps to Writing a Powerful Business Plan,* by Joseph A. Covello and Brian J. Hazelgren (Naperville, IL: Sourcebooks Trade, 1994). Five-star reviews.
- *The Instant Business Plan Third Edition, Twelve Quick and Easy Steps to a Successful Business,* by Gustav Berle and Paul Kirschner (Santa Maria, CA: Puma Publishing, 2000). Includes free downloadable Macintosh and Windows business-planning software.
- *The One Page Business Plan: Start with a Vision, Build a Company!* edited by James T. Horan and Rebecca S. Shaw (El Sobrante, CA: One Page Business Plan, 1998). Tom Peters calls *The One Page Business Plan* "an out and out winner."
- *Online Business Planning: How to Create a Better Business Plan Using the Internet,* by Robert T. Gorman (Hawthorne, NJ: Career Press, 1999). Includes a complete, up-to-date resource guide.
- *Your First Business Plan: A Simple Question and Answer Format Designed to Help You Write Your Own Plan,* 3rd edition, by Joseph Covello and Brian J. Hazelgren (Naperville, IL: Sourcebooks Trade, 1998). Best-selling guide for the novice.

Software

- *Adams Streetwise Complete Business Plan,* Adams New Media
- *Business Plan Pro,* versions 3.0 and 4.0, Palo Alto Software
- *Business Plan Writer Deluxe,* Macmillan Digital Publishing
- *Business Plans Made E-Z,* E-Z Legal Forms
- *Cortext Software Business Plan Deluxe,* Cortext Limited
- *Officeready Business Plans,* Canon Computer Systems

Web Sites

- <http://www.sba.gov> (home page for the Small Business Administration [SBA]). A search of that site for the key words *business plan* results in several helpful sites, including the SBA's online courses in business plan development listed below.
- <http://classroom.sba.gov/xtrainx/BPLAN914/ie.htm> (the site for SBA's online course for Internet Explorer users)
- <http://classroom.sba.gov/xtrainx/BPLAN914/ns.htm> (the site for SBA's online course for Netscape users)
- <http://www.sba.gov/hotlist/bplan.html> (the SBA Hotlist for business plans)

Note: Because the Internet is a constantly changing media, these addresses are subject to change. If any one address does not work for you, try using the keyword search from the SBA home page.

FRANCHISING OR BUYING THE PERFECT IDEA

Let's say that you have followed all of the suggestions provided in this chapter and still the perfect idea escapes you. Should you give up your dream of becoming an entrepreneur, or is there another route to business ownership? Actually, there are two other routes available to you. You could buy a franchise or purchase an existing business. Here is what our gurus have to say about these two options.

Going the Franchise Route

Would the franchise route be a good option for you? First, some words of wisdom from Earl Graves about the ins and outs of franchising. Then, we will look at some advice from Dave Thomas on checking out a franchisor before signing on the bottom line.

Earl Graves's Advice on Buying a Franchise

- *Franchises do not encourage independent thinking.* The first thing to know about franchising, says Graves, is that franchises do not encourage independent thinking; so, if your bent is to be a free spirit, franchising may not be right for you. Be aware, cautions Graves, that the franchise owners will lay down strict rules for you to follow, including rules covering your approach to marketing and the delivery of goods and services.

- *Don't think of franchise ownership as a part-time job.* As a franchise owner you are responsible for your business 24 hours a day, seven days a week. It is not a nine-to-five job. You'll have deadlines and quotas to meet. You will be expected to learn about and stay abreast of developments in your market. The franchisor will probably insist that you attend training workshops. And on a day-to-day basis you won't be able to just sit back and give directions. If you can't see yourself cleaning the rest rooms or sweeping the parking lot late at night, a franchise may not be for you.

- *Don't think that franchising is a way to avoid the unpleasant task of drawing up a good business plan.* You still need one, says Graves, so you should ask the franchisor for all the details about start-up costs and working capital you will need. Crunch the numbers. Can you avoid borrowing the start-up fees and still retain enough money in reserve to last at least three years without profits? If not, advises Graves, you need to do some more analysis. Think it though. Plan.

■ *Get expert advice.* In addition to a well-thought-out business plan, Graves advises you to get the counsel of smart legal and accounting professionals who can help you fine tune your b.s. detector. In particular, says Graves, never sign an agreement without first having your attorney review it thoroughly. Make sure you completely understand your rights and obligations and those of the franchisor.

■ *Know exactly what it takes for you to get out of the deal.* Graves notes that some tough contracts allow termination only if it is initiated by the franchisor. That means you could be locked in for life even if you want out.

■ *Check out the franchisor carefully.* Read all of the fine print in the Uniform Franchise Offering Circular (UFOC) that the franchisor is required to give you by Federal law. Then ask questions. A lot of questions.[81] What should you ask? Let's turn to Dave Thomas, the founder of Wendy's, for some more advice about how to check out a franchisor.

Dave Thomas on How to Check a Franchise Out

Dave Thomas has the distinction of having been on both sides of the franchise fence, first as a franchisee for KFC and then as the franchisor for Wendy's. Here are his suggestions for checking out a franchise.

■ *Learn everything you can about the franchisor.* Ask the franchisor for a copy of its annual report and study it carefully. Check trade and business magazines to see what has been written about the franchisor over the last few years. Ask your stockbroker for any investment research that he or she may have about the company.

■ *Visit the franchise.* Visit several different units of the franchise to see how they operate. How well are standards followed from one place to the next? If you find big differences between the way different locations are run—for example, one is clean and efficiently run and another is sloppy and slow—then there may be a problem with the franchisor's system.

- *Talk to franchisees.* Thomas suggests you ask franchisees questions such as the following:

  □ What do you like and dislike about the franchisor?
  □ Does the franchisor keep his or her commitments to you?
  □ Is the franchisor a tough inspector? Does he or she make franchisees operate their units according to the system? (Thomas says you want a franchisor to be tough because that is the only way standards will be maintained across the system, protecting your investment.)
  □ Is there any difference in how company-owned and franchised units are run? (In the best franchises, says Thomas, you will see very little if any differences.)

- *Investigate the background of franchisees.* Do most of the current franchisees actually run their units themselves, or are they primarily just investors? Thomas advises you to look for a franchisor who has the minimum number of absentee franchise owners. As he puts it, "A franchise isn't just an investment, it's a way of life. You can't play this game from the sidelines."

- *Find out about how well the franchisor communicates with franchisees.* Do franchisees have the opportunity to get together and share information? Is there a good dialogue between franchisees? According to Thomas, you want to be part of an organization that maintains a good and open flow of communication so that ideas are shared and problems can get solved fast.

- *Check out the size of the franchise.* Thomas warns you to be especially cautious about buying into a franchise with only a few units. A small chain will not be able to give you the kind of operating, marketing, advertising, and other support you will need. If the franchise is just starting, says Thomas, you should be sure to find out about expansion plans. Does it plan to grow fast? How does the franchisor plan to accomplish that?

- *Find out how the franchisor deals with a franchisee who gets in trouble.* The big danger, explains Thomas, is that a franchisee can get into deep trouble before the franchisor discovers what is happening. The key to avoiding such disasters is communication. Thomas suggests that you find out how the franchisor keeps tabs on franchisees so that he or she can detect problems before they get out of hand.

- *Find out about any hidden charges.* Are you going to be forced to buy supplies or equipment exclusively from the franchisor? Such an arrangement can provide extra profits for the franchisor and add tons of extra costs for the franchisee.

- *Work for one of the franchisees before you invest.* The best way to learn about the franchisor, says Thomas, is to go to work for one of the existing franchisees. That way, you learn the system from the inside before you put up your money.[82]

Warren Buffett on Buying an Existing Business

Suppose you find the whole prospect of following someone else's game plan confining. You want a little more independence to do things your way than you would have as a franchisee. In that case, buying an existing business might be right for you. Someone has already developed the idea and made it work. You buy their assets, learn their system, and still have the ability to tailor it to your liking. How do you make sure you don't make a mistake and pick the wrong business to buy? Here is some advice from Warren Buffett.[83]

Mistake #1: Buying Because the Price Looks Cheap

Buffett cautions you not to get carried away with a bargain purchase. "Unless you are a liquidator, that kind of approach to buying businesses is foolish," writes Buffett:

> First, the original "bargain" price probably will not turn out to be such a steal after all. In a difficult business, no sooner is one problem solved than another surfaces—never is there just one cockroach in the kitchen. Second, any initial advantage you secure will be quickly eroded by the low return that the business earns. For example, if you buy a business for $8 million that can be sold or liquidated for $10 million and promptly take either course, you can realize a high return. But the investment will disappoint if the business is sold for $10 million in ten years and in the interim has annually earned and distributed only a few percent on cost. Time is the friend of the wonderful business, the enemy of the mediocre.[84]

Mistake #2: Buying a Business with Problems, Even If You Think You Know How to Fix Them

As Buffett puts it, "good jockeys will do well on good horses, but not on broken down nags." No matter how good a business manager you may think you are, says Buffett, you are better off avoiding difficult business problems rather than trying to solve them.

Mistake #3: Buying a Business When You Don't Like the People

No matter how attractive the business, Buffett says, he has never been successful in making a good deal with a bad person. His advice: If you don't like the people you have to work with in making the deal, walk away from it.

THERE IS NO FINISH LINE

Here are a couple of final words from our gurus that apply whether you start a business from scratch, buy one, or go the franchise route.

First, our gurus warn that even with the best advice there is nothing certain about what you are doing. Richard Branson puts it this way:

> There aren't ingredients and techniques that will guarantee success. Parameters exist [such as those presented in this chapter] that, if followed, will ensure that a business can continue, but it's not as if you can clearly define . . . business success and then bottle it as if it's a perfume. It's not that simple. To be successful, you have to be out there, you have to hit the ground running, and if you have a good team round you and more than a fair share of luck, you might make something happen. But you certainly can't guarantee it just by following someone else's formula.[85]

Second, there is no finish line. You are going to have to reinvent your company over and over to survive. Bill Gates estimates that every product in his company becomes obsolete in three years; so, he sees himself constantly reinventing his game plan. We are confident that you will find, like Gates, that your company needs constant attention. You will just have to keep trying because, as Arthur Blank likes to say, every entrepreneur quickly learns that "those that don't make dust, eat dust."[86]

KEY IDEAS

- There are no perfect ideas for businesses.

- Real entrepreneurs gather ideas for creating and reinventing their businesses everywhere and all the time. They are constantly on the lookout for products or services that might satisfy needs.

- One source of ideas is the competition or potential competition. Real entrepreneurs make it a practice to visit their competitors' stores and shop their businesses in order to discover what their competitors are doing wrong and what they are doing right.

- Successful entrepreneurs have well-tuned antennae for detecting business opportunities. They constantly ask themselves, "How could this problem be turned into profit?"

- Successful entrepreneurs recognize that irritants are often the genesis of good ideas. If something bothers the entrepreneur, it probably bothers others also. Removing the irritant may be a solid basis for a new business.

- Successful entrepreneurs are not surprised when their ideas for businesses are rejected by friends, relatives, and business associates. They take the rejection only as a sign that they must check out their idea in more detail.

- Entrepreneurs who buy a franchise should:

  □ Treat the franchise as a full-time business and not as an investment.
  □ Check out the franchisor carefully before proceeding.

- Entrepreneurs who decide to buy an existing business should:

  □ Not shop for bargains.
  □ Not buy a business with problems, even if they feel they know the solutions.

▫ Not buy a business if they dislike or do not trust the existing owners or managers.

⊶ Successful entrepreneurs know that even the best business idea will need attention over time. There is no finish line. All businesses have to be reinvented every day.

Arthur Blank, cofounder of Home Depot

Ben Cohen, cofounder of Ben & Jerry's Ice Cream

Cecil B. Day, cofounder of Days Inn of America, Inc.

Walt Disney, cofounder of Disney Brothers Studio (later Walt Disney Productions, Ltd.)

Charles Ferguson, cofounder of Vermeer Technologies, Inc.

Debbi Fields, founder of Mrs. Fields Cookies, Inc.

Bill Gates, cofounder of Microsoft Corporation

Earl Graves, founder, publisher, and editor of *Black Enterprise*

Jerry Greenfield, cofounder of Ben & Jerry's Ice Cream

Bud Hadfield, founder of Kwik Kopy

Wilson Harrell, founder of over one hundred companies, columnist for *Success Magazine,* and former publisher of *Inc. Magazine*

Chris Larsen, cofounder of E-Loan

Bernie Marcus, cofounder of Home Depot

Tom Monaghan, founder of Domino's Pizza

Robert Mondavi, founder of Robert Mondavi Winery

Ross Perot, founder of Electronic Data Systems (EDS) and of Perot Systems Corporation

Stephen M. Pollan, financial consultant and writer

Anita Roddick, founder of The Body Shop

Howard Schultz, founder of Starbucks Coffee Company

Thomas Stemberg, cofounder of Staples, Inc.

R. David (Dave) Thomas, founder of Wendy's International, Inc.

Ted Turner, founder of Turner Broadcasting System, Cable News Network (CNN), and Turner Network Television (TNT)

Lillian Vernon, founder of Lillian Vernon Corporation

3

Money Matters

Money matters. It is as simple as that. The money you have or can get from someone else makes all the difference in your ability to start a business and keep it going. All entrepreneurs learn that lesson, and almost all entrepreneurs hate it. Of all the activities entrepreneurs hate the most, raising and managing money are at the top of the I-can't-stand-to-do-it list. The fun for entrepreneurs is thinking up ideas, taking prudent risks, winning and losing, wooing customers, inspiring employees, creating, and innovating. Accounting, financial analysis, running the numbers, wooing bankers, and romancing venture capitalists are rarely tasks entrepreneurs enjoy. If you are like most entrepreneurs, you will find this chapter—well—necessary. So, let's begin with the most necessary of necessary things. Just how much is it going to cost to get your "perfect idea" off the ground and keep it running until it can take care of itself?

ESTIMATING START-UP COSTS

So far in this book we have relied exclusively on entrepreneurs as our gurus because we wanted to present the ideas of people who had been there and done it. This chapter is a little different. We will be turning to the advice of two well-known business writers as we discuss methods for estimating your start-up costs. As we already noted, real entrepreneurs don't find the ins and outs of money matters that enjoyable, so they rarely go into great detail about how they crunched their numbers. In addition, our entrepreneurs' approaches to such matters as estimating start-up costs are often decidedly unsophisticated compared with those recommended by the experts in small-business development. Because we want to be true to our entrepreneur gurus, while not giving you bad advice, we include both approaches in this chapter.

First, we share with you an example of the typical entrepreneur's method for calculating start-up costs, based on the experiences of Ben Cohen and Jerry Greenfield of Ben & Jerry's. As you will see, it is rich with imprecision. Next, we share the recommendations of Stephen M. Pollan and Mark Levine, coauthors of *The Field Guide to Starting a Business*. Their approach is much more precise. The difference between these two approaches is somewhat analogous to the differences between the approach most of us use to jump-start a car and the method recommended by battery manufacturers. Faced with getting the car going on a cold and snowy day, most of us pay little attention to the order in which we attach the cables. The manufacturer's guide, on the other hand, gives precise instruction amid dire warnings of the possible consequences should you not follow their steps. We all know that both methods have worked in the past. We also know that the manufacturer's way is a lot less dangerous. That said, here is the way start-up costs are usually calculated, followed by the way some notable experts recommend.

The Ben & Jerry Approach to Estimating Start-Up Costs

When Ben Cohen and Jerry Greenfield decided to open a homemade-ice-cream parlor in Burlington, Vermont, in 1978, they had exactly $8,000 between them to invest in the business—$4,000 from Jerry, $2,000 from Ben, and $2,000 from Ben's father. They knew that $8,000 wouldn't be enough but had no idea how much they would really need. Here is how they calculated their start-up cost, as explained in their 1997 book, *Double Dip*.

> We sent away for some of the inexpensive little six-page brochures the Small Business Administration publishes. The brochures gave us formulas to figure out how much money we needed to start out with, and what our break-even point would be. Everything we needed, and in those days they [the brochures] cost only twenty-five cents each.
>
> We used those brochures to fill in the blanks on the pizza parlor business plan we were using as a template. Unfortunately, we read one of the

brochures wrong, which caused us to make a basic error in our planning. We thought you were supposed to double your cost of ingredients to come up with your retail price. In fact, for an ice cream parlor, you're supposed to triple it.

Also, the business plan called for us to estimate how many ice cream cones we were going to sell in an hour, a week, or a month. That stumped us. How were we supposed to know how many people were going to patronize a homemade-ice-cream parlor in a town that had never had one? There was no rational basis for coming up with an estimate of sales—but writing a business plan, applying for a bank loan, required us to do that. . . .

Later we realized that our initial calculations were based on sales projections that were unprojectable, on the wrong formula for figuring selling price, and on a huge underestimation of the number of ice cream cones we would end up selling in a typical day. Not surprisingly, our financial model showed the business couldn't be successful. . . .

In those moments it helps to be a person like Ben, who realizes facts and figures don't tell the whole story—and may be downright misleading. . . .

But there's always that choice to make. You can just as easily say, "I don't believe the numbers," as, "I don't believe my own qualitative judgments based on my observations of the marketplace."

After all, it wasn't instinct alone that told us to go ahead despite the projections. We couldn't afford to hire anyone to do market research, so we'd done our own—visiting homemade-ice-cream parlors up and down the East Coast. We counted the revolutions per minute of the ice cream freezers at Steve's. We learned how other shops made ice cream. We saw ice cream parlors that were successful in towns similar to Burlington. We familiarized ourselves with the competition they faced, their pricing, the kind of products they were serving. We had reason to believe we could be successful too. So we changed the numbers to project first-year sales of $90,000 and a pretax net profit of $7,746.[1]

As Greenfield says, it's easier to go with your instincts—just like attaching the battery cables. In this case, everything worked out okay. They got their bank loan, although as we will see later in this chapter, not on the basis of their financial projections and not for the amount they thought they needed. Would it have been different if they had used a more sophisticated formula in estimating their start-up costs, or are all such projections just wishful thinking anyway? Let's look at the way Pollan and Levine say you should perform your calculations.

The "Expert" Approach to Estimating Start-Up Costs

Stephen Pollan and Mark Levine are coauthors of *The Field Guide to Starting a Business.* Pollan is a financial consultant who has appeared on such television programs as *Good Morning America* and *Today.* Pollan and Levine suggest you calculate your start-up cost as follows:[2]

Step One: Prepare a Personal Austerity Budget

Calculate your living expenses—food, housing, clothing, utilities, and so on. Then cut your expenses to the bone. What is the minimum amount you actually have to have to stay alive for 18 months? Do you have that much money readily available to you in a savings, checking, or money-market account? If your answer is yes, proceed to step two. If no, stop now. You're not ready to start your business.

Step Two: Determine Your Initial Cash Outlay

Make an estimate of all of the one-time costs you will incur in starting your business. The types of expenses Pollan and Levine say you should consider are listed in Exhibit 3.1.

Step Three: Determine Your Working-Capital Requirements

Working capital is the amount of money you will need each month to make up for the shortfall between the money you take in from selling your products and/or services and the money you must pay out in operating expenses. During the early days, months, or even years of your new business, you should expect your shortfall between income and expenses to be sizable. Later, as your business improves, the difference between income and expenses should narrow until you reach breakeven, that is, you can pay all of your monthly expenses based on the money you have taken in that month. In order to calculate the working capital, you will need you need to prepare a cash-flow analysis. Here is how Pollan and Levine suggest you do that: (1) determine your monthly fixed costs, (2) determine your monthly vari-

EXHIBIT 3.1. Initial Cash Outlay

ITEM	AMOUNT	ITEM	AMOUNT
Deposits:		Office supplies	
Rent		Transportation equipment	
Telephone		Professional fees:	
Utilities		Legal	
Insurance		Financial	
Other		Other	
Machinery and equipment		Advance advertising and publicity	
Office equipment		Leasehold improvement	
Office furniture		Inventory (one turn)	
Stationery		**Total Initial Cash Outlay**	

Source: Stephen M. Pollan and Mark Levine, The Field Guide to Starting a Business (New York: Fireside, 1990), pp. 124–125.

Note: In making your estimates, include only the amounts you will have to pay up front. If you will be paying for some of these expenses over time, include them in your estimate of working capital in step three.

able costs, (3) estimate what you can charge per item, (4) determine your contribution margin, (5) determine how much sales you need to break even, (6) forecast your cash flow, and (7) estimate your working-capital requirements.

Determine Your Monthly Fixed Costs

Fixed costs are monthly expenses that you will have that do not vary according to your volume of sales. (See Exhibit 3.2.)

Determine Your Monthly Variable Costs

Variable costs are those costs that will vary based on your volume of sales. (See Exhibit 3.3.)

Estimate the Price You Can Charge per Item

To arrive at a price for the product or service you plan to sell, Pollan and Levine suggest that you ask yourself the following:

- Is the product or service unique enough to command a high price?
- Are there any legal limits on how much I can charge?

EXHIBIT 3.2. **Fixed Costs**

Item	Amount	Item	Amount
Rent	_____	Exterminating	_____
Salaries	_____	Garbage collection	_____
Fees	_____	Telephone	_____
Advertising	_____	Cleaning and maintenance	_____
Promotion	_____	Professional dues	_____
Taxes	_____	Continuing education	_____
Water	_____	Upkeep of business libraries	_____
Electricity	_____	Other	_____
Insurance	_____	**Total Fixed Costs**	_____
Window cleaning	_____		

EXHIBIT 3.3. **Variable Costs per Item or Sale**

Item	Amount	Item	Amount
Raw materials	_____	Credit card fees (2 to 15% of sales)	_____
Packaging	_____	Other	_____
Sales commissions	_____	**Total Variable Costs**	_____

- How will competitors respond to my pricing?
- Are there market conditions—such as new technology, pending legislation, or new sources of supply—that could affect the price?
- Will I have to work through middlemen to get my product or service to the public? If so, what is their pricing policy?
- If I have to purchase items for resell, what is the industry standard markup? (The markup is the difference between the selling price and amount the reseller paid for the item. For example, if you buy an item for $10 and then turn around and sell it for $15, the markup is 50 percent. Higher-quality items command a higher markup than lower quality items, particularly if they are accompanied by exceptional service.)

EXHIBIT 3.4. **Cash Flow**

Month	1	2	3, etc.	Breakeven
Sales	xx	xxxx	xxxxxxx	xxxxxxxx
Income	$xx	$xxx	$x,xxx	$xx,xxx
Expenses	$xx,xxx	$xx,xxx	$xx,xxx	$xx,xxx
Difference	$xx,xxx	$xx,000	$x0,000	$0

Note that Pollan and Levine warn that you should take into consideration such things as customer-payment terms, supplier-payment terms, loan- or investment-payback terms, and your requirements for cash to reinvest in your business when estimating your income and expenses.

Determine Your Contribution Margin

Your contribution margin is the difference between your variable costs in producing an item or providing a service and the price you can charge for the item or service. For example:

$$\text{Sales Price} - \text{Variable Cost} = \text{Contribution Margin}$$
$$\$3.00 - \$1.00 = \$2.00$$

Determine the Volume of Sales You Need to Reach A Break-even Point

To find out what volume of sales you need to break even, divide your monthly fixed costs by the contribution margin. For example:

$$\text{Monthly Fixed Costs} / \text{Contribution Margin} = \text{Break-even Volume}$$
$$\$10,000 / \$2.00 = 5,000 \text{ items}$$

Forecast Your Cash Flow

To forecast cash flow, project your income and expenses month to month until you reach breakeven. (See Exhibit 3.4.)

Estimate Your Working Capital Requirements

Your working capital requirements represent the sum of the shortfall (income minus expenses) for the period from start-up until breakeven.

Step Four: Determine the Amount You Need for Start-Up

To determine how much money you need for start-up, add together your initial cash outlay and your working capital requirements.

Step Five: Double It!

Pollan and Levine don't suggest this step, but our entrepreneurs do. Take whatever amount of capital requirements that your calculations indicate you will need and double it. Arthur Blank explains, "I always tell people starting new companies to secure twice the capital they think they need. Not because they need the money, but because it gives you the confidence and the strength to do what you think is right instead of being pushed by external financial forces."[3]

Most people are amazed at how much working capital it will take and the number of imponderables you have to consider just to come up with your estimates. They typically decide about halfway through Pollan and Levine's calculations that Jerry Greenfield just might be right: It's easier to go with your instincts. But if you're still interested in being an entrepreneur, you need to go on to the next step—coming up with the money.

RAISING THE MONEY

There are two sources of funds to provide you with working capital: debt and equity. Debt is money you borrow and have to pay back. Equity is money you obtain from investments people or institutions make in your company in return for some share of ownership. Debt and equity financing have both advantages and disadvantages.

The advantage of equity financing is that you don't have to pay it back if things don't work out. The disadvantages are (1) it's hard to get, (2) you have to give up some ownership and perhaps control of your company to get it, and (3) we repeat—it's hard to get.

The advantage of debt financing is that you keep control of your business, at least until you find you can't make the payments on your loan when they come due. The disadvantages of debt financing are (1) it's hard to get, (2) you have to make payments on your loan regardless of whether your business is making any money or not, and (3) we repeat—it's hard to get. Pollan and Levine state that it is essential that you achieve a balance between these two types of financing. They explain:

> If your business is highly leveraged—has a large amount of debt financing as compared to equity financing—cash flow can become a major problem be-

cause of the interest and amortization you'll have to pay. If your business is minimally leveraged—has a large amount of equity financing compared to debt financing—you won't be taking full advantage of the invested dollars [since you could carry some debt and free up the investment money to use elsewhere]. Businesses funded solely on debt financing are very risky. . . . Equity financing gives you some strength and protection.[4]

In short, you want a mix of financing. It's okay to take out some loans, but get as much equity financing as you can. Just realize that getting money—debt or equity—is going to be hard and that you are going to have to do it repeatedly. You will need money to get started; you'll need another influx of money when your business starts to grow; and you'll need another and another as you try to expand your business and become even bigger. The whole task of money raising just isn't going to end.

There are only two ways of raising money: the hard way and the very hard way!

Anita Roddick[5]

Dealing with Rejection

We discussed rejection in the first two chapters, but certain aspects of rejection bear repeating. You should expect to be turned down often when you approach people and institutions for money. Howard Schultz recalls that, in the course of the year he spent trying to raise money for his coffee bars, he spoke to 242 people and was turned down by 217 of them. "Try to imagine how disheartening it can be to hear that many times why your idea is not worth investing in," writes Schultz. "Some would listen to my hour-long presentation and not call me back. I'd phone them but they wouldn't take my call. When I finally got through, they would tell me why they weren't interested. It was a very humbling time."[6]

For Schultz, the hardest part of fund-raising was just keeping an upbeat attitude rejection after rejection.

You don't want to pay a visit to a prospective investor and not display the full measure of passion and enthusiasm about what you're proposing to do. You can't be dejected when you meet with a landlord to begin negotiations about leasing a location. But if you've had three or four fruitless meetings that week, how do you whip yourself up? You really have to be a chameleon. Here you are in front of somebody else. You're depressed as hell, but you have to sound as fresh and confident as you were at your first meeting.[7]

Schultz writes that raising money was always difficult and that he never really felt that he was good at it because it took him so long. Over time, he says, he did get better at his presentation and at anticipating and responding to objections and concerns. He learned a lot because he got plenty of practice, and you will, too. One of the things you will learn is that, while some entrepreneurs are also bankers and investors, typically, bankers and investors are not entrepreneurs. They have a different mindset.

Bankers and Investors Aren't Entrepreneurs

According to Wilson Harrell, if you ask an audience of entrepreneurs who they distrust and detest the most, their immediate answers will most often be "bankers," "venture capitalists," and "Wall Streeters." Similarly, if you bring together a group of bankers, venture capitalists, and Wall Streeters and ask them who they dislike and distrust most, their most likely response will be "entrepreneurs," although they would also admit that these same entrepreneurs have made their financial institutions the most money. Why do these two groups, who are so dependent on each other, dislike and distrust each other so much? The answer, says Harrell, is mind-set.

Let's take a moment to compare them: They, the money providers, believe with every morsel of their being that "growth" and "profits" are the same words; that "net revenue" is the only barometer for success. The idea that a business person would pour every dime of potential profit back into growing a company is simply not acceptable.

On the other hand, entrepreneurs know that showing a profit and paying taxes is stupid during the fast-growth years of a company. The word "risk" to the financial community is synonymous with Black Friday, AIDS, the Bubonic Plague and getting fired. To entrepreneurs, "risk" is a way of life. We eat it for breakfast. To entrepreneurs, "security" means the "company," and its continued growth. To them, it means mortgages on homes,

liens on everything that's not nailed down and, above all, "personal guarantees." To them "success" means "pay back." To entrepreneurs, it means foot-
prints in the sands of time. On and on it goes. Mindsets from different
worlds.[8]

It is crucial, however, for the entrepreneur to develop and maintain a
working relationship with these people who have such a different mind-set.
So, let's take a look at each of three groups to whom you will undoubtedly
go again and again for financial support—your friends and relatives, bankers, and venture capitalists.

Dealing with Friends and Relatives

We start with your friends and relatives for a simple reason. It is with them
that you will most likely be forced to start raising money, whether you like
it or not. After emptying out your bank account—minus what you need to
live on for those 18 months (see step one on calculating your start-up costs
discussed previously)—your next stops will be your mom, dad, brother,
sister, uncle, aunt, next-door neighbor, tennis buddy, doctor, dentist, attorney, accountant, or some such person. Why not go first to your friendly
neighborhood banker or venture capitalist? Simple. Practically all—99.9
percent of them—will turn you down. Your best shot at getting financing is
from the people who know you best and who have the greatest faith in you.
Once you have secured their loans and investments, say our gurus, then you
can think about other sources of funding.

Keep in mind as you approach friends and family that what you are discussing is a business transaction, even though the loan or investment that
you receive may be based more on emotion than on cold-blooded financial
ratios. As Earl Graves puts it, "blood may be thicker than water, but don't
take it for granted. Why risk touching off a family feud in the event of a
misunderstanding over money."[9] Graves suggests that you have your attorney draw up a promissory note for every loan from a friend or family
member, detailing, among other things, the following:

- The amount of the loan.
- The date of the loan.

- The interest rate.
- The frequency of payments.
- The period over which the loan will be repaid.
- The collateral you are offering should you not be able to pay back the loan.[10]

You and the friend or relative making the loan should sign the document, and, advises Graves, it should be witnessed by a notary who is not a family member.

Such attention to detail may seem excessive, considering that you are dealing with a close friend or relative. In fact, says Graves, it is critical for a reason that has nothing to do with keeping peace in the family—tax consequences. He explains:

> The agreement must be not only formal but legal as well. Entrepreneurs risk IRS audits if the Feds suspect things aren't quite right.
>
> Remember that all bank deposits of more than $10,000 in cash are automatically reported to the IRS. When you deposit Uncle Joe's check for $30,000 in your bank account and fail to report it on your personal or business tax form, you'll have some explaining to do.
>
> The relative providing you with the loan should base the interest rate on current rates in the market. Otherwise the loan might be considered a gift and subject to federal gift taxes. Federal tax laws allow individual taxpayers to give up to $10,000 a year tax-free to any individual. A married couple can give up to $20,000 a year to each individual. Amounts above that can be subject to gift taxes for the borrower.
>
> To be certain you don't run afoul of the tax man, consult section 7872, subsection D of the IRS code. Each month the IRS also publishes rates for loans ranging from short term to long term. Your accountants, too, should be consulted regularly to make certain that they are monitoring your business and keeping you out of trouble, which is what they are paid to do.[11]

What our gurus are saying about loans also applies to investments. You should have your attorney draw up a document spelling out how the investors will share in the profits, roles and responsibilities, survivorship, buy-out rights, and so on. In short, dot the i's and cross the t's on all of these issues. You will be glad you did.

Dealing with Bankers

Okay, you've tapped your friends and relatives for all of the funds they are willing to or can loan you or invest in your company. Maybe you've been lucky and found an affluent "angel" who is willing to invest a sizable amount because he or she thinks the adventure would be fun or a way to display financial expertise. Regardless, you have assembled a pool of cash. But you still need more. You don't yet have the working capital your estimates indicate you need, much less double your estimates as our gurus advise. It's time now to approach your local banker.

You are now armed with the reality that your banker's answer will likely be "no." Not only that, but you will probably get a lecture on how perilous it is for a bank to do business with someone like you. Dave Thomas recalls an unpleasant experience with a banker in the early 1960s, shortly after Thomas had taken over a group of Kentucky Fried Chicken franchises in Columbus, Ohio:

> One of the first things I wanted to do was to install air-conditioning systems in the four restaurants because I know how air conditioning could build traffic. But, instead of going downtown to the commercial loan department and talking with somebody who knew something about business, I went to the local branch that did our banking. The loan officer there knew about loans for cars and refrigerators but couldn't understand air conditioning as a business principle. Instead of a loan, what I got was a big lecture on how late these restaurants were in paying their bills and what a lousy risk I was.[12]

Thomas says that experience and others like it left him pretty sour on banks and the judgment of bankers. Tom Monaghan reports a similar banking experience in the early 1960s:

> I wanted to borrow $250 to buy a used refrigerator for my DomiNick's store [the forerunner to Dominos Pizza]. I asked [the bank president] for the money in a very humble way.
>
> "Nope," he said.
>
> I begged and pleaded, but he just leaned back in his big leather swivel chair and tossed his head from side to side for emphasis as he slowly repeated, "Nope . . . nope . . . nope."

He gave me a long lecture about all these ratios, and what it amounted to was that I had to have $500 in the bank in order to borrow $250.

"If I had five hundred dollars," I asked, "why would I want to borrow two hundred fifty dollars from you? Why don't you take that refrigerator I want to buy as collateral?"

"Nope."

Monaghan says he came away feeling humiliated and switched banks at the first opportunity. He eventually got the money for his refrigerator elsewhere and says he had forgotten about the incident until one day in 1985 when the chairman and president and the senior vice chairman of the National Bank of Detroit (NBD) paid him a visit. They sought out Monaghan to invite him to sit on NBD's board of directors. As he accepted the offer, Monaghan writes, he couldn't help thinking, "This is my revenge for being turned down on that refrigerator loan, and as Jackie Gleason used to say, 'How sweet it is!' "[13]

Most of our other gurus have had similar unpleasant experiences with banks and bankers, yet all agree that banking relationships are critical. "Bankers," says Monaghan, echoing the sentiments of most of our gurus, "are the keepers of the keys to success for an entrepreneur. They can help you more than anyone else. They can also hurt you most, because all creditors and potential creditors check with the bankers first. A negative word from a banker can block all your plans. In times of trouble, it's doubly important to have a good relationship with your bank, because you must be able to write checks to stay in business."[14] At times, the survival of your company may depend on the quality of the relationship you have with your banker. Consider the example of Home Depot.

Arthur Blank and Bernie Marcus opened their first four Home Depot stores in Atlanta in 1979. By 1983, with the help of a friendly banker at Security Pacific National Bank by the name of Rip Fleming, they had grown their business to 19 stores and $250 million in revenues. Then disaster struck. Fleming reached 65 years of age and was forced into retirement. The Home Depot account was turned over to a new loan officer who viewed the company as just another small business with limited potential for growth. "We were being handled in a traditional manner by the bank's small-business group," Blank recalled. " We were numbers and points to them, not people with unique personalities."[15]

Recognizing that the good banking relationship they had enjoyed in the past was now all but gone, Blank and Marcus appealed to Fleming for help. Fleming responded by asking a young loan officer he had been mentoring, Faye Wilson, to get involved in the Home Depot account. Wilson agreed to take on the account as a favor, and Marcus and Blank soon discovered that she was quite different from the banker they had been assigned. Blank recalled that Wilson came across as quiet and unassuming but that she was extremely articulate and could speak with great passion about something if she believed in it. Perhaps more important, Wilson was interested in getting to know Home Depot and seemed open to working with its founders. Unlike the other loan officer who had been primarily interested in achieving maximum guarantees and protection for the bank, Wilson was more of a customer advocate. The change in bankers was to prove extremely fortuitous for Home Depot just two years later.

In 1985 Marcus and Blank were seeking a $200 million to $225 million line of credit in order to grow from 50 Home Depot stores with $700 million in annual sales to 100 stores. Because the loan was too large for Security Pacific to take on by itself, Wilson had organized a consortium of banks to share the risk, including C&S Bank in Atlanta. Everything was going well until the last minute, when disaster struck. Blank explained what happened this way:

> The problem came when Wilson received a call from the C&S loan officer who had been in the syndication meetings with us. We later learned that he thought our expansion into California was too risky, so at the last minute, he unilaterally made the decision that the bank would not participate in the deal.
>
> This set off alarms because here was a local bank, one that knew the company, knew the management, presumably had an ability to physically be involved day-to-day, looking at operations if they wished, and we had other business with them. Their withdrawal—for unexplained reasons—was less an issue of their share of the cash but the appearance of a problem at home. What would another bank, one we didn't already have a relationship with, say? "C & S must know something we don't know." It created a potential blackball effect.[16]

Wilson told the Home Depot founders that she would take care of the problem. Calmly, she began working the phones, reassuring loan officers at

---

EXHIBIT 3.5.   **Banking Rules**

Rule #1: Bankers make loans to people, not to companies.

Rule #2: You have to get to know your banker.

Rule #3: You have to learn to speak your banker's language.

Rule #4: Sometimes, you have to make them sweat.

---

the other banks in the consortium that all was well a Home Depot. Perhaps more crucial, Wilson went to her bosses at Security Pacific in an effort to convince them to pick up the C&S share of the loan. The bank's chief credit officer asked Wilson one thing, "Are you willing to put your job on the line for this?" She said she was, and she did. The bank consortium stayed together, and Home Depot got its loan. Writing about Wilson's contribution years later, Arthur Blank put it simply, "She literally saved our company."[17] Wilson was later to become the first woman on the board of Home Depot.

Rules That Govern the Relationship with Your Banker

What makes the difference? Why were Dave Thomas and Tom Monaghan turned down for relatively minor loans whereas Bernie Marcus and Arthur Blank found a banker who was willing to put her job on the line for them? The difference, say our gurus, has to do with following the four rules that govern the relationship you have with your banker. (See Exhibit 3.5 for a summary.)

Rule #1: Bankers Make Loans to People, Not to Companies

Bankers don't make loans to companies. They make loans to people. Consider Debbi Fields's experience, for example. Fields recalls that, when she got the idea for her cookie company, she went looking for a banker to loan her start-up money. Fields and her husband, Randy, had a mortgage from Bank of America and had gotten to know a banker there by the name of Ed Sullivan—not the television host. Initially, says Fields, she and her husband had decided not to approach Sullivan for their business loan because they wanted to keep their mortgage holder separate from their business banker. After repeated turndowns from other bankers, the Fields decided that keeping their business and personal banking separate just wasn't going to work out. They decided to turn to Sullivan for the loan.

Ed was that very rare thing, a kind and understanding banker. His kindness was not based on the fancy little phrases they teach people in bank school, it was based on a personal approach to what turns out, in fact, to be a very personal transaction—the lending of money, the establishment of trust between individuals, perhaps the ultimate test of intuition.

Ed Sullivan was a gentleman of the old-fashioned variety, warm and courtly, nearing sixty at the time, with thin graying hair. He'd had several hip surgeries and walked with difficulty. His counterpart at the bank was a young man named Bob Derenzi, whose smile was the real thing, backed up with easy laughter, a guy who had a knack for making you feel like the most important person in the entire world.

We invited Ed over for lunch, with a plateful of chocolate chip cookies for dessert. After lunch, it became clear to me that Randy and Ed wanted to talk privately, so I acted the part of the little woman and left them in the kitchen. Later on, Randy told me what was said.

The tone was man-to-man. "Randy," Ed said, getting down to business right away, "how much are you going to put into this?"

Randy shrugged. "I don't know. Maybe twenty-five, fifty thousand."

Ed nodded, accepting Randy's figures. "You know it isn't going to work, of course, but there are some positives. It'll be a good education for Debbi. You'll know where she is every day, it will give her something to do, something she can call her own and, last but not least, it'll become a terrific tax shelter for the money you make in your consulting practice."

Randy agreed.

"Look," Ed went on, "my bank, the Bank of America, was built on the basis of investing in people. A.P. Giannini had at the heart of his building this bank one basic idea: you invest in people, you don't invest in businesses and numbers."

So Ed Sullivan, Bob Derenzi and the Bank of America went against their business instincts and made the loan because they trusted Randy and me to pay back the money when the business flopped. They trusted us, not cookies, and certainly not projections or marketing surveys. And if I'd suspected in my heart that the whole process was really based on emotion all the mumbo jumbo about numbers and graphs aside—I was absolutely sure of it now. Banking is nine-tenths instinct. When it comes right down to it, these people have to decide whether you're going to turn them into kings or paupers. It's a gut-level decision and anybody who tells you different is kidding you.[18]

You may recall the earlier description of Ben Cohen and Jerry Green-field's mumbo-jumbo exercise in creating their own business plan. Like the Fields, they discovered that the numbers in their spiffed-up plan were less important in getting them their loan than was their relationship with their banker. Ben tells the story this way:

> Plan in hand, we went to Fred Burgess at the Merchants Bank in town and asked him for $18,000. Fred said he'd submit the loan to the Small Business Administration because the SBA would guarantee it. If we couldn't pay it back (which many small business start-ups never manage to do), the SBA would repay the bank 90 percent of what it had loaned us.
>
> The SBA agreed to give us the $18,000 if we found a "suitable location" in Burlington. We thought the gas station was a fine choice, but the SBA didn't agree, because we couldn't get more than a one-year lease. When we went back for our loan, the SBA wouldn't approve it. Fred offered us $4,000 instead. We took it.
>
> Fred's loan didn't seem like the greatest vote of confidence, but we weren't too proud to accept it. All we had was $8,000, and the extra $4,000 gave us just enough to open. Looking back on it now, it's clear that Fred didn't expect to get paid back. He probably thought it was worth the $4,000 just to watch how we spent it. Maybe he figured he'd get some amusing stories out of it.[19]

Rule #2: Get to Know Your Banker

How do you build the kind of relationship with a banker that Debbi and Randy Fields had with Ed Sullivan, that Bernie Marcus and Arthur Blank had with Faye Wilson, and that Ben Cohen and Jerry Greenfield had with Fred Burgess? Well, advises Earl Graves, you don't wait until you need the money. Long before you approach them for a business loan, says Graves, you should try to get to know your local banker as an individual. Find out what interests he or she has in common with you. What charities does he or she support? Establish a connection any way you can. Once you get a loan, writes Graves, don't just send the loan officer quarterly statements. Instead, you should make it more personal. "Invite the banker to visit your plant or distribution center. Let the banker meet your key people. Face-to-face contact with the banker helps build a bond of friendliness and trust that will go a long way toward winning approval on the next and undoubtedly larger loan request."[20] Graves says you should notify your banker when you get a major new account, purchase a new piece of equipment, or hire new management talent. "And, of course," he notes, "if there's bad news, don't sugarcoat it. Explain what happened and how it will be remedied."[21] In short, you have to work at the relationship constantly.

> If you are in debt to a man, you owe it to him to let him know exactly how your business stands. And when he knows you aren't holding anything back, he isn't going to be hard on you if occasionally you can't pay a bill the day it falls due.
>
> *Howard Johnson*[22]

Rule #3: Learn to Speak Your Banker's Language

Part of working at your relationship with bankers is learning to speak their language or finding someone to translate "bankese" for you. Bankers speak the language of accounting and finance, a language that is foreign to most entrepreneurs. Anita Roddick recalls that her first experience in getting a business loan was a disaster simply because she didn't understand bank-speak. It was in the early 1970s, and Roddick had decided to open a little shop to sell cosmetics. Working with her husband, Gordon, she calculated that she would need about four thousand pounds to get started. She assumed that getting the loan would be no problem because she was prepared to use a small hotel she and her husband owned as collateral. Unfortunately, writes Roddick, she went about the whole loan process in the wrong way.

> I made an appointment to see the bank manager and turned up wearing a Bob Dylan T-shirt with [my daughter] Samantha on my hip and [my other daughter] Justine clinging on to my jeans. It just did not occur to me that I should be anything other than my normal self. I was enthusiastic and I gabbled on about my great idea, flinging out all this information about how I had . . . discovered these natural ingredients when I was traveling, and I'd got this great name, The Body Shop, and all I needed was £4,000 to get it started. I got quite carried away in my excitement, but I was on my own. I discovered that you don't go to a bank manager with enthusiasm—that is the last thing he cares about. When I had finished, he leaned back in his

chair and said that he wasn't going to lend me any money because we were
too much in debt already.[23]

Roddick was stunned. She couldn't believe she had been turned down.

I went home to Gordon absolutely crushed. "That's it," I said. "It's hopeless.
The bank won't give me any money." I was ready to give up, but Gordon is
much more tenacious than I am. "We will get the money," he said, "But we
are going to have to play them at their own game." He told me to go out
and buy a business suit, and got an accountant friend to draw up an
impressive-looking "business plan," with projected profit and loss figures
and a lot of gobbledegook, all bound in a plastic folder.
    A week later we went back to the same bank for an interview with the
same manager. This time I left the children behind and Gordon came with
me. We were both dressed in suits. Gordon handed over our little presentation, the bank manager flipped through it for a couple of minutes and
then authorized a loan of £4,000, just like that, using the hotel as collateral.
I was relieved—but I was angry, too, that I had been turned down the first
time. After all, I was the same person with the same idea. It was clear to
me that bank managers did not want to deal with mothers with babies.[24]

Experiences such as those reported by Roddick and other entrepreneurs
he has known convinced Wilson Harrell that many entrepreneurs just should
not try to interface with members of the financial community. "If you know
in advance that the chances of 'getting along' are small or nil," writes Harrell, "why risk blowing a relationship that's so vitally important? Wouldn't it
be better to employ the services of someone who could speak for you—
someone with *their* [the banker's] mindset—someone who could act as in-
terpreter?"[25] Would such an approach work? It did for Tom Monaghan.
    Remember that Monaghan had problems with bankers from the begin-
ning—he couldn't even borrow $250 to buy a used refrigerator. Monaghan
writes that he found his inability to communicate with bankers enormously
frustrating. Then, in 1977 he met a financial consultant by the name of John
McDivitt who found a way to translate Monaghan's vision into bankese.

I'm not sure what John thought of Domino's potential, but I was fascinated
by his response when I explained the hard times I'd had in dealing with
bankers. [John's] principal contribution was a penetrating financial analysis

of our business and a presentation of it that allowed bankers to understand, for the first time, what a dynamic company they were looking at in
Domino's.

John constructed an economic model of our business, demonstrating its
organization from a single working unit, a store, through all the various levels of consolidation we had at that time. He analyzed the variable costs at
the store level, showing how they changed and related to each other at dif-
fering volumes of business. These models became templates to overlay reports from the stores so we could interpret what was happening in them. I
was fascinated by the logic of this exercise and how it clearly demonstrated
the economic functioning of our stores as if they were machines with observation windows cut into them to show their working parts.

John then drew a numerical picture in which he channeled the cash trib-
utaries produced by all our operating units into a single stream. Collec-
tively, this grew into a broad river of money. I wasn't surprised. I knew what
a powerful cash producer Domino's was, but this was the first time I had
seen it depicted so objectively. Now I understood what John meant when
he talked about explaining our business in economic terms.

No wonder bankers had failed to appreciate my passionate appeals for
money. I might as well have been speaking Swahili, because the words I was
using to describe our business simply weren't meaningful to them. The per-
suasive power of John's economic model was immediately self-evident.[26]

Like Monaghan, you may be able to find a translator to help you communicate with the money changers. On the other hand, you may be stuck
doing what Roddick terms the "hell-raising, hair-raising, money-raising"
yourself. If you are, here are five questions Earl Graves suggests that you
ask yourself before you keep that appointment with your banker.[27]

1. **How much money do you need?** If you want to borrow $50,000,
   only ask for $50,000. Never ask bankers how much they are willing to
   lend. It's important to collect the most precise calculations possible
   and then explain why you need every penny.
2. **How will you repay the loan if things go as planned?** Will it be
   from your business's cash flow, proceeds, or the conversion of assets?
   To demonstrate to the banker exactly how you'll make good on the
   money owed, you should present at least a year of monthly cash-flow
   statements and quarterly projections for the term of the loan.

3. **How will you repay the loan if things go sour?** In most cases you'll have to surrender collateral such as equipment or property. Bankers will consider the market value of the collateral you have pledged against the value of the loan. Regardless of how the bank is compensated, it's important to have a contingency plan.

4. **How will the loan help your business?** Bankers want to be assured that the infusion of cash into the business will help it build cash flow, expand the sales force, or lead to cost controls. Count on a rejection letter if you tell the banker the money will be used to increase your salary or buy a fancy new vehicle.

5. **What's your personal stake?** If your own finances aren't on the line, bankers won't be interested in risking any of their cash. Banks prefer a personal investment of at least 20 percent.

Rule #4: Sometimes You Have to Make 'Em Sweat

Our final banking rule is drawn from the experiences of Cecil B. Day, the cofounder of Days Inn of America. In 1972 Day was trying to arrange financing for his string of motels. He was having particular trouble with one banker who stubbornly refused to loan money for construction. Frustrated, Day decided some unorthodox tactics were in order. He knew that this particular banker was very fond of air-conditioning and had frequently bragged about his air-conditioned office, home, and car. "Air-conditioning did for the south what furnaces did for the North," the banker was fond of saying. Day asked the banker to ride with him to one of the motel construction sites where he could see what was being done and where they could discuss Day's pending loan. The banker agreed, and Day arranged to pick him up the next morning. The trip to the construction site would be one the banker would never forget.

The day of their meeting, Day departed his home not in his normal automobile but driving his son's 1971 Pinto. The Pinto had no radio, no cigarette lighter, and most important for Day's purposes, no air conditioning. Day picked up the banker at the appointed time, and they began their hourlong trip to the construction site. As they drove, the temperature began to rise—80, 85, 90. The banker, who by now was beginning to sweat profusely, kept giving Day one excuse after another as to why the loan couldn't be made. Day was uncomfortable also, but he just kept driving and pitching his case for the loan. The banker still refused. Day kept driving and pleading his case. The sun kept climbing in the sky, and the temperature kept creeping up—92, 95, 98. Sweat poured off the banker. His suit was drenched. Still, Day just kept driving and pitching his case. Finally, near heat exhaustion, the banker yelled "Okay, okay. You can have the loan. Just get me back to the bank where it's cool."[28]

Day knew that, in dealing with bankers, sometimes you just have to make 'em sweat.

Dealing with Venture Capitalists

There are two sources of funds for your business—debt and equity. You go to bankers for debt financing. At some point, you will likely have to go to venture capitalists for your equity financing. If you are like most entrepreneurs, you've probably heard about venture capitalists. You may even have read some stories about them, but chances are you don't really know much about the process of obtaining venture capital. That is what makes Charles Ferguson's 1999 book *High Stakes, No Prisoners* so helpful.[29] Ferguson is a cofounder of Vermeer Technologies, Inc., the company that created Front-Page, a software tool for creating Web sites. Ferguson's book chronicles his involvement with Vermeer from the time of its founding in 1993 until it was sold to Microsoft in 1996. Our interest here centers around the events of August through December of 1994, when Ferguson was looking for funding for his dream. Here, in summary and in Exhibit 3.6, is what happened and, more important, what Ferguson, a novice at starting companies, learned about venture capitalists.

Lesson #1: Venture Capital Is a Rough Game

August 1994: Ferguson met his first venture capitalist (VC), Andy Marcuvitz, whom he describes as the ideal VC type—heavyset, badly fitting suit, no discernible personality, no sense of humor, no compassion, never makes a joke, rarely smiles, argues relentlessly, but keeps his voice even and never loses his temper. At their first meeting, the two attempted to dazzle each other with their technical and business credentials. Finally, Ferguson announced that Vermeer was a "paradigm-shifting" company and that if Marcuvitz wanted to hear more he would have to sign a nondisclosure

EXHIBIT 3.6. **Lessons about Venture Capital**

- Lesson #1: Venture capital is a rough game.
- Lesson #2: Unless you have an introduction from someone they know, most venture capital firms won't even talk to you.
- Lesson #3: Venture capitalists don't invest in financial projections; they invest in people.
- Lesson #4: Expect premoney valuation to be a major stumbling block.
- Lesson #5: Venture capital presentations are grueling.
- Lesson #6: Venture capitalists will drag the process out.
- Lesson #7: Venture capitalists drive a tough bargain.
- Lesson #8: If a venture capitalist suggests a party, he'll stick you with the bill.

agreement. Anyway, Ferguson continued, he had some private investors who might be an alternative to VCs. Regardless, he intended to drive a hard bargain and would never give up control.

To Ferguson's surprise, Marcuvitz was decidedly unimpressed. In fact, Marcuvitz began to lecture:

Kid, if you think you can do it that way, be my guest. But you're already raising warning flags for VCs. In the first place, we don't like nondisclosure agreements: They're generally a sign of trouble, like husband-and-wife boards of directors. Founders who are obsessed with secrecy tend not to understand what's really important to a company's success, and sometimes they're just crazy. You should be letting us get to know you. You don't seem to have much business experience, and what little you do have is not in startups. That's okay, but be sure that you don't make a big mistake. For example, raising money from random rich people is usually bad: It's dumb money, and it takes too much time to service. If you do manage to fool someone, your valuation will be too high. So then, when you try to get serious VC money, either you'll have to explain to your friends why you overcharged them, or you'll try to get the VCs to accept a huge setup for no reason. VCs don't play that game, so you could ruin your whole deal. And anyway, your fears are misplaced: We don't want to control you—we just want to make money.[30]

The rest of their meeting was a sparring match, with the participants trading shots about the industry, the Internet, what's possible and impossible in seeking VC capital, and so on. Ferguson came away rating the meeting as a draw. Over the next few months, he learned several more hard lessons about raising venture capital.

Lesson #2: Unless You Have an Introduction from Someone They Know, Most Venture Capital Firms Won't Even Talk to You

August and September 1994: Ferguson attempted to contact other venture capital firms with no luck. He learned quickly that he didn't have the experience or contacts to get most of them even to return his phone calls.

Lesson #3: Venture Capitalists Don't Invest Based on the Financial Projections: They Invest in People

September 1994: Ferguson and Marcuvitz met again, and Marcuvitz agreed to arrange a presentation at the offices of Matrix Partners in Waltham, Massachusetts. Ferguson provided an overview of the market—on-line services, the Internet, growth of the Web, and so on. His staff followed with a demonstration of the software, technical discussion, and review of financials. Marcuvitz listened politely to the numbers then announced that the financials didn't mean anything. They only indicated that the entrepreneur had thought seriously about the size of the market and the cost of designing and developing the product.

Lesson #4: Expect Premoney Valuation to Be a Major Stumbling Block

Mid-September 1994: At Marcuvitz's request, Ferguson met with Paul Ferri, the founder of Matrix and a longtime VC game player. Ferguson describes Ferri as "clearly a tough guy—even more laconic and poker-faced than Marcuvitz." Ferri had a number of questions for the entrepreneur:

- Do you plan to be CEO?
- How much money does the company need for the first round of financing?
- What premoney valuation do you place on the company?

The latter question set off an argument. Premoney valuation is the value of the company before the VC investment. It determines how much of the company the venture capital company owns. For example, if the prevaluation is $2 million and the venture capital firm puts in $4 million, then the total value of the company after the investment is $6 million and the venture capital firm owns two-thirds of the company. On the other hand, if the prevaluation is $8 million and the venture capital firm puts in the same $4 million, they end up owning only one-third of the company. Obviously, VCs push for a low prevaluation. The danger for the entrepreneur is not only losing control but ending up making very little money. Ferguson recalled a friend who had joined a start-up owning 2 percent of the company. Four years later the company was sold for $18 million, but because of a low prevaluation, his original shares were so diluted that the friend received only $76,000 for his original 2 percent stake.

Determined not to lose control and end up with a paltry sum after years of 70-hour weeks, Ferguson told Ferri he wanted a premoney valuation between $20 million and $30 million. Marcuvitz and Ferri smiled and explained that Ferguson was naive. Such an evaluation was ridiculous and maybe even dangerous. Venture-capital valuation rules of thumb, taking into account Ferguson's experience, the experience of his team, and the vagaries of the market, they said, placed the prevaluation closer to $2 million than $20 million. Ferguson argued back with a list of reasons why $2 million was too low, but Marcuvitz and Ferri were unmoved. They suggested that Ferguson talk to other VCs, if he didn't believe them. They even provided some introductions to other VC firms.

Lesson #5: Venture Capital Presentations Are Grueling and Can Drain Your Personal Bank Account

Mid-September to early December 1994: Ferguson and his team presented to more than 20 VC firms, half on the West Coast and half on the East Coast. Travel expenses were eating into their remaining funds. The presentations were filled with tension and anger. Most of the VC firms didn't know anything about the Internet and had to be educated. Most were uninterested. Occasionally, conflicts of interest arose. For example, just before one meeting Ferguson discovered that a VC firm for which they were scheduled to present was already an investor in a potential competitor. He learned to research VC firms carefully before doing a presentation.

Lesson #6: Venture Capitalists Will Drag the Process Out, Assuming That the Longer It Takes for You to Get Funding, the More Willing You Will Be to Agree to Their Terms

November 1994: Ferguson was getting scared. Many of his best people were working without cash compensation, and he didn't know how long he could retain them that way. He needed to buy computers, acquire office space, hire more people, and reserve space at trade shows. The Internet was exploding, and he was running out of time and money. To make matters worse, the VCs had raised new issues. They didn't want the founder to be the CEO; they wanted to bring in someone from the outside who was experienced running a start-up. Plus, they wanted Ferguson and cofounder Randy Forgaard to agree to a period of vesting.

Lesson # 7: Venture Capitalists Drive a Tough Bargain

Late November 1994: Ferguson was in California again for another round of presentations. He was exhausted and anxious to head home. Late on the afternoon before he was scheduled to leave, he got a call from Wade Woodson from Sigma Partners, a small VC firm to which Ferguson had been talking for several months. Woodson wanted a meeting as soon as possible.

Ferguson was testy. He told Woodson that he already had a meeting that night and that he would be flying out first thing in the morning. He said he could meet Woodson at the airport at 6 A.M. but he mumbled, "What's the point if this is just another turn down?" Woodson replied: "I don't think I would get up at 5 A.M. for that. If I was just going to say no, I think I'd sleep in." "Oh!" thought Ferguson.

At six o'clock the next morning, Woodson handed Ferguson a term sheet. Sigma Partners was proposing a $4 million investment with a prevaluation of $4 million. The proposal was contingent on several conditions: (1) Ferguson must find two other VC firms willing to be coinvestors; (2) he must take a 20 percent cut in his personal stock holdings in the company; and (3) the stock-option pool for future employees must come out of Ferguson's and Forgaard's shares, not those of Sigma Partners. Ferguson calculated that he would be left with just 12 percent of the company and Forgaard would own only 4 percent. They wouldn't be getting nearly what they wanted, and a number of issues, such as vesting, CEO selection, control, remained to be solved. But Ferguson and Forgaard were exhausted and almost out of funds. They accepted. It was just a handshake deal, with no papers signed, and Sigma Partners could walk away anytime it wanted. As for Ferguson, Woodson cautioned him: "Now Charles . . . we have a deal. You can't use this to go out and shop for a better offer. No reputable firm will give you better terms once they know that you've got a handshake deal with us. And we will certainly walk away if we find out that you're using our offer as a bargaining lever. If we were to pull out under those circumstances, no one else would be interested in you."[31]

Lesson #8: If a Venture Capitalist Suggests a Party, He'll Stick You with the Bill

December 1994: Ferguson made a round of telephone calls to the few VC firms that still seemed interested, hoping to line up the coinvestors that Sigma demanded. Matrix finally agreed to come in on the deal, as did Atlas Venture in Boston. The investment would consist of $1.6 million each from Sigma and Matrix, plus $800,000 from Atlas Venture. Ferguson spent the Christmas season on the phone, day and night, trying to resolve the remaining outstanding issues of vesting, CEO selection, and so on. He got to be CEO at a salary that was one-fifth of what he made before starting the company. Finally, the deal was done and a conference table full of papers were signed. Marcuvitz even suggested a pizza party for the whole company to celebrate. Ferguson recalls, "My goodness. . . . Marcuvitz has a human side. But just before the dinner ended, he stood up, shook hands, and departed. He had stuck me with the bill. That's more like it, I thought."[32]

A venture capitalist's answer is "No, No, No" until it's "Yes." At which point they add, "I'm going to pay you as little as possible for as much of your company as I can get."

Thomas Stemberg[33]

Maintaining Control

Whether the debate is over prevaluation, CEO selection, vesting, or any of numerous other issues, conflict between investors and entrepreneurs usually centers around one central issue—control. Our gurus have one piece of advice when it comes to that issue. Fight as long as you can and as hard as you can to maintain as much control as you can. And beware of what Wilson Harrell called the "hooey." Here are three examples from Harrell:

> Most investors will try and persuade the entrepreneur that they won't exercise the control prerogative; that they'll let the entrepreneur continue running the company. That's a bunch of hooey. Others will say that they only want control until they get their money back, or make some predetermined profit. That's more hooey.
>
> In rare instances, an investor will suggest that you become partners, with equal control. That's equal hooey. It just means you get to spend all your time arguing or hiring lawyers. Entrepreneurs become entrepreneurs for one simple reason: to be free. If you give that up, then you stop being an entrepreneur, and to hell with that.[34]

In the pursuit of funding, you will have to deal with Harrell's "hooey" repeatedly. You'll have to decide how much control you are willing to give up to get the money you desperately need. Sometimes your best option, say our gurus, is to reject the hooey outright. Just say no. Bernie Marcus says he had to make that call at least twice while seeking funds to get Home Depot going. The first instance involved none other than another of our gurus—Ross Perot.

In the late 1970s, Ken Langone, a Park Avenue investment banker and later cofounder of Home Depot, was helping Bernie Marcus in his search for $2 million to fund the opening of the first four Home Depot stores. Langone knew Ross Perot because he had helped Perot take EDS public in 1968. Langone arranged for Marcus to meet Perot, and after some sparring, Marcus and Perot reached an understanding. Perot would put up the entire $2 million. In return he would own 70 percent of Home Depot, Langone would get 5 percent, and Marcus and Blank would retain 25 percent, with which they would have to bring in additional people to run the business. Marcus's "hooey" decision came during the course of a meeting with Perot in Dallas at which they were to hammer out the final details. Marcus describes the confrontation this way:

> During a discussion of what perks would go with my salary, I told Perot I had a small problem. While my salary and perks would be similar to those I enjoyed at Handy Dan [Marcus's previous employer], there was the matter of a company car.

The leased car I had been driving was still being paid for by Handy Dan, but the company would repossess it unless I planned to take over the lease or buy it for the depreciated value. This was a good deal for a new company.

"We ought to try to save as much money as we can," I said. "I would like to buy it outright at the depreciated value. Would you like me to buy it, and then I will just charge it to our entity, or do you want to give me a check, and I will pay for it?"

"That's fine," Perot said. "You can either do that or buy a new car, I don't really care."

But then Perot decided to test me. "What kind of a car is it?" Perot asked in that peculiar Texas drawl of his.

"It's a Cadillac."

Perot didn't like that answer at all.

"My people don't drive Cadillacs," he said. "My guys at EDS drive Chevrolets."

"That's fine," I said. "I think it's a good policy for you, but this is a new company we're forming, not EDS. Look, this is a four-year-old car and I'm a big guy. It is cheaper to have an old Cadillac than it is to go out and get a new Chevrolet. So how do we pay for it?"

Not that the question meant anything.

"My people don't drive Cadillacs," Perot said again. And again, "My people don't drive Cadillacs."

And when he said it the third time, I realized this was never going to work.[35]

Marcus recalls sitting across the table from Perot and thinking, "What he is really saying is 'I am the boss; I control your life. I will tell you what to do and what not to do.'" It was more than Marcus could take, so he called a halt to the meeting.

I smiled. "Ross, I have to talk to Kenny for a minute. Would you mind if we step outside?"

Ken was perplexed.

"Look, Kenny," I whispered, "I know Perot is a very important person in your life, but you have to understand something. If this guy is going to be bothered by what kind of car I am driving, how much aggravation are we

going to have when we have to make really big decisions? If we can't be free
to run the business the way we know it has to be run, it isn't going to
work. I am never going to have this man for a partner. I would rather starve
to death. No way."

Now it was Ken's turn to wonder whose brains were scrambled. "You
must be out of your mind! Are you crazy? My God, he is going to give you
$2 million!"

"Kenny, I wouldn't touch it with a ten-foot pole. I am out of here," I said
and headed down the hall.[36]

Marcus walked away from the deal leaving Langone to make excuses to
Perot for his abrupt departure. Perot seemed to have no hard feelings about
the aborted deal, but Marcus later calculated that Perot's 70 percent share in
Home Depot would have been worth about $58 billion in the late 1990s. It
was a high price for being hung up about Cadillacs and Chevrolets. As for
Marcus, Langone was eventually able to get the $2 million by selling pre-
ferred stock to a group of investors.

Marcus's second turndown of a funding offer came not long after the
Perot episode. The $2 million in start-up capital that Langone had raised
from his investors proved sufficient to get Marcus and Blank to the point of
opening their stores. They had been able to acquire leases on four Atlanta-
area stores. What they didn't have was the $3 million they estimated they
needed to purchase inventory and actually open the stores. "We needed that
$3 million," writes Marcus, "the way someone dying of stab wounds needs
blood in their veins."[37]

One potential source of funds that Langone lined up was a Boston-based
venture capitalist. He came to Atlanta, discussed the deal, and he and Marcus reached an agreement. Marcus agreed to drive the VC back to the airport while the Home Depot staff celebrated. Then the hooey started.

I happily drove our new investor to the airport. But in the car, the man
turned very serious again.

"Listen, there are things I didn't want to talk about in the office because
they are very sensitive, and I want to discuss them with you," he said.

"What are they?" I asked

"First, I need two men on the board of directors."

That was easy, something I anticipated. "Okay, you got it."

"Now, when I make an investment, I like people to invest with me, and I need an investment on your part."

"What do you mean 'investment'?"

"Well, I need to have you invest."

"We started the business, we left everything in California, especially our support system," I said, puzzled. "We are sacrificing our lives here."

"No, I mean more than that," he said. "First of all, you should not have company cars."

We all had leased company cars because so much of our time was spent in cars, driving all over Georgia on company business, and none of us could afford to buy cars. Pat [Farrah, another founder] was broke and I was broke, attorneys having sucked us both dry. Arthur and Ron [Brill, another member of the founding team] had no money either.

"That would be kind of tough for us," I said. "But if we could figure out a way to pay for auto expenses, maybe we can do that."

"Okay," the man said. "Another thing is that everybody needs to take a 10 percent cut in salary."

I stared at him in disbelief. "Everybody?"

"Yes."

"Do you know what I just went through to hire these people? I hired them from all over the United States. I brought them here. I sold them on this dream. They took less money than they ever had made before, and they left their security, all of those things, and you want me to cut their salaries by 10 percent?"

"Yes."

"Well, I guess we could do that, if that's so important to you. I don't think it's fair, but what choice do I have?"

"Now," the man said, "is the best of all. I am not paying your employees' or managers' medical insurance. I think they should get it on their own."

The blood rose up in my eyes. I swerved and pulled the car onto the shoulder of the highway. My gut told me this was a terrible mistake, and my premonitions so far had been right. "Get out of the car," I said. "Get out of the G-damn car!"

The man just looked at me. He thought I was crazy. We were in the middle of nowhere; cars and trucks were zipping by.

"I said, get out of the car! You are a stupid sonuvabitch! Do you think I would get in bed with an imbecile like you? Get out of the f-ing car. You can walk to the airport for all I care.

I then got out of the car and, as the man timidly got out, I tossed his luggage by the side of the road.

"Please don't leave me here!" the man pleaded. "I have to catch a plane."

After several minutes, still fuming, I relented and allowed the man back in. "Don't talk to me for the rest of the trip. I will have nothing to do with you. We are finished. This partnership is over before it has begun."[38]

Marcus eventually got his $3 million in funding in the form of a line of credit with Security Pacific Bank, thanks to the help of Rip Fleming, the loan officer we mentioned earlier. He also retained control, which is, of course, what our gurus say you should do.

Ideally, say our gurus, you want to own 51 percent or more of the business. Depending on your industry, that may or may not be possible. Howard Schultz, for example, notes that if you have a retail business like his and you want to expand rapidly with company-owned stores, you'll require repeated injections of capital to cover expenses, inventory, rents, and so on. It will be almost impossible to expand without giving up some of your stake in the business. Schultz says he would have liked to have retained 50 percent ownership of Starbucks, but at the time, he felt he had no choice but to relinquish some control in order for Starbucks to grow.[39]

If you can't retain 50 percent ownership for reasons such as Schultz outlines, our gurus urge you to negotiate for control of the company anyway. How can you do that? Robert Mondavi had few funds of his own and needed a substantial investment to get his winery going. Therefore, he agreed to take a 20 percent equity share at the outset, provided that he retained 50 percent of the vote on substantive issues. His investor agreed.[40] Wilson Harrell was once in a situation in which he was desperate for funds. He negotiated his heart out but still could not get the investor to budge. Finally Harrell agreed to give up 51 percent of the stock but with some conditions. He insisted that the company bylaws be changed to allow him to appoint two members of the board of directors. The investor would appoint the other two members. The four directors would then pick a fifth acceptable to all. As compensation for serving as president and CEO, Harrell negotiated stock options that would be earned based on performance. Over a period of years, Harrell was able to exercise these options and ultimately regain 51 percent ownership.[41] In short, say our gurus, keep fighting for control any way you can.

Do anything, but don't give up control. For example, agree to give up 60, 70 or 80 percent of the profits until the investor has recovered his or her investment, plus a reasonable return. Agree that you won't increase your salary, or put your girlfriend on the payroll, or buy a yacht, or whatever. In other words, agree that all the investor's money will go exclusively to building the business. Agree to those kind of controls, but do everything possible to keep 51 percent of the stock out of the control of any single individual.

Wilson Harrell[42]

MANAGING THE MONEY ONCE YOU GET IT

Let's assume that you have dealt with all the hooey. You hung tough and retained, if not 50 percent ownership, at least 50 percent control. You have the money in your hands or bank account. Now you have to use it. More important, you have to manage it. Entrepreneurs usually aren't very good at that either. If venture capitalists are wary about allowing entrepreneurs to be the CEOs in start-up companies, they are terrified at the prospect of having a true entrepreneur serve as the chief financial officer. Here is how Fred Lager, former president and CEO of Ben & Jerry's and author of *Ben & Jerry's: The Inside Scoop,* describes Ben Cohen and Jerry Greenfield's approach to money management during the early years of their company. While funny, the Ben-and-Jerry approach to accounting is anything but atypical.

Neither Jerry nor Ben liked to keep the books, and their recordkeeping was almost nonexistent. Within two months of opening, there was a sign on the front door of the gas station [the site of their first ice cream shop] that read "We're closed today so we can figure out if we're making any money." They spent the day with an accountant, who tried to set them up with a system that would keep track of their sales and expenses.

At first Jerry paid the bills, but when they ran into cash-flow problems, Ben took over. Ben stopped paying the bills, and cash flow improved immediately. The deposits were made up by whichever of the two closed up at night. The cash got counted, stuffed into a night bag, and dropped off at the Merchants Bank, where it was opened and deposited into their account the next morning. The bank's count almost never agreed with theirs, and they put candy bars in the bags to compensate the tellers for the extra work involved in reconciling their account.[43]

Our gurus, being true entrepreneurs, don't have sterling records as money managers. However, they do have four pieces of general advice on that topic:

1. Be a miser.
2. Know your numbers.
3. Reinvest in the business.
4. When all else fails, be creative.

Let's take a look at each of these pieces of advice.

Be a Miser

Lillian Vernon echoes the advice of our other gurus, "Do not spend your hard-earned cash on anything but necessities—stylish office furnishings and the like are peripheral to the ultimate success of your business."[44] Vernon recalls that, when she started her mail-order business, she composed advertising copy on a $25 manual typewriter, cranked out mailing labels on an old Addressograph, used the backs of order forms for scratch pads, and even recycled paper clips. Your major aim when you are starting out, says Vernon, should be *liquidity*.

> *Liquidity* [is] the business world's term for actual cash. There are misunderstandings about the word cash; profits are not cash, accounts receivable are not cash until they are received, and physical assets are not cash. Although your computer system is a company asset, it can't pay the utility bills or meet your employees' salaries. Think of cash for your company as you think of the money in your checking account: it is always available. You use it to pay bills, to tide you over in an emergency: suppose a labor strike hits your product-delivery system and you can't get the goods to the customer on time. Once your business is established, only cash can give you the wherewithal to expand.[45]

The other point to remember about cash, says Vernon, is that it takes time to arrive. Just because you are showing a profit on paper doesn't mean you can pay your bills. "Suppose you paid off your bills for inventory and you have sold enough product to show, on paper anyway, a profit. Until your customers actually pay you, however, you have no cash on hand. There may be a time lag ranging from two to three months between your outlay and your cash income. That is the harrowing time for a beginning business.[46]

The best way to make the time less harrowing, say our gurus, is to conserve your cash.

Know Your Numbers

Of course, you can't conserve cash unless you know exactly how much cash you have. That means you have to know your numbers. "'Know your numbers' is a fundamental precept of business," writes Bill Gates. "The business side of any company starts and ends with hard-core analysis of its numbers. Whatever else you do, if you don't understand what's happening in your business factually and you're making business decisions based on anecdotal data or gut instinct alone, you'll eventually pay a big price."[47] Learn to read your balance sheets and income statements. Most important, say our gurus, set aside a specific time on a regular basis to analyze all of the numbers about your business—financial and nonfinancial. Debbi Fields says she starts every business day playing Sherlock Holmes with her sales figures:

> I get to my office early in the morning—in winter it's still dark and cold in the mountains—and I go right for the coffee.
>
> Next stop: the store controller's office. Steaming cup in one hand, computer printout in the other, I read down long lists of numbers, sometimes stopping, sometimes backing up.
>
> The computer tells the story of one day in the life of a company, who won and who lost, successes and failures in more than five hundred Mrs. Fields Cookies stores spread over twenty-five states and five foreign countries, on four continents, spanning sixteen time zones. By 6:00 A.M., Utah time, all this information has flowed into a terminal in Park City, high in the Utah Mountains.
>
> For the next hour or so, I play Sherlock Holmes. Hidden among these numbers are special problems that need to be fixed. I need to find them, and, because I am the chief executive officer of this company, it's up to me to fix them. Fix them now. The way I've come to think about it, last month's profit and loss statements are ancient history; that's all over and done with.

What matters to me is what happened yesterday and what I can do about it today. . . .

As I read across the columns for a certain store or district, a picture of the problem begins to form in my mind and, close beside it, an idea of what the solution might be. My hand begins to wander toward the telephone— the day is beginning.[48]

Notice that while reviewing the numbers Fields is simultaneously developing a plan of action to make them better. That's another key, say our gurus. "The analysis should always support action," advises Bill Gates, "not just more analysis. Analysis should lead you step by step to a decision and to action. You have to think, act, evaluate, adapt."[49]

Reinvest in the Business

As you review your numbers, you should be able to identify the liquidity that Vernon mentioned. You will be tempted to take some of that wonderful liquidity for yourself. After all, you have worked hard, you've sacrificed for it, and you've earned a few treats for yourself—a little indulgence. Resist the temptation, say our gurus. When you are starting a business, you shouldn't be taking money out. Any money the business earns, over and above the bare essentials you need to survive, should be reinvested in the business. Vernon declares that it is the single piece of advice she would give new entrepreneurs. She recalls taking enough out of her business in the early years to eat, live, and educate her children. Beyond that, all the money went back into the business. "Just as real estate people tell you that location, location, and location are the three essential considerations when buying a house, so do I believe that reinvest, reinvest, and reinvest are the three rules of starting up a business and keeping it going. . . . There is a line in Thornton Wilder's play *The Matchmaker* to the effect that money is like manure, it should be used to make things grow."[50]

A fellow who hasn't been in business before looks in the cash register and thinks, "That's all mine." But it isn't. It belongs to the vendors, to his employees, to debt retirement, to interest, to royalties.

Bud Hadfield[51]

When All Else Fails, Be Creative

Of course, you can do your absolute best at managing cash flow and still find yourself broke. Despite your best intentions, your liquidity may solidify. What then? Then you do what you do best. You're an entrepreneur, an innovator, and a creator. Innovate and create. Almost all of our gurus at one time or another have had to resort to unusual tactics to pay their bills, and you will too. Here are three examples to get your creative juices flowing.

Ted Turner's "Beg-a-Thon"

After purchasing a money-losing television station in Atlanta and turning it around with innovative and often irreverent programming and promotion, Ted Turner attempted to do the same with a station in Charlotte, North Carolina. This time, Ted's superstation formula didn't seem to be working as well. The station was bleeding red ink. Desperate for cash, Turner decide to go directly to his viewers for help. He launched a 24-hour fund-raising "beg-a-thon," as he called it, during which Turner personally went on the air and asked his viewers to send in whatever they could afford to help save his station. Over 35,000 people responded to his appeal, sending in contributions that ranged from 25 cents to as much as $100. Turner raised nearly $50,000 for his ailing station.

In typical entrepreneurial fashion, Turner is said to have used the money to build a new parking garage for the station rather than paying off his debts. Nevertheless, Turner kept the station alive. When he ultimately sold it eight years later, he paid back every dime to the 35,000 contributors to his "beg-a-thon." It seems he had kept the names and addresses of all those who had made a contribution.[52]

Fred Smith Goes to Las Vegas

In the early 1970s, Fred Smith met with representatives of General Dynamics in New York, seeking funding for his struggling overnight delivery service, Federal Express. Smith left the meeting discouraged, having been turned down again by a source he had been sure would come through with some badly needed cash. As Smith tells the story, he went to the airport to catch his flight back to Memphis. As he was checking in, he saw a TWA flight schedule announcing a departing flight to Las Vegas. On impulse, Smith opted for the flight to Vegas.

On landing, Smith proceeded to the nearest casino and began placing bets. He had all of $100 in his pocket. Over the next few hours, he won $27,000, which he immediately sent back to Memphis. By various accounts, the money was used to make the payroll or purchase fuel for the planes. Smith recalls that the $27,000 wasn't decisive, but as he puts it, "it was a omen that things would get better."[53] And they did.

Ben & Jerry's Ice-Cream-for-Life Payment Program

Ben Cohen and Jerry Greenfield opened their first ice-cream parlor in an old abandoned gas station that Fred Lager describes as "the embodiment of funk. . . . It had been built in the 1940s, and the exterior walls were covered by a white baked-enamel aluminum skin that was sectioned off into large, two-foot squares, giving the station an almost igloo-like appearance. The roof was flat, and the right front corner of the building was curved in a wide, sweeping arc that visually softened the impact of the structure as it protruded into the lot."[54] The station had no heat and obviously needed a lot of work to be turned into anything resembling an ice-cream parlor. Because they had limited construction skills, the pair hired Darrell Mullis, an employee of a local building contractor to help with the work. The only problem was that they had no money to pay Mullis. Needing the help anyway, Cohen and Greenfield came up with an innovative proposition. Would Mullis be willing to perform the work in return for ice cream? Mullis thought it over and agreed, thus becoming the first charter member of Ben & Jerry's "Ice-Cream-for-Life-Club."

They later offered a similar deal to their plumber, Lanny Watts. Lager describes Watts as Burlington, Vermont's, "alternative, hippie plumber." He didn't advertise and wasn't listed in the Yellow Pages. He was also innovative. For example, while repairing the plumbing in Cohen and Greenfield's broken-down gas station, soon-to-be ice-cream parlor, Watts discovered a broken urinal in the bathroom. Concerned that ripping it off the wall might lead to other repairs that the pair couldn't afford, Watts simply left the urinal in place and built a plywood box to cover it. Watts' original arrangement with Cohen and Greenfield was to work for his regular hourly rate plus materials. The problem was that he quickly lost track of how much and which materials he had used. Watts didn't want to have to reconstruct everything from scratch, so he asked Jerry Greenfield if he could just ballpark it. Jerry thought for a moment and then made a counteroffer. Would Watts be willing to accept the same deal they had given Darrell Mullis—free ice cream for life or as long as Ben & Jerry were in business, whichever came first? Watts considered the offer for a moment and then said he had some questions. Did the offer apply just to the original store or did it include any subsequent franchises? Never having thought about franchises, Greenfield readily agreed. "Sure, Lanny, it includes our franchises," answered Greenfield. But that wasn't enough for Watts, who wanted further clarification. "Well, I'm not just talking about your Vermont franchises now, I'm talking about all the franchises, coast-to-coast." Standing in the rubble of what he thought would be his first and only outlet, Greenfield agreed. "Sure Lanny," he said, "coast to coast. No problemo." Watts thus became the second member of the ice-cream club. But it wasn't to last. About six weeks after Cohen and Greenfield opened their store, Watts came by to say that he had run into some cash-flow problems of his own and wanted out of the ice-cream club. The pair reluctantly agreed and bought back Watts's membership for $350. Lager notes that it was one of the most shortsighted business transactions a plumber had ever made—"Lanny's fish story. The one that got away."[55]

GOING PUBLIC

"For most entrepreneurs," writes Thomas Stemberg, "taking their company public is the Holy Grail. An initial public offering, or IPO, betokens acceptance by the financial community and credibility among corporate peers." Of course, there is another benefit—"It turns company founders into multimillionaires."[56] Correction—it can turn young founders into billionaires. For a notable example, look to Bill Gates. Microsoft stock went on sale on March 15, 1986, at $21 per share. Almost immediately it went to $55.50 and then to $90.75. At the age of 31, Bill Gates became the youngest billionaire in history.

Okay, you're saying, this is what I have been waiting for—making it big, becoming a billionaire. After all of the drudgery—finding seed money, begging bankers, wooing VCs, watching every nickel and dime, and working, working, working, and working some more with little pay and less sleep—

now is the time to cash it all in and get rich. But hold on just a moment, say our gurus. Going public can lead to riches for the founders, and it can have other advantages. But it also can have some disadvantages. Here is what Howard Schultz discovered when he took Starbucks public:

The Advantages

Being a public company has lent Starbucks a certain patina, taking it to the big leagues. Our stock market listing provided the liquidity that has allowed many people at Starbucks, including me, to cash in stock options and buy things we need or have long wished for. It has likewise served as a great incentive to attract talented people, who join us not only because of the excitement of building a fast-growing company but also because of the value we are creating.

Our success on Wall Street also added dimension to the brand. It allowed us to go back to the market almost every year and ask investors for more money to underwrite our growth. We've raised close to $500 million since going public, by issuing new stock or selling bonds that convert into stock if the price goes above a certain level. I personally enjoy the intellectual stimulation of interacting with the bright people I've met on Wall Street, people who have done their homework and understand the company. I also like the challenge of formulating a strategy for Starbucks to finance its growth.[57]

And the Disadvantages

It exposes your business to a high degree of scrutiny and your personal life to a sudden lack of privacy. Most importantly, it increases the weight of responsibility to shareholders and imposes a burden of meeting Wall Street's expectations. . . . Alongside the exhilaration of being a public company is the humbling realization, every quarter, every month, and every day, that you're a servant to the stock market. That perception changes the way you live, and you can never go back to being a simple business again.[58]

Going public is the financial and legal equivalent of stringing up your underwear for everyone to examine. And the examination is endless.

Thomas Stemberg[59]

Still interested? Still convinced going public is the Holy Grail? Okay, then, exactly what is the process for taking your company public? Well, say our gurus, it ain't as easy as it looks. "Taking a company public," declares Bernie Marcus, "requires a magical, mystical combination of dazzling numbers, personality, and a little sleight of hand."[60] It's somewhat like finding venture capital, only tougher. Here is how two young Internet entrepreneurs recently did it.

Their names are Chris Larsen and Janina Pawlowski. Larson, a former auditor for Chevron, and Pawlowski, a former mortgage broker, quit their jobs in 1992 to start a mortgage business. In 1995 they took their business on-line as E-Loan. The business model was simple. They would save home buyers as much as 50 percent on mortgage fees by cutting out the loan agent and handling the process over the Internet. By December 1998 they had revenues of $6.8 million, and although they had not shown a profit, they were confident that it was time to take their company public. Here's the chronology:[61]

> *January 13, 1999:* E-Loan's board approves an IPO, and Larsen and Pawlowski begin their search for investment bankers to help them. Seven investment banks compete for the honor of underwriting the E-Loan offering and taking 7 percent of proceeds as their fee. The pair is anxious to select an investment banker with analysts who can spur investor interest. By February they settle on Goldman Sachs and Company because of its knowledge of E-Loan and the mortgage industry. The participants agree to take E-Loan public by Memorial Day so they can catch investors before the summer-vacation season.
>
> *February–March 1999:* Larsen and Pawlowski undertake the arduous task of drafting a prospectus. The prospectus will be the only document that E-Loan can use to attract investors. Every word must be precise. Risks to investors must be spelled out. If something goes wrong with the stock, the prospectus will be E-Loan's and its founders chief defense. Getting the wording right is tough because the bankers, lawyers, and executives all have to agree. Larsen describes the process as like 35 people trying to write a term paper. The final draft is hammered out during one long 32-hour session in late March, and the prospectus is sent to the printer.

As E-Loan's vice-president for business development puts it, "everything begins to happen at warp speed." E-Loan rushes to close some expansion deals in Japan and Europe and to reach agreement on credit lines to fund consumer loans.

Larsen and Pawlowski start getting calls from friends and relatives they have never known—including none other than Barbra Streisand. Streisand, like the rest, wants to be put on the "friends-and-family" list so she can purchase shares at the initial offering price. Pawlowski is impressed and puts Streisand's name on the list. Other new friends and family don't fare as well.

April 1999: Larsen, Pawlowski, and their chief financial officer, Frank Siskowski, begin preparing for two weeks of presentations they will be giving to potential investors in June. They hire a communications consultant to help them and run through several practice sessions while she watches. Her verdict: Siskowski seems okay. Larsen talks too fast. Pawlowski sounds tentative. All need more practice.

While Larsen, Pawlowski, and Siskowski are practicing, E-Loan's prospects turn south. Refinancings that drove E-Loan's performance in the first quarter are slowing due to rising interest rates. As a consequence, E-Loan's revenues for the quarter are likely to be flat. That's bad news for the IPO because it may spook investors. Worse, two IPOs for Internet companies "break" or fall below their offering price on the first day, and the Dow Jones industrial average dives 235 points in a single day. The signs look very bad for E-Loan's IPO.

Reluctantly, the parties involved decide to hold off. They won't be going public before Memorial Day. The question is, When will they be going public? Goldman Sachs suggests waiting until the end of July, but Pawlowski and Larsen are worried about such a long delay. They finally reach an agreement—they will go public June 29 but drop E-Loan's filing range by $2 a share to between $9 and $11 to keep investor interest. It could cost E-Loan up $7 million in what they raise from the offering, but, they reason, they can always raise the filing range closer to the time of the IPO if market conditions improve.

June 15, 1999: Larsen, Pawlowski, and Siskowski kick off two weeks of presentations to investors with a meeting at T. Rowe Price Associates in Baltimore. Then it's on to investor meetings in Milwaukee, Minneapolis, Kansas City, Denver, San Diego, Los Angeles, San Francisco, Chicago, Houston, New York, Boston, and so on. They give 58 presentations to nearly two hundred money managers in 12 days. Sometimes they are scheduled for eight presentations in a single day, starting as early as 7 A.M. Pawlowski describes the experience to company employees in a message on the company Intranet this way: "Drive, drive, drive. Park. Go to the bathroom. Present [to the investors]. Get feedback. Go to the bathroom. Drive, drive, drive . . . Park, run, run, run, sweat, run. No time for the bathroom! . . . Whew! . . . Do we have to do this again tomorrow?"[62]

Pawlowski compares the experience to that of actor Bill Murray in the movie *Groundhog Day*. Her life is just one day lived over and over.

The road show ends on Friday, June 25. Larsen and Pawlowski sweat out the weekend. They are hoping for a offering price of $16 a share. They will hear from Goldman Sachs on Monday.

Monday, June 28, 1999: A Goldman general partner calls to say that Goldman is worried that some potential investors may be wavering. That being the case, they want to bring E-Loan out at $12 to $14. Larsen and Pawlowski are crushed, but it is out of their control. By the end of the day Goldman Sachs decides on $14. It's at the top of the range and much better than the $9 to $11 that they had agreed to back in the spring. Still, the E-Loan founders are disappointed.

June 29, 1999: Larsen, Siskowski, and Pawlowski, who is accompanied by her nine-year-old son, are gathered at Goldman Sachs near Wall Street, staring at computer screens, waiting for trading to begin. Suddenly, E-Loan's symbol snakes across the screen. The price—20 7/8. They are already up 50 percent. Larsen and crew rush to call the troops back in California. E-Loan's entire staff of 250 is glued to the ticker. Someone calls out the E-Loan price. The stock just hit $23—now it's at $30—$38—$43. By the time the market closes, E-Loan's stock is up 164 percent, and 41 of E-Loan's employees find that they are suddenly millionaires. Larsen and Pawlowski do even better—over $200 million each. (See Exhibit 3.7 for a summary of the results of E-Loan's IPO.)

EXHIBIT 3.7.	Results of E-Loan's IPO
Total amount raised	**$56,300,000**
Minus fees:	
Underwriters	*$3,900,000*
Attorneys	*$700,000*
Accountants	*$550,000*
Prospectus printer	*$500,000*
Listing, filing, and IPO registration	*$118,000*
Miscellaneous	*$132,000*
What E-Loan took home for selling 10 percent of its equity	**$50,300,000**

Source: Robert D. Hof, "Inside an Internet IPO," Business Week, September 6, 1999, p. 63.

DEALING WITH WALL STREET

With their successful IPO, Larsen and Pawlowski joined the ranks of successful entrepreneurs. They created a company and saw it legitimized by the market. Welcome, say our gurus, to a new experience, one that Howard Schultz describes as an emotional roller coaster. "In the beginning," writes Schultz, "you accept the congratulations [for your company's stock performance] as if you really deserve them. Then, when the stock price falls, you feel you have failed. When it bounces back, it leaves you dizzy."[63] What's so frustrating about the ride, says Schultz and our other gurus, is that you have very little control over it. Your stock goes up. Your stock goes down. But the true value of your company stays the same. All the time you are either being praised or damned. By way of example, Schultz recalls dramatic fluctuations in Starbucks's stock price during the first part of 1996 that seemed to have no relation to what was actually happening with the company. His story is typical.

In early December 1995, Starbucks' stock price reached a record high—the sort of news that normally lifts moods around the office. But in fact, we had just learned that our Christmas merchandise was not selling as well as we had predicted, and tension ran high as we waited for the final results of the critical holiday selling season.

In early January, when we announced December comps of only 1 percent, the stock fell dramatically, from $21 to $16. In just a few days, we lost $300 million in market value, even though we had announced only a $5 million shortfall in sales. Concerned investors called me up, asking: "Why is the company performing so poorly?" The *Wall Street Journal* declared that we were a "shining light" that "may now be fading." Analysts seemed sure that our growth days were over, that the bloom was off the rose.

In fact, Starbucks hadn't changed in that month. Although our sales were lower than expected, our overall annual sales growth was nearly 50 percent. We were still buying and roasting coffee. We were opening a store a day. We continued with our plans to enter new cities and introduce new products.

Three months later, the stock rose to another all-time high. Comps were healthy again for the first three months of the year.

Goldman Sachs, one of the pedigree bankers on the Street, with no vested interest in Starbucks, predicted even higher profit margins and a higher stock price.

Investors were now phoning to congratulate me—some of them the same people who had called with serious concerns during the Christmas season.

What had changed? Again, nothing substantial. Starbucks was the same company in April that it was in January. The difference was that Wall Street suddenly decided the company was worth a lot more.[64]

At some point, advises Schultz, you have to come to grips with the irrational nature of Wall Street. Relax and just focus on running your business. Try to remain calm through the "heady highs and sickening lows." And when the financial press calls to ask you what happened and what might happen and why, just maintain your composure. No one does that better than Ben Cohen. Maybe that's a good way to end this chapter. Here are highlights of one of Cohen's most notable interviews with the Wall Street press. This time it was the *Wall Street Transcript* (*TWST*). Notice how calm Cohen remains throughout the interview, brilliantly fielding each question. Learn from it. You may have to do this some day.[65]

TWST: Do you believe you can attain a 15-percent increase in earnings each year over the next five years?

BEN: I got no idea.

TWST: Umm-hmm. What do you believe your capital spending will be each year over the next five years?

BEN: I don't have any idea as to that either.

TWST: I see. How do you react to the way the stock market has been treating you in general and vis-à-vis other companies in your line?

Ben: I think the stock market goes up and down, unrelated to how a company is doing. I never expected it to be otherwise. I anticipate that it will continue to go up and down, based solely on rumor and whatever sort of market manipulation those people who like to manipulate the market can accomplish.

TWST: What do you have for hobbies?

BEN: Hobbies. Let me think. Eating mostly. Ping-Pong.

TWST: Huh?

BEN: Ping-Pong.

See, we told you Ben Cohen was brilliant.

KEY IDEAS

- Money matters, but raising it is the activity that entrepreneurs hate most.

- Most entrepreneurs go with their instincts in estimating start-up costs.

- Most experts recommend a process similar to the following to arrive at start-up costs:

  - Step one: Prepare a personal austerity budget.
  - Step two: Determine your initial cash outlay.
  - Step three: Determine your working-capital requirements.
  - Step four: Determine the total funds you will need.
  - Step five: Double your estimate.

- There are two sources of funds—debt and equity. Entrepreneurs should strive for a balance of both.

☞ Bankers and investors have a different mind-set from that of entrepreneurs. As a result, entrepreneurs should expect frequent rejection as they seek funding.

☞ Your best sources of initial funding are friends and relatives. Just be sure that all loans and investments are documented.

☞ Bankers don't make loans to companies; they make loans to people. Therefore, the relationship you develop with a banker will be critical to your success in obtaining financing.

☞ Entrepreneurs who do not speak the accounting and finance language of bankers should employ an intermediary who does.

☞ Venture capitalists don't invest based on financial projections. They invest in people. Therefore, it is important that any venture capitalists you approach get to know and like your team.

☞ Premoney valuation will always be a stumbling block in negotiations with venture capitalists.

☞ Conflicts between entrepreneurs and venture capitalists normally center around issues of control of the company. You should fight long and hard to retain as much control of your company as possible. If you cannot retain 51 percent ownership, at least try for an arrangement that gives you freedom to make the most important decisions about company operations without interference.

☞ Walk away from any deal if you feel you are sacrificing too much control or if you are not comfortable with the investors.

☞ The following are keys to managing money:

- Be a miser.
- Know your numbers.
- Reinvest in the business.
- When all else fails, be inventive.

☞ Going public can make you rich and legitimize your company. The disadvantages are that you lose your privacy and become a servant to the stock market.

☞ Taking a company public requires a magical, mystical combination of dazzling numbers, personality, and a little sleight of hand.

○━┯ Running a public company is an emotional roller coaster with dizzying highs and lows. As the founder, you have no control over the direction of the roller coaster, but you will receive both praise and blame for whatever happens.

○━┯ The only way to cope with an irrational Wall Street is just to relax and focus on running your business.

J. Walter (Walt) Anderson, cofounder of White Castle

Marc Andreessen, cofounder of Netscape Communications

Mary Kay Ash, founder of Mary Kay Cosmetics

Phineas Taylor (P.T.) Barnum, founder of "The Greatest Show on Earth"

Arthur Blank, cofounder of Home Depot

Richard Branson, founder of the Virgin Group

Jim Clark, founder of Silicon Graphics and cofounder of Netscape Communications

Ben Cohen, cofounder of Ben & Jerry's Ice Cream

Debbi Fields, founder of Mrs. Fields Cookies, Inc.

Earl Graves, founder, publisher, and editor of *Black Enterprise*

Jerry Greenfield, cofounder of Ben & Jerry's Ice Cream

Wilson Harrell, founder of over one hundred companies, columnist for *Success Magazine,* and former publisher of *Inc. Magazine*

Masaru Ibuka, cofounder of Sony Corporation

Edgar Waldo (Billy) Ingram, cofounder of White Castle

Phil Knight, cofounder of Nike Corporation

Ray Kroc, founder of McDonald's Corporation

Edwin Land, founder of Polaroid Corporation

Bernie Marcus, cofounder of Home Depot

Robert Mondavi, founder of Robert Mondavi Winery

Akio Morita, cofounder of Sony Corporation

David Packard, cofounder of Hewlett-Packard

Anita Roddick, founder of The Body Shop

Pleasant Rowland, founder of Pleasant Company

Colonel Harland Sanders, founder of Kentucky Fried Chicken (KFC)

Thomas Stemberg, cofounder of Staples, Inc.

R. David (Dave) Thomas, founder of Wendy's International, Inc.

Ted Turner, founder of Turner Broadcasting System, Cable News Network (CNN) and Turner Network Television (TNT)

Sam Walton, founder of Wal-Mart Stores, Inc.

4

Getting Customers

I f you have worked your way through our first three chapters, by now you should have done the following:

- Explored whether you have what it takes to join Club Terror.
- Started searching for, and maybe found, your perfect idea.
- Considered how you can scrape together enough money to get your business started.

Your next step will be to open the door to your business, launch your Web site, announce your wonderful new product or service, and—have customers avoid you in droves. Contrary to the fantasy of the movies, if you build it, they will *not* necessarily come—at least not initially and not without some prodding. Don't panic, our gurus advise, it happens to most entrepreneurs.

When Bernie Marcus and Arthur Blank opened their first Home Depot stores in Atlanta, they sent their children into the parking lot to hand out dollar bills to potential customers. Their idea was to lure customers into the stores by giving them the opportunity to win prizes by matching the serial numbers on the bills to numbers posted on signs inside the stores. The kids started the day with $700. They ended the day with almost $700. Marcus and Blank had so few customers, they couldn't even give their money away.[1]

Thomas Stemberg had a similar problem wooing customers when he opened his first Staples. In an effort to entice office managers into his store, he distributed coupons good for discounts on office supplies to office managers at businesses in the area surrounding the store. Then he waited and waited and waited. It took more than a month before the first office manager showed up with one of Stemberg's coupons. It seemed the office managers in the area had little, if any, interest in Stemberg's office superstore.[2]

The experiences of Marcus, Blank, and Stemberg are common. Like investors, customers are hard to attract, but don't despair. Our gurus have plenty of advice to offer. Here is how they recommend that you get customers.

USE PROMOTIONS AND GIMMICKS TO GET ATTENTION

Your first priority, say our gurus, is to let your potential customers know that you exist. You have to announce your business. Most of our gurus started with some type of short-term promotion intended to create customer awareness and build traffic. Marcus and Blank's dollar bills and Stemberg's coupons are two good examples. A list of others is shown at Exhibit 4.1. The following sections discuss each idea.

Give Your Product Away

When Debbi Fields opened her first cookie store, she recalls standing behind the counter hour after hour with no customers and no sales. The cookies that she had baked early that morning lay in the display case becoming less fresh and less warm with each passing minute. Fields knew she would have to throw them away because they no longer met her standards. She was mad at the world. "Here I had something wonderful to share," she remembered, "and all people seemed to care about was price." At that point, Fields says, she made a critical decision. "I thought, if I can't sell

---

EXHIBIT 4.1. **Short-Term Promotional Ideas**

- Give your product away.
- Use contests and games.

- Celebrate the holidays.
- Do something mysterious.

them, I'm going to give them away." Fields called a friend to come and tend the store, "just in case some disoriented consumer attempted to buy a cookie," loaded up a tray of cookies, and went out on the street. Fields credits what happened next as a critical component to her business that, in a few years, would begin grossing over a hundred million dollars annually.

I was bound and determined to get a reaction. I simply couldn't believe that years of compliments and smiles on behalf of these cookies counted for nothing. I was afraid of rejection, embarrassed that I might meet someone I knew.

What I really wanted to do was crawl into one of my new cabinets, slam the door, and cry until I fell asleep. But the idea of failure absolutely terrified me. I was so afraid to fail that I physically forced myself to take my plastic tray and head out into the busy Palo Alto streets.

"Sir, would you try these cookies, please?"

"Mmm, these are good. Where can I buy them?"

Not everybody was willing to taste a free cookie, but eventually the braver souls finished up what I had on the tray. I went back to the store and started baking. An hour later, some of the people who'd tried a cookie on the street wandered into the arcade and presented themselves at the counter. They'd found me! And they bought cookies.

By the end of the day, I had exactly fifty dollars in sales in my cash drawer and I won my bet with Randy [Fields's husband had bet her she couldn't sell fifty dollars worth of her cookies the first day]. When I came home, flushed with victory, he bet me I couldn't sell seventy-five dollars' worth the following day.

That day, after giving away some more cookies, I did seventy-five dollars in sales.[3]

Fields says that, since the first day in Palo Alto, she has been a true fan of giving the product away.

Ever since that first sunny morning in Palo Alto, I've believed in giving free samples to the public, and that is the ongoing policy of Mrs. Fields Cookies today, wherever the stores might be found. It's a very simple statement: here's a cookie sample, and I'm betting my business that once you've had a taste, you'll be back as a customer. I'm also saying, You are the judge of this product. We are not selling by hype or high pressure, and we are betting that we can please you enough to make you buy what you just got for free.[4]

Sound good? Just give away some of your product or a little of your service and customers will beat a path to your door. Well, not necessarily. Fields argues that this approach works only when it is treated as more than just a product giveaway. She continues:

> Offering a sample to a potential customer is a pleasant sort of exchange. It involves human contact, a few words back and forth, an act of giving that takes the chill off the marketplace. . . .
>
> The idea is based on my experiences as a shopper at the friendly stores in Menlo Park. Every person who comes to a Mrs. Fields counter is important, really important. It's become quite the fashion for service personnel, in a certain type of restaurant, for instance, to be terribly chummy. Only one way will this work: if it's really meant. Insincere patter turns people off like crazy—you have to hire individuals who have an instinctive affection for other human beings, and you cannot teach them some line of formula chit-chat to use on the customer. Spontaneity is everything; it must come from the heart!
>
> In my little store in Palo Alto, I did what I meant to do the whole time I was planning the business: I made friends everywhere. Apparently, I wasn't the only person in the world tired of being treated like a detached hand with a dollar in it. Every day more and more people discovered the store, every day more and more of them came back. I had customers who came every morning, five days a week at 10:00 A.M. for their coffee break. Sometimes, when they couldn't make it, they would telephone to let me know they wouldn't be in. I got to know many of my customers by name, I knew where they worked, I knew about their families, I knew about their lives.
>
> At one time, the neighborhood diner or cafe worked in exactly the same way. But that concept was put aside—lost in the anonymity of mass feeding, and fast food restaurants. So I didn't create the idea—I just woke it up.
>
> Maybe the food-service business had changed, but I discovered that people hadn't changed at all. They still wanted and needed recognition. The store worked. The idea worked.[5]

Debbi Fields says her idea can work for you if you remember one simple thing—it is the pleasant exchange, the sincere human interaction, that makes the difference. People get to sample your product or service, that's true. But more important, they feel the chill being removed from the marketplace. They associate your business with warmth and friendship— and that's not a bad association.

Use Contests and Games

Next to product giveaways, games and contests are probably the most popular attention getters our gurus have tried and recommend. Sam Walton was a particular fan of contests and used them frequently to attract customers to his Wal-Mart stores. Among his favorites were these two:

- **Hidden item.** An expensive item is hidden somewhere in the store and the person who finds it gets to buy it for a ridiculously low price. Note, however, that this particular type of promotion once caused real headaches for one of Walton's store managers, as explained in Walton's 1993 book *Sam Walton: Made in America.*

> One year, on George Washington's birthday, Phil Green [a store manager] ran an ad saying his Fayetteville store was selling a television set for twenty-two cents—the birthday being on February 22. The only hitch was that before you could buy that television set you had to find it first. Phil had hidden it somewhere in the store, and the first person to find it, got it. When Phil arrived at the store that morning, there was such a crowd out front that you couldn't even see the doors. I think all of Fayetteville was there, and a lot of them had been there all night. Our folks had to go in through the back. When they finally opened the front doors, there was a stampede like you wouldn't believe: five hundred or six hundred people tearing through that store looking for one twenty-two-cent television set. Phil sold a ton that day, but the place was so totally out of control that even he admitted playing hide-and-seek with merchandise was a terrible idea.[6]

- **Kiss the pig.** Jars with each of the store managers' names written on them are set out in the store. Customers are asked to vote for the manager they would most like to see kiss a pig by dropping money into the glass jars. The money that is collected is donated to a charity, and the winning manager gets the honor of kissing a pig at a special ceremony held at the store for all of the customers to witness.

EXHIBIT 4.2.   **Sam Walton's Favorite Games and Contests**

- **Plate drops.** Store employees write the names of prizes on paper plates and sail them off the roofs of the stores into the parking lots.

- **Balloon drops.** Same idea as plate drops, with slips of paper identifying the prizes placed inside balloons.

- **Shopping-cart bingo.** Every shopping cart is given a number. Numbers are drawn at random and announced over the store's public-address system. The customer whose cart has the correct number receives a discount on all items she or he has in the cart at the time.

- **Travel giveaway.** Boxes of candy are given to the customer who has traveled the farthest to get to the store. (This is a popular game for store openings.)

- **Coins in the haystack.** A Wal-Mart store in Ardmore, Oklahoma, once placed a pile of hay in front of the store and mixed $36 worth of coins in it. Customers' kids were invited to dive into the haystack in search of the money. Each kid could keep as much as he or she could find.

Source: Sam Walton, with John Huey, Sam Walton: Made in America (New York: Bantam Books, 1994), pp. 205–207.

Then, of course, there is the classic World Championship Moon-Pie-eating contest that got started by accident and ended up becoming an annual tradition at Wal-Mart's Oneonta, Alabama, store. Walton recalled the origin of the contest this way:

The Moon Pie contest started back in 1985, when John Love, an assistant manager . . . accidentally ordered four or five times more Moon Pies than he intended to and found himself up to his eye balls in them. Desperate, John came up with the idea of a Moon Pie Eating Contest as a way to move the Moon Pies out before they went bad on him. Who would have thought something like that would catch on? Now it's an annual event, held every fall—on the second Saturday in October in the parking lot of our Oneonta store. It draws spectators from several states and has been written up in newspapers and covered by television literally all over the world. As of this writing, by the way, the world record for Moon Pie eating is sixteen double deckers in ten minutes. It was set in 1990 by a guy named Mort Hurst, who bills himself as "the Godzilla of Gluttony."[7]

As Walton freely admitted, many of the games and contests Wal-Mart holds, such as those just described and shown in Exhibit 4.2, are corny. After all, what could be sillier than grown men and women stuffing themselves with Moon Pies or kissing pigs? Yet, they work. Customers love them. Why? Because it's fun, writes Walton: "When folks get together and do this sort of silly stuff it's really impossible to measure just how good it is for their morale. To know that you're supposed to have a good time, that there's no place for stuffed shirts . . . is a very uplifting thing for all of us."[8] It's also, we might add, good for the cash register.

Celebrate the Holidays

True entrepreneurs never let a holiday go by without offering some kind of promotion or gag to garner attention. Phil Green's 22-cent television set promotion was a tie-in to Washington's birthday. Other Wal-Mart stores make it a practice to field entries in every local holiday parade. For example, the Fairbury, Nebraska, store sponsors a precision shopping-cart drill team that marches in all local parades. Wearing Wal-Mart smocks, members of the team execute a complex series of whirls, twirls, circles, and crossovers. In Fitzgerald, Georgia, the local Wal-Mart store has a float in the Irwin County Sweet Potato Parade. The float features seven store volunteers dressed in costumes depicting various fruits and vegetables. As the float passes the judging stand, the volunteers launch into their favorite company cheer.

Wal-Mart isn't alone in exploiting holidays for customer attention and good will. Most of our other gurus do the same. For example, its first year in business Ben & Jerry's gave free ice-cream cones to moms on Mother's Day. As Fred Lager explained, "any woman who came in with her kids, pictures of her kids, gray hair, or stretch marks qualified. Visibly pregnant women got two cones."[9]

As in the case of games and contests, many of the holiday attention getters sponsored by our gurus are silly. What makes them work? Like games and contests, say our gurus, the holiday stunts are devoid of cynicism and loaded with fun. They are silly but sincere.

Do Something Mysterious

Holiday celebrations are often just staged, good-natured, silliness—people dressing up in costumes and so on; but there is another kind of staged attention-getting silliness that has a slightly more serious undertone. It may be the most difficult type of attention-getter to pull off because it involves some degree of trickery. The idea is to attract attention by doing something unusual or mysterious. Your customers' curiosity literally leads them to your door. The master of this kind of attention-getting stunt was none other than P.T. Barnum.

Barnum used a wide range of attention getters to attract customers to his New York museum in the mid-1800s. For example:

- He placed bright-colored flags and a huge revolving light on the roof of the museum. People could see the flags waving in the breeze, illuminated by Barnum's spotlight, for miles around. They would search out Barnum's building just to see what the flags were all about.

- In constructing his building, Barnum had the contractor build a balcony on the second floor. Visitors to the museum were encouraged to step out on the balcony to get a breath of fresh air and to enjoy the view. Barnum knew that the sight of so many people congregated on the balcony high above the street would attract the attention and rouse the curiosity of nearly every passerby on the street below.

- Barnum hung signs and banners on the walls of his building and at night projected eerie images onto the side of his building. No one walking down the street could possibly miss them.

Of course, today, signs, banners, lights, and flags are nothing new. Along with balloons, they are used as attention getters by almost every start-up retailer. Often, however, they aren't very effective. Passersby do, indeed, pass by without giving the business a thought. Why? Our gurus answer simply that they have become common. They are no longer mysterious. Barnum understood that the device itself is not as important as the way the device is used and the curiosity it produces. In fact, part of his genius was his ability to turn a simple object into a source of mystery and intrigue. Take the common brick as an example. Barnum is said to have hired a young man one day and given him several bricks along with the following instructions:

Now go and lay a brick on the sidewalk at the corner of Broadway and Ann Street; another close by the Museum; a third diagonally across the way at the corner of Broadway and Vesey Street, by the Astor House; put down the fourth on the sidewalk in front of St. Paul's Church, opposite; then, with the fifth brick in hand, take up a rapid march from one point to the other, making the circuit, exchanging your brick at every point, and say nothing to no one. . . .

You must seem to be as deaf as a post; wear a serious countenance; answer no questions; pay no attention to any one; but attend faithfully to the work and at the end of every hour by St. Paul's clock show this ticket at the Museum door; enter, walking solemnly through every hall in the building; pass out, and resume your work.[10]

Somewhat confused by these strange instructions but nevertheless eager to earn his wages, the young man did as he was told. Within half an hour over five hundred people had assembled to watch the young man complete his mysterious chores, and at the end of the hour, when he presented his ticket and walked through the museum doors, most bought tickets and followed him. The brick stunt worked so well that the police eventually put an end to it, complaining that the huge crowds in front of the museum were blocking traffic.

Over one hundred years later, Anita Roddick used a similar stunt to attract attention to her first Body Shop stores. This time the device was perfume instead of bricks, but the goal was the same, as Roddick explains:

Brighton shopkeepers opening up for business in the spring of 1976 occasionally had cause to sniff the air, then pause and scratch their heads at the curious sight of this odd woman in dungarees with unruly dark hair walking down the street intently spraying strawberry essence on to the pavement. It was not a madwoman—it was me, laying a scented trail to the door of The Body Shop in the hope that potential customers would follow it.[11]

Passersby sniffed the air and did follow the scent, all the way to front of Roddick's shop, which itself was drenched in the most exotic perfume oils she could find. Roddick's scented trail worked not because of the device she used but because of the effect it engendered. The smell of exotic perfume on the street was different, curious—mysterious. Her ploy was also simple. That's the last lesson our gurus teach about your efforts to attract attention.

Keep It Simple

Our gurus say you should try to keep your promotions and attention-getting efforts as simple as possible. If you don't, not only do you run the risk of customers missing the point of your complex promotion but you may find that administering it becomes a nightmare. That's what happened to Ben Cohen and Jerry Greenfield during one of their earlier efforts to attract customers to their fledgling ice-cream store. It was winter in Vermont, and ice-cream sales had sagged. In an effort to boost sales, the pair came up with the idea for a promotion they called POPCDBZWE (pronounced "pop sid biz we")—Penny Off Per Celsius Degree Below Zero Winter Extravaganza. As the name implies, the promotion was to offer a penny off on the price of ice cream for every degree the temperature was below zero in Celsius. As you might expect, the promotion became a nightmare for the employees, who were expected to convert Fahrenheit to Celsius while scooping ice cream. Customers didn't understand the calculations or find the few cents discount motivating.

Eventually, Cohen and Greenfield replaced the POPCDBZWE promotion with another one that Cohen concocted. He proposed what he called the First Law of Ice-Cream-Eating Dynamics. This breakthrough in thermal physics held that a person's sensation of cold was a result of the difference between their internal temperature and that of their surrounding environment. Thus, one way to warm up in cold weather, argued Cohen, was to eat a lot of ice cream. Because the ice cream was cold it would lower your internal temperature and thus make you feel warmer. Cohen is said to have lectured on the subject extensively but to no avail. Sales did not improve.

COURT THE PRESS FOR FREE PUBLICITY

The promotions and gimmicks discussed so far are aimed at capturing the attention of the passerby—the shopper in the mall who might be enticed into Debbi Fields's cookie shop by a sample, the person on the street who might impulsively buy a ticket to Barnum's museum out of curiosity, or the shoppers who might return to their local Wal-Mart store to see the manager kiss a pig. These types of promotions are all necessary attention getters, say our gurus, but they pale when compared to the most powerful attention-getter of all—press coverage.

According to Wilson Harrell, press relations are so important that you shouldn't leave them to chance: "If I could relive my marketing life, I would never begin a business, or deploy a new idea, product or service, without retaining a professional PR firm. . . . As a matter of fact, I would re-tain them before I hired my first vice president, lawyer, or accountant. From day one, I would have someone devoted to getting 'free' publicity for what-ever I was trying to do."[12] What can a professional public relations (PR) person do for you? Harrell provides the following example:

It was in 1969. Art Linkletter and I had become involved both financially and emotionally in marketing Toasta Pizza [a frozen pizza that could be pre-pared in a home toaster]. After incredible test-marketing results, we were ready to roll out nationally. By then, I had learned the value of PR, and re-tained a small but brilliant PR firm. One day, just as our roll-out was about to begin, the two partners come dancing into my office unannounced—full of fire and vinegar. With bouncing excitement, they told me their idea: "We want to proclaim to the world that this year (1969) is the 100th anniver-sary of pizza." I asked a logical question: "So what?" Twenty minutes later, after they unfolded their plot, I sat at my desk dumbfounded—while it began to sink in. Then I jumped up and yelled, "Let's do it!" and started dancing with them.

Their plan was to contact every TV talk show in America, and volunteer to appear on their programs to celebrate the 100th Anniversary of Pizza, to talk about its origin and progress down through history until today, when a brand-new innovation would thrust pizza into every household in the world that had a toaster. Of course, when they appeared on the show, they would have a home toaster and demonstrate how easy it was to produce instant Toasta Pizza, which everyone present would gobble up.

The idea became a plan, the plan became an outrageous PR campaign. It worked like magic. They hired a beautiful young woman, Italian of course, with the gift of gab and a sexy accent. She traveled the country appearing on TV and radio programs, telling all about the history of pizza, while she sold the hell out of Toasta Pizza. As part of the campaign, the PR firm had also written news releases and stories, which newspapers and magazines picked up and ran all over the country.

All the PR activity was carefully planned to coincide with the efforts of our sales force. It was an entrepreneurial marketing coup, *par excellence*. Every supermarket buyer in America must have seen or heard or read about Toasta Pizza, because we got a 95-percent supermarket acceptance on the first roll. Voila! That one idea was worth more than all the millions we spent on advertising . . . at about one-hundredth the cost.[13]

OUR VIEW

The reality is that neither Harrell, nor Linkletter, the PR firm, nor anyone else knows when the first pizza was concocted, but the concept dates to pre-history. There is ample evidence that the Greeks and Etruscans ate flat bread topped with a variety of condiments—an early version of pizza—long before 1869. Regardless, the media didn't question Harrell's claims, and he got his publicity, thanks, of course, to the PR guys and their outrageous idea.

Like Harrell, Jim Clark, founder of Silicon Graphics and cofounder of Netscape, favors bringing a PR specialist into a company at start-up. Marc Andreessen, Clark's cofounder at Netscape, recalls that he was skeptical when Clark first mentioned the idea: "I was like, 'We're a start-up company and we don't need to hire a full-time PR person.'" Still, Clark insisted, and they brought in Rosanne Siino, a PR specialist from Clark's previous company, Silicon Graphics, as the 19th Netscape employee. Siino was soon able to get a story about Andreessen in a local California paper under the headline: "He's Young, He's Hot, and He's Here." That was followed by a story in *Fortune* heralding Netscape as one of "25 Cool Companies" and featuring a large photo of Clark, Andreessen, and the entire Netscape development team. Within a few months and prior to shipment of Netscape 1.0, Marc Andreessen was being proclaimed as the next Bill Gates. *People* magazine included him as one of the most intriguing people of 1994, along with other notables such as Tiger Woods, the golf pro, and *Time* gave him a prominent spot on their list of 50 future leaders. Given Siino's performance, it is hardly surprising that Andreessen later changed his mind about the wisdom of hiring a PR specialist and declared the decision to hire Siino "one of the smartest investments [Netscape] had ever made."[14]

You Are Your Own Best Publicist

Of course, one of the reasons Siino was successful is that she really did have a story to tell. Clark and Andreessen were interesting people doing interesting things. In a sense, they were their own best publicists; they could use themselves to promote their company. That's an important lesson to learn, one that Richard Branson says he learned from Freddie Laker, foun-

---

EXHIBIT 4.3.   Tips on Becoming Your Own Publicist

- Help the press.
- Put on a flashy show.

- Find an angle.
- Celebrate everything.

---

der of Laker Airline, which later went out of business. When Branson was forming Virgin Atlantic, he recalls going to Laker for advice on how to compete against British Airways. Laker told Branson to use himself, which is exactly what Branson did. In fact, he was so successful in getting free press attention from publicity stunts, ranging from daredevil balloon expeditions to April Fools' pranks, that the term *Bransonesque* (meaning "flamboyant") became part of the British vernacular. In characteristic fashion, Branson argued that he was just trying to help, because he recognized that reporters and editors needed stories and pictures. When he disguised a balloon as a UFO, filled it with midgets dressed as little green men, and landed it on a field near London, he was only trying to make the British press's jobs a little easier.[15] Likewise, say our gurus, you should try to help out your local and national press. A few tips on how to do that are listed in Exhibit 4.3, then discussed in the sections that follow.

PR Tip #1: ~~Manipulate~~ Help the Press

None of our gurus are as adept at ~~manipulating~~ helping the press as Richard Branson. In fact, most writers site Branson's skill in dealing with the press as one of the key reasons for the success of his various enterprises. Branson's secrets for dealing with the press are summarized in Exhibit 4.4.

1. **Be available.** From the beginning of his entrepreneurial career, Branson has made himself available to the press. He doesn't hide behind press officers or PR specialists, and reporters and editors have come to appreciate his availability and reward him with positive stories.

EXHIBIT 4.4.   Richard Branson's Secrets for Dealing with the Press

- Be available.
- Treat reporters well.

- Plan for meetings.
- Tell them what you want them to know.

2. **Treat reporters well.** Branson is not only available; he treats the press well. When reporters come to interview him, Branson meets them promptly, welcomes them with refreshments and a smile, and is direct and straightforward with his answers. He takes an interest in their opinions, going so far as taking out his notebook occasionally and writing down some point they make. Reporters go away impressed—this successful and busy man is very nice and surprisingly normal.

3. **Plan for the meeting.** What most of the reporters don't realize is that their visit with Branson is carefully staged. Branson plans the encounter down to the last juicy tidbit of information he will drop, as though by accident, into the conversation. Every spontaneous funny line is prepared in advance. Even the setting and Branson's wardrobe are carefully selected for maximum visual appeal.

4. **Tell them what you want them to know.** Branson recognizes that most reporters are busy and are unable or unwilling to spend time carefully checking facts. As a result, explains Tim Jackson, author of *Richard Branson; Virgin King,* Branson often hoodwinks journalists.[16] For example:

   ▫ In the course of an interview, Branson repeatedly has to excuse himself to take phone calls. The reporter assumes, and writes in his column, that Branson is in great demand and his business is booming. The reporter doesn't know that all the calls are coming from the same public telephone and that all are being made by one of Branson's employees.

   ▫ During the filming of a BBC documentary, Branson produces a musician who explains in solemn terms why he has decided to sign with the upstart Virgin Records rather than a larger record company. No one on the production team thinks to check the background of the "musician." As a result, they never learn that, in fact, he is the husband of Branson's secretary and that Virgin not only has not signed him to a contract but they haven't signed anyone else either.

OUR VIEW

While the above stories are true, at least according to our source, we can't help but caution our readers that hoodwinking the press may not always be the smartest move. You could get caught, you know.

PR Tip #2: There's Nothing Better Than a Flashy Show

One of the secrets of Branson's success with the press has been his visual flair. Branson notes that he has worn almost every costume imaginable, including dressing as Peter Pan, a pirate, an airline stewardess, and a bride in wedding dress and high heels. Fancy dressing, says Branson, "makes a back page photo into a front page one."[17]

> As long as you don't hurt anyone and are creative, the authorities are usually fairly forgiving.
>
> *Richard Branson*[18]

Of course, dressing up is not the only way to dazzle the press. For those who may be a little squeamish about cross-dressing, there are other ways to make a visual impact. For example, Branson is said once to have hired a team of jokesters to sneak onto the Heathrow runway and drape a canvas sheath with the Virgin Airlines logo over the tail of a British Airways aircraft.[19] And when he opened his Virgin Records store on Broadway, Branson had himself lowered into Times Square atop a big lighted globe similar to the one dropped on New Year's Eve. The photographers, of course, flashed away as a close-up of Branson's image was broadcast to the giant Sony Jumbotron. Followed by the mass of reporters, Branson strode into his 75,000-square-foot megastore and up to one of the store's thousand listening stations, where he began listening to selections from Liza Minnelli's latest album. Suddenly, someone tapped a "startled" Branson on his shoulder. Who would have guessed it—Liza herself asking how Branson liked her new record. "Great," said Branson, as the reporters scribbled notes and the photographers took their front page photos of the smiling duo.[20]

PR Tip #3: Find an Angle

Our gurus caution that being visual, by itself, is not enough. You can shoot off rockets, drop illuminated balls from the sky, and still have the reporters yawn. What you need in addition to a flashy show is an angle, a hook, something to pique the news editor's curiosity. Dave Thomas believes that Colonel Harland Sanders, founder of Kentucky Fried Chicken (KFC), had one of the best angles he has ever seen.

Because the Colonel was such a personality, we were able to get him on local TV and radio shows, which led to plenty of free publicity. He really attracted attention in his famous double-breasted white suit with black string tie. It could be the middle of winter, and there'd be this guy in a white suit and goatee, a likable grandfather-type, a master showman, talking about his "secret" recipe of eleven herbs and spices for cooking chicken, America's hospitality dish. Everybody wants in on a secret, so people listened. He'd get all riled up about the difference between bad fried chicken and good fried chicken, so you'd think it was a federal case.

If we promised to bring a bucket or two of chicken along, we could get him on plenty of shows. Sometimes, we could trade them for an outright ad. This was back before the "payola" stink, so maybe it was "chicken-ola," I don't know. When he was on the radio, sometimes I used to nudge him to keep him awake. I was always worried he'd go to sleep. I used to think, I'm sure glad he's doing those interviews and not me! And today I'm doing the same thing that he was doing.[21]

Sanders had the look, a mysterious secret recipe, and of course, a couple of buckets of tasty "chicken-ola" to clinch the deal.

PR Tip #4: Celebrate Everything

A final way our gurus say you can garner free publicity is by participating in—or better yet, creating—a public event or celebration. Wal-Marts' Moon-Pie-eating contest mentioned earlier is such an event. It not only got local media attention, but after several years it began to attract the attention of the international press. Ben Cohen and Jerry Greenfield are masters at this type of promotion. Here is how Fred Lager described one of their first such celebrations. Cohen and Greenfield put on an end-of-summer celebration with the help of several other local merchants:

The celebration, called "Fall Down," was held at or near the of St. Paul and College streets [in Burlington, Vermont], and spilled out from in front of the gas station into City Hall Park, across the street. It featured a round-the-block stilt-walking contest, an ice-cream-eating and an apple-peeling contest in which the person with the longest unbroken peel won a dinner for two at a local restaurant. . . .

By far the highlight of the day was the Burlington debut of the dramatic sledgehammer-smashing of a cinder block on the bare stomach of "Habeeni Ben Coheeni, the noted Indian mystic." It was a routine that Jerry had learned in a carnival techniques course he'd taken his senior year at Oberlin [College]. Fall Down marked the second time they had done the act. . . . Jerry had given Ben the option of whether he wanted to be the smasher or the smashee. ("There was no hesitation on my part," said Ben. "I didn't want the responsibility.")

As the crowd gathered in anticipation, the song "RubberbandMan," by the Spinners, was cranked out over the makeshift PA system, Ben (aka Coheeni), draped in a bed sheet and perched on a platform in the lotus position, was carried onto the scene by six bearers, while chanting incoherently, a cross between a hum and a groan. "Feel the vibrations. The profound mound of round, here before us," Jerry exhorted to the crowd. "His ever-expanding consciousness exceeded only by his ever-expanding width. . . .

While Jerry invited a few kids up to verify that the cinder block and sledgehammer were real, Coheeni went metabolic, falling backward into the hands of his attendants, who suspended him in a supine position between two chairs. Once settled in place, Jerry looked for an appropriate opening in the sheet so as to expose only the belly, on which he placed the cinder block.

"And now I ask for your total silence as I bring the sledgehammer above my head. No loud noises, no lighting of matches, no flash. Keep your eyes on the belly, as this will be over in an instant. Ladies and gentlemen, one time, and one time only. . . ."

Whereupon, Jerry took the sledgehammer and, in one fell swoop, brought it crashing down on the cinder block, smashing it into lots of pieces that, fortunately for insurance purposes, didn't go hurtling into the crowd, but fell away harmlessly.

"Habeeni Ben Coheeni, ladies and gentlemen, the noted Indian Habeeni Ben Coheeni," Jerry shouted over and over, as "RubberbandMan" once again cranked out over the speakers.

Habeeni, restored to his platform, left in triumph, carried out by handlers and tossing flower petals to the pumped-up crowd.[22]

Before the cinder-block trick, Jerry had done his part in warming up the crowd with his "Dr. Inferno" routine. He had lined up several cotton-tipped torches, each of which had been dipped into 151-proof rum. He told the audience that he would attempt the "tongue transfer," wherein he would transfer the fire from one torch to another using only, as the name implies, his tongue. Jerry lit one of the torches and, as he reflected later, all would have gone well if he had just put a little less rum on the cotton. Some of the flaming rum dribbled out of his mouth and caught his chin on fire. The crowd didn't sense Jerry's panic and thought his flaming chin was a great addition to the act. Fortunately, Jerry was able to extinguish his face and even finish his act with a flourish, swallowing three flaming torches at once in a "flaming triple." Jerry's experience does, however, illustrate the dangers of this kind of self-promotion and prompts us to issue a warning.

◆◎ OUR VIEW

Don't try these types of gags without adequate training or, at a minimum, adequate insurance.

MARKET RESEARCH AND A FORMAL MARKETING PLAN

Short-term promotions and publicity stunts are effective and—perhaps even more important for the start-up business—low-cost ways of attracting attention and recruiting customers, but you may find that you want to consider more sophisticated marketing and promotion efforts. At that point, you will have to determine how much and what type of market research you should conduct and whether you should develop a formal marketing plan. Our gurus have mixed opinions about these issues. Some, like Earl Graves and Wilson Harrell, say that you definitely should conduct market research and develop a formal marketing plan. They even offer advice on how to go about doing both. Many other gurus, including Pleasant Rowland, Ted Turner, Richard Branson, Akio Morita, Edward Land, and Mary Kay Ash, warn that you may find traditional marketing research and planning of little if any use, particularly when you are just starting your business. Let's look at both sides of this argument, starting with the recommendations of Graves and Harrell.

Study the Market and Develop a Plan

Earl Graves and Wilson Harrell argue that you should conduct at least some formal market research and develop a marketing plan, particularly if your venture involves bringing a new product to market. Exhibit 4.5 contains Harrell's process for conducting market research. Harrell notes that only 1 in 1,000 consumer products succeed, so bringing any new product to market is always risky. The best way to reduce that risk, he says, is to conduct some research to gauge likely consumer response to your great idea. You can then use that information to develop a marketing plan in which Earl Graves says you should discuss the following:[23]

- **Your product.** Discuss the product's design and development, branding, and packaging. Who are your competitors? What does your product or service offer that your competitors' products/services do not? To whom will the product be sold? Who is the target customer? Earl Graves suggests that you include information on their per capita income, age, sex, geographic location, and attitudes. You should be able to describe the size of the market for your product/service in dollars and provide an estimate of the share of the market your product can obtain.

- **Pricing.** What will you charge for your product/service? Graves notes that pricing is rarely easy because "much psychology goes into properly pricing a product or service. [For example,] a premium product that is discount priced may not sell, because people won't perceive its true value."[24] Also, advises Graves, the price you place on your product or service must be consistent with your business concept and image. In other words, Neiman Marcus and Wal-Mart probably could not successfully charge the same price for the exact same product.

- **Distribution channels.** What channels of distribution will you use to move the product from manufacturing to the buyer? Will you sell your product through normal retail outlets, over the Internet, through infomercials, via telemarketing, or through a combination of these channels? Graves warns that not all distribution channels are appropriate for all products and services.

- **Promotion.** What methods will you use to garner attention and promote your product or service? This includes your use of advertising, publicity stunts (such as discussed earlier in this chapter), and general public relations. The key to successful promotion, say our gurus, is that all of your promotion activities are integrated and are consistent with the image you hope to convey. For example, a Moon-Pie-eating contest may work well for Wal-Mart but would not fit with the image Tiffany seeks to convey.

- **Actions.** The key to the success of your marketing plan, say our gurus, is for you to go beyond the plan to actions. You should map out specific marketing goals and action plans and then carry them out. "A marketing plan's success," writes Graves, "depends on the extent to which goals and action plans become a daily part of the business."[25]

EXHIBIT 4.5.   **Wilson Harrell's "Marketing for the Amateur"**

Step #1: Conduct the "Well, I'll Be Damned!" Test

Assemble a sample of your product or service (or if a sample would be too expensive to build, create a sketch and/or description) and show it to 20 objective people (i.e., people who are not your relatives or friends and therefore won't just tell you what you want to hear). "If most of them don't say 'Well, I'll be damned!' or 'Why didn't I think of that?' " writes Harrell, "stop right there. . . . If most of the people you ask say the magic words, you're on the right track." Ask your 20 objective people the following questions:

- What would you be willing to pay for this product if it were on the shelf of a local store? Insist that they give you a specific price.
- If this product were available at the price you suggested, would you:

  1. Buy it for sure?
  2. Maybe buy it?
  3. Not buy it?

- If you would buy the product, how many times a year would you buy it?
- What similar product are you using now?
- Are you happy with your present product?

Make careful notes on the answer each person gives to these questions. Finish by obtaining the age, occupation, income level, and marital status of each person.

(continued)

EXHIBIT 4.5.   (continued)

Step #2: Determine What You Can Charge for Your Product or Service

Rank in order answers to the question, "What would you be willing to pay for this product?" Drop the top and bottom 10 percent of answers. Average the rest to come up with the "perceived value" of your product. Subtract the approximate amount the retail store or other distributor will want to make for its markup. Harrell notes that you should plan on a 25 percent markup if your product is something you eat, drink, or clean your house with; 35 percent if it is a household item like an appliance or something you put on your face, hair, or body. Then, says Harrell, subtract 15 percent for what it will cost you to sell the product to your distributor, 15 percent for advertising, 10 percent for warehousing and transportation, 5 percent for administration, and 5 percent for miscellaneous things such as your salary. The remainder, if any, is your profit.

Step #3: Determine the Market for Your Product

Tabulate responses to the question, "Would you buy this product?" Take 100 percent of the "for sure" answers and 50 percent of the "maybe" answers. According to Harrell, if that total is over 50 percent of all the answers, you have fighting chance; 65 percent is okay; over 85 percent is great. You can go on to the next step. If your total is under 50 percent, advises Harrell, you should stop here. You're wasting your time.

Step #4: Conduct the Rube Goldberg Test

Make enough finished and packaged copies of your product to fill small displays in five or more retail outlets. Visit independently owned stores and ask the owner to allow you to display your product in his or her store. Promise to set up and maintain the display yourself and not to charge the store owner for the product during the period of the test. In return for letting you run your test, the store owner gets to keep 100 percent of the proceeds from any sales. The selling price will be the perceived value you calculated in step two. Your purpose is not to make money from the sales of your product at this stage but rather to get some idea of how many customers out of every 100 who buy a product similar to yours will buy your product. Harrell notes that this test will not be easy to arrange because most store owners will think you are nuts. Still, he insists that you keep trying until you get at least five or more store owners to agree to go along with your crazy scheme.

   At the conclusion of the test period, pick up your display and ask the store owners to compare your product sales to the sales of the slowest-selling competing product. If your product didn't sell as well as the slowest-selling competitor's, declares Harrell, you are finished. No store owner is ever going to agree to stock a new product that sells worse than his or her slowest-moving product. On the other hand, if your product sold better than the slowest-selling competitor, you have a fighting chance. Ask the store owners if they would consider continuing to stock your product given the volume of sales they have seen. According to Harrell, if three out of five agree, you have a potential winner.

(continued)

EXHIBIT 4.5.   **(continued)**

Step #5: Play the "What If" Game

Contact the appropriate national association of producers of the type of product you will be selling and request information on the total annual dollar sales for products of that type nationally. (Harrell notes that advertising agencies and people who sell that type of product locally can also help you arrive at an annual sales figure.) Now, says Harrell, do some calculations. First, calculate your share of the product sales in your market test. For example, if a total of 100 products were sold during your test in the five retail stores and your product accounted for 10 of those, then your market share in the test was 10 percent. If your product accounted for only 1 of the 100 sales, your market share was only 1 percent. Next, multiply the national sales figure provided by the national association by the percentage market share you obtained in your test to come up with an estimate of your dollar volume of sales should you take your product nationally. Finally, apply some of the percentages discussed in step two to see what profit you might make and how much you would have available for advertising, to support a sales force and so on. For example, you need roughly 15 percent for advertising. If annual national sales are $200 million and your estimated market share from your test is 10 percent, then you could expect $20 million in annual sales. Fifteen percent of that or $3 million would be available for advertising. Ask yourself, or experts in the field, if $3 million is enough to support a national advertising campaign. (Harrell says it isn't.) Keep playing with the numbers and running different calculations until you get a good feeling for the sales and profits your product is likely to produce.

Step #6: Design a Marketing Plan

At this point, Harrell recommends that you seek the help of someone experienced in marketing products like yours. Ideally, he advises, you should seek a retired marketing executive from a company that produces products similar to yours. Harrell suggests you consult the national association you approached earlier, advertising agencies, and even the local telephone yellow pages to find an individual to help you. Once you have found the expert, negotiate a fixed price for his or her help in developing a marketing plan. Give your expert the results of your "Well, I'll be damned!" test, your "Rube Goldberg" test, and all of your calculations. Ask your expert to study all of the data and tell you how much money he or she feels you will require to launch your product, how slowly or quickly you can roll out your marketing campaign, whether you must go national right away or whether you can roll out your product market by market, and so on. Your expert should help you put together a rollout plan that will include the level and types of media advertising you will need and the financing you will require.

Source: Wilson Harrell, For Entrepreneurs Only (Hawthorne, NJ: Career Press 1994), pp. 67–74.

Go with Your Intuition

Although Graves and Harrell offer sensible advice on market research and market planning, many of our gurus don't agree with their approaches. For instance, Mary Kay Ash notes that, although Mary Kay Cosmetics does highly sophisticated market research today, when she started out she relied almost exclusively on her intuition. She writes:

> In the beginning, my intuition was my only guide. I didn't conduct marketing surveys to find out what other women thought of the cosmetics they bought over the counter at their local department stores. I didn't have the money for such research. But I did know I felt embarrassed to try on makeup in a store in front of other shoppers. And when I did, no one bothered to teach me how to apply it myself. Sure, the store cosmeticians could make you look like Elizabeth Taylor, but once they were finished, you had no earthly idea what they had done or how to repeat it.
>
> The more I thought about it, the more I thought it would be wonderful for a skin care expert to come to my house and, in the privacy of my home, show me what would be the best look for my face. Then, if she instructed me on how to do it myself, I would be able to do it tomorrow and every day. I believed other women would feel this way, too. Based on that belief, I decided to conduct skin care classes. Right from the start, instinct told me a woman wouldn't mind experimenting with makeup when she was with a few close girlfriends. How did I know they would feel that way? Because that's the way I felt about it.[26]

Ted Turner and Richard Branson echo Ash's comments. They both went with their instincts in starting new businesses. Seldom, if ever, did they rely upon market research.

> Where's the fun in making a bunch of studies? I usually know what I want to do. . . . I never even did a marketing study on Cable News Network. . . . If everybody . . . had said that they hated the idea, I wouldn't have given a damn. There's never a reason for a study if your idea is conceptually sound.
>
> *Ted Turner*[27]

Pleasant Rowland, creator of the American Girl series of dolls, books, and magazines, states that, in the area of market research, she was the test. She recalls holding exactly one focus group when she was starting her company. Giving in to the advice of so-called experts, she says she produced some sample products, went to Chicago, and hired a person to lead a fancy focus group. The participants were all mothers of girls, and the question on the table was "Would anyone buy these products?" Rowland recalls that the results were awful:

> For the first 45 minutes of the focus group it was dreadful. The group hated everything about The American Girl Collection because we were merely talking about the idea as a concept. Then we brought out the products. It was a 180-degree turn. I learned a great lesson. Forget the focus group. Go do what you believe you're going to go do. Come from a place of heart. Come from a place of mission. There will be people out there who will love this and admire it, if you love it and admire it.
>
> So, the whole criterion for developing our products for a long, long time—longer than most people would ever have believed and still a huge part of it today—is, "Do I, Pleasant Rowland, like it?" "Would I have liked it when I was eight years old?" And if the answer is "yes," we make it. Bottom line, if I think it should be pink, it's pink.[28]

> I do not believe that any amount of market research could have told us that the Sony Walkman would be successful, not to say a sensational hit that would spawn so many imitators.
>
> Akio Morita[29]

So, what gives here? Are gurus like Turner, Branson, Ash, Morita, and Rowland just stubborn, or do they recognize something about entrepreneurship that Graves and Harrell overlook? Maybe the answer is a little of both. There is no doubt that these gurus in particular can be very stubborn about pursuing ideas that others reject. It is also true that they offer an important insight. Morita explains the insight this way: "Our plan is to lead the public with new products rather than ask them what kind of products they want. The public does not know what is possible, but we do. So instead of doing a lot of market research, we refine our thinking on a product and its use and try to create a market for it by educating and communicating with the public."[30]

Morita, Turner, Branson, and many of our other gurus argue that the kind of market research and planning gurus such as Graves and Harrell propose is simply worthless and unproductive for many entrepreneurs for one simple reason—the product or service they are proposing is so new and unique that there is no market for it that such research can reveal. "Markets," says Edward Land, "are what you look back to. A market is something that has been created."[31] If your product is sufficiently new or different, such as Turner's CNN, Rowland's American Girl Collection, Ash's skin-care classes, Land's instant camera, and Morita's Walkman, then it is unlikely that traditional market research will be of much help.

David Packard on the Origin of the HP Color Printer

[The] DeskJet single-handedly created the revolution in color printing. Prior to the introduction of the color DeskJet 500C in 1991, color printers were expensive, purchased only by users whose special needs justified the price. Our market research clearly showed that customers were not looking for color printers. Asked to prioritize their requirements for printers, customers consistently put color printing way down the list. But, when we asked, "If we satisfied all your black printing requirements and offered you the ability to print in color as well for little or no price penalty, would you buy such a printer?" the overwhelming response was "Yes." Our customers didn't want color printers, but they were very interested in printers that could print in color too. In short, HP should offer color as a feature.

David Packard[32]

In fact, say these gurus, market research might convince you to abandon an idea that has real potential. Better, then, just to move ahead with your gut instincts, recognizing, of course, that if there is no existing market for your product, you are going to have to educate your customers. What do you do if you have a product or service your customers don't understand or view negatively? How do you change their minds? How do you, in effect, create a market for an innovative new product or service when none exists? Let's look at three situations and examine how our gurus responded to each of them. In the first, you have created a product or service that is so new or unique that would-be buyers simply don't see its value. Your situation is similar to that faced by Akio Morita in marketing Sony's early tape recorder. We will show you how Morita convinced Japanese buyers that his recorder had value. Second is a situation in which you find yourself with a product or service that has to be repositioned in the customers' minds. They associate your new product with an older established product. You have to convince them of the uniqueness of what you have to offer. White Castle founders Walt Anderson and Billy Ingram faced such a situation, as did Robert Mondavi. We will see how they changed their customers' minds. Finally, we will examine a situation that many entrepreneurs face. Your product or service has a decided negative. Ted Turner had such an obstacle to overcome with his SuperStation. We will show you how he responded by turning not one, but in fact two, severe negatives into positives.

Situation #1: The Customer Doesn't Perceive the Value of What You Have to Offer

Akio Morita recalls that he and Masaru Ibuka faced the problem of customers seeing no perceived value in selling one of Sony's first products, a tape recorder.

> We were engineers and we had a big dream of success. We thought that in making a unique product, we would surely make a fortune. I was determined to make this tape recorder a success; when it was ready I demonstrated it every day, wherever I could find an audience. I took it to businesses, to the universities. I loaded it into the truck and took it to friends and recorded their voices talking and singing, every day. I was like an entertainer, setting up this machine and recording people's voices and playing them back to their delight and surprise. Everybody liked it, but nobody wanted to buy it. They all said, with variations, "This is fun, but the machine is too expensive for a toy."[33]

Morita says he was baffled by the response. He just couldn't figure out what he was doing wrong. He knew he had this great product, and yet no one seemed to want to buy it. Then, he says, a chance incident helped him see the light and taught him an important lesson.

I was still trying to figure out what we were doing wrong in trying, but failing, to sell our tape recorders, when I happened to stroll by an antique shop not far from my home in Tokyo. I had no real interest in antiques and I didn't then appreciate their value. As I stood there looking at these old art objects and marveling at the high prices marked on them, I noticed a customer buying an old vase. Without hesitation, he took out his wallet and handed over a large number of bills to the antiques dealer. The price was higher than we were asking for our tape recorder! Why, I wondered, would someone pay so much money for an old object that had no practical value, while a new and important device such as our tape recorder could attract no customers. It seemed obvious to me that the value of the tape recorder was far greater than that of an antique because of its ability to enhance the lives of the many people who might come in contact with it. Few people could appreciate the fine lines of the vase, and something that expensive could hardly be handled by many people, for fear of breaking it. One tape recorder, on the other hand, could serve hundreds, or even thousands of people. It could entertain them, amuse them, educate them, help them improve themselves. To me there was no contest the tape recorder was the better bargain—but I realized that the vase had perceived value to that collector of antiques, and he had his own valid reasons for investing that much money in such an object. Some of my ancestors had done the same, as I would do later. But at that moment, I knew that to sell our recorder we would have to identify the people and institutions that would be likely to recognize value in our product.[34]

Morita and his associates began searching for customers who would more readily derive benefit from their recorder. Tamon Maeda, one of Morita's associates, quickly identified such a group.

We noted, or rather Tamon Maeda did, that during that early postwar period there was an acute shortage of stenographers because so many people had been pushed out of school and into war work. Until that shortage could be corrected, the courts of Japan were trying to cope with a small, overworked corps of court stenographers. . . . Those people had no difficulty realizing how they could put our device to practical use; they saw the value in the tape recorder immediately; to them it was no toy.[35]

Morita and his associates quickly arranged to demonstrate their machine to the Japanese Supreme Court. Almost instantly they sold 20 machines. Armed with that success, they went on to discover an even more lucrative market.

> It seemed to me a logical step to go from the courts into the schools of Japan. Ibuka pointed out to us in one of the many meetings we had on the subject of sales that Japanese education had traditionally been centered on reading, writing, and abacus skills. But when the Americans came at the end of the war, they felt that verbal communications and audio/visual training were very important, and the Japanese Education Ministry followed their lead. But there was little media available in Japan, only some sixteen-millimeter films with English language soundtracks, which were of very little use because [they were in] English. . . . Ways had to be found to do the instruction in Japanese. The tape recorder was the logical medium.[36]

Morita later wrote that his experience with the tape recorder taught him an important lesson about marketing: "A sale cannot be achieved if only the seller understands the value of the merchandise. The buyer has to understand its value also."[37] A fundamental principle of attracting customers to new products with which they might not be familiar, explains Morita, is communication—your ability to effectively and accurately convey to your customers the value and usefulness of your product.

> We used to think that everything started in the lab. Now we realize that everything spins off the consumer. And while technology is still important, the consumer has to lead innovation. We have to innovate for a specific reason, and that reason comes from the market. Otherwise, we'll end up making museum pieces.
>
> *Phil Knight*[38]

Situation #2: You Find that You Have to Reposition Your Product or Service in Customers' Minds

Morita's challenge was to convince customers of the value of a totally new product. The second situation is slightly different. In this case, your product or service isn't entirely new; a similar but inferior product or service has been around for some time. People have become accustomed to thinking about the product or service in a certain way. You need them to see your product in a new light, to reposition it in their minds. How do you accomplish that? Let's look at the experiences of three of our gurus—White Castle founders Walt Anderson and Billy Ingram and Robert Mondavi Winery's founder, Robert Mondavi. Each of these gurus faced a similar problem.

For Walt Anderson and Billy Ingram, the problem was finding a way to expand their customer base.[39] Anderson and Ingram had founded the White Castle hamburger chain in 1921. Throughout the 1920s, their business grew as hamburgers became increasingly popular, but almost all of the growth was coming from sales to working-class males. The original White Castles were located near factories or in industrialized areas that women and the middle class didn't frequent. They were small, smoke filled, and awash with a constant banter about sports, hunting, and other manly diversions. Ingram and Anderson even refused to hire women to operate their restaurants fearing that their predominantly male customers would use language inappropriate to those of delicate sensibilities. Women and middle-class people largely avoided White Castle and thought of it as decidedly blue collar. As the country entered the 1930s, that avoidance became a problem.

As the Great Depression deepened, it brought more and more layoffs and troubling times for the largely male industrial workforce. Ingram quickly realized that his traditional customer base was rapidly diminishing. If he was to expand his base and keep growing, he had to reposition his restaurants to appeal to the middle class, especially women. Somehow these potential customers had to be convinced that White Castle hamburgers were a viable and nutritious mealtime option. That was going to be a significant challenge for two reasons. First, the middle class in general regarded hamburgers as very much blue-collar fare. Second, and perhaps more important, most middle-class women had read essays about the dangers of ground meat and hamburgers, which convinced them that ground meat was inedible and that the quality and nutritional value of hamburgers was not to be trusted.

For some time, Ingram had been working to change this image. He insisted that White Castles be kept scrupulously clean; even the name White Castle was intended to signify cleanliness. Additionally, he ordered that only special cuts of shoulder meat (now called "ground chuck") be used in their hamburgers, and he insisted upon frequent deliveries from butcher shops to ensure that the meat would be fresh. Still, Ingram knew that he had to do something to win over women and the middle class. He had to reposition the product in their minds, so he hired Ella Louise Agniel to help him do it.

Agniel was a former secretary with no direct experience in the food industry, but she was outgoing, confident, and most important, a housewife herself. Ingram gave her the pseudonym of Julia Joyce, a crash course on White Castle, and sent her out to educate the women of America on the virtues of hamburger sandwiches. Throughout the 1930s, Agniel traveled constantly from city to city, speaking to women's clubs about the nutritional benefits of White Castle products and demonstrating how the "non-fattening, highly digestible, energy and strength enhancing, vitamin-rich burgers" could be easily incorporated into weekly menus. Thanks in part to Agniel's propagandizing, Ingram was able to gradually remove the stigma from the hamburger. By 1937 the president of the National Restaurant Association was proclaiming that the hamburger had taken its place alongside apple pie and coffee as a truly national food. Through Agniel, Ingram had changed the customers' perception of the product. He had educated the consumer.

Robert Mondavi had a similar problem some 30 years later. After clashing with his brother (Charles Krug) over the direction the family winery should take, Mondavi left Krug and started his own winery in 1965. He was determined to produce California wines that would match the finest European varieties. His problem was that wine drinkers at that time didn't think of California wines as being of particularly high quality; and they weren't. Mondavi thus had two challenges. First, he had to produce a high-quality wine. Second, he had to convince wine drinkers that he had actually done so. To accomplish the first, he launched a series of experiments to enhance the subtleties in flavor that American wines lacked. To accomplish the second, Mondavi just did what came naturally—he talked:

> In the late 1960s and early '70s . . . when I was on the road two or three weeks at a time, promoting our wines, what was I doing? Talking and repeating myself over and over, at sales meetings, with customers, with anyone who would listen to what I had to say about fine wines and the Napa Valley.

When I went on the road with our sales reps and distributors, and even when I was alone, I had something else I loved to do. . . . [A]t night I'd go to one of the best restaurants in town. I'd sit down and order dinner and with it I'd order a bottle of fine Bordeaux, maybe even a First or Second Growth. Then I'd order another fine Bordeaux. When everyone started to get interested, I would invite the owner or the chef or the sommelier over for a taste of these great French wines.

"So what do you think?"

"Lovely," they'd say, or some such. Then I'd open a bottle of our cabernet sauvignon and offer them a taste. Chances are they'd be impressed and often they were downright shocked! Here was a truly fine wine, made in California, and more reasonably priced than a top-quality French chateau wine. And they could taste the quality![40]

Mondavi's talking and tasting paid off. By the late 1970s, the Robert Mondavi Winery was not only producing some good wines but like a number of other California wineries, was being recognized for doing so. The customer had been educated. Perceptions had changed.

Situation #3: Your Product Has a Decided Negative

Ingram and Mondavi were battling perceptions. In reality, the White Castle hamburgers were safe and nutritious, and Mondavi's California wines were actually better wines. It was just that the customer wasn't aware of the change and had to be educated. But what do you do if your product really does have a negative? What if, in some ways, it really isn't as good? Well, say our gurus, you just have to turn a negative into a positive. Here is how Ted Turner did just that.

It was in the early 1970s. Over almost everyone's objections, Ted Turner had bought a debt-ridden UHF television station in Atlanta, Channel 17, which he christened WTCG. The station showed mostly wrestling, old movies, and old syndicated shows. In addition, it had two major negatives going for it when it came to appealing to prospective advertisers. First, at a time when most other stations were broadcasting in living color, almost all of WTCG's programs were available only in black and white. Second, being a UHF station, WTCG was hard for viewers to find and tune in. With an amazing bit of entrepreneurial reasoning, Turner was able to turn both negatives into positives. Black and white wasn't a problem, Turner told his prospective advertisers. On the contrary, it was a benefit. "You want to avoid clutter? . . . You want shock value?" he shouted while pounding on their desks. "You want your message to stand out the way it never could on any other station? Then run your color commercials on WTCG, where all [the] programs are black and white!" And, argued Turner, being a UHF station wasn't a problem either. In fact it was a guarantee of intelligent viewers. How so? "Because," insisted Turner, "it takes a genius to figure out how to tune a UHF set, dummy!"[41]

Well, maybe "dummy" is not the best thing to call your prospective customer, but you get the point. For every negative, say our gurus, there is always a positive you can stress. It's your job to find that positive and point it out to your customer. That's a necessary skill in getting customers. It's also fundamental to advertising, our next topic.

USING ADVERTISING EFFECTIVELY

It is highly likely that advertising will be a key vehicle you will use both to garner attention and to educate your customer. Ray Kroc once said that there are two kinds of attitudes about advertising—that of the "begrudger" and that of the "promoter." Begrudgers, he said, always treat every cent paid for ad campaigns as if they are strictly expenditures, and they are reluctant to spend money for promotions unless they can see an immediate return. Promoters, on the other hand, are never hesitant to spend money on advertising because they have a broader vision of its benefits. Kroc viewed himself as a promoter:

> I never hesitate to spend money in this area, because I can see it coming back to me with interest. Of course, it comes back in different forms, and that may be the reason a begrudger can't appreciate it. He has a narrow vision that allows him to see income only in terms of cash in his register. Income for me can appear in other ways; one of the nicest of them is a satisfied smile on the face of a customer. That's worth a lot, because it means that he's coming back, and he'll probably bring a friend. A child who loves our TV commercials and brings her grandparents to a McDonald's gives us two more customers. This is a direct benefit generated by advertising dollars. But the begrudger has a hard time appreciating this."[42]

Our gurus urge you to be more of a promoter than a begrudger when it comes to advertising, but, they warn, don't treat your relationship with advertising agencies lightly. This is an area of your business that requires your personal involvement. How then should you go about such tasks as selecting an ad agency, finding the right account executive, working with the creative department, avoiding excessive commissions, and measuring the success of your ads? Here are four advertising success secrets our gurus offer.

Advertising Success Secret #1: Hire the Biggest Ad Agency in Your Community

Your first task is to find an advertising agency. Wilson Harrell suggests that you should begin looking for one even before you open shop. Harrell notes that, "whatever your product or service, you must tell potential customers why they need whatever you're selling. From calling cards to yellow page ads to full-blown TV campaigns, you need creative ideas that project your message. [And] that's not a place for amateurs, specifically not you and/or your spouse."[43] Start your search for an agency, suggests Harrell, by seeking out the biggest and best advertising agency in your community. Don't be intimidated by size, and don't talk to their lower-level employees. Go right to the top, to the owners of the agency. Tell them your company is headed for the Fortune 500 and that you want to develop a long-term relationship with an ad agency that can help you get there. Don't assume that they won't be interested because you don't have a lot of money to spend on ads at the moment, says Harrell; agency owners are usually entrepreneurs themselves, and entrepreneurs love entrepreneurs. Harrell recalls one small company he worked with that was able to secure the services of a large and powerful agency even though the owners of the start-up had very little money to spend on ads.

> I was a consultant to a small company that had developed a dynamite consumer product. What they didn't have was money. They desperately needed a lot of startup creative work, such as package design, copy and layout for sales kits, etc. If things went well, they would soon need print ads, as well as radio scripts and story boards for TV commercials. Obviously, they needed a fully staffed advertising agency. But, they figured, no money, no agency. Right? Wrong.

We met with the owners of an outstanding agency. They liked the product and the people. When the meeting was over, we had an agency that was willing to bet on the future; to invest their creative talent to accomplish all the in-house work with no up-front cost. A home run. How? Simple. We signed a long-term contract, based on sales. Not only did we get a great agency, but we were assured of special attention. A win-win for everyone. You see, I knew that an ad agency's greatest nightmare is to build an account and then lose it. We swapped money for security.[44]

Advertising Success Secret #2: Avoid the Top-Dog Ad Executive

Once you have landed an agency, your next critical task is to make sure that you get the right account executive. He or she is the person in the agency that will coordinate all of your relationships with the other people in the agency, such as those in the creative department. The account executive is also responsible for two other tasks: (1) keeping your account and (2) increasing your ad budget. Harrell offers the following advice to guide your search for the right account executive:

Don't try to get any of the top dogs. Agencies are like any other company; their top management is snowed under. That means you won't get the time you need when you need it. On the other hand, if they try to palm off some "junior" or the owner's brother-in-law, give them your old tried-and-true CEO "silent stare" until they try again. What you want is someone who is bright, who knows the agency well, and who isn't loaded down with 50 other accounts. Keep staring until they produce someone who gives you a warm feeling.

Once you're satisfied, help your account executive to be a better politician within your company. The more they know about you and your key players, the better they will function. Encourage your senior executives to spend time with the AE [account executive].[45]

Advertising Success Secret #3: Make Sure the Creative Types Are People You Would <u>Not</u> Hire

Once you have found the right account executive, your next stop is with the agency's creative department. You'll have no trouble recognizing people from the creative department, declares Harrell, since they rarely, if ever, look normal. "Don't act surprised to meet some strange-looking individual, with hair down to his waist (if it's a man), or a crew cut (if it's a woman). If they remotely resemble someone you would hire, the chances are you've got the wrong person."[46] Also, don't expect the creative people to be very politic. They will probably treat you like a worm and laugh at any ideas for ads you suggest. Harrell says you should insist on meeting the agency's creative people for two reasons:

> First, because it will make your day, but more importantly, because they are one of the major reasons you hired the agency in the first place. Let the creative people show you their work, face-to-face. What you are looking for is something that is fresh and different, even outrageous. Contrary to the advice you may have received, you are not looking for practical or solid creative ideas. What you are looking for are new and exciting ideas that stir the imagination. What you don't want is warmed-over copies of past efforts. Or, even worse, something that was designed to please you, and wouldn't sell grits in Georgia.[47]

When it comes to your ads, you want something that is clever. But you also want something that isn't so clever that no one gets the point. Anita Roddick learned that lesson with one of the Body Shop's first environmental ad campaigns. This one was intended to warn about the dangers of acid rain, as Roddick explains:

> We hired a brilliant Polish instructor who produced an extraordinary surreal poster showing a dead tree sprouting from a decomposing human head against an industrial background of smoking chimneys. The quirky copyline said "Acid Reign," which we thought was really clever. It was very, very sophisticated: the trouble was that our customers and the public hadn't got a clue what we were getting at. (In fact, someone came into one of our shops—I think it was in the Channel Islands—and asked if we were now selling LSD. I still don't know if it was a joke or not.) Ninety-eight posters went up in the UK shops and another 217 abroad, and all we achieved was to mystify everybody. . . .
> We learned from that experience, and we learned very quickly, that simple, emotive imagery was the key to getting a message across. We learned that the first bite is taken with the eye and that something very graphic and

very striking is needed to grab attention. We did better with the next . . .
campaign, on the dangers to the ozone layer with a poster showing a child
in a huge desert landscape, dressed in aluminum like a spaceman and carrying an aluminum umbrella with holes. It bore the copyline "Ozone or no
Zone?" We had a quote from a Roger McGough poem to go with it: "The
way we mistreat the earth, Anyone would think we owned it."[48]

Ben and Jerry had a similar experience with a clever advertising slogan
they adopted during their first year of business. The slogan was simple,
consisting of only two words, "Lick It," referring, of course, to their ice
cream. They printed the slogan on bumper stickers that they gave away and
on the backs of T-shirts that they sold. Then some of Ben and Jerry's customers began to object. Fred Lager recalls the incident this way:

> [The slogan] created a bit of an uproar in the local lesbian community, who
> had taken to hanging out at the gas station in relatively large numbers.
>
> *Commonwoman,* an alternative weekly newspaper, cited the bumper stick-
> ers as an example of offensive behavior in the local business community.
> Ben and Jerry responded by placing an ad in the newspaper that read as fol-
> lows:
>
>> Despite the fact that *Commonwoman* displayed our bumper sticker as an
>> example of sexism in Burlington, and
>>   Despite the fact that *Commonwoman* published an article advocating
>> stealing from businesses, and
>>   Despite the fact that *Commonwoman* disapproves of and threatens
>> not to accept this ad because they fail to see the humor in it,
>>   Ben & Jerry's would like to thank *Commonwoman* for its service to
>> the community and would like to thank its many readers for supporting
>> our store these many months.
>
>> Ben thought the slogan too good to drop, but Jerry . . . prevailed upon
>> him, and "Vermont's Finest" replaced "Lick It" as the slogan of choice on
>> the bumper stickers and shirts. With the change in slogans, amicable rela-
>> tions with the lesbian community were restored.[49]

As you work with the creative department to design, or at least to ap-
prove, ads that get your message across, and with the hope that they don't

offend anyone, you may also face the issue of picking a spokesperson. Someone may even suggest that you take on that role yourself, like Lee Iacoca did for Chrysler. If you do decide on such a role, don't be surprised if your first efforts at doing a commercial for your company don't turn out so well. Asked to evaluate Dave Thomas's initial foray into spokesmanship, Jim McKennan, an official at Wendy's ad agency, could only exclaim, "Those first commercials, *oy gevalt!*"[50] It seemed that a major problem was Thomas's propensity to scramble syntax, mix verbs, and invent words as he spoke. The agency's writers had difficulty coming up with complete sentences that Thomas was able to deliver, and *Advertising Age* proclaimed his early ads "thoroughly pathetic in every respect."[51] Eventually, however, the agency learned to adapt the ads to Thomas's unique style, and his delivery improved. Within a few years, *Advertising Age* had changed its opinion and was now calling Thomas's ads "hilarious, pointed, tactically sharp, and beautifully performed."[52] More important, Thomas's ads were working. Thanks partly to the advertising campaign, by early 1991 Wendy's was earning its highest profit in years. Exhibit 4.6 illustrates what Thomas learned about making a good ad.

EXHIBIT 4.6. Dave Thomas's Rules for Making a Good Ad

1. **Don't make claims for something you really can't deliver.** No matter who is speaking for a company, an ad has to be credible. . . .

   You have to be very careful that you deliver what you claim in an ad because customers really measure your products against your claims. If you can't make a claim you can live up to, I guess you're just better off with an ad full of smiling faces.

2. **Show a sense of humor.** People say I'm funny. They say I'm good at making them smile. Well, maybe. I know I'm not real good at telling jokes or gags and delivering a great punch line. My sense of humor has more to do with smiles than with going for the big laugh. . . .

   Some of you remember an ad for the Dave's Deluxe sandwich. I'm at a cocktail party, where the waiter shoves these ridiculous hors d'oeuvres under my nose. You don't want to be rude, but you don't know what's in it, and you definitely don't want to eat it. You say to yourself, "Who comes up with these crazy ideas?" "Whatever happened to peanuts or cheese and crackers?" Or: "Why am I here? I'd rather be someplace where I would feel comfortable." We were making the point that a Dave's Deluxe sure beats a crab puff. People relate to that. It makes them smile.

(continued)

EXHIBIT 4.6. (continued)

3. **Don't think that a down-home, easy-going ad is either cheap or easy to make.** A typical four- or five-day production for a series of television commercials costs about a million dollars. That's just to film, edit, and finish the commercials, not the cost of running them on television. A million-dollar investment can make anybody look good. The last one I made had dozens of takes and took ten hours to produce. That's for a commercial that is only thirty seconds long. So far, I've made over a hundred TV ads for Wendy's. None of them were made without a lot of effort. Not once did I ever feel that I got it all right.

4. **Don't pretend to be an actor if you're not.** Whether you're making a presentation or a commercial, it's all the same. The big thing is not to be phony. . . . The biggest risk that a company president or chairman faces when they do a commercial is that they will come across as having a big ego. You can always tell when the ad agency talked the boss into starring in the commercial because they wanted to flatter his ego. Everything looks staged, the boss pretends he's an actor, and everything falls flat. That's real risky for the company because the manager isn't credible, and the commercial can't convince the audience to buy the product.

5. **Talk in a believable way.** Some companies do "image advertising" that you couldn't believe in a thousand years. The employees all look like fashion-show models, the sound track sounds like it came from Ben Hur, and you get the feeling that the company does more good works than Mother Teresa. Remember, the words in your message can be honest and real, but if you overdo the effects and visuals, you lose being believable.

6. **Make sure your customers can recognize you.** In the early days of Kentucky Fried Chicken, we had all kinds of people coming up with the way Colonel Sanders was supposed to look. In ads, on bags, and in menus, we had fat Colonels and skinny Colonels, dark-haired Colonels and fair-haired ones. We had to standardize his image into one professional look. Only then did we get the real benefits of being a brand. People know how to find you then.

7. **Be controversial.** At last count, there are 2,931 brands of products competing for attention on American television. Getting people interested enough to watch your commercial these days is very tough. Marketing people say good ads have to "bust through all the clutter." To do that, they conclude, you have to be controversial. But some of these marketing geniuses go too far. There's plenty of suggestive, risqué advertising on TV today. We think you can be controversial without forgetting about good taste. One time, an agency wanted me to say "up to your keister in biscuits," and I wouldn't do it because I felt it would offend some people.

8. **Don't try to please everyone.** This may be the most important marketing lesson I know. I've sat in on plenty of marketing meetings where people tried to make everyone happy, and it doesn't work. Go after the customers who will make a difference to your business. Expect some people not to like you and many more not to even notice that you exist. Spend your time thinking about the people you really want to be your customers. Then do everything you can to talk to those customers in a way that will make them feel good about you.

Source: R. David Thomas, Dave's Way (New York: Berkley Books, 1992), pp. 163–164.

Advertising Secret #4: Beat the Commissions

Whether you appear in your ads yourself or hire someone to do the job, our gurus caution you to pay attention to the commissions you are paying. One of the things Harrell disliked about the commission structure of most advertising agencies is that they continue to collect a 15 percent commission on media buys even though most media buying today is accomplished by media-buying firms. If such commissions are the principle source of an agency's income, writes Harrell, the possibility exists for a conflict of interest about how much advertising to buy. Instead, there is a better and simpler way to compensate ad agencies for their efforts:

> Agree with your agency that all advertising will be billed to you at their net cost, no commissions. Instead, you agree to pay them for services performed by the job, or hour, . . . the same way you pay for most professional services. By all means, let them make a profit on your account; even give them an incentive kicker based on sales results! I'm not suggesting that you try to save money, but rather that you try to get more bang for your bucks.[53]

Another way to reduce your costs, according to Harrell, is to authorize your agency to have its media-buying service make "opportunistic" media buys for your company. Such buys occur when television or radio stations have a last-minute cancellation or difficulty selling a particular spot or space. For example, a few years ago, the media-buying company his agency was working with was able to secure a $200,000 prime-time spot on a major network for his company for just $40,000 due to a last-minute cancellation. Although such fantastic buys don't come along often, notes Harrell, you want to be able to take advantage of them when they do.[54]

NEVER LOSE SIGHT OF YOUR GOAL

One final word from our gurus—as you go about the process of buying advertising, starring in your own television and radio ads, coming up with clever print ads, courting the media, and pulling off really funny publicity stunts, just remember one thing. You're not doing all of this to win advertising awards or to get your face on the cover of *Time* as "the most interesting person of the decade." You're doing this to make sales and to build a long-term brand image. "Marketing," says Phil Knight of Nike, "is just getting people to buy things."[56] It's about getting customers. Period.

> The indicator of how well . . . marketing is working is whether people are buying the product. . . . Marketing done well results in sales. Effective short-term marketing results in a short-term sales boost—a cents-off promotion or a six-week run of ads, for instance, can create a short-term lift. Long-term, image marketing results in ongoing, sustained sales. Image marketing is a slow build over time, and it's based on communicating the essence of the brand. The positioning statement of Ben & Jerry's—the essence of the brand—would be, "Two regular, caring guys living in Vermont, the land of cows and green pastures, making some world-class ice cream in some pretty unusual flavors."
>
> *Ben & Jerry*[55]

KEY POINTS

- Most entrepreneurs have to use promotions and gimmicks to get the attention of potential customers.

- Successful promotional efforts should be easy to administer and easy to understand. Customers may miss the point of complex promotions.

- Successful entrepreneurs court the press.

- Gurus disagree on the usefulness of traditional market research for entrepreneurs. Some argue that all entrepreneurs should conduct market testing and develop a formal marketing plan. Others argue that marketing studies are useless for determining the viability of products that are truly new because there is no market for such products that market research can reveal. For really new products, entrepreneurs must go with their instinct and create a market by educating the consumer.

- Educating the consumer involves one or more of the following:

  - Demonstrating a need for the new product by illustrating how the product solves a problem or delivers a benefit.

□ Repositioning the product in the customers' minds by showing how it is better or different from existing competing products.

□ Turning a perceived negative into a positive.

⊶ Advertising is a key vehicle for garnering attention and educating the customer. Successful entrepreneurs never hesitate to spend money on advertising because they recognize its benefits.

⊶ Try to avoid paying unnecessary commissions to ad agencies, and use opportunistic media buys to reduce your costs.

⊶ Remember that the real reason for advertising, promotions, and press relations is not to win awards or get your face on the cover of *Time*. The real reason is to make sales and build a brand image. The real reason is to get customers.

Mary Kay Ash, founder of Mary Kay Cosmetics

Arthur Blank, cofounder of Home Depot

Richard Branson, founder of the Virgin Group

Michael Dell, founder of Dell Computer Corporation

Debbi Fields, founder of Mrs. Fields Cookies, Inc.

Bill Gates, cofounder of Microsoft Corporation

Earl Graves, founder, publisher, and editor of *Black Enterprise*

Bud Hadfield, founder of Kwik Kopy

Howard Johnson, founder of Howard Johnson Company

Herb Kelleher, founder of Southwest Airlines

Ray Kroc, founder of McDonald's Corporation

Bernie Marcus, cofounder of Home Depot

Konosuke Matsushita, founder of Matsushita Electric Industrial Company

Edward Miller, cofounder of Spic and Span, Inc.

Tom Monaghan, founder of Domino's Pizza

Bill Rosenberg, founder of Dunkin' Donuts

Howard Schultz, founder of Starbucks Coffee Company

5

Keeping Customers

Having been through all that we discussed in the last chapter and, as a result, having gotten some customers to venture into your store, access your Web site, or sample your products, our gurus have one piece of advice for you at this point:

For goodness sake, don't lose them!!!

That's what this chapter is about—keeping customers. Our gurus say that the effort you expend to keep customers may be the most important thing you can do to help your business succeed. Of course you recognize that customers are vital, but just how valuable is a single customer? Quite valuable. Our gurus have done the calculations.

EVERY SINGLE CUSTOMER HAS VALUE

In November 1995, *LUV Lines* (the corporate newsletter for founder Herb Kelleher's Southwest Airlines) featured an article that put the importance of customer service in perspective. It read in part as follows:

> How important is every Customer to our future? Our Finance Department reports that our break-even Customers per flight in 1994 was 74.5, which means that, on average, only when Customer #75 came on board did a flight become profitable!
>
> Aside from that statistical data, let me share with you a down-to-earth formula . . . [that] utilizes our annual profit and total flights flown to clearly

illustrate how vital each Customer is to our profitability and our very existence.

When you divide our 1994 annual profit by total fights flown, you get profit per flight:

$$\frac{\$179,331,000 \text{ (annual profit)}}{624,476 \text{ (total flights flown)}} = \$287 \text{ (profit per flight)}$$

Then, divide profit per fight by Southwest's system wide average one-way fare of $58:

$$\frac{\$287 \text{ (profit per flight)}}{\$58 \text{ (average one-way fare)}} = 5 \text{ (one-way fares [Customers!])}$$

The bottom line, only five Customers per flight accounted for our total 1994 profit! In other words, just five Customers per flight—only 3 million of the 40 million Customers we carried—meant the difference between profit and loss for our airline in 1994. To take it a step further, to have lost the business of only one of those Customers would have meant a 20 percent reduction in profit on that flight. That's how valuable each Customer is to Southwest and you! . . .

Studies reveal that, on average, for each Customer who was "wronged," there are 25 others who remained silent. The studies claim that each person in this silent majority will, by word of mouth, tell between 8 and 16 people—an average of 12—of their complaint. (Over 10 percent will tell more than 20 people!) When you do the math, a potential 300 people can be influenced by just one negative situation. Here is what that factor means to Southwest Airlines:

Last year, we heard from about 60,000 Customers who were dissatisfied with some aspect of their experience with us. . . .

$$\begin{array}{r} 60,000 \text{ ("wronged" Southwest Customers)} \\ \times\ 25 \text{ (silent majority)} \\ \hline = 1,500,000 \text{ possible dissatisfied Southwest Customers} \end{array}$$

Now if those 1.5 million dissatisfied Southwest Customers told 12 others of their experience:

$$\begin{array}{r} 1,500,000 \\ \times\ 12 \text{ (word of mouth)} \\ \hline = 18,000,000 \text{ potential "influenced" Southwest Customers} \end{array}$$

Do you think that 18 million is enough Customers to put us out of business? And, when you compare that 18 million potentially lost or never-reached Customers with the 3 million which accounted for our total 1994 profit, the significance of each and every Customer becomes even more apparent.

There is, however, a positive aspect of Customer complaints! The aforementioned research also indicates that if you make a sincere effort to remedy complaints and regain Customers' good will, 82 to 95 percent of those Customers will stay with you![1]

That may sound good for Kelleher's airline, but do the same kinds of statistics about the marginal value of each additional customer apply to other businesses? They sure do, say our gurus. Let's look at a business that is about as far from running an airline as you can get—selling pizzas.

Tom Monaghan claims that in the pizza business the care and attention you give to existing customers is as important, if not more important, than all the money you spend on advertising and promotions to attract new customers. In fact, he declares, caring for existing customers may be the most important single thing you can do to help your company grow. He explains:

Suppose a store is delivering 95 percent of its pizzas within thirty minutes. Sounds pretty good. But let's look at that 5 percent of orders that are delivered late. Let's say it comes to fifty late orders per week. We know that more than 10 percent of late deliveries result in lost customers, which means that this store is losing, at minimum, five customers per week. If you multiply that out for the year, then multiply that by twenty-six, which is the average number of times a customer buys from us during the year, you get 6,760 lost orders. It would take a lot of time and money spent on advertising and promotion to bring in that many orders. And there's no way to atone for bad word-of-mouth from the disgruntled customer. . . .

I've always said that if you just take care of every single customer, your business will grow by 50 percent a year. Make sure every pizza gets there in thirty minutes, make sure every one is good—no burned pizzas and no raw pizzas—and don't skimp on the ingredients. That's it. You don't need any sophisticated marketing programs. The solution is simple, and it's right before your nose.[2]

Sound too simple? Maybe, but Monaghan swears that it works. In fact, he points to an example from the early 1980s. Monaghan had visited with a Domino's franchisee whose sales at the time were only $2,446 per week and who wanted some advice on how to grow his business. Monaghan responded with his "take-care-of-existing-customers" speech. The franchisee later considered that advice in light of the teamwork he had seen in professional sports. Teams with a solid defense didn't get scored on as often, so even if their offense only scored occasionally, they still had a good chance of winning games. From that day forward, the franchisee devoted himself to "defensive management." He made sure his pizzas were well prepared and delivered promptly. He took care of every single customer, day in and day out. Within seven months, his sales doubled to $5,600 per week, without advertising.[3]

> When you're too busy for customers . . . don't worry about it. In time, you won't be busy at all.
>
> *Bud Hadfield*[4]

THE NINE KEYS TO CUSTOMER RETENTION

If, as our gurus say, every single customer has value, then how do you avoid losing them? Are there secrets to customer retention? Yes. Our gurus maintain that there are nine keys to making sure customers come back again and again. They are summarized in Exhibit 5.1.

EXHIBIT 5.1.	**Nine Keys to Customer Retention**
1. Be a tough boss.	5. Exceed expectations.
2. Get the itty-bitty, teeny-weeny things right.	6. Guarantee 100% satisfaction.
	7. Spend time with your customers.
3. Be nice.	8. Make bad news travel fast.
4. Become a trusted advisor.	9. Put employees first.

In the following sections we look at each of these keys to customer retention in more detail.

Key #1: Be a Tough Boss

Successful entrepreneurs are almost always obsessed with treating their customers right. Consequently, they can get a reputation for being tough bosses. Bill Rosenberg, founder of Dunkin' Donuts, admits that his employees often find him demanding, but, he writes, "anybody who has truly succeeded had a similar philosophy. They tell you that Howard Johnson was tough to work for. They tell you that Ray Kroc was tough to work for. They tell you that Willard Marriott was tough to work for; what they really mean is that we are all demanding. We will not let you screw our customers."[5] No self-respecting entrepreneur will. In fact, company legends develop around instances of the founding entrepreneur's anger at shoddy work. For example, Howard Johnson is said to have had a problem with one of his franchisees not keeping his restaurant clean. Johnson had complained several times without results, so one day Johnson went to the restaurant, called everyone outside, including the franchisee, and padlocked the door. He then pointed to the sign over the restaurant and said, "You see that sign up there, it says Howard Johnson and the way you're keeping this place says Howard Johnson is a slob. I'm not removing the lock until you clean up."[6]

Debbi Fields describes a similar experience as follows:

> I remember walking into our third store . . . and seeing a very unhappy-looking batch of cookies laid out for the customers. They were flat and overbaked. A perfect Mrs. Fields cookie is half an inch in thickness, and these were a quarter of an inch. A perfect Mrs. Fields cookie is three inches in diameter, and these appeared to measure three and a quarter inches. They were also a little more golden brown than they should have been—they'd been left in the oven too long.
>
> My initial response was curiosity, no more than that. As a manager, I try not to jump to conclusions. Perhaps these people thought the cookies were perfect. If they did, it was my fault, because it meant they hadn't been properly trained. So I turned to the young man standing next to me and said, "Tell me, what do you think of these cookies?"
>
> "Aw," he said, "they're good enough."
>
> I nodded. I had my answer. One tray at a time, I took the cookies—five or six hundred dollars' worth—and slid them gently into the garbage can. "You know," I said to him, " 'good enough' never is."[7]

Key #2: Get the Itty-Bitty, Teeny-Weeny Things Right

Like our other gurus, Fields is obsessed with getting every detail right for her customers. Only the best raisins, nuts, and other ingredients should be used in her cookies. From the beginning, she says, her cookies had to be just right.

> From the very first, I set up a policy that we still follow today. Our cookies had to be warm and fresh and when they were two hours out of the oven, what hadn't been sold was donated to the Red Cross to be given to blood donors, or to other deserving charities, and we baked a new batch. We guaranteed everything we sold. If a customer was not happy with an order, we replaced it. Whatever it took to serve warm, fresh cookies all day long, that's what we did. That meant a lot of staffing, and that made the cookies expensive. We could have had all our cookies baked by six in the morning; that would have made them cheaper, but then we'd have been like everyone else.[8]

Fields recalls that even her husband couldn't always understand her obsession with the quality of ingredients in her cookies.

> [A rep for one of our suppliers once] called me and said, "Debbi, you've got to taste this new product! We think it's terrific. It's fifty percent butter and fifty percent margarine. Do you have any idea how much money that will save you? This is a brand-new product—everybody is using it, they love it, they can't tell the difference."
>
> "I can't believe you're even calling me," I said. "We are definitely not interested."
>
> I told Randy [Fields's husband] the story and, playing devil's advocate, he insisted that I wouldn't really know what was going on unless I actually tried the butter-margarine blend. Finally I agreed, called back, and they sent some over. I baked up a test batch of cookies with it and they were dreadful. The difference was night and day. Couldn't people tell? I refused to believe they wouldn't taste the difference.[9]

Ray Kroc was also obsessed with getting every little thing right at McDonald's, laying out elaborate guidelines for constructing the perfect hamburger. Hamburger patties were to weigh precisely 1.6 ounces and measure 3.875 inches in diameter—not 4 inches, but 3.875 inches. Each pound of meat was to make 10 hamburgers, and the meat was to contain no lungs, hearts, or cereal and only 19 percent fat. The meat patty was to be placed on a bun that had to be exactly 3.5 inches wide and was to be topped with precisely one-quarter ounce of onions. Everything was to be kept fresh. French fries were to be thrown away if not sold within 7 minutes. Hamburgers could be kept only 10 minutes and coffee only 30.[10]

For Bud Rosenberg, getting the teeny-weeny things right comes down to being obsessed with something as seemingly mundane as the cream in his coffee:

> I go into Hollywood Circle in Hollywood, Florida, and I go into a store to taste the coffee many years ago. I say to the operator, "Geez, this coffee don't taste right. There's something wrong, it doesn't meet Dunkin' Donuts' standards."
>
> The franchise owner tells me there's nothing wrong with the coffee. So I said, "Let me see the coffee, let me weigh the grind. Geeze, it smells good, it weighs right, it's fresh, what the hell is wrong with it?" So I call up the coffee company and they say everything is alright; so I asked the owner what kind of cream he uses. So he showed me these little creamers made of vegetable fat, the kind that never goes bad. So I say to him, "Did you ever read your manual?" He says, "Yeah." So I say to him. "The manual says you got to use 18% butterfat cream."
>
> The man responds indignantly, "Hey, there's nothing wrong with these. You know the Hollywood Beach Hotel; they use these. All the best hotels, they all use these." I said to him, "Yeah, well how many rooms do you have to rent?"
>
> The franchise owner said, "What do you mean?"
>
> I say this to all of my people that we have two things to sell: coffee and doughnuts. And if we don't have the freshest coffee and the finest doughnuts then we have no reason for existing. We have nothing else to sell. We don't have any rooms to rent. So why should the people come here to get a superior cup of coffee if your coffee is no better than theirs. . . .
>
> Some people just don't understand. You've got to have a niche in life; you've got to satisfy the customer.[11]

Truly successful entrepreneurs never lose their commitment to their customers, even after their business is a resounding success. Take the case of Edward Miller, cofounder and chairman of Spic and Span, Inc., Milwaukee's premier dry cleaner. Until he died at the age of 93, Miller still showed up each week at his factory, greeted his employees, and settled in to study the numbers—for example, 21 garments returned from customers: three pants, two skirts, one dress, three shirts folded instead of on hangers. That wouldn't be such a bad report, considering that Spic and Span handles over ten thousand garments a day. Still, Miller would personally visit with each department head to discuss what happened to the 21 problem garments and why. He would also remind them of the key to Spic and Span's success—"Quality comes first, service comes second, and cost comes last." "I don't care how long it takes for them to get it right, Miller would say, "quality comes first."[12]

> Quality comes first, service comes second, and cost comes last. I don't care how long it takes . . . to get it right; quality comes first.
>
> *Edward Miller*[13]

Key #3: Be Nice

Howard Schultz claims that the success of Starbucks has as much to do with relationships as it has to do with the quality of the coffee. Of course, product quality must be superior, notes Schultz, but Starbucks' success is "more than great coffee. It's the romance of the coffee experience, the feeling of warmth and community people get in Starbucks stores. That tone is set by our *baristas,* who custom-make each espresso drink and explain the origins of different coffees."[14]

Part of world-class quality and service, say our gurus, is treating customers with respect—creating that feeling of warmth and community that Schultz says makes Starbucks tick. Fred Smith adds that each daily interaction with a customer is particularly critical in a service-oriented business such as his. As he explains: "A positive interaction adds value—a negative experience can be devastating. And the kicker is [a provider of services] can't . . . [reverse] a bad experience with a customer like a manufacturer can recall a faulty part, fix it, and put it back into service so it works right the second time."[15]

For that reason, Tom Monaghan tells all of his franchisees that the biggest little thing they can do to help their businesses succeed is just to be nice to their customers.

I've often remarked in speeches that my objective is to have everyone say that Domino's Pizza people are nice. Not brilliant or charming or models of efficiency, just nice. How can that be achieved? Simply by getting employees to take every opportunity to be friendly, to smile at the customer and say "please" and "thank you" and "sir" and "ma'am." I am very serious about the proper technique for taking telephone orders, how to say the right words and get as much friendliness into your voice as possible. It sounds very basic, and it is. But it's one of those fundamentals you have to stress over and over again, like a football coach harping on blocking and tackling. And though it's a little thing, it pays off big and in unexpected ways. If you are nice to other people, they'll be nice to you. Not only will your business prosper, but your customers' return of courtesy will bolster your self-image and you'll become a happier person.[16]

> Treat people you do business with as if they were a part of your family. Prosperity depends on how much understanding one receives from the people with whom one conducts business.
>
> *Konosuke Matsushita*[17]

Earl Graves relates how the importance of treating customers with respect was forcefully brought home to him a number of years ago by none other than his mother. Graves had been visiting his mother before going to a sales meeting with Jack Welch, the CEO of General Electric (GE). When he told his mother about his upcoming trip, Graves recalls that he was surprised at her response. "I always liked that man," was her reply. "But you have never met Jack Welch," Graves said. "Oh no, not him," said Graves mother, "[I mean] the other man from GE, the man who took off his hat to me and called me Mrs. Graves when he came to fix the refrigerator in our old house." Then it dawned on Graves. That visit from the GE repairman had occurred when he was just two years old. Ever since, his mother had bought GE products whenever she could. "That's product loyalty," writes Graves.[18] Indeed it is. And, say our gurus, it is just the kind of loyalty a little heartfelt respect can breed.

Even our gurus admit to being vulnerable to a little attention. Debbi Fields recalls how, during the early days of her company, one chocolate salesman won her loyalty and another quickly lost it based not on the quality of their chocolate chips, which were equivalent, but on the quality of their respect for her and attention to her company's needs.

I called up a certain very large and very famous chocolate company. "Hi," I said brightly, "my name is Debbi Fields and I'm opening up a new cookie store and before I open the store I want to test your chocolate. Could you send me, uhh, maybe twenty-five pounds? I'll pay for it, of course, and if I like it I might even buy three hundred pounds."

The salesman never missed a beat. "Listen, sweetheart, when you want ten thousand pounds of chocolate, call me. Otherwise, we're not interested." He hung up on me.

I was crushed. Here I was trying to show the world my best business style, so proud that I was actually going to open a store, and this man had just stuck a pin in the balloon. I felt three inches tall—just some overambitious female—"sweetheart"—who had deluded herself into believing that she had the ability to open a business. It was like the bankers all over again except this guy wasn't smooth and slippery. He said what he thought and slammed the phone down.

Anxiously, I looked up another very large and very famous chocolate company in the telephone directory and dialed the number. . . .

A salesman answered the phone and I didn't even try to sound sophisticated. "I have a tiny little company," I said, "and I was wondering if I could maybe taste a little of your chocolate. I really can't buy much."

"Where are you?" he asked. I gave him the address of the store. He said he'd be right there.

He arrived with the back of his car loaded with chocolate chips, and staggered into the store with a double armload of plastic bags. He introduced himself and shook my hand. "Well," he said, "what can I do for you?" . . .

The salesman listened with all his attention as I told him what I was trying to do, how I envisioned the product, and what my ambitions were for the little business. All for a sale of twenty-five pounds. . . . He treated me like the only customer he'd ever had. . . .

Well, guess what. I happen to believe in loyalty and this salesman and his company still have the Mrs. Fields account today. We did buy more than twenty-five pounds of chocolate from this man. We bought tons of chocolate every year, for ten years, simply because he took the time and energy to be interested in and involved with a new business run by a very young woman. And it's worth noting that this particular company was the second call I made. The first salesman I encountered was just too important to deal with somebody he considered beneath his interest. Too bad, really, because this year alone we'll be buying about seven million dollars' worth of chocolate.[19]

Key #4: Become a Trusted Advisor

Ultimately, say our gurus, respect and attentiveness to customers means becoming their trusted advisor and taking responsibility for their investment in your product or service. In his presentations to Home Depot trainees, Bernie Marcus loves to tell stories. One of his favorites concerns the do-it-yourselfer who needs a saw.

> Say there's a customer. . . . He gets in his car and drives down the street, stopping at lights and intersections. The do-it-yourselfer gets on the highway. He drives for several miles and then gets off the highway and enters this huge Home Depot parking lot. He finds a parking spot—the store is crowded so the space is not near the door and gets out of his car and walks into the store. . . .
>
> You say, "What are you building today?" Or if you ask, "What are you looking for today?" and the customer says, "a hacksaw," you take him to the hacksaw. . . .
>
> If the customer is building a window frame, what he really needs is another saw. Maybe the customer thinks the saw he needs is called a "hacksaw," . . . but if he buys the hacksaw and takes it home and can't do the job, he's going to be frustrated when he can't finish the project. That do-it-yourselfer will likely blame Home Depot for not pointing out the right tools and the right way.[20]

Instead of simply helping the customer find the hacksaw he thinks he needs, says Marcus, why not go a step further and offer the customer some real advice and assistance? Take the example of a do-it-yourselfer who might arrive at a Home Depot to buy some two-by-fours and a roll of screening to build a rabbit hutch. The associate could show the customer where the two-by-fours and screening are located, or he or she could go further. Marcus explains:

> With our expert knowledge, we might say, "Well, instead of using white pine, I would recommend pressure-treated lumber. You can use it outside. It won't rot. It will last longer."
>
> "Oh," the customer will say, "I didn't know there was such a thing."
>
> "Next, I would recommend using hardware cloth. It is galvanized, so rabbit feet won't go down through it. And let me show you how to put a door on that hutch, how to hang hinges."
>
> What the customer will go home with are different products that he or she probably wasn't aware of, and how-to knowledge of how to assemble them a little bit smarter. The project will come together easier and we hope the end product will be better. When the project is done, our ten minutes of guidance probably increased the customer's self-confidence.
>
> Along the way, we might also sell the customer a new handsaw or drill to complement the hammer, screwdriver, and pair of pliers in the kitchen drawer.[21]

Marcus says that in his experience the customer who is given the additional advice and support, like that given the rabbit-hutch builder, will come back to Home Depot a month or so later with a bigger project. Soon the customer will start returning again and again. A bond will be formed. A strong relationship will be developed. And Home Depot will win the customer's loyalty.

It's the difference, explains Marcus, between merely offering the customer good service—"Let me help you find the two-by-fours"—and *customer cultivation:* "Let me share my knowledge to help you succeed at what you are trying to do." "*Customer cultivation,*" writes Marcus, "is just like cultivating a tomato plant. Prepare the soil, maybe put some additives in it. Plant the seed. Water it. Prune it. Fertilize it. Apply insecticides. It will always grow bigger if you cultivate it. If you cultivate it, it will bear fruit."[22] Marcus declares it was cultivation, not just service, that helped Home Depot grow from 2 stores to 4, from 4 to 8, from 8 to 16, and so on. And, he says, customer cultivation can help you grow your own business.

Michael Dell sees customer cultivation as critical to his industry because it is easy for the customer to become confused with the wide variety of constantly changing technology. Consequently, it isn't enough for Dell Computers just to provide high-quality products and responsive service. Dell has to act as an advisor.

> In an average month, a customer might hear about new operating system transitions on the server/workstation side, Intel's latest micro-processor, changes in LCD display technology, as well as the latest development in battery technology and weight for notebook computers. The industry is constantly coming up with improvements in technology, and many of these improvements end up in our products. But it's easy for customers to end up with too much technology—or technology that doesn't meet their needs—if they're not careful.
>
> In acting as our customers' advisor, we try to help them make the right decisions, so that technology actually adds value to their business. It's simply a function of looking at our customer's challenges as our challenges. If our customers are challenged by the problem of having to support their PCs, it's not enough to say, "Here's your PC. It's got a manual. Good luck." If we don't take responsibility for their problems, those very same problems will inevitably resurface in some form—most notably, in our losing them as customers.
>
> We try to take responsibility for how our customers' investment is used. We look at the entire value chain of events and ask: How can we help customers manage the complexity of the technology so that it drives their costs down? How can we influence the industry to bring down the cost of this technology? . . .
>
> We aim to be more than just a computer supplier. We try to become a customer's advisor on technology strategy. . . . We help steer our customers through the storm of technological options. And our customers help us stay humble. Together, we work to figure out the difference between the next thing and the next useful thing.[23]

"In becoming a valued advisor to your customers," adds Dell, "you need to look beyond the product you're selling and seek ways to enhance the total customer experience."[24] See Exhibit 5.2 for some suggestions.

Ultimately, states Dell, your goal shouldn't be just to please customers with quality products and good service but, through the advisor role, to build a meaningful, memorable total experience that will win customers for life. At Dell, he writes, "we've always tried to exceed [our customers'] expectations."[25] That's another key to retaining customers, say our gurus.

EXHIBIT 5.2. **Michael Dell's Tips on Becoming a Valued Advisor to Customers**

- *See the big picture.* It's not enough to just respond piecemeal to your customers' problems. You've got to be willing to invest in coming up with a solution to the immediate problem *and* look beyond it to see its bigger potential.
- *Run with the suggestions your customers provide.* Ask yourself, "Is this a onetime event, or indicative of a trend? Is this an opportunity ripe for development?" Go even one step further and ask, "Is there another whole business here?"
- *Always think bottom line—but not just yours.* Consider your customers' bottom line as well. Can you save them money, while enhancing your partnership with them? Think strategically about your customers' businesses, and find ways to help them cut costs and increase profits, all the while improving how they can serve their customers.
- *Go beyond selling your products or services, and make yourself valuable to your customers as an advisor.* Delivering expert advice with no strings attached does much to demonstrate that you are a trustworthy partner.
- *Be a student.* It's as important to listen as to counsel. Customers can provide a much-needed perspective on products and services you may be too invested in to evaluate objectively. Since they're the ones who'll be buying, it's always better to know sooner rather than later.

Source: Michael Dell and Catherine Fredman, Direct from Dell: Strategies That Revolutionized an Industry (New York: HarperBusiness, 1999), pp. 168–169.

No Aisle Numbers!

You won't even see aisle numbers in our stores. There is not a retailer on the face of the globe with 100,000-square-foot stores other than The Home Depot without some aisle numbers. Why? Well, if we had aisle numbers, when a customer asks, "Do you know where I can find this widget?" it would be very easy for our associates to point and say, "Aisle eight." If there are no aisle numbers, the employee has to say, "Let's take a walk and we'll find it together."

Bernie Marcus[26]

Key #5: Exceed Expectations

To illustrate what it takes to retain customers, Bud Hadfield likes to tell the story of a man he once knew who owned a small delicatessen. Hadfield writes:

[It was] the kind where the walls and counters were covered with yellow Formica. His place was so small, he served only sandwiches.

All his business was take-out, but people lined up at the counter and out the door to place their orders. He had some sandwiches made ahead of time, and he passed them across the counter as fast as he could. You would see him grab a big handful of corned beef, roast beef, and salami, slap it on the bread, wrap it in waxed paper and slide it back in the bag.

This fellow was so successful that he decided to expand. He built a restaurant 20 times the size of his original deli.[27]

Years later, says Hadfield, the delicatessen owner's promising business hadn't grown at all. Why? Hadfield believes he has an idea.

I stopped in shortly after he opened. The owner was at the cash register, but now he had a man in a white hat behind the counter, putting the meat on a scale. The customers stood there and watched him carefully weigh the meat and take a little off.

My guess is that the scale cost $50, but in reality, it may have cost him $50 million. If he had kept giving the customers what they wanted, he might have a chain of delis all over the country. He was in business before Ray Kroc, selling those thick sandwiches as fast as he could bag them. If he hadn't decided to measure them, there might be corned beef under the golden arches instead of hamburgers.[28]

The moral of the story is that you aren't going to be very successful if you repay customer loyalty by teaspooning your services. And surprisingly, says Hadfield, it doesn't require a lot to go from mere satisfaction to delightful surprise. The simplest gesture can make a tremendous difference. It did for him.

In my early days as a printer, I bought an oversupply of air mail envelopes. Even my customers couldn't buy enough to make any appreciable dent in the stock. One of the men in the shop had an idea that seemed worth trying. He suggested giving them away by including some with every order for plain envelopes. We tried it. The results were astonishing; our business soared. In less than a year we were printing more envelopes in a single week than we had printed in the busiest month of the previous year.

What happened? What caused our sales to jump? There were several reasons, but in talking with our customers, one factor surfaced more than any other. Those few air mail envelopes were something extra; they were more than the customer believed was part of the bargain.[29]

And Then Some

A very successful businessman was once asked, "To what do you attribute your success?"

"I can tell you in three words," he answered. "And then some."

"What do you mean, 'and then some'?" he was questioned.

"Do everything that's expected of you," he explained, "and then some."

Mary Kay Ash[30]

For Herb Kelleher, exceeding expectations has much to do with getting all the teeny tiny things right while simultaneously exhibiting an air of insouciance and effervescence. Instead of meeting efficient but serious flight attendants and gate agents, reasons Kelleher, why shouldn't passengers be greeted by ticket agents who, during flight delays, entertain them by awarding prizes for the passenger with the largest hole in his or her sock? Instead of standing at the doorway to welcome passengers as they board, why shouldn't flight attendants hide in the overhead luggage bins and pop out with a greeting? And instead of having to endure another boring safety lecture delivered by an equally bored flight attendant, why shouldn't passengers be treated to something like the following, which was once delivered by Southwest flight attendant Karen Wood:

If I could have your attention for a few moments, we sure would love to point out those safety features. If you haven't been in an automobile since 1965, the proper way to fasten your seat belt is to slide the flat end into the buckle. To unfasten, lift up on the buckle and it will release.

And as the song goes, there might be fifty ways to leave your lover, but there are only six ways to leave this aircraft: two forward exit doors, two over-wing removable window exits, and two aft exit doors. The location of each exit is clearly marked with signs overhead, as well as red and white disco lights along the floor of the aisle. (Made ya look!)

Located in the seatback pocket in front of you or to the side of you in the lounge area, among the peanut wrappers, coffee cups, and newspapers, you should find an emergency information card supplementing our safety features. Take note on the back that in the event of a water evacuation, your bottom . . . your seat bottom, that is, can be used as a flotation device by removing the cushion, holding onto the straps underneath it, and choosing your favorite stroke.

Please check at this time to make sure your seat belts are securely fastened, seat backs and tray tables are in their full upright and most uncomfortable position, and all the carry-on luggage you've brought in is crammed underneath the seat in front of you, or in one of the overhead bins.

FAA regulations require passenger compliance with all lighted passenger information signs, posted placards, and crew member instructions regarding seat belts and no smoking. In other words do exactly what we say!

Speaking of smoking, there's never any smoking aboard our flights. You know what happens if we catch you smoking here at Southwest, don't you? You'll be asked to step out onto our wing and enjoy our feature movie presentation, Gone with the Wind. There is never any smoking, even in the lavatories.

Finally, although we never anticipate a change in cabin pressure, should one occur, four oxygen masks will magically appear overhead. Immediately stop screaming, please deposit a quarter, and unlike President Clinton, you must inhale! If you're seated next to a child or traveling with someone who is acting like a small child, secure yourself first and then assist him or her. Please continue wearing the mask until otherwise notified by a uniformed crew member—yes, believe it or not, these are uniforms! And we do need to tell you that the bag does not inflate, but you still are receiving oxygen. Sit back, relax and enjoy a one-hour flight to San Diego on the best airline in the universe—Southwest.

Southwest Airlines is determined to offer Positively Outrageous Service to customers. . . .

Oh, my airline has a first name, it's S-O-U-T-H; my airline has a second name, it's W-E-S-T. Oh, I love to fly it every day and if you ask me why, I'll say, 'cause Southwest Airlines has a way of bringing sunshine to your day.[31]

"Beyond winning and satisfying your customer, the objective must be to delight your customer—and not just once, but again and again," advises

Michael Dell. "The total customer experience is the next competitive frontier."[32]

Key #6: Guarantee 100 Percent Satisfaction

One way to exceed your customers' expectations, say our gurus, is to offer a guarantee of 100 percent satisfaction. Bill Gates makes a case for such a guarantee in his 1999 book *Business @ the Speed of Thought*. Interestingly, he does not cite the software industry or his own company, Microsoft, as good examples of such a practice. Instead, he recommends the practice adopted by Promus Hotels, a Memphis, Tennessee–based operator of a family of hotels that includes Hampton Inns, Embassy Suites, and Doubletree Inns.[33] Promus, notes Gates, was the first hotel chain to guarantee that customers would not be charged for their rooms if they had a complaint about any aspect of their stay. Additionally, all Promus employees, including desk clerks, maids, and even maintenance engineers, are empowered to make good on that promise. Gates explains that a guarantee of satisfaction such as that offered by Promus is a powerful inducement to customer loyalty for several reasons.

> [First,] a no-questions-asked guarantee from a service company such as Promus makes complaints mean something. Customers like the guarantee going in even if they're a little skeptical about how hard it will be to get you to deliver on it and when you do deliver on it, you have a very gratified customer.
>
> Equally important, the guarantee creates a financial incentive to fix the underlying problem right away. Because it costs the hotel money immediately, the problem doesn't get overlooked. It doesn't get filed away. Tying complaints to immediate payouts "lowers the water and exposes the rocks" relating to service quality.
>
> [Finally,] because every employee is empowered to act on the guarantee, everybody is on the hook for quality. The everyday hotel workers who make or break quality and who can administer the guarantee, have more pride in their own jobs and pride in the hotel. Peer pressure comes into play within the different groups to hold up their end. And if you're going to give all hotel employees the power to make a customer's stay free—a lot of

power for service personnel—then you'd better train them all to do a good job.[34]

Gates notes that Promus management faced considerable skepticism from their franchisees when they first proposed the total-satisfaction-or-no-charge policy. The general response was: "You're nuts. Deadbeats will just take advantage of us. They'll kill us." As it turned out, however, refunds from the program were much lower than expected—averaging only 0.3 percent of revenues—and the "intent to return" for customers who exercised the guarantee was 50 percent higher than for other customers. The Promus guarantee even gained the corporate business of one of our gurus. Gates reports that Debbi Fields complained about the lack of soap and towels in her room during one visit to a Hampton Inn. On hearing the complaint, the desk clerk immediate tore up her bill. Fields was so impressed with the response to her complaint that she designated the Hampton Inn as her company's corporate hotel chain. In addition, she later became a member of the Hampton/Promus board.[35]

As Gates mentions, companies such as Promus that offer a 100 percent guarantee occasionally are taken advantage of by customers who return "broken" items that aren't broken or complain of problems that aren't really problems at all. Still, argue our gurus, being taken advantage of can be a good thing. How? Here is the way Bernie Marcus explained it to a young Home Depot employee.

We have a return policy that says you can bring a product back for any reason. No gimmick, no tricks. . . .

Lina Khano, all of 18, was working our return desk when a woman brought in a product that she claimed was defective. Somehow, Khano decided the customer was lying through her teeth.

When she turned away from the woman to get approval for the return from a manager, an indignant Khano found me standing behind her.

"I can't believe this woman is doing this!" she said under her breath.

"If it were me," I said, "I would give her her money back."

Khano did just that, smiled and gave her the money. But as the woman walked away, Khano was fuming. I put an arm around her shoulders.

"I am going to teach you a lesson that you will remember for the rest of your life," I said. "Sometimes, in this business, you have to accept things that you believe are totally wrong."

"Excuse me?" Khano said.

"Sometimes, in this business, you have to do distasteful things," I repeated.

"Uh, okay."

"Just think about it, Lina," I continued. "This woman, she brought this thing back even though it is not defective. Don't worry about it. Even if we have to eat the cost of it or throw it away, it is no big deal, because from now on, she will have the confidence to come and buy here, and even if she goes home and tells everybody that we are stupid, that's okay, too, because now everybody is going to come shop here and take advantage of us."

The key to our no-holds-barred return policy is that people talk about it. It gets them hooked; they know they can never make a bad purchase at The Home Depot, because we don't ever want to give them a reason not to come back. There are probably some dishonest people that will take advantage of us. But they are a tiny minority. We are not going to punish the honest folks who need to trust us.[36]

Like Marcus and Blank, Mary Kay Ash insists on a 100 percent money-back guarantee for her customers. She tells her people to honor the guarantee regardless of the length of time between the purchase and the request for refund and even if the product being returned has been used and its container is empty. Why does Ash offer such a generous return policy? She replies, "We make outstanding products, so refund requests affect a very small percentage of our total sales. [More important,] our refund policy is generous because we want our customers and company employees to be happy and proud of what we do. If any one of them isn't happy, we all suffer. In our business, satisfying people's needs is what we're all about."[37] And sometimes what customers need is the reassurance that a 100 percent no-questions-asked, money-back guarantee offers.

Key #7: Spend Time with Your Customers

The 100 percent satisfaction guarantee offered by many of our gurus' companies is, as Gates says, a vivid demonstration of the commitment to get all the little things right. It is also a way of listening to the customer, and listening, really listening, is extremely important for retaining customers. Where does listening begin? Well, say our gurus, just like having a commitment to world-class quality and service, listening begins with you.

A very important part of our philosophy . . . is letting the customers provide the yellow brick road to success. . . . We have always felt that if we
listen, they'll give us the answer we need.

Arthur Blank[38]

Michael Dell notes that, when he tells people he spends nearly 40 percent of his time with customers, the reaction he usually gets is, "Wow—
that's a lot of time to spend with customers." His response? "I thought that
was my job."[39] This is the response our gurus say you should give. Almost
all of our gurus report spending much of their time out of their offices,
meeting with and talking to customers. For example, Bernie Marcus and
Arthur Blank donned orange aprons and worked in their Home Depot
stores, waiting on customers, listening to complaints, and asking questions.
Marcus says it was through those personal experiences that he and Blank
found out what they were doing right and wrong during the early years of
building the company. In the beginning, he reports, he would even chase
down customers in the parking lot to find out what they needed.

> We had so few customers that if I saw someone leaving a store empty-
> handed, I took it personally.
>
> "What is it that we don't carry that you need? Why didn't you buy
> something?" I'd say, doggedly pursuing them to the parking lot. "I didn't find
> what I came in for," was usually the answer. "What is it that you need?" I
> asked. And whatever the answer, I would say the same thing: "Oh my gosh,
> I'm so sorry you didn't find it. We carry it, we just happened to be out. If
> you give me your name and address, I will deliver it to you."
>
> That's how I often expanded our merchandise selection. First I would
> run back inside and order it so we'd have it in the future. Then I would per-
> sonally go buy whatever it was at West Building Supplies, Handy City, or a
> wholesale house and personally deliver it to the customer's home, carefully
> removing the other store's price sticker and charging the customer a lower
> price than I paid out of pocket.[40]

Richard Branson took a similar hands-on approach to listening to customers when he was starting Virgin Atlantic Airlines. Among other things,
Branson would call Virgin reservations to see how his people were handling

calls. He frequently boarded Virgin flights and spent the time aloft talking to the passengers and cabin crew. He insisted that every Virgin flight have a visitor's book where passengers could record their comments. Each month Branson picked 50 passengers at random who had written comments in the book and called them to apologize for the airline's mistake or to comment on their idea. And when a station manager informed him that a Virgin flight had been severely delayed, as they had standing orders to do, he would call the departure lounge and ask his staff to pass along his personal apologies for the delay. Customers were often astonished at Branson's personal involvement. Here was the chairman of Virgin Group on the telephone with an apology. Some were so surprised that they refused to take the call or believe it was really Branson, thinking it was just a practical joke.[41]

> One of the most surprising things we learned early on from our customers was that they really valued being asked [their opinion.]
>
> *Michael Dell*[42]

Our gurus believe that listening to customers is so important that many require their entire top management team to spend at least some time each year working directly with customers. Herb Kelleher, for example, requires each officer of Southwest Airlines to work in the field as a reservation agent, baggage handler, dispatcher, or in some similar position where he or she has hands-on contact with customers. The officers must report back to Kelleher on what they did, what they found, and the steps they took to improve the job they performed. Kelleher declares that the exposure senior managers get to line operations can have enormous benefits. For example, he credits the development and implementation of a major proprietary sales system to the experience one group of Southwest officers had while working a late-night shift at the airport. This night there were an unusual number of weather-related problems and delays. The officers stood helpless as their employees shuffled through mounds of forms while the passengers became increasing irritated. They came away from the experience convinced that the system had to be changed, and it was.[43]

If you have business customers, one of the best ways to learn how your product or service does or does not meet their needs, say our gurus, is to visit them in their place of business. Michael Dell explains that not only has he picked up good ideas about how to improve customer service by making such personal on-site visits but he has created whole new opportunities for his company as a result of what he has learned. He cites the following example:

> I remember being in the U.K. once in the late 1980s and visiting one of our customers, British Petroleum in London. The London real estate market at that time was very overheated and space was expensive, yet BP's information technology (IT) guy showed me a whole floor in their headquarters building that they had devoted to configuring PCs. I saw some of their people taking PCs out of the boxes, installing special features, such as job-specific software and network interface cards (NICs) and removing the features they didn't use. I was amazed. Not only was BP spending inordinate amounts of money to configure their machines, but they were also having to do so in high-cost real estate space that they probably could have used for other purposes.
>
> We were watching his people custom-configure these PCs when he asked me, "Do you think you guys could do this for me, so that we don't have to be in the PC business?" I gave it a moment's thought, then replied, "Absolutely, we'd love to do that." What was both expensive and time-consuming for our customer, was relatively easy for us to execute. It also provided a terrific opportunity for us to add the kind of value we knew our customers in other industries would benefit from as well.[44]

Dell states that the key to making your customer contact work for you is to really make an effort "to engage in a cooperative, mutually beneficial dialogue—not just talking at, or talking to, your customers, but talking with them—and really listening to what they have to say." "When you engage directly with customers," explains Dell, "you begin to develop an intimate understanding of their likes, needs, and priorities. You find out what's working for them—and why. You can try out new ideas on them—ideas worth millions of R&D dollars and countless hours of your people's valuable time—and they'll tell you whether you're on track or not."[45]

According to Dell, listening to customers is a job that you will likely find both redeeming and refreshing, not to mention lucrative—the BP learning experience, for example, eventually led Dell to create Dell Plus, a multi-million-dollar program of system-integration services. But what happens when your chain of businesses grows so big that you can't fly on every flight,

chase down disenchanted customers in every parking lot, or personally visit
every corporate customer's business? What do you do then? You create the
infrastructure to keep listening, say our gurus.

When Home Depot began to grow, Marcus and Blank decided they
needed a more formal mechanism for listening to customers, so they
created the position of director of consumer affairs and staffed it with the
now-famous Ben Hill. They posted large signs and freestanding sandwich
boards at the front of every store with a silhouetted profile of Ben and the
words: "Are you satisfied? If not, contact the store manager, _____, or call
me, Ben Hill, director of consumer affairs, at 800-533-3199." Dissatisfied
customers who called that number reached a main-office switchboard at
Home Depot's corporate headquarters in Atlanta. What they didn't know
when they asked to speak to Ben Hill was that there was no such person.
Ben Hill was fictitious. The words "Ben Hill," however, were a code-red
signal to "expedite the call right now." And who took those expedited calls?
Bernie Marcus, Arthur Blank, or if they were not available, the
highest-ranking person in the company free to take the call. Whoever was
free dropped whatever they were doing, even if it was signing a million-
dollar deal, to take the call. It didn't take long, says Marcus, for word to get
around Home Depot stores that, if you let a customer leave unhappy, the
next call you got could be from Marcus or Blank that might go something
like this: "I just got a call from a customer on the Ben Hill line, and we're
in trouble. . . . I would like you to run to one of our other stores, get the
product the customer needs, drive it over to the customer's house, and apologize."[46] Marcus reports that the Ben Hill system has worked extremely
well, and Home Depot continues to monitor those calls very closely. Stores
with the fewest Ben Hill calls get awards. Those with too many calls . . .
well, as Marcus says, a store doesn't want to have too many Ben Hill calls.

Herb Kelleher came to realize that Southwest Airlines needed a more
formal structure for listening to customers several years ago during a meeting between his maintenance department and ground-operations personnel.
Maintenance wanted to resolve a particular problem one way. Ground operations wanted to resolve it another. Suddenly, states Kelleher, it occurred
to him that the only person who wasn't being heard from was the most-
important person of all—the customer. Kelleher immediately set up a
consumer-relations function in his own office through which he could personally monitor all customer complaints. Having customer relations reporting directly to him, says Kelleher, means that he can keep close tabs on

what customers are actually saying about all facets of Southwest Airlines' operations. It also means that he can make phone calls when he thinks they are needed. "Hey, wait a second. Six letters have shown up in the last two months about inadequate baggage service in Albuquerque. What's wrong? What's changed?" or, "We never used to get a complaint on your ticket counter in Las Vegas. How come we suddenly had eight complaints in the past month?" [47]

Key #8: Make Bad News Travel Fast

The practice that Michael Dell refers to as not "perfuming the pig" is the same as what Bill Gates talks about as making bad news travel fast. Both see it as a sometimes painful but always critical requirement for listening to customers. What's the practice? Identifying problems, facing the disappointment, hunting down the bad news, and then doing something with that information to change things and make your customers' experiences improve. Dell admits it is a hard thing to do. After all, he says, "it's human nature to shrink in the face of bad news or disappointments and to hope that something will just happen to make the situation better."[48] The problem, explains Dell, is that things don't usually get better by themselves, and in the meantime, you have lost valuable time. It is a lot better to find out right away when something isn't going right and then get to work fixing it—fast.

> Don't tell me about the good things, tell me about the problems and I don't want any surprises.
>
> *Wayne Huizenga*[49]

Bill Gates echoes Dell's sentiments.

I have a natural instinct for hunting down grim news. If it's out there, I want to know about it. The people who work for me have figured this out. Sometimes I get an e-mail that begins, "In keeping with the dictum that bad news should travel faster than good news, here's a gem."

A lot goes wrong in any organization, even a good one. A product flops. You're surprised by a customer's sudden defection to another vendor. A competitor comes out with a product that appeals to a broad new market. Losing market share is the kind of bad news that every organization can relate to.

Other bad news may have to do with what's going on internally. Maybe a product is going to be late, or it's not going to do what you expected it to do, or you haven't been able to hire enough of the right kinds of people to deliver on your plans.

An essential quality of a good manager is a determination to deal with any kind of bad news head on, to seek it out rather than deny it. An effective manager wants to hear about what's going wrong before he or she hears about what's going right. You can't react appropriately to disappointing news in any situation if it doesn't reach you soon enough.

You focus on bad news in order to get cracking on the solution. As soon as you're aware of a problem, everybody in your organization has to be galvanized into action. You can evaluate a company by how quickly it engages all of its available intellect to deal with a serious problem.[50]

The problem, note Gates, Dell, and many of our other gurus, is that bad news travels too slowly in most companies. People have to dig information out of paper files, find someone they can talk to who knows something about the problem, and then muster up the courage to telephone or meet with their boss to discuss it. By the time the boss finds out that a problem exists, it's already serious. Fortunately, say our gurus, things don't have to be that way. You can harness modern technology to flood yourself with bad news. Gates and Dell have a lot to say about harnessing technology for customer listening. They also sell the hardware and software to help you do it, something you may want to factor into your evaluation of their advice. Regardless, they recommend three steps for effective, "high-tech" listening:

1. Collect and immediately digitize feedback on customer needs, problems, concerns, and performance results on key metrics such as on-time delivery.
2. Segment your data to focus on the needs and expectations of different types of customers.
3. Analyze the data and take action to improve your company's performance.

Each step is discussed in more detail in the subsections that follow.

Step #1: Collect and Immediately Digitize Customer Feedback

Gates recommends that you seek to create a "digital customer feedback loop" for your company like the one he created at Microsoft.

"We began collecting data about customer problems from support engineers in 1985 and began the steps to create a regular feedback loop in 1991. First we used a phone system and then developed different tools for gathering data from sources such as e-mail, Internet newsgroups, and the Web. Then we began to consolidate the data. We're now in our third generation of computer-based customer feedback tools. . . .

"[We have] a tool for incident management and analysis that makes sense of seven to eight million pieces of raw customer data per year. Six million pieces of data come from support incidents, mostly by phone but also from the Web. One million come in from Premier, our more sophisticated support service for enterprise [large] customers. The rest of the customer data comes from a variety of other sources. Support engineers enter problems reported via phone into the database as they handle calls. Online problem reports go directly into the database. E-mails, already electronic, are easily converted into a structured format for entry."[51]

In addition to entering data on customer comments and complaints into a computerized database, says Dell, you should enter results on key measures of product quality, responsiveness, and so on that define your customers' experience with your company. He writes:

"Not all feedback is created equal. To many companies, feedback means anecdotal evidence and comments from which they can feel or sense a trend. But that kind of qualitative feedback is limiting. It's a self-reinforcing question to ask someone whether he is satisfied with the computer he just bought. It's like asking someone if he's smart. You're not going to get a lot of objective—or constructive—feedback. The real answer to the question comes when he buys a second time. Would he buy from you again? Would he recommend your product to his friends? We use aggregate data to sharpen our sense of what customer satisfaction means, and continue to take their pulse many times over the course of our relationship.

"We try to take the process one step further. We have defined a series of metrics that define the customer experience in very measurable terms; we track the order and delivery process, product reliability, and also service and support from the customer's point of view. Our results are data-driven and based on real-time customer input. And we've designed our business to be flexible enough to respond to those metrics quickly, and to deliver what we believe to be the best customer experience."[52]

The key to making this system work, explains Gates, is creating computer databases containing—or "digitizing," as Gates refers to it—data on customer needs, problems, concerns, and performance results on key metrics such as on-time delivery early on in the process. That's important, he argues, because critical information won't otherwise get to the right people soon enough. "You can collect information from customers even if you don't have a digital system" writes Gates, "but you can't analyze it quickly. You can't make nondigital information integral to the development process for a service or a product. Nondigital systems won't enable you to route information directly to product developers. Digital systems give companies the ability to do all these things and transform into adaptive learning organisms. Customer service changes from add-on activity to an integral part of product development."[53]

Step #2: Segment Your Data

Once you have digitized your data, say our gurus, your next step is to segment the data to focus on the needs and expectations of different types of customers. "No matter what your business," notes Dell, "it's important to remember that not all customers are exactly the same."[54] For example, Dell has learned that among his customers, large businesses and consumers, notebook and desktop users, all have different requirements.

"A large company, for instance, is most interested in consistency and will trade minor upgrades in speed and performance for stability in its computing platform. It also wants to feel some modicum of control over its PC use across a wide number of users. It seeks consistency and reliability in its network, whether it's a bank or an airline or a law firm.

"Consumers, on the other hand, have very different concerns. Consistency isn't as high a priority because a consumer generally has only one computer. What's important to a consumer is having the fastest computer, the latest performance, and the hottest peripherals—like the latest graphics chip, the latest DVD drive, the fastest connection to the Internet.

"We've also found that different customers require vastly different levels of service and support. A large company often requires a relatively low volume of support, but support that is very sophisticated and high value-add. When they call us, they want their technical person to speak to ours. For example, one of the biggest issues for the NASDAQ stock exchange is that they have to provide a stock quote within a few milliseconds—and it has to be the same quote on both the East and West Coasts. They can't experience technical difficulties! So we have dedicated systems engineers who work onsite with NASDAQ.

"That's a very different level of communication from that which is required for an individual consumer who generally needs higher volumes of support, and support that is clear, but that can most often be delivered easily by one of our service technicians.

"Service and support requirements also differ by product. Desktop, notebook, or workstation problems typically occur during the day, when people are using them. Servers, however, are installed in the middle of the night because you can't take them down during the day when people are relying on them. As a matter of course, most server questions come up in the middle of the night, so we provide twenty-four-hour, seven-day-a-week service."[55]

You need to uncover similar idiosyncrasies among your customers, say our gurus. You do so by subdividing the data you collect by ever-narrower customer types, for example, segmenting your data by customer size or some other distinguishing characteristic.

Step #3: Analyze the Data and Take Action

Finally, say Dell and Gates, you must get the data you have collected, digitized, and segmented into the hands of people who can do something with it to actually improve your company's performance. For Microsoft that means getting the data to the product improvement (PI) team in Microsoft's technical services area. Gates calls Microsoft's PI team the "voice of the customer" and describes their function this way:

"The people in this group sift through a lot of bad news and some good news all day long. They focus exclusively on what our customers are telling us that we might not want to hear but should. They analyze customer feedback and lobby on behalf of the customers for fixes and new product features to improve the customers' experience with our software. Although they sit in the customer support group, they're not in the customer support business. They're in the product improvement business. . . .

"By analyzing the aggregate data, the PI team develops prioritized lists of problems and recommends to each development team a variety of solutions, including new product features. This structured feedback gets to our development teams early enough in the development cycle for appropriate corrections or new features to be included in the next release. . . .

"We also use our corporate intranet to disseminate information to all interested parties, integrating Web pages with e-mail. For our major products, any employee can go to our Web site to see the current status of the data on customer complaints and requests. When a product is released, PI posts reports on immediate customer reaction. More detailed reports are posted monthly, organized by major product groups. These monthly reports include a problem's symptoms, a short-term solution, recommendations for a longer-term fix, and any response from the product group. Microsoft subscribers get e-mail with links to new monthly reports as they are done. Other employees will see the most current reports when they browse the intranet site. The most frequent visitors are the program managers, developers, and testers for various products. Writers of online articles regularly review the site to ensure that they develop content focused on the most important issues to customers, and another team uses the site to evaluate what new software tools customers may need. The status of customer issues is included in the major quarterly product reviews that go to senior management."[56]

At Dell a major part of analyzing customer feedback is performed at a regular Friday morning customer-advocate meeting of 175 people representing all parts of the company. During the first 90 minutes of the meeting, attendees review key statistics on various indicators of customer satisfaction. Then, the group as a whole may call a customer to discuss a difficult problem that occurred during the previous week or call Dell itself and pretend to be a customer in order to get a sense of what it is like to do business with the company.[57]

Ultimately, says Gates, your performance improvement team or customer-advocate group should be seeking answers to some basic questions, such as the following:[58]

- What do customers think about your products?
- What problems do they want you to fix?
- What new features do they want you to add?
- What problems are your distributors and resellers encountering as they sell your products or work with you?
- Where are your competitors winning business away from you, and why?
- Will changing customer demands force you to develop new capabilities?
- What new markets are emerging that you should enter?

Key #9: Put Employees First

Putting employees first may be the strangest customer-retention secret of all, but it is one that at least some of our gurus, including Herb Kelleher and Richard Branson, think is critical. You may have heard the phrase "the customer comes first." Wrong, say Kelleher and Branson. Customers come second. Employees are, or at least should be, the number-one "customer" of every company. Here is how Kelleher explains his reasoning:

> Once you do determine what customers want, . . . how you deliver it makes the difference. That difference depends on your employees. We've always felt that we not only deliver a good product, the best on-time performance, the baggage always arrives with the customer, and that sort of thing, we also deliver the product at a very reasonable price, which is value.
>
> However, we wanted still more than that, something that you might call a spiritual element—a warmth, good humor, entertainment quality, hospitality, altruism. There are a lot of words that you can apply but they amount to those things that will produce a sense of dedication and togetherness that leads each employee to believe that he or she is doing something worthwhile as an organization and for society. And we don't believe a company can have that kind of atmosphere and that kind of customer service unless it first realizes that the employees are its number-one customers. Years ago, business gurus used to apply the business school conundrum to me: "Who comes first? Your shareholders, your employees, or your customers?" I said, "Well that's easy," but my response was heresy at that time. I said employees come first and if employees are treated right, they treat the outside world right, the outside world uses the company's product again, and that makes the shareholders happy.
>
> That really is the way it works and it's not a conundrum at all. Your employees should be your first customers and it's very important to communicate that to everyone.[59]

Kelleher backs up his commitment to putting employees first with action. For example, he has been known to invite customers who abuse his employees to fly other carriers, as in the story of the rather unpleasant lady SouthwestAirlines employees nicknamed "Pen Pal."

This particular woman seemed never to be satisfied. After every flight she would file a complaint. She didn't like not having a meal in flight. She didn't like unassigned seating. She didn't like the absence of a first-class section. She didn't like the boarding procedures, the color of the airplanes, or the uniforms worn by the flight attendants. She didn't like the casual atmosphere on the planes, and most of all, she didn't like peanuts! In keeping with company policy, Southwest employees responded to each complaint, patiently explaining why the company did this and did not do that. Still, the woman continued to bombard them with her grievances. Eventually, in frustration, Southwest's customer-relations people sent Pen Pal's latest diatribe to Kelleher with a note: "This one's yours." Kelleher read the complaint and quickly drafted a response:

> Dear Mrs. Crabapple,
> We will miss you.
> Love, Herb[60]

> If the employees come first, then they are happy. A motivated employee treats the customer well. The customer is happy so they keep coming back, which pleases the shareholders. It's not one of the enduring Green mysteries of all time, it is just the way it works.
>
> *Herb Kelleher[61]*

What Kelleher and Branson recognize is that it is unreasonable to expect employees to go out of their way to treat customers well if they themselves are treated poorly. On the other hand, when employees feel that they are respected, that their opinions are valued, and that their employer demonstrates a genuine concern for their welfare, then they pass that good feeling and attention along to customers. Ultimately, customer retention comes down to employee retention. And that is the focus of our next, and final, chapter.

KEY POINTS

- Every single customer has value. Taking care of existing customers may be the most-important thing you can do for your business.

- You should be a tough boss. You set the standard of customer care and attention that your employees will follow.

○━┳ Insist on getting every minor detail of product quality and service right. You must set exceedingly high standards for your products and services.

○━┳ You should view every interaction with customers as critical, particularly in a service-oriented business. You must be willing to go to extraordinary lengths to ensure that every customer interaction turns out positively for the customer. Be respectful of customers and highly attentive to their needs and insist that your employees behave in the same fashion. Understand that customer loyalty can be built on something as simple as a kind word.

○━┳ Ultimately, you should seek to become your customers' trusted advisor. To that end, you must take responsibility for your customers' investments in your product or service. Your goal should be not just to please customers with quality products and good service, but through your advisory role, to build a meaningful, memorable, total experience that will win the customer for life.

○━┳ Always try to exceed your customers' expectations.

○━┳ Offer your customers a 100 percent money-back guarantee, and make it easy for customers to take advantage of the guarantee.

○━┳ Spend up to 40 percent of your time interacting with your customers and insist that all of the top managers in your company do the same.

○━┳ Make sure that bad news travels fast. Hunt out grim news so you can fix problems quickly.

○━┳ Harness modern technology to improve customer listening.

○━┳ Put your employees first. It is unrealistic to expect employees to go out of their way to treat customers well if they themselves are treated poorly.

Paul Allen, cofounder of Microsoft Corporation

Mary Kay Ash, founder of Mary Kay Cosmetics

Arthur Blank, cofounder of Home Depot

Richard Branson, founder of the Virgin Group

Charles M. Brewer, founder of MindSpring Enterprises

Ben Cohen, cofounder of Ben & Jerry's Ice Cream

Michael Dell, founder of Dell Computer Corporation

Roy Disney, cofounder of Disney Brothers Studio (later Walt Disney Productions, Ltd.)

Walt Disney, cofounder of Disney Brothers Studio (later Walt Disney Productions, Ltd.)

Debbi Fields, founder of Mrs. Fields Cookies, Inc.

Bill Gates, cofounder of Microsoft Corporation

Jerry Greenfield, cofounder of Ben & Jerry's Ice Cream

Wilson Harrell, founder of over one hundred companies, columnist for *Success Magazine* and former publisher of *Inc. Magazine*

Soichiro Honda, cofounder of Honda Motor Company, Ltd.

Masaru Ibuka, cofounder of Sony Corporation

Ken Iverson, former president, chairman, and CEO of Nucor Corporation

Steven Jobs, cofounder of Apple Computer, Inc., and cofounder of NeXT

Howard Johnson, founder of Howard Johnson Company

Herb Kelleher, founder of Southwest Airlines

Ray Kroc, founder of McDonald's Corporation

Charles Lazarus, founder of Toys "R" Us

Konosuke Matsushita, founder of Matsushita Electric Industrial Company

Robert Mondavi, founder of Robert Mondavi Winery

Akio Morita, cofounder of Sony Corporation

David Packard, cofounder of Hewlett-Packard

Ross Perot, founder of Electronic Data Systems (EDS) and Perot Systems Corporation

Anita Roddick, founder of The Body Shop

Colonel Harland Sanders, founder of Kentucky Fried Chicken (KFC)

Howard Schultz, founder of Starbucks Coffee Company

Ricardo Semler, president and CEO of Semco, S.A.

R. David (Dave) Thomas, founder of Wendy's International, Inc.

Sam Walton, founder of Wal-Mart Stores, Inc.

6

Managing People

When Ben Cohen and Jerry Greenfield were about to open their first ice-cream parlor, they asked their landlady-to-be what she thought the hardest part of running a business would be. Her reply was "managing people." The boys write that after she left they said to each other: "That's not going to be a problem for us. We're going to be really good at that. We'll have employee meetings weekly. We'll talk with everyone about what's going on, and they'll feel part of the business. It's not going to be a hierarchical thing. It's going to be a team thing."[1] Their noble intentions aside, Cohen and Greenfield admit that they soon learned their landlady was right. Managing people quickly became the hardest part of running their business. It's a lesson most of our gurus say they had to learn, usually the hard way. Therefore, it seems fitting to end this book of entrepreneurial lessons with the toughest subject of all. From hiring to firing and through all that goes in between, what follows is the collected advice and wisdom from the people who have been there and done it. (See Exhibit 6.1 for a summary of our gurus' "people lessons.")

EXHIBIT 6.1. **Fourteen People Lessons**

People lesson #1: Your employees are the spinal cord of your business.

People lesson #2: Hire smarts and attitude.

People lesson #3: Inspire those you hire.

People lesson #4: Demand excellence.

People lesson #5: Be open and candid.

People lesson #6: Treat employees as equals.

People lesson #7: Cement a team spirit.

People lesson #8: Listen to employees.

People lesson #9: Empower employees to do the right thing.

People lesson #10: Trust your employees.

People lesson #11: Small is beautiful.

People lesson #12: Praise people to success.

People lesson #13: Share the financial rewards.

People lesson #14: Firing people is the hardest part of managing.

PEOPLE LESSON #1: Your Employees Are the Spinal Cord of Your Business

It has become popular in recent years for most CEOs to say that employees are their company's most-valuable resource. In fact, says Ken Iverson, former president and CEO of Nucor Corporation, proclamations attesting to the value of employees have become so common that most people now react to such pronouncements with a barely disclosed chuckle. While everyone knows executives like to "say the words," they also feel that few executives believe the words, much less act in concert with them.[2] Well, say our gurus, you had better start believing the words, because they are true.

> People are definitely a company's greatest asset. It doesn't make a difference whether the product is cars or cosmetics. A company is only as good as the people it keeps. And in order to attract and retain good people, a business must treat people right. Without people skills, no organization and for that matter, no manager can make it in today's highly competitive business environment.
>
> *Mary Kay Ash*[3]

Our gurus repeatedly emphasize that their employees made the fundamental difference in their company's successes. For example, Richard Branson argues that based on his experience he is absolutely certain that no company can be successful unless it hires the right kind of people and motivates them in the right way.[4] Konosuke Matsushita adds that, "over the long term, the skill, determination, and motivation of employees is almost always key" to success and that "the idea that a few individuals could build a great business only by themselves, through one or two clever strategic decisions is absurd."[5] And Sam Walton maintained that, as much as people like to talk about the elements that went into Wal-Mart's success, such as merchandising, distribution, technology, market saturation, real estate strategy and so on, the truth was that none of those things were the real secret to the company's unbelievable success. What carried the company and made the difference, according to Walton, was the relationship the company developed with its employees. Interestingly, the "partnership" Walton and other managers at Wal-Mart developed with their employee "associates" wasn't part of some master plan or grand vision for the company.[6] It was something that developed over time—a lesson they had to learn—and one that our gurus say all entrepreneurs must learn. As Arthur Blank puts it, your employees are the spinal cord of your company. They are what holds it upright.[7]

PEOPLE LESSON #2: Hire Smarts and Attitude

Early in his company's history, Michael Dell tried very hard to hire just the right people for every job vacancy. Looking back on the experience, he notes that he found it both frustrating and futile. Even though his company was small, it was growing rapidly. Before he knew it, the people he had so carefully selected for specific jobs found themselves out of their league. Although they were talented, they soon became overwhelmed as the job for which they had been hired changed. That early experience, explains Dell, taught him a lesson about hiring that he still applies today—don't hire people for a specific job; hire them with the long term in mind. Invite them to join your company and to grow with it. "If you hire them to grow far beyond their current position, you build depth and additional capacity into your organization."[8] Almost all of our gurus echo these sentiments. Hire for potential, they say, don't just hire for the moment. What does it mean to hire for potential? What should you be looking for in prospective candidates? Two things, say our gurus—smarts and attitude.

> It's not enough to hire to fill a job. It's not even enough to hire on the basis of one's talents. You have to hire based upon a candidate's potential to grow and develop.
>
> *Michael Dell*[9]

Hire Smarts

When hiring people for the long term, Dell first looks for "people who have the questioning nature of a student and are always ready to learn something new."[10] These are people who have an open and questioning mind, who have a healthy balance of experience and intellect, and who aren't afraid to make a mistake in the process of innovating. They are "people who expect change to be the norm and are liberated by the idea of looking at problems or situations from a different angle and coming up with unprecedented solutions."[11]

Bill Gates describes these ideal long-term candidates as simply being "smart." When asked in a 1994 interview to explain what he meant by "smart," Gates replied, "There's a certain sharpness, an ability to absorb new facts. To walk into a situation, have something explained to you and immediately say, 'Well, what about this?' To ask an insightful question. To absorb it in real time. A capacity to remember. To relate to domains that may not seem connected at first. A certain creativity that allows people to be effective."[12] Gates's bias for "smarts" over almost anything else is said to have led him to devalue previous programming experience, particularly mainframe experience, in favor of inexperienced young people with degrees in math and the sciences. His hiring theory, which seems to have been proven right by Microsoft's success, is that candidates with backgrounds in math or the sciences have proved their intellectual mettle by virtue of their degree and could easily apply their smarts to computers. To reinforce his commitment to hiring smarts, Gates insists that Microsoft managers hire fewer people than they need for a project—"n minus one"—reasoning that his managers will be forced always to hire only the smartest people because they know they will never be able to hire as many people as they want.

In addition to looking for academic degrees, Dell likes to ask the following questions in his pursuit of smarts.

> When I interview people, the first thing I do is find out how they process information. Are they thinking in economic terms? What is their definition of success? How do they relate to people? Do they really understand the strategy of the business they're involved in today? Do they understand ours? It's surprising how many people already in the workforce contribute in some way to their company's strategy but don't really understand it that well. It's important to me to know whether potential candidates have the capacity to understand Dell's strategy and if they can help us evolve and develop it.
>
> I usually ask candidates to tell me about something they did that they are particularly proud of. This gives me a few insights into whether they are

focused on the success of the company they're currently working for or on their own personal aggrandizement.[13]

Hire Attitude

In order to gauge the attitude of job candidates, Dell makes a point of disagreeing with them during the course of their interview. "I want to know if they have strong opinions and are willing to defend them," he says. "At Dell, we need people who are confident enough of their abilities and strong in their convictions, not people who feel the need to give in the face of conflict."[14]

Like Dell, Bill Gates frequently interjects tough questioning and disagreement into interviews with job candidates. In his 1996 book *The Microsoft Way,* Randall Stross describes one infamous exchange between Gates and an aspiring candidate for a Microsoft position: "Once, a senior vice-president of a leading computer company who was being interviewed for a position at Microsoft told Gates that she would have to research the answers to some of his questions. He is said to have demanded of her, 'Why don't you have an answer? Are you stupid?'"[15] Stross notes that the exchange was widely reported in the press, and when most people read about it, they took it as simply another example of Microsoft's hostile "macho" culture. Yet, writes Stross, there was more to the "Are you stupid?" remark. "[The] remark obscures the real issue at the heart of Gates's displeasure, which was not lack of smarts, which hardly could be determined by Gates's question, but lack of another attribute that Gates sought: verbal facility."[16] Gates's combative posturing, writes Stross, could be taken as just a way of emphasizing that Microsoft wanted to hire people who were smart *and* "who were also pragmatically inclined, verbally agile, and able to respond deftly when challenged."[17] He was just putting the candidate to a test of attitude, according to Stross.

OUR VIEW

Well, maybe. Regardless of how you feel about the appropriateness of such childish remarks as "Are you stupid?" the point our gurus are making is that the candidate's attitude must match the company's culture. The "right" attitude might be "self-confidence" for one company, "combativeness" for another, and "arrogance" for still another. Every company is unique, so the key is to match the attitude to your unique culture. Take Southwest Airlines as an example.

Herb Kelleher explains that he looks for a sense of humor coupled with the ability to work in a collegial environment and a need to excel. He says: "We look for people who are unselfish and altruistic and who enjoy life. The focus is on the intangibles, the spiritual qualities, not an individual's educational experience. We can train anybody to do a job from a technical standpoint. We're looking for an esprit de corps, an attitude. We try to hire and promote people who have a humane approach."[18] Kelleher believes that a person's values are more important than their experience:

> We say, "OK, here's a guy with 30 years' experience in the field, a very distinguished record. The contender is someone with five years' experience in the field and doesn't have the laurels the other guy does." But what are their values? We'll take the one with less experience if he has the values we're looking for, and someone else can take the expert. We look for attitudes. We'll train you on whatever you need to do, but the one thing we can't do is change inherent attitudes in people.
>
> I've often said, if I could do that, if I could change attitudes, I'd be on Park Avenue making $5,000 an hour as a psychologist. But you can't. Once we've got people with the right attitudes, we can do almost anything we want thereafter.[19]

And so can you, say our gurus. Of course, it isn't going to be easy to hire people with both smarts *and* the right attitude. Ross Perot notes that, when he describes the kind of person he is trying to hire, recruiters insist that finding that person would be like looking for needles in a haystack. Wrong, Perot replies, I want "needles in a haystack with a red dot—very special people."[20]

> Entrepreneurs need employees who are racehorses. We need chargers who can make things happen. We need people who are creative and innovative, and who don't know what it means to say something can't be done. It helps if they are workaholics with an excess of nervous energy, and even better if they never sleep. But, above all, they can't be the kind of people

who like to follow "proper procedures," or who value security over the thrill of the chase.

Wilson Harrell[21]

PEOPLE LESSON #3: Inspire Those You Hire

According to Michael Dell, "it's not enough to just hire well. You need to engender a sense of personal investment in all your employees."[22] If you want your business to prosper, say our gurus, then you must inspire those you hire. Ricardo Semler, CEO of Semco, S.A., likes to illustrate the difference between an employee who is simply hired and one that is inspired by recalling the parable of the stonecutters. It goes like this:

> Three stone cutters were asked about their jobs. The first said he was paid to cut stones. The second replied that he used special techniques to shape stones in an exceptional way, and proceeded to demonstrate his skills. The third stone cutter just smiled and said: "I build cathedrals."[23]

Sounds great, you say, but suppose you're not in the business of building cathedrals. Suppose, instead, you manufacture pumps or dishwashers like Semco, sell cosmetics like The Body Shop and Mary Kay, or make ice cream like Ben & Jerry's. Suppose your product or service isn't inspirational in itself. Suppose it is just plain mundane. Can you still inspire your people? Can you turn your crew of stonecutters into energetic cathedral builders? Yes you can, say our gurus. In fact, they say, you must, and you do it by making the workplace inspirational. When asked how she was able to inspire her employees to sell something as inconsequential as cosmetic cream, Anita Roddick responded:

> You do it by creating a sense of holism, of spiritual development, of feeling connected to the workplace, the environment and relationships with one another. It's how to make Monday to Friday a sense of being alive rather than slow death. How do you give people a chance to do a good job? By making them feel good about what they are doing. The spirit soars when you are satisfying your own basic material needs in such a way that you are also serving the needs of others honorably and humanely. Under these circumstances, I can even feel great about a moisturizer.[24]

Likewise, at Mary Kay Cosmetics, the inspiration comes from the work environment and not necessarily the product line. As Mary Kay Ash puts it, the thrill of Mary Kay Cosmetics comes from "teaching bumblebees to fly." She explains:

> Aerodynamics has proven that the bumblebee cannot fly. . . . The body is too heavy, and the wings are too weak. But the bumblebee doesn't know that, and so it goes right on flying. Without a doubt, my biggest thrill in this business is seeing women have their own personal dreams fulfilled in a career. So many women don't know how great they really are, that [like the bumblebee] they really can fly! They come to us all Vogue on the outside—and vague on the inside. In the beginning, many women just have no confidence at all. . . .
>
> A woman usually comes into our organization as a tight little rosebud, sometimes appearing at my door too timid to even tell me who she is. Then I watch her after six months of praise and encouragement and she's hardly recognizable as the same person.[25]

The secret of inspiration, declares Howard Schultz, is to provide your employees with a larger purpose for their day-to-day activities. "If people relate to the company they work for," he states, "if they will form an emotional tie to it, and buy into its dreams, they will pour their hearts into making it better."[26] "If people understand that the work they do produces more than just profits," explain Ben Cohen and Jerry Greenfield, "and they're in alignment with the values of the company, there's no end to what they can contribute."[27] You'll tap the discretionary beyond-the-call-of-duty effort everyone is capable of giving if they are inspired to do so. Cohen and Greenfield equate the extra effort to that you often see from workers at some nonprofit agencies.

> Most people who work at nonprofit agencies take those jobs—despite the fact that they earn less money than they would in the private sector—because they're highly motivated by what the agency does. Their work has meaning for them because they're addressing an issue they're concerned about. . . .
>
> Employees can bring the same passion that's usually reserved for nonprofits to a for-profit workplace, if they see the work they're doing as supportive of goals and values they believe in.[28]

Where do these values and goals come from? From you, say our gurus. From day one, whether you realize it or not, you will shape the values of your company through your words and behavior. You will create an environment in which your stonecutters will either shape stones or build cathedrals. Just be aware, warns Schultz, that whatever values you convey are likely to be part of your company for a long time: "Once the . . . people of the company have absorbed those values, you can't suddenly change their world view with a lecture. . . . It's difficult, if not impossible, to reinvent a company's culture! If you have made the mistake of doing business one way for five years, you can't suddenly impose a layer of different values upon it. By then, the water's already in the well, and you have to drink it."[29] Consequently, advise our gurus, it is important to establish the right tone from the beginning. You may even want to draft and distribute a statement outlining your values. (See Exhibits 6.2 and 6.3 for value statements from Ben & Jerry's and from MindSpring's founder, Charles Brewer.)

EXHIBIT 6.2. Ben & Jerry's Aspiration

- **To be real:** We need to be who we say we are, both inside and outside the company. We are all custodians of the reputation of Ben & Jerry's. We will strive to put into practice the words we use to describe ourselves: Friendly, Enthusiastic, Exciting, Caring, High-Quality, Progressive, Off-beat, Innovative, Cutting-Edge, Funny, Lighthearted, Encouraging, Informal, Activist, Honest, Childlike, Down-Home.
- **To be the best:** If our customers are euphoric about our products, we will prosper. Our future together depends upon our ability to outperform the competition. That's our business strategy. We want to be the best ice cream company in the world. We want to be viewed as master ice cream makers. We are passionate about giving customers what they want, when they want it, every single time.
- **To improve continuously:** Every time we do something, we should be checking to see if our methods worked and figure out how we can do it better the next time. From the minute we join the company we are responsible for helping to shape and improve what goes on around us.
- **To learn continuously:** We want people to have the opportunity to develop their potential to contribute to the company. We'll need to keep growing skills in three areas: technical skills to achieve excellence in day-to-day work, personal skills to give life and vitality to these aspirations, and business knowledge to understand the companywide implications and importance of what each of us does.

(continued)

EXHIBIT 6.2.　(continued)

- **To be inclusive:** We embrace individual differences. The right to be ourselves contributes to our sense of ownership. We perform better and serve the marketplace better when men, women, gays, lesbians, and people of different races, nationalities, ethnicities, and backgrounds work together. Building a diverse staff contributes to excellent performance, not just to societal good.
- **To be creative:** Our creativity is our strength. We want to see beyond conventional thinking and come up with ideas that work, that excite our customers and reflect our values.
- **To build community:** No one at Ben & Jerry's should feel alone or apart. When one of us needs help, we reach out to help. People from outside feel our energy when they visit us. We have a zest for life, a sense of humor, and we enjoy one another's company. We share the excitement of succeeding at the game of business and we'll try to have fun while we do it.
- **To be open and trusting:** Rationales, strategy, and the truth should be shared. We want to be open about our concerns and admit our mistakes and failings. We need to make sure people feel safe to speak up about things they care about. If we trust one another's good intentions, we'll feel better about trying new things and about speaking up about things that concern us. It's expected that we'll all do the right thing even when nobody is looking.
- **To celebrate and to give meaningful recognition:** When we reach or exceed our targets, we should cheer. Celebration establishes a sense of accomplishment, which leads to more accomplishments. Celebrations don't need to be elaborate. Recognition is the currency of leadership. We should make recognition a contagious part of everyday life.
- **To use consultive decision making and active listening:** When making decisions we'll involve people with special expertise and people likely to be affected. We'll also give those with a contrary point of view an opportunity to be heard. However, Ben & Jerry's is not a democracy. Leaders need to make calls based on facts, data, and input. In order to practice consultive decision making and to create the conditions for people to contribute their best thinking, we must be active listeners.
- **To hold ourselves accountable:** We all need to do what we said we were going to do and be clear about who's responsible and what's expected. When we don't do our part it affects everybody. We put the company at risk when we tolerate poor performance.
- **To be great communicators:** Leaders are responsible for effectively and consistently communicating pertinent information in a timely way. Good leaders have well-informed teams. We're each responsible for absorbing the information offered through company communication vehicles like postings, staff meetings, and The Rolling Cone.
- **To be up-front:** People aren't going to do better unless they understand what they need to do to improve. Good straight feedback is essential to improvement. Talking about someone's performance to people other than the person does harm to the individual and to the company.
- **To be profitable by being thrifty:** We believe in investing wisely and with a sense of frugality. When we save the company money, we do a service to our shareholders and ourselves.

Source: Ben Cohen, Jerry Greenfield, and Meredith Maran, Ben & Jerry's Double-Dip: How to Run a Values-Led Business and Make Money Too (New York: Simon & Schuster, 1997), pp. 173–175.

EXHIBIT 6.3. **MindSpring's Values**

- We respect the individual, and believe that individuals who are treated with respect and given responsibility respond by giving their best.
- We require complete honesty and integrity in everything we do.
- We make commitments with care, and then live up to them. In all things, we do what we say we are going to do.
- Work is an important part of life, and it should be fun. Being a good business person does not mean being stuffy and boring.
- We are frugal. We guard and conserve the company's resources with at least the same vigilance that we would use to guard and conserve our own personal resources.
- We insist on giving our best effort in everything we undertake. Furthermore, we see a huge difference between "good mistakes" (best effort, bad result) and "bad mistakes" (sloppiness or lack of effort).
- Clarity in understanding our mission, our goals, and what we expect from each other is critical to our success.
- We are believers in the Golden Rule. In all our dealings we will strive to be friendly and courteous, as well as fair and compassionate.
- We feel a sense of urgency on any matters related to our customers. We own Problems, and we are always responsive. We are customer-driven.

Source: Brad Grimes, "Lessons from MindSpring," Fortune, June 21, 1999, p. 186[F].

PEOPLE LESSON #4: Demand Excellence

In the previous chapter, we noted that many of our gurus have reputations for being tough bosses who are obsessed with treating customers right. Howard Johnson locked a franchisee out of his restaurant because it wasn't kept clean. Debbi Fields dumped hundreds of dollars worth of "unhappy-looking" cookies into the garbage to teach her employees a lesson about quality. And Ray Kroc insisted that every little thing about his hamburgers be perfect. This determination to accept nothing less than the highest standard of performance is a people lesson taught by almost all of our gurus. Their reasoning, explains Steven Jobs, cofounder of Apple Computer, is that "people get far more excited about doing something as well as it can be done than about doing something adequately. If they are working in an environment where excellence is expected, then they will do excellent work without anything but self-motivation."[30]

> If you don't like to work hard and be intense and do your best, this is not the place to work.
>
> *Bill Gates*[31]

Our gurus frequently carry their obsessions with perfection to extremes. For example, Dave Thomas says that Colonel Harland Sanders was a really nice man but that he had a mean temper. "If something wasn't right, he'd let loose with a string of cuss words that could make you feel two feet high."[32] According to Thomas, the colonel didn't want to cuss and felt really bad about it. He even prayed to stop but couldn't.

Soichiro Honda is said to have had a similar fiery temper that actually on occasion led him to strike workers when their performance didn't live up to his expectations. Hideo Sugiura, an engineer who worked with Honda, recalls one of his scariest encounters with his boss:

> On many occasions Honda struck me. One time, he hit me in front of twenty or thirty of my subordinates. Earlier that day, I was working in my office when an employee ran in with a panicked expression, saying that the president was asking for me. I ran out and asked Honda what was wrong. Without saying a word, he suddenly hit me.
>
> It turned out that the cause of his anger was a bolt that was supposed to stick out by a maximum of 2mm but was protruding by 5mm. Honda screamed, "Who was in charge of such a ridiculous design? It was you!"
>
> Before I could say anything or apologize, wham! He hit me again. Frankly, I was seething with resentment. As the chief leader of a thousand employees at the research lab, I had my pride, too. Sure, what he was saying was true, but he didn't have to hit me in front of everyone.[33]

A former president of Honda recalls that the founder would also throw things at people who displeased him. "When he got mad, he blindly reached for anything lying around, and started throwing whatever was in reach randomly at people; it was dangerous! The desks in our office were covered with dents and scratches from the wrenches and hammers that the boss threw around."[34]

Despite such tirades, Soichiro Honda is said to have been worshiped and respected by many, if not most, of his employees. How could that be true?

Hideo Sugiura provides an explanation as he recalls the second half of the hitting incident. Sugiura says he was standing there after being hit the second time, thinking that he couldn't take such abuse any more and was just going to quit right then. But, recalls Sugiura, when he raised his head to glare at Honda, he saw something that changed his mind.

> His eyes had welled up with tears. When I saw that, I couldn't say anything. I thought, he's serious. The boss just wanted to convey to me how important vehicle design was, and how rigorous we must be at every step. It was a small detail, but if we slacked off with even a small part, we could not make reliable products.
>
> That's the point he wanted to make. And to teach not just me, but all the engineers, he hit me.
>
> Believe me, I learned an important lesson that day.[35]

Many of Honda's employees learned similar lessons. As Masaru Ibuka notes, Honda "was a demon when it came to business . . . [who] set goals, berated people, and even hit them when they made excuses—but all his subordinates understood how sincere and serious he was about work."[36] Presumably, Honda could get away with such behavior because his employees understood that he was responding not out of arrogance or meanness but out of concern for their welfare and the welfare of the company that employed them.

OUR VIEW

Setting high standards for performance is a good idea, but, as you should have learned in kindergarten, cussing, hitting, and throwing things are not nice. They may get you sued or even arrested. They may even get you shot. Consequently, it may be wiser to find a less-aggressive way to show your displeasure with your employees' failure to meet your exalted standards.

> People . . . generally do what you expect them to do! If you expect them to perform well, they will; conversely, if you expect them to perform poorly, they'll probably oblige.
>
> *Mary Kay Ash*[37]

PEOPLE LESSON #5: Be Open and Candid

Of course, say our gurus, if you are going to hold your people to high standards of performance, you must tell them what those standards are and how well they are performing in respect to them. In short, explains Herb Kelleher, "if you want your employees to do their best for the company, then you have to give them the necessary information."[38] That means you have to share information about your company's performance openly and freely, and that's not something most companies do. The arguments against sharing information are endless: Employees will use the numbers to argue for higher raises, sensitive information will be improperly disclosed to competitors, bad news will frighten employees. Well, maybe, say our gurus, but the advantages of being open and candid with employees far outweigh the potential disadvantages.

In reality, maintain our gurus, the more an employee knows about the operations of a company, the better prepared he or she is to serve the company's and the customers' interests. Herb Kelleher notes that Southwest Airlines is known for saturating its employees with information about the company, its customers, and its competition. Such openness, Kelleher believes, leads directly to better customer service.

> Access to critical information grants customer-contact people the knowledge and understanding they need to take ownership and responsibility for doing the right thing. For example, a Southwest customer service agent who understands how the company makes its money, where profits come from and what they mean to the company, is in a better position to serve a customer who is making a special request. An agent who doesn't have access to this knowledge is limited by the company's rules and regulations.
>
> Customers who deal with Southwest employees rarely get the runaround. Instead, they are likely to deal with a person who is well informed, makes sound decisions, and has a flexible, creative problem-solving approach. Their solid knowledge of the company gives the people of Southwest Airlines the confidence and power to truly make a difference in the lives of their customers.[39]

What kind of information should employees be seeing on a regular basis? Just about anything and everything, say our gurus. For example, every month at Semco each employee gets a balance sheet, a profit-and-loss analysis, and a cash-flow statement for his or her division that they are taught how to read.[40] At Wal-Mart, employees (associates) receive regular reports on their store's purchases, sales, profits, and markdowns.[41] If you get the information, say our gurus, your employees probably should get it also.

> There are really just two ways to go on the question of information-sharing: Tell employees everything or tell them nothing. Otherwise, each time you choose to withhold information, they have reason to think you're up to something. We prefer to tell employees everything. We hold back nothing.
>
> *Ken Iverson*[42]

PEOPLE LESSON #6: Treat Employees as Equals

Sharing information is an important first step in treating employees as equals. It is a way to begin building the partnership between employees and management that all of our gurus believe is necessary for superior performance. Exhibit 6.4 summarizes some other ways our gurus suggest you can treat your employees as equals. These are discussed in detail in the sections that follow.

Get Rid of Executive Limos and Executive Parking Spaces

Ken Iverson recalls that, when Nucor acquired a new plant several years ago, one of his first actions was to sell off the company limousine and elim-

---

EXHIBIT 6.4. **Three Ways to Treat Employees as Equals**

1. Get rid of executive limos and executive parking spaces.
2. Eliminate executive dining rooms, executive bathrooms, and exclusive executive offices.
3. Don't employ receptionists, executive secretaries, personal assistants, or other support staff.

inate the executive parking spaces. Soon afterward, he was greeting his new employees outside the plant one morning when he was approached by a young man who pointed back toward the parking lot and said:

> "Look where I'm parked. That's the *boss's* spot."
>
> "You mean, that *was* the boss's spot," replied Iverson.
>
> "Yeah, I guess so," responded the young man. Then, turning serious, he continued, "You know, that makes me feel a whole lot better about working here."[43]

If you are having difficulty with the idea of giving up your reserved spot, just pause for a moment, suggests Iverson, and think how your employees will feel on a rainy day when they have to park all the way across the parking lot and walk past your reserved space as it sits empty because you are out of town on business.[44] Keep in mind that these rain-soaked workers are the same ones you are depending on to make products, respond to customers, and generally make your company succeed.

> Respect is not a function of the distance from car door to plant door.
>
> *Ricardo Semler*[45]

Eliminate Executive Dining Rooms, Executive Bathrooms, and Exclusive Executive Offices

Ross Perot recalls that an executive from a big company who was visiting him at EDS was shocked to learn that there was no executive dining room. "I can't believe you eat in the cafeteria," said the executive. "It's the only place to eat," replied Perot. Later, as the executive and Perot went through the cafeteria line, the visitor tapped him on the shoulder and whispered, "I can't believe you stand in line." "Well," said Perot, "these guys are bigger than I am. I have to." As they sat eating, the executive remarked on how good the food was. "What do you do to make the food so good in your cafeteria?" he asked. "I eat here," replied Perot.[46]

Don't Employ Receptionists, Executive Secretaries, Personal Assistants, and Other Support Staff

The elimination of support staff is one of our gurus' more-controversial suggestions, but it is one that Ricardo Semler particularly favors. Semler recalls that the idea to eliminate, or at least significantly reduce, so-called support staff came to him one day when he heard about an assistant cashier who had applied for work at Semco. When asked to describe the job she was leaving, the clerk responded, "I stamp the pink copies and hand them to another girl." Pressed to describe her work in greater detail, the clerk couldn't. The only thing she seemed to know was that she was paid to stamp the pink forms, but she had no idea what the forms were for or what happened to them once they left her desk. As Semler thought about the hapless clerk, several questions came to mind: "Can people truly be inspired by purely repetitive clerical work performed without any sense of context? How much of it is really necessary? What if we could eliminate all those dead-end jobs and keep only positions with the potential for making people feel gratified? Could we run our company without secretaries, receptionists, and personal assistants?"[47]

Determined to seek answers, Semler decided to try an experiment. He would ask his support staff to send a copy of a 10-page *Harvard Business Review* article to a fellow executive whose office happened to be on the same floor and, coincidentally, right next door to his own. Semler calculated that the article would have to travel a grand total of 10 feet. The question was, How long would it take for the article to make the trip?

First, I gave the article to Irene Tubertini, one of my secretaries, and asked her to have it copied, then to bring it back to me so I could write a short comment on it, then to send it on to Clovis [the executive next door]. But because the article was long, it first had to go to our central mailroom to be copied by a clerk who handled long documents. The mail is only picked up twice a day—between nine and ten in the morning and four and five in the afternoon. Since my test began at 11 A.M., the article sat in Irene's outbasket for most of the first day. By the time it got to the mailroom, the clerk had left for the day, so it wasn't copied until the next morning. By then it missed the morning pickup and sat in the mailroom for most of that day.[48]

In total, it took 22 hours for the article to travel 10 feet—a rate of some 2.2 hours per foot. Armed with the results of his research, Semler announced his decision to phase out most receptionist and secretarial positions over a period of two years. Existing receptionists and secretaries would be offered different jobs in marketing, sales, or other parts of the firm.

As you might expect, Semler's proposal was met with opposition from most receptionists and secretaries and from almost all of Semco's managers. Still, Semler persisted. As a result, most clerical positions were eventually eliminated, and managers learned to fetch their own guests, make their own photocopies, send their own faxes, type their own letters, dial their own phones, and even do their own filing. Semco not only saved the cost of all the previous clerical help, but there were other side benefits. Forced to file his own papers, Semler found to his amazement that fewer papers needed filing. He went from filing 50 or 60 documents per week to filing just 2 or 3. Other managers did the same. As a consequence, Semco was able to cancel an order for $50,000 worth of new filing cabinets and even sold off some the company no longer needed.

> I do not like to have my managers think they are a special breed of people elected by God to lead stupid people to do miraculous things.
>
> Akio Morita[49]

PEOPLE LESSON #7: Cement a Team Spirit

A side benefit of stripping away the unnecessary perks and privileges of management and treating people equally is that you begin to build a team spirit, which our gurus consider crucial to the success of their companies. The ultimate team-spirited company, Southwest Airlines, published the following—based on naturalist Milton Olsen's description of the behavior of geese—in their employee newsletter, *LUV Lines*, to emphasize the importance of teamwork.

> This spring when you see geese heading back north for the summer flying along in "V" formation, you might be interested in knowing what scientists

have discovered about why they fly that way. It has been learned that as each bird flaps its wings, it creates an uplift for the bird immediately following.

By flying in "V" formation, the whole flock adds at least 71 percent greater flying range than if each bird flew on its own.

Basic Truth No. 1: People who share a common direction and sense of community can get where they are going quicker and easier because they are traveling on the thrust of one another.

Whenever a goose falls out of formation it suddenly feels the drag and resistance of trying to go it alone and quickly gets back into formation to take advantage of the lifting power of the bird immediately in front.

Basic Truth No. 2: There is strength and power (safety, too) in numbers when traveling in the same direction as others with whom we share a common goal.

When the lead goose gets tired, he rotates back in the wing and another goose flies point.

Basic Truth No. 3: It pays to take turns doing hard jobs—with people or with geese flying north.

These geese honk from behind to encourage those up front to keep up their speed.

Basic Truth No. 4: Those who are exercising leadership need to be remembered with our active support and praise.

Finally, when a goose gets sick or is wounded by gunshot and falls out, two geese fall out of formation and follow him down to help and protect him. They stay with him until he is either able to fly or until he is dead, and then they launch out on their own or with another formation to catch up with their group.

Basic Truth No. 5: We must stand by those among us in their times of need.[50]

So, how do you go about cementing such a team spirit? The following sections discuss some techniques our gurus have employed (summarized in Exhibit 6.5.)

EXHIBIT 6.5. **Team-Building Tips and Techniques**

- Parties.
- Retreats.
- Other fun activities.

- Sing-alongs.
- Company cheers.

Source: Adapted from Tips & Traps for Entrepreneurs, Courtney Price and Kathleen Allen, New York: McGraw-Hill, 1998.

Parties, Retreats, and Other Fun Activities

In his book *Richard Branson, Virgin King,* Tim Jackson reports that one of the primary vehicles Branson used to cement a team spirit during the early days of Virgin Records was to hold weekend retreats.

> Starting on a Friday and ending on a Sunday night, the entire staff of the record company, publishing company and studio management team would decamp to a country house hotel. Attendance was in theory optional, but those who did not come were told jokingly that they were expected to spend the week-end working in the office. At the hotel, other record companies might fill the days with talk of sales targets or new products. At Virgin, business was banned. Instead, the guests would spend the weekend playing tennis or golf, swimming and sunning themselves, eating and drinking with great gusto.[51]

Similarly, Arthur Blank recalls some festive weekends during the early days of Home Depot. Once the last customer went home and the doors were closed, employees would crank up the music on the public address system and haul out stacks of pizza and six-packs of beer to celebrate the week's sales.[52]

OUR VIEW

Although after-hours parties and weekend retreats may be a good idea, heavy drinking and other questionable behaviors are not recommended for obvious moral, ethical, and legal reasons. In fact, Arthur Blank reports that Home Depot banned alcoholic beverages at company functions following a holiday party at which an exceptionally drunk young man grabbed the microphone away from Bernie Marcus and proceeded to insult everyone at the party—including Marcus's wife.[53]

Singing Songs

Mary Kay Ash is such a fan of songs as a way to build esprit de corps that she initiated a song contest when she started her company. Employees are invited to write their own words to well-known tunes and submit them for consideration. The best are sung at company gatherings. One of the most popular Mary Kay songs is said to be entitled, "I've Got That Mary Kay Enthusiasm." Another is "If You Want to be a Director, Clap Your Hands," which ends with the line, "If you want to be a Director, you've got to be a 'perfecter,' so do all three, clap your hands, stomp your feet, and yell *hooray*."[54] Mary Kay reports that guests who have never before attended her company's gatherings sometimes find the singing a bit strange. Eventually, however, even they are caught up in the enthusiasm and join in the singing.

A Company Cheer

One of Sam Walton's favorite methods for kicking off company meetings was to do the University of Arkansas Razorback cheer:

Whooooooooooooooooooooooo Pig. Sooey!
Whooooooooooooooooooooooooooo Pig. Sooey!
Whoooooooooooooooooooooooooooooooo Pig. Sooey!
Razorbacks!!!!!

He would then follow up with the official Wal-Mart cheer:

Give Me a W!
Give Me an A!
Give Me an L!
Give Me a Squiggly! (Here, everybody does a little twist.)
Give Me an M!
Give Me an A!
Give Me an R!
Give Me a T!
What's that spell?
Wal-Mart!
What's that spell?
Wal-Mart!

Who's number one?
The CUSTOMER!

Walton admitted that guests at company events sometimes found the cheers—well, unusual. For example, during a visit to Bentonville, Arkansas, Wal-Mart's headquarters, President and Mrs. George Bush were treated to a rousing rendition of the hog calling followed by the Wal-Mart cheer. Walton said he could tell by the expression on the first couple's faces that they weren't used to witnessing such enthusiasm. [55]

Remember: You'll be left with an empty feeling if you hit the finish line alone. When you run a race as a team, though, you'll discover that much of the reward comes from hitting the tape together. You want to be surrounded not just by cheering onlookers but by a crowd of winners, celebrating as one.

Victory is much more meaningful when it comes not just from the efforts of one person, but from the joint achievements of many. The euphoria is lasting when all participants lead with their hearts, winning not just for themselves but for one another.

Success is sweetest when it's shared.

Howard Schultz[56]

PEOPLE LESSON #8: Listen to Employees

Mary Kay Ash relates the story of a friend who once purchased a small manufacturing company at a bargain price. When he asked the previous owner why he had been willing to sell the company so cheaply, the owner reported that he was driven to do so by his lousy employees. "My employees have become very militant, and they just don't appreciate all I've done for them over the years," complained the seller. "They're going to vote for a union any day now, and I don't want to deal with those union people." Not knowing what kind of trouble he had gotten himself into, reports Ash, her friend decided to hold an open meeting with his new employees. "I want you all to be happy," he told them. "Tell me what I can do to make that happen." "We need new fixtures in the bathrooms," they replied. "And larger mirrors in the locker rooms. And, we would like some vending machines in the recreation area." "And, what else?" asked Ash's friend. "Nothing," said the employees, "that's all—just the bathrooms, lockers, and vending machines." Ash's friend was amazed. These were all minor issues and easily remedied. He fixed the bathrooms, put up new mirrors in the locker rooms, and installed vending machines. The union was never voted in. Everyone was content. Ash's friend had gotten an excellent company at a bargain price because the previous owner just hadn't listened.[57] Don't make that mistake, say our gurus. Listen to your employees. You will probably learn a lot, and you may even save your company.

> You don't learn nothing while you're talking.
>
> Ross Perot[58]

An important first step in listening to your employees is to get out of your office and roam around. Intentionally put yourself into situations where you will have chance encounters with your employees and hear their spontaneous remarks. Michael Dell describes how he uses this technique.

Some days I show up at our headquarters building; other days, I'll go to some of our other facilities. I show up at the factory unannounced to talk to the people on the floor and to see what's really going on. I go to brown-bag lunches two or three times a month, and meet with a cross-section of people from all across the company. It's easy to sit in a product meeting and say, "We have these new products and our salespeople will sell them." But this may not be the reality. So I go to a brown-bag lunch and listen carefully to what the sales force has to say. It's a great way of learning what people are really dealing with on a day-to-day basis, and provides a forum for the exchange of ideas and solutions.

I believe you can learn a lot from incidental interactions. I might be in a car with an account executive as we drive from one customer to another. That's a great opportunity to find out what's really going on. I'll ask, "What are your customers telling you? How do you think the company's products are doing? What are you seeing in the competitive market? What are our biggest challenges? What are the threats to your success? How can the company support you better?"[59]

PEOPLE LESSON #9:
Empower Employees to Do the Right Thing

While you are out listening to your employees' ideas, our gurus suggest that you spend part of that time encouraging your employees to take initiative and put their ideas into action. How, you may ask, do you empower employees to do things their way without ending up with total chaos? Arthur Blank believes that the best way is to think in terms of the "three bundles"—an idea he credits to GE Chairman Jack Welch:

> **Bundle 1:** This is the nonnegotiable bundle. There are very few Bundle 1s in The Home Depot; those are the things we do the same across the company. Many of these are operational in nature, areas where investment in systems dictates a more uniform compliance. They are usually transparent to the customer, things that have to be done to maintain key consistencies between the stores.

> **Bundle 2:** This is the entrepreneurial bundle. Entrepreneurship comes into play here because this involves challenges in which the company provides only a minimum standard. If a store can extend that standard, great! We say, "Your store will carry such-and-such product lines. How you sell or display them is up to you." As a result, we get the benefit of some extraordinary creativity in this bundle; many of these ideas get distributed company wide as part of the "Best Practices" program.

> The entrepreneur[ial] bundle works at every level of the company. We even use it to further our community programs by giving the stores a budget for spending in their own communities. We don't tell them exactly how to spend the money. Instead, they find causes and become attached to those causes, emotionally and financially. The empowerment is great.

> **Bundle 3:** This is when we give associates complete autonomy to make their own decisions in the way they operate their store. They don't make the decision about the assortment in the store, although they do talk to the merchants about what their customers are looking for, so in a sense they're responsible for the fine-tuning of the assortment. But they're totally responsible for the amount of merchandise that we have in stock. They're responsible for being sure our pricing is right in the stores, for building the

displays, for signing, hiring, and training. And they're responsible for paying people what they're worth, which is the backbone of our entire organization. The people in our stores are responsible for moving people along in the company and for deciding who doesn't move along. All of those things come from the individuals making those decisions in their stores.[60]

Your goal, say our gurus, should be to make Bundle 3 as big as possible. That means inverting the traditional organizational pyramid. You put your employees on top and give them the power to make decisions. You support them; they don't support you. Herb Kelleher puts it this way:

Take the [organizational] pyramid—and turn it upside down. Turn it on its point. Down here, at the bottom, you've got the people at headquarters. Up there, at the top, you've got the people who are out there in the field, on the front lines. They're the ones who make things happen, not us. The people out there are the experts. You can compare our roles in the front offices to the military: We're the supply corps, we're not the heroes. We supply the heroes, period. The heroes are out there.[61]

PEOPLE LESSON #10: Trust Your Employees

Ultimately, it's about trust. It is the firm belief that, as Arthur Blank writes, "with the right value system and the right knowledge to do their job people can be trusted to make the right decisions." "If you can operate with that kind of trust," he goes on, "you don't have to micromanage. And people will do more good for the company than anyone could ever dictate."[62] Lack of trust between managers and employees, our gurus warn, causes all kinds of problems. David Packard says he learned this lesson early in his career.

In the late 1930s, when I was working for General Electric in Schenectady, the company was making a big thing of plant security. I'm sure others were, too. GE was especially zealous about guarding its tool and parts bins to make sure employees didn't steal anything. Faced with this obvious display of distrust, many employees set out to prove it justified, walking off with tools or parts whenever they could. Eventually, GE tools and parts were scattered all around town, including the attic of the house in which a number of us were living. In fact, we had so much equipment up there that when we threw the switch, the lights on the entire street would dim.

The irony in all of this is that many of the tools and parts were being used by their GE "owners" to work on either job-related projects or skill-enhancing hobbies—activities that would likely improve their performance on the job.[63]

Packard recalls that, when he started HP with Bill Hewlett, the memories of GE were still strong, and he was determined that parts bins and store-rooms at HP would be kept open. From a practical standpoint, according to Packard, keeping the parts bins and storerooms open made it easier for product designers to get access to the parts and tools they needed to work on new ideas at home and on the weekends. More important, the open bins and storerooms were symbols of trust.

Perhaps the most-publicized example of trust at HP occurred in the 1960s when it became the first company in the United States to implement flextime. Workers were allowed to come to work early in the morning or as late as 9:00 A.M. "To my mind," asserts Packard, "flextime is the essence of respect for and trust in people. It says that we both appreciate that our people have busy personal lives and that we trust them to devise, with their supervisor and work group, a schedule that is personally convenient yet fair to others."[64] That trust, says Packard, has paid off, and HP has rarely had a problem with work schedules.

Ricardo Semler reports similar results from flextime at his company. At Semco factory workers are allowed to arrive anytime between 7 A.M. and 9 A.M. Semler recalls that when the system was first initiated a number of people expressed concern that workers wouldn't coordinate their schedules and that production would suffer. Consequently, the company set up a task force to mediate any scheduling conflicts. But the task force never met. "Our workers knew that production would suffer if they didn't coordinate their schedules," writes Semler, "so that's what they did."[65]

PEOPLE LESSON #11: Small Is Beautiful

Of course, it's easier to trust people you know. That's not such a problem when you are just starting. You know everyone well. After all, you work with them every day. But, what do you do when your company starts growing? You can't personally know thousands of employees. How do you grow big while still keeping the intimacy that allows trust to flourish? Easy, say our gurus; think small to grow big. Every time your company starts getting big, break it into smaller pieces, which is exactly what many of our gurus did with their companies. Richard Branson is a good example.

Branson's Virgin Group as a whole employs over twenty thousand people, but it is in reality just a collection of small companies. Every time a venture starts to get big, Branson breaks it into several new companies. By the time he sold Virgin Music, Branson had created as many as 50 different subsidiary record companies under that label, and none had more than 60 employees. Virgin Records was big, but it didn't feel big to its employees.

> Think small and act small and we'll get bigger.
>
> *Herb Kelleher*[66]

How small is small enough? Semler doesn't think there is a magic number. For some companies the limit may be only a few dozen people. In others, it might be as many as five hundred. The key, advises Semler, is to keep the organization small enough so that everyone knows and can therefore trust almost everyone around them. Generally, he maintains, that means you will want to limit the size of your company or subsidiaries to no more than perhaps 150 people.[67] Branson places the figure even lower. He recommends that, "[o]nce people start not knowing the people in the building and it starts to become impersonal, it's time to break up a company. . . . I'd say the number is around 50 or 60 people. By keeping it small, you give people a chance. A company operates at its peak when people are able to know each other's strengths and weaknesses. I don't want people to get lost in the corridors of power."[68]

> When you increase the size [of the company], the important thing to do is when you see a new product opportunity, have a small team go after that opportunity. That's what we always did at Microsoft. We had small teams working on different areas.
>
> *Paul Allen*[69]

But, you might ask, don't you lose economies of scale when you keep breaking the company up into ever smaller chunks? Of course you do, replies Branson, "But . . . look at what you get! People who have worked for small companies and then big companies will tell you that it's not as much fun. In a small company, you can create a different type of energy. People feel cared for."[70] That's the next people lesson.

> The smaller you make your company, the better. The only advantage to large is muscle, but you lose motivation.
>
> *Richard Branson*[71]

PEOPLE LESSON #12: Praise People to Success

When is the last time you said to somebody at work, "You know, you're really terrific! I admire the fine job that you are doing," asks Mary Kay Ash.[72] Can't recall? Well, warn our gurus, you are violating a fundamental principal of people management. You can literally praise people to success. As Ash likes to say, people respond to praise like a thirsty plant to water.

Mary Kay Ash admits that, when she endorses praise as a valuable and universal people-management strategy, she often encounters skeptics. "Come on, now, Mary Kay," they say, "it may work for you to award ribbons, honor sales leaders on stage before large audiences, and name top achievers in your publications, but this kind of thing doesn't work with men." When she hears such remarks, she just smiles and asks, "Did you ever notice the stars on a six-foot-seven-inch, 275-pound linebacker's helmet? Or the medals on a soldier's uniform? Men are willing to risk bodily injury and even their lives for praise and recognition!"[73]

Other gurus add that the ways to making praise work are being sincere—don't say it unless you mean it—delivering the praise in public, and making the praise or reward fit the recipient. Ash relates the story of how she came to understand the importance of making praise public several years ago when she was attending a sales convention for a multibillion-dollar corporation.

> I noticed several of the salesmen wearing green sports jackets. I could tell the coats were brand-new because many of the men's sleeves were too long or too short, or their jackets simply needed some tailoring.
>
> "What are all these green jackets for?" I asked one of the company's vice presidents.

"This year's top salesmen received the jackets as a gift."

"When was the ceremony where the jackets were awarded?" I asked.

"Oh, there was no ceremony," he explained. "The jackets were just sent to their rooms."

That evening, at the convention's main banquet, I eagerly waited for the big moment when the company would recognize its top salesmen. Finally, at the end of the meal, hundreds of balloons fell from the ceiling, and I thought, "Oh, good opening. Now the awards are going to be presented." But much to my surprise, the evening ended there. Not a mention of achievement was made. No applause, no recognition, nothing!

As a guest, I couldn't say anything, but I thought, "This company missed a golden opportunity to proudly award the jackets to their star performers in the presence of their peers!" I was certain the salespeople would have valued the recognition much more than the actual green jackets.[74]

To make praise effective, you also need to make sure the praise or tangible reward you bestow fits the person being honored. Early in her career, Ash worked very hard to win a sales contest and was excited to discover that she had won. When her sales manager, an avid fisherman, presented her with her prize, she accepted it gracefully, although she later admitted that she had no idea what it was. Then someone explained it was a flounder light, which would come in handy the next time she tried to gig fish while wading into water wearing hip boots. Ash was proud of winning the sales contest but had to admit that a flounder light was somewhere near the bottom of her list of preferred prizes.[75]

PEOPLE LESSON #13: Share the Financial Rewards

A flounder light may not be right for everyone, but our gurus generally agree that one prize is on just about everyone's approved list—money. They have learned—many of them the hard way—that some form of bonus, profit-sharing, and/or stock-ownership plan is the best way to reward employees. Sam Walton, for example, admitted that in the early days of Wal-Mart he was far from generous when it came to sharing the financial rewards.

We didn't pay [our employees] much. It wasn't that I was intentionally heartless. I wanted everybody to do well for themselves. It's just that in my

very early days in the business, I was so doggoned competitive, and so determined to do well, that I was blinded to the most basic truth, really the
principle that later became the foundation of Wal-Mart's success. You see,
no matter how you slice it in the retail business, payroll is one of the most
important parts of overhead, and overhead is one of the most crucial things
you have to fight to maintain your profit margin. That was true then, and it's
still true today. Back then, though, I was so obsessed with turning in a profit
margin of 6 percent or higher that I ignored some of the basic needs of our
people, and I feel bad about it.

The larger truth that I failed to see turned out to be another of those
paradoxes like the discounters' principle of the less you charge, the more
you'll earn. And here it is: the more you share profits with your associates—whether it's in salaries or incentives or bonuses or stock discounts—the more profit will accrue to the company. Why? Because the
way management treats the associates is exactly how the associates will
then treat the customers.[76]

According to Walton, one of his biggest single regrets in his whole business career was that he didn't include his employees in the initial managers-
only profit-sharing plan that his company put in place in 1970. That is a mistake other gurus, such as Bill Gates, didn't make. Microsoft offers stock
purchases at a 15 percent discount and has long used stock options as a recruiting and retention tool. In the late 1980s, for example, the company offered options for up to three thousand shares of Microsoft stock to pro-
grammers who joined the company right out of college. Although the details
of stock purchase and options packages have changed over time, stock ownership by Microsoft employees has been called one of the most-important
employee benefits the company has ever offered. It's a benefit that has made
Microsoft a financially lucrative place to work. It is, notes Gates, one of the
key things that tie Microsoft employees together and create a common
bond.[77] It has also made many of Gates's employees millionaires.

PEOPLE LESSON # 14:
Firing People Is the Hardest Part of Managing

As we noted at the beginning of this chapter, Ben Cohen and Jerry Greenfield quickly learned that managing people is the hardest part of running a

business. A corollary to that lesson is that firing people is the hardest part of managing. No one likes to do it. In fact, Cohen and Greenfield grew to hate the task so much they invented a persona—the Monster—to do it for them. Whenever it became obvious that, due to overscooping or slow scooping, one of their college-student employees wasn't making the grade as an ice-cream server, they would begin saying to each other, "The Monster is hungry, the Monster must eat." That would be the cue for Cohen—who had accepted the job of firing people because his employment history gave him the most experience with the matter—to launch into his speech. "You're a wonderful person," he would say. "We really like hanging out with you. But you don't scoop fast enough. Therefore, you shouldn't take this personally, but you can't work here anymore."[78]

Although Cohen tried to be compassionate, the situation was always difficult. Some of the college students would even begin to cry. He would try to reassure them that all wasn't lost. "Look," he would say, "you're in college. You're looking to become a philosophy major. Scooping quickly is not a skill you need for what you're trying to do with your life."[79] Still, firing was never easy for Cohen, Greenfield, or the hapless students, and it won't be for you. Firing will be the meanest part of your job, but, say our gurus, it is part of your job and you must do it. Also, don't think you can avoid it by trying to change the person in question. It is unlikely that you can.

Robert Mondavi tells us that when he started out in business he operated on the assumption that he could change people. He was convinced that he could encourage them, ride them, inspire them, offer them incentives, and that eventually their performance would improve. For years, Mondavi says, he tried to do just that. On occasion he was even able to see some improvement in an errant employee's performance. Yet, he almost always found the effort frustrating. He finally came to accept a cold, hard truth: "You cannot change people. Influence them a little, yes. But truly change them, no—unless they themselves deeply want to change."[80] His advice? When you find yourself with a problem employee, work with him or her to see if they can improve. But if your initial efforts don't seem to work, face reality. Do what you have to do. As Cohen and Greenfield put it, let the Monster eat. And sometimes firing people is the kindest thing you can do even if the reason for their firing isn't their fault. Walt Disney said that he learned that lesson in the early 1940s.

The Disney brothers found themselves in financial trouble during the pre–World War II years. Their banker had proposed a 20 percent reduction in expenses, including laying off anyone who could be released without affecting work on films already in progress. Roy Disney agreed, citing lay-offs as preferable to their other options, such as selling their product out through a franchise or going through receivership or bankruptcy. Walt resisted, not wanting to fire anyone. Years later he recalled how personally difficult the eventual decision to cut their workforce was for him.

> My brother went through as much hell as I did. I became all confused. I didn't know where I was. I had a big staff. I hated to lay off anybody. I tried to hold on to 'em. I tried to think for different ways. The war was not here yet. But they were still drafting; some of my boys had to go. It was a terrible period.
>
> I just became so darned confused that I just didn't know what the heck I was doing. I should have had a big layoff. I should have practically closed the doors until I straightened the mess. But no, I tried to keep 'em. The boys should have had increases because of their time. I couldn't give 'em an increase; I was fighting like the devil even to pay 'em.[81]

Disney explained that the experience taught him a lesson. It's a lesson our other gurus say they have had to learn and one they recommend your heeding:

> You don't do a person good sometimes by keeping them. I learned a lot on that. I think the best thing is to face up to it. I always hated to fire anybody. I'd always think, "Well, gee, he's got five kids." I began to let that enter into it, and it's wrong. The best thing is to face up to it. Because sometimes I've seen some of those kids go out and be very successful outside. In other words, it could have been a favor.[82]
>
> The most difficult thing which I have had to do, and I think I have done well, but it was hard, was look at the people who have helped me build this company, get to half a billion, then billion and so on, and recognize that at some point along the way, they ran out of steam. They were terrific people, but they did not have the capacity to take me from a billion to $5 billion, from $5 billion to $10 billion. Recognizing that and dealing with it will be your greatest challenge.
>
> *Charles Lazarus*[83]

Of course, say our gurus, the best thing is to never have to have layoffs or fire anyone at all. How do you do that? Well, there is the advice in Chapter 1 on how to decide if you should start a business at all. And the advice in Chapter 2 about picking the right idea. And, of course, the ideas in Chapter 3 about. . . . Enough said. We think you get the idea.

KEY POINTS

- Managing people is the hardest part of running a business.

- Your employees are the spinal cord of your business. If they do not perform well, your business cannot succeed.

- Don't hire people for a specific job; hire them with the long term in mind.

- Hire smarts—people who have an open and questioning mind, who have a healthy balance of experience and intellect, and who aren't afraid to make a mistake in the process of innovation.

- Hire attitude—people whose personality matches the culture of your organization.

- It is not enough just to hire well. You must inspire those you hire. Even the production and sale of mundane products and services can be inspirational if you create a work environment in which people feel they are accomplishing something worthwhile for themselves and others.

- Hold people to high standards of performance. They will get more excited about doing something as well as it can be done than about doing something just adequately. If they work in an environment in which excellence is expected, they will do excellent work.

- Share as much information about company performance with employees as possible. The more an employee knows about the operations of the company, the better prepared he or she is to serve the company's and the customers' interests.

- Eliminate all signs and symbols of status such as executive limos, parking spaces, and dining rooms. Treat people as equals.

- Eliminate or significantly reduce the use of receptionists, secretaries, and personal assistants for managers and executives.

- ☞ Use parties, songs, cheers, and other social activities to generate a sense of team spirit.

- ☞ Manage by roaming around. Get out of your office and get to know your employees where they work. Listen and learn.

- ☞ Encourage employees to take the initiative and put their ideas into action. Provide them with as much authority as possible to do what they think needs to be done to satisfy customers.

- ☞ Trust people to make the right decisions and do the right thing.

- ☞ Stay small to grow big. Limit the size of your company or its individual subsidiaries to a few hundred people at most.

- ☞ Praise people to success. Be sincere with your praise, do it in public, and match the tangible rewards to the person being honored.

- ☞ Share the financial rewards of success. Use bonuses, profit sharing, and/or stock ownership to reward employees.

- ☞ Firing is the hardest part of managing, but it is part of your job, and you must do it when it is required. Don't assume you can change people if they do not want to change. You can't. Sometimes the kindest thing you can do is let someone go so they can find success elsewhere.

The Gurus

Paul Allen, cofounder of Microsoft Corporation, was born in Seattle, Washington, in 1954. He attended the same Seattle high school as Bill Gates and belonged to the same group of computer "geeks." Allen and Gates first collaborated on a computerized traffic-volume analysis system in 1971. Allen later told *Fortune,* "We were always interested in business. . . . We talked about being entrepreneurs. Obviously, it was on a smaller scale, because we were kids."[1]

In 1973 Gates left for Harvard, and Allen moved to Boston to work as a programmer for Honeywell. Two years later Gates dropped out of Harvard to join Allen to work together as "Micro-Soft." Allen recalls: "We both took part in every decision, and it's hard to remember who did what. If there was a difference between our roles, I was probably the one always pushing a little bit in terms of new technology and new products, and Bill was more interested in doing negotiations and contracts and business deals."[2]

As executive vice president of research and new development at Microsoft, Allen contributed to the development of such products as Microsoft Word, Windows, and the Microsoft mouse. He left Microsoft in 1983, at the age of 30, after being diagnosed with cancer, which was ultimately treated successfully. Following his recovery, Allen invested in a variety of businesses, including the investment research firm Vulcan Ventures, the Egghead retail software chain, the National Basketball Association Portland Trailblazers, the National Football League Seattle Seahawks, and an 80 percent stake in Ticketmaster. Vulcan Northwest is the umbrella organization that oversees all of his vast holdings. Allen retains his seat on Microsoft's board, and he remains the company's second-largest stockholder. In 1999 he was declared to be the second-richest American, second only to his old school pal and business partner Bill Gates.

J. Walter (Walt) Anderson, cofounder of White Castle, was born in 1880 on a farm outside St. Mary's, Kansas. He attended a small business college in Sedalia, Missouri, then transferred to Baker University for two years. While attending college, he supported himself working as a school janitor and lived in an abandoned house. He spent several years wandering through the Midwest, working odd jobs as a dishwasher or cook in restaurants.

In 1905 Anderson's father bought him his own restaurant in Marquette, Kansas. That lasted only one year, after which Anderson sold the restaurant and started a traveling stage show—another failure. He then returned to the kitchen, working as a cook for the Southern Pacific Railroad and for a series of local diners.

At a diner in Wichita, Kansas, Anderson experimented with grilling and serving ground meats in a variety of ways and with a variety of condiments. The most-popular item on the menu was a flattened meat patty that was smothered with onions, seared on both sides, and served on a bun. Legend has it that Anderson stumbled on to this idea while cooking a meatball that was sticking to the skillet. In a moment of exasperation, he supposedly smashed the meatball flat with a spatula. To Anderson's amazement, not only did the resulting patty cook faster, but his customers actually preferred it. Regardless of the accuracy of the legend, the modern hamburger was born.

Anderson borrowed $80 in 1916 to buy and partially refurbish an old shoe-repair stand, which he equipped with a counter and three stools, a flat piece of iron he used as a griddle, and a variety of cooking utensils. He hung a simple sign over the door that read "Hamburgers 5¢."

In 1921 Anderson met Edgar Waldo (Billy) Ingram, an insurance and real estate broker and former employee of Dun and Bradstreet. Ingram and Anderson forged a partnership by cosigning a lease for property held by a reluctant owner. Thus began a partnership that would change the nature of fast food in America. (See Billy Ingram's biography.)

Marc Andreessen, cofounder of Netscape Communications, was born in New Lisbon, Wisconsin, in 1971. He showed an early interest in computers, mastering the Basic programming language at the age of eight or nine. In the sixth grade, he used his school's personal computer to write his first program, designed to help him to do his math homework. Unfortunately, the janitor turned the power off at the end of the day, and the program was lost.

After graduating from high school, Andreessen enrolled at the University of Illinois at Urbana-Champaign to study computer science. During his stay there, he developed a fascination for the Internet but was unhappy with the cumbersome software that accessed this seeming wealth of information. He suggested to a colleague at the university's National Center for Supercomputing Applications (NCSA) that they develop an easy-to-use interface to the on-line material. In early 1993, the resulting NCSA Mosaic interface was released on the Internet, free of charge.

Shortly after the release of Mosaic, Andreessen earned his bachelor of arts degree and received a fateful e-mail message from James Clark: "You may not know me, but I'm the founder of Silicon Graphics. I've resigned and intend to form a new company. Would you be interested in getting together to talk?" A *Fortune* reporter noted, "For Clark, the partnership was a chance to start over; for Andreessen, twenty-three, it was a once-in-a-lifetime opportunity to form a company with a Silicon Valley legend."[3]

Clark invested $4 million in the new company, which was christened Mosaic Communications Corporation but was later changed, as part of a legal settlement with the University of Illinois, to Netscape Communications. In December 1994 Netscape released its browser, Navigator.

On August 9, 1995, Netscape made an initial public offering of 10 percent of the company's stock, amounting to 3.5 million shares at an opening price of $28 per share. Within minutes, the per-share price had grown to $74\frac{3}{4}$ but settled to $58\frac{1}{4}$ by the end of the day. Even with that decline, Netscape's market value was $2.3 billion.[4]

Mary Kay Ash, founder of Mary Kay Cosmetics, was born Mary Kathlyn Wagner, in 1918, in Hot Wells, Texas. Mary Kay had to assume responsibility for many household tasks and for the care of her invalid father at the age of seven because her mother had to work to support the family. She recalls this as a positive experience and remembers her mother's inspiring words: "Honey, you can do it" and "Anything anyone else can do, you can do better."

Ash's first experience with direct sales occurred in the late 1930s when she was made an offer by a door-to-door salesperson: If she could sell 10 sets of books, she would receive a free set. Ash sold all 10 sets in a day and a half. She continued in direct sales for the next 25 years, selling everything from expensive pots and pans to floor brushes and cleaning materials (for Stanley Home Products Company). In 1952 she joined the World Gift Company as the national training director, where she was repeatedly passed over for promotion. Finally in 1963, when yet another man she had trained was made her supervisor, she resigned.

In her third marriage—and with her three children grown—Ash didn't need the income from work. So, she decided to "retire" and write a career guide to help other women avoid some of the pitfalls she had encountered. Instead, she started her own company.

With her $5,000 in life savings, the support of her family, and the direct help of her son Richard and her husband, who, tragically, died just before her company's opening, Ash opened Beauty by Mary Kay on September 13, 1963. She and her nine consultants gave facials and demonstrated the company's cosmetics, primarily in people's homes. Within three-and-a-half months, sales totaled $34,000. In the first calendar year, wholesale revenues topped $198,000 and reached $800,000 in the second year. Her 9 consultants have become 475,000 in number, and her cosmetics are sold in 25 countries.

The success of Ash's company allowed her to achieve her goal of helping women succeed in the business world. Estimates are that more women have become millionaires from their Mary Kay careers than at any other company in the world. It has also allowed Ash to fund The Mary Kay Foundation, which gives large sums of money to support social-service programs and medical research and treatment facilities like the Mary Kay Ash Cancer Research Laboratory.

Among Ash's many honors are the Dale Carnegie Leadership Award and the Horatio Alger Distinguished American Citizen Award. Mary Kay Cosmetics was listed in both editions of *The 100 Best Companies to Work for in America* and was listed as one of the top 10 companies for which women can work.

James L. (Jim) Barksdale, investor and former president and CEO of Netscape Communications, was born in Jackson, Mississippi, in 1943. He was one of six sons of a well-to-do banker and a mother with high expectations for her children. The Barksdale parents handed out a weekly "Boy of the Week Award" for good deeds and were never fully satisfied with anything short of perfection.

Barksdale was president of his eighth-grade class and president of his fraternity at the University of Mississippi, from which he graduated with a degree in business in 1965. After graduation he took a sales job with IBM, then served as vice president of Cook Industries, Inc., from 1973 to 1979. He was senior vice president information systems and chief information officer at Federal Express Corporation (FedEx) from 1979 to 1983, when he was named chief operating officer. The quality program Barksdale established won FedEx the coveted Malcolm Baldrige National Quality Award.

In 1992 Barksdale became chief operating officer of McCaw Cellular, and in 1995 he became CEO of Netscape Communications. The sale of Netscape in March 1999 netted Barksdale $700 million, much of which he has invested either in up-and-coming Internet companies or in his native Mississippi. The Barksdales donated $5.4 million to the University of Mississippi in 1996 and have since increased their endowment to $130 million.

Phineas Taylor (P.T.) Barnum, was founder of The Greatest Show on Earth®, a best-selling author, politician, showman, investor, entrepreneur, and marketing genius. He was born on July 5, 1810, in Bethel, Connecticut. A bright student, excelling in mathematics, he showed a flair for salesmanship at an early age. He worked as a clerk in his father's country store, and at the age of 12 he sold lottery tickets.

When he was 25, Barnum bought Joice Heth, a black slave who claimed to be the 161-year-old nurse to George Washington. Barnum exhibited her in New York and New England, amassing about $1,500 per week for the show. In 1841 he bought Scudder's American Museum in New York City—a sort of Disneyworld of the nineteenth century—where he exhibited curiosities from every corner of the globe. The next year, he added "The Feejee Mermaid," supposedly an embalmed mermaid, and General Tom Thumb (Charles Stratton) to the exhibit.

In 1850 Barnum departed temporarily from his curiosity shows to sponsor the successful U.S. tour of European opera star Jenny Lind, "The Swedish Nightingale," but he returned to the world of curiosities with P.T. Barnum's Grand Traveling Museum, Menagerie, Caravan, and Circus. His traveling museum grossed $400,000 the first year of operation.

By 1872 Barnum was referring to his show as The Greatest Show on Earth. P.T. Barnum's Traveling World's Fair, Great Roman Hippodrome and Greatest Show on Earth seated 10,000 people in a five-acre area. In 1881 he joined forces with James A. Bailey and James L. Hutchinson, creating P.T. Barnum's Greatest Show on Earth, and The Great London Circus, Sanger's Royal British Menagerie and The Grand International Allied Shows United, soon to become known simply as the Barnum & London Circus. While Barnum and Bailey went their separate ways in 1885, they rejoined in 1888 to create the Barnum & Bailey Greatest Show on Earth.

Because of Barnum's vast fame in show business, people often overlook his many other accomplishments. Among other things, he started the first illustrated newspaper in New York City, and he became a famous public speaker, a best-selling author, a politician, and a successful investor. He also made a fortune in real estate. But he was always consumed by his shows. It was reported that, just before he died on April 7, 1891, his last words were about his show that was appearing at Madison Square Garden: "Ask Bailey what the box office was at the Garden last night."

Jeffrey P. Bezos, founder and CEO of Amazon.com, was born in New Mexico about 1964. He showed an early interest in computer science and finance and later studied electrical engineering and computer science at Princeton University. After earning a bachelor's degree, summa cum laude, in 1986, he worked briefly for a fiber-optics company. He then worked for Bankers Trust Company and for the investment-banking firm D.E. Shaw and Company, where he earned the reputation of being a computer whiz kid. By the age of 30, he became what is assumed to be the youngest senior vice president ever at Shaw.

In 1994 Bezos read a report that claimed that the World Wide Web was growing at a rate of 2,000 percent per year. He then compiled a list of some twenty products he thought might sell well on the Internet. The overwhelming product of choice was books for several reasons, including (1) the large number of titles in existence and (2) the ability of potential purchasers to "sample" the product electronically. After settling on his product, Bezos quit his Wall Street job and, along with his wife, headed for Seattle.

The decision to start Amazon.com—named after the world's second-largest river—in Seattle was based on the availability of skilled technology professionals and on the presence of the large book wholesaler, Ingram. In July, 1994, Bezos and his four newly hired employees set up shop in the Bezos's garage and sold their first book.

With an investment of $8 million to $10 million by the venture-capital firm Kleiner Perkins Caufield & Byers, Amazon.com became the most-successful retailer on the Internet in only four years. It also became the third-largest bookseller in the country, behind Barnes & Noble and Borders. The value of the company's stock at the time of its initial public offering, May 14, 1997, was $18 per share. One year later it had reached almost $100 per share and has since ridden the tide of Internet stocks upward. Net sales in 1998 were $610 million, and the company claimed to offer 16 million items for sale to its 8.4 million customer base.

Despite this phenomenal growth, however, Amazon.com has yet to show a profit. From the beginning, Bezos emphasized establishing brand-name recognition before profits. He has chosen to use the company's revenues for advertising and for product expansion, adding a virtual "drugstore," toys, videos, greeting cards, and music to his product mix.

Arthur Blank, cofounder of Home Depot, was born in the early 1940s in Flushing, New York. He graduated from Babson College in 1963 with a bachelor of science, with distinction, in business administration, after which he took a position in New York with the accounting firm Arthur Young & Company. In 1967 he became controller of his family's business, Sherry Pharmaceutical, which was bought in 1970 by Daylin Corporation. While at Daylin, Blank served as controller of a discount drugstore chain, a subsidiary called Elliott's Drugs, and two years later was made president and chief operating officer. Then in 1974 he became controller of Daylin's largest subsidiary, Handy Dan, where he met future business partner Bernie Marcus.

For more information about the evolution of Home Depot, see the biography of Bernie Marcus.

Richard Branson, founder of the Virgin Group, which includes Virgin Atlantic Airways, Virgin Records, Virgin Megastores, Virgin Cola, and numerous other Virgin companies, was born in 1950 in a suburb of London. Of his parents, Branson says, "My parents brought me up with this philosophy: You must *do* things—you mustn't watch what other people are doing; you mustn't listen to what other people are doing."[5]

Branson's first entrepreneurial experience as a child was growing Christmas trees. At the age of 15, he began an "alternative-culture" magazine, *Student,* but he quickly gave up his editorial responsibilities to take over the day-to-day operation of the magazine. Branson tenaciously turned *Student* into a huge albeit brief success. From the corner telephone that he used as an office, he sold tens of thousands of dollars in advertising space for the magazine. He also persuaded writers like Jean-Paul Sartre, Alice Walker, and John Le Carré to contribute articles, and he orchestrated interviews with celebrities like actress Vanessa Redgrave and novelist and essayist James Baldwin. The first issue of *Student* reportedly sold 50,000 copies. Branson dropped out of his exclusive English boarding school, Stowe, at the age of 16 to commit himself full-time to the magazine.

When *Student* began to lose money in the late 1960s, Branson came up with a scheme to raise capital selling discount records by mail. Virgin Records, born in 1970, experienced explosive growth in the recording business, largely by taking chances on unknown artists. The label eventually signed such names as Boy George, the Culture Club, Human League, and Phil Collins. But Branson's biggest challenge lay ahead.

In 1984 Branson was approached about financing a new airline that would provide all-business-class service between London and New York. He ignored his advisers and reasoned that the airline business was closer in spirit to the entertainment industry than one might think: "Obviously you've got to make sure you've got somebody running it who can safely get your airplane from A to B, but once you've sorted that out, the airline business has everything to with entertainment."[6]

Virgin Atlantic Airways started with one leased Boeing 747 that flew round-trip daily between Gatwick Airport, south of London, and Newark International Airport in New Jersey. The airline's lack of advertising budget pressed Branson into the position of unofficial spokesman. Branson staged outrageous stunts to get media coverage and to distinguish his airline from his stodgy competitors. For instance, in 1985 he attempted to break the transatlantic speed record for powerboats, following this with his 1987 crossing of the Atlantic in a hot-air balloon and his 1991 attempt to cross the Pacific in a 196-foot-tall balloon.

Despite bitter battles with rival British Airways, Virgin has expanded routes to Singapore, Hong Kong, Sydney, and Los Angeles. The retail division has expanded the presence of the Virgin Megastore, and Branson has started innumerable other companies. His vast wealth has funded the Help Advisory Center, which provides counseling on birth control and sexually transmitted diseases, and the Healthcare Foundation, which concentrates on AIDS education.

Charles M. Brewer, founder of MindSpring Enterprises, was born in Louisville, Kentucky, about 1960. He received a bachelor's degree in economics from Amherst College, graduating Phi Beta Kappa. From November 1981 until October 1984, he was employed by the investment banking firm of Wertheim & Company, after which he returned to college to pursue a masters in business administration (MBA) from Stanford University. After graduating from Stanford in 1987, Brewer became a vice president of Sanders & Company, a venture capital firm. In 1989 he became the chief financial officer of Atlanta-based AudioFax, Inc., a fax server software provider, and subsequently served as that company's CEO from May 1989 until April 1992. When he became disillusioned with what he considered an unfulfilling job, he resigned.

While contemplating what to do next with his life, Brewer decided to join a growing number of Internet surfers. He spent the next three months simply attempting to log on. "Once I got on," says Brewer, "it was great. It was the setup that was absurd—the lack of help, the busy signals, the poor quality of the network. It was obvious that it didn't need to be that way."[7] In the spring of 1994, with $150,000 of his own money and the assistance of one software developer, Brewer founded MindSpring Enterprises.

MindSpring's first customers were actually beta testers who received the service free of charge. By the end of the summer, the company had a few hundred paying customers and a growing reputation for quality service and support. An influx of capital from ITC Holding allowed Brewer to expand the network and continue to hire development and support staff. The company went public in March 1996 and subsequently grew to more than a half million customers, 750 employees, and revenues in excess of $100 million before its 1999 merger with former rival EarthLink.

Warren Edward Buffett, chairman of Berkshire Hathaway, Inc., was born in Omaha, Nebraska, in 1930. His father, Howard Homan Buffett, was a stockbroker and fiscally conservative four-term representative to the U.S. House of Representatives. While growing up in Washington DC, young Buffett delivered papers for the *Washington Post,* gathered lost golf balls from a golf course and sold them, and even, at the age of 11, dabbled in the stock market. In high school, he and another student started a pinball-machine business that grossed $50 dollars a week. Before graduating he accumulated enough money to buy a 40-acre farm in Nebraska.

Buffett attended the University of Pennsylvania from 1947 to 1949 and graduated with a bachelor's degree from the University of Nebraska in 1950. During his studies, he read the works of Benjamin Graham, a proponent of the value approach to portfolio management—as opposed to the traditional growth approach. Buffett decided to do his graduate work with Graham at Columbia University and received his MBA in 1951. Buffett paraphrases a lesson he learned from Graham: "You're not right or wrong because 1,000 people agree with you or disagree with you. You're right because your facts and your reasoning are right."[8]

Buffett returned to Omaha to work as a salesman in his father's investment company from 1951 to 1954, and he worked in New York as a security analyst for Graham from 1954 to 1956. By the age of 25, Buffett had accumulated $5,000 of his own money and $100,000 from relatives and friends to establish the highly successful Buffett Partnership investment fund.

Donald Keough, who later became president of Coca-Cola, was a young executive in Omaha at the time. In a 1985 interview with *New York,* Keough relates the following story: "I had five small kids and left for work each day. Buffett had three and stayed home. He had a marvelous hobby, model trains, and my kids used to troop over there and play with them. One day, Warren popped over and asked if I'd thought about how I was going to educate these kids. . . . I told him I planned to work hard and see what happened. Warren said that if I gave him $5,000 to invest, he'd probably be able to do better [for me]. My wife and I talked it over, but we figured we didn't know what this guy even did for a living—how could we give him $5,000? We've been kicking ourselves ever since. I mean, if we had given him the dough, we could have *owned* a college by now."[9]

While Buffett Partnership invested in many high-profile companies like American Express, it also invested in companies like Berkshire Hathaway, a troubled textile manufacturer in New Bedford, Massachusetts. After dissolving the partnership in 1969, Buffett began to build Berkshire Hathaway into a diversified conglomerate of insurance companies, department stores, banks, and so on. Even when the textile company became less and less profitable, Buffett kept it going for the sake of the employees he thought were too old to retrain. He did not close the textile operation until 1985.

In the 1970s, Buffett began investing in media and advertising. He bought into a number of newspapers like the Omaha *Sun,* the *Washington Post,* Affiliated Publications (which owns the *Boston Globe*), and Time, Inc. He also bought into General Foods Corporation (1983), purchased See's Candy Shops, and became involved in the Capital Cities Communications' takeover of the American Broadcasting Companies (ABC). These and many other highly successful investments contributed to Buffett's being declared the third-richest person in America in 1999 with $31 billion in assets, following only Bill Gates with $85 billion and Paul Allen with $40 billion.

Washington Atlee Burpee, founder of Burpee Seed Company, was born in Philadelphia, Pennsylvania, in 1858. His boyhood hobby was breeding poultry—chickens, geese, turkeys, pigeons—and by the time he entered high school, he was contributing articles to poultry trade journals. One story recounts the following:

In 1872 an English poultry fancier traveled to Philadelphia to meet a fellow breeder-exhibitor with whom he had been corresponding for several years. The two knew each other only through letters, and the Briton was eager for the opportunity to sit down over some brandy with his learned friend and exchange ideas on the care and mating of high-class fowl. When he arrived at the train station, however, there was no one to greet him but an ungainly fourteen-year-old boy. "Would you happen to be the son of W. Atlee Burpee, the poultry authority?" asked the fancier. "No sir, I am the son of Dr. David Burpee. *I* am W. Atlee Burpee, the poultryman," came the startling reply.[10]

At the age of 17, Burpee started a mail-order business selling purebred fowl and two instructional manuals. His parents were not impressed by his entrepreneurial venture and insisted that he enroll in medical school. He entered the University of Pennsylvania in 1875 but made it only one year. He dropped out when a wealthy investor offered him $5,000 to start a purebred poultry and livestock business. The partnership was a rocky one, and Burpee finally convinced his father to lend him the money to start his own business.

W. Atlee Burpee & Company was established in 1878 as a mail-order house for purebred livestock and fowl. Burpee, who continued to provide his customers with instructional material, also offered several varieties of seed in his catalog. As it turned out, most of the orders he received were for his seeds and not for his livestock, so Burpee became a seed salesman who also offered poultry.

Burpee traveled the world in search of new and better varieties of fruits, vegetables, and flowers. Among the most widely known produce introduced through the Burpee catalog are iceberg lettuce (introduced in 1894) and the bush lima bean (introduced in 1907).

Burpee turned over the company to his son David in 1915 and died two years later.

Thomas Matthew (Tom) Chappell, cofounder of Tom's of Maine, Inc., was born in 1943 in Pittsfield, Massachusetts, the son of a textiles entrepreneur. He graduated from the Moses Brown School, a Quaker high school in Providence, Rhode Island, then attended Trinity College in Hartford, Connecticut. He received his bachelor of arts degree in English in 1966 and spent the next two years selling insurance. Of this experience he later said, "I grew up in a family where venturing was normal, and I needed a more creative environment than a large corporation has to offer."[11]

In 1968 Chappell and his wife and cofounder, Kate Cheney Chappell, moved to Kennebunk, Maine, in search of a community that shared their concerns for the environment. Two years later, with a $5,000 loan from a friend, the couple opened the Kennebunk Chemical Center, predecessor to Tom's of Maine, in the town's former Boston and Maine railroad station. Their first product was a nonpolluting tar remover and cleaner for dairy equipment, which sold poorly, as did their second product—a phosphate-free laundry detergent that failed to clean effectively. In 1972 the Chappells decided to try their hands at personal-care products.

Tom, Kate, and their friends were concerned about products that contained artificial colors and preservatives, chemicals, and animal-based ingredients. They were also frustrated in their search for alternatives, so the idea of producing such a line of products seemed logical. Over the next several years they developed and successfully marketed products like Coco Orange Soap, Pure Skin Lotion, Apple Shampoo, a nonalcoholic mouthwash, an all-natural baby shampoo, and the market's first natural toothpaste.

By 1981 Tom's of Maine dominated the all-natural, personal-care products market, with more than $1.5 million in sales of more than forty products, but their competition was growing. In an effort to ward off their competitors, Chappell raised $75,000 in equity capital, wrote a new business plan, created a board of directors, and hired marketing professionals. He wanted Tom's of Maine to compete as the natural alternative to products like Crest and Colgate. His strategy appears to have worked because the company's annual sales climbed to $5 million by the mid-1980s. Unfortunately, while Tom's of Maine prospered, Tom Chappell became more and more unhappy with himself. He had founded the company to create effective, health-oriented products in a pleasant workplace without harming the environment, but he found himself chasing the bottom line and losing sight of his goals.

In 1987 Chappell did something to change his situation—he reduced his involvement in the company and enrolled in Harvard Divinity School. His studies there reinforced many of his original ideas and had a significant impact on the way Chappell ran his company. Employees were encouraged to donate paid time as volunteers in charitable activities. The company committed 10 percent of its pretax earnings each year to nonprofit groups and made substantial donations to environmental and other organizations. It also redoubled its efforts to reduce the amount of packaging it used and to use recycled or recyclable materials. Because of his efforts, Chappell and his company have received a number of awards and honors including Entrepreneur of the Year by CNBC Television, Corporate Conscience Award for Charitable Contributors by the Council on Economic Priorities, being named among the "thirty great companies for dads" by *Child* magazine (June–July 1992), and among the "one hundred best companies for working mothers" by *Working Mother* magazine every year, starting in 1993. Chappell received his master's degree in theology in 1991 and continues to influence the direction of his company.

James (Jim) Clark, founder of Silicon Graphics (1982) and cofounder of Netscape Communications, was born in 1944 in Plainview, Texas. He was suspended from high school "for antics such as sneaking in whiskey on a band trip"[12] but eventually earned a master's degree in physics from Louisiana State University (1971) and a doctorate in computer science from the University of Utah (1974).

Clark taught both at the University of California at Santa Cruz and at Stanford University. While at Stanford he worked with a group of graduate students to develop microchips that enhanced computer images. In 1982 he started the firm Silicon Graphics, Inc., along with his graduate students. The company manufactured computer workstations that appealed primarily to engineers and architects, but they soon caught on with filmmakers and animators. Industrial Light & Magic used Silicon Graphics computers to create the dinosaurs in the movie *Jurassic Park.*

In 1994 Clark resigned over a disagreement about the direction the company should take in the future. Although a wealthy man, he immediately started looking for a new challenge. That challenge turned out to be the Internet.

Clark e-mailed a recent graduate of the University of Illinois who had worked on the hottest new software on the Internet—Mosaic. He offered Marc Andreessen an opportunity to join him in a new venture. Their resulting partnership became Netscape Communication. (See Marc Andreessen's biography for information about the evolution of Netscape.)

Bennett (Ben) Cohen, cofounder of Ben & Jerry's Ice Cream, was born in Brooklyn, New York, in 1951. He attended public school in Merrick, Long Island, where, in a junior high school gym class, he met his future business partner, Jerry Greenfield. According to Greenfield, "We were the two slowest, chubbiest guys in the seventh grade. . . . We were nerds."[13] And so the friendship began.

During his senior year in high school, Cohen had a part-time job driving an ice-cream van and selling ice cream to neighborhood children. Following high school, he attended Colgate University for a year and a half, then returned to work as an ice-cream vendor. He later enrolled at Skidmore College and worked at a variety of part-time jobs, including cashier at a McDonald's, guard at a racetrack, night janitor, and assistant superintendent of an apartment complex.

In 1977 Cohen hooked up again with his old friend Jerry Greenfield. They decided to try their hand at the food business, and according to Greenfield, "We wanted to do something that would be . . . fun."[14] After dismissing the idea of making and selling bagels, they agreed on ice cream as their product. Of course, neither knew how to make ice cream, so they both signed up for a five-dollar correspondence course in ice-cream making from Pennsylvania State University. They later claimed to have received a perfect score on their final exams—which happen to have been open book.

Early in their partnership, the pair agreed that they wanted to locate their business in a small, rural college town, so they moved to Burlington, Vermont. On May 5, 1978, with an investment of $12,000 (one-third of which was borrowed), they opened the first Ben & Jerry's Homemade Ice Cream Shop in a renovated gas station.

Cohen and Greenfield were as committed to social issues as they were to their business. In fact, "when Jerry and I realized we were no longer ice-cream men but businessmen, our first reaction was to sell," says Cohen. "We were afraid that business exploits its workers and the community. We listed the company with a broker and actually had a buyer. We ended up keeping it, but we decided to adapt it so we could feel proud to say we were the businessmen of Ben & Jerry's."[15]

Contrary to their wishes, however, the company's rapid expansion meant bringing in senior executives who did not fully agree with their approach to the bottom line. In June 1994 Ben Cohen announced that he was giving up his position as CEO. Today, Jerry Greenfield is the chairperson of the board and Ben Cohen is vice chairperson of the company.

Finis Conner, cofounder Shugart Associates (purchased by Xerox in 1978), cofounder Shugart Technology (later renamed Seagate Technology), and founder Conner Peripherals, was born in rural Alabama in 1943. He grew up in various locations in Alabama, Texas, and Florida and later admitted that his high school education consisted mainly of "going to the beach almost every day."[16] In 1961 he headed for California with $100 in his pocket, half of which he lost in a poker game before arriving. Conner explained, "I was just a naive country boy."[17]

That same naive country boy enrolled in San Jose State University's industrial management program and took a job as a clerk/typist for IBM to support himself. It was during his time at IBM that Conner had his first entrepreneurial experience with a small company that designed circuit boards. Conner later took his experience and his degree to Stewart Warner Microcircuits and eventually to the Memorex Corporation, where he met his future and long-time business partner Alan Shugart.

When Memorex refused to fund their idea for developing and marketing floppy disk drives, Conner and Shugart formed Shugart and Associates. The company was so successful that Xerox Corporation bought it in 1978. Although he stayed with the company until 1979, Conner needed a new challenge. While working at International Memories, Inc., Conner found his next product—the hard disk drive. He contacted his old friend and partner, Alan Shugart, and the two founded Shugart Technology, Inc., later renamed Seagate Technology, Inc. By 1984 Seagate was the leading manufacturer of 5.25-inch hard disk drives, but Conner was getting restless. He felt that Seagate had lost its innovative edge, and he resigned.

After a year of spending time with his family, playing golf, and sailing his yacht, Conner, 42, decided he was not ready to retire. He founded Conner Peripherals in 1985 and went in search of a product to sell. That product was the 3.5-inch hard disk drive. The next year he met an old business acquaintance, Rod Canion (cofounder of Compaq Computers, Inc.), at the Comdex trade show and came away with $12 million with which to develop and market his product. Conner Peripherals' revenues soared to $113 million in 1987, $256 million in 1988, and $700 million in 1989, becoming the undisputed leader in the hard disk drive industry. On February 5, 1996, Seagate Technology and Conner Peripherals merged under the name Seagate Technology, Inc., forming the single-largest company in the storage industry.

Joshua Lionel Cowen (originally Cohen), cofounder of Lionel Manufacturing Company, was born in 1877 in New York to Eastern European Jewish parents who immigrated to the United States in the mid-1860s. Cowen's father became a prosperous hatmaker and expected his son to excel in school and in a profession. His parents enrolled him in the Peter Cooper Institute, but Cowen was bored with all of his classes except technical shop class.

Cowen was always a tinkerer and was attracted to gadgets. He even developed an early electric door bell while at Peter Cooper. He also invented an "electric flowerpot," which illuminated a plant inside, and sold the invention to Conrad Hubert. (When Hubert failed to sell the gadget, he decided to detach its tubes and sell them for their illuminatory value. He renamed his product the Eveready Flashlight and became a multimillionaire.)

Cowen enrolled for a short time both at the City College of New York and at Columbia University, but he dropped out to take an apprentice position assembling battery lamps. He received the first of his many patents for a device that ignited a photographer's flash—the Flash Lamp—in 1899, and in the same year he received $12,000 from the U.S. Navy for a mine detonator he had developed. With that money, he and his friend Harry C. Grant cofounded the Lionel Manufacturing Company on September 5, 1900.

The partners initially attempted to sell a portable electric fan, but Cowen came up with another idea based on a childhood fascination. He wanted to develop an electric train that merchants could use in their display windows to attract attention. The train would pull merchandise around a circular strip of track. A Manhattan toy-store owner bought the first of Cowen's trains and returned the next day with an order for six more, explaining that customers wanted to buy the display out of his window.

In 1902 Lionel issued its first catalog featuring two electrically powered rail cars, a metal suspension bridge, and various track configurations. By the 1950s, Lionel's became the third most popular catalog in the country, surpassed only by Sears and Montgomery Ward in distribution. Although hit hard by the depression, the company survived to introduce a new streamlined train and another with a realistic whistle in 1935. They later introduced their biggest seller, a handcar with Mickey Mouse and Minnie Mouse, and following World War II they introduced their all-time bestseller, the Santa Fe diesel. By 1952—the company's 50th anniversary—it was producing 622,209 engines and 2,460,760 cars. But this popularity wasn't to last.

By 1958 railroads had been replaced by airplanes, and the toy-railroad industry suffered the consequences. The next year a disillusioned Cowen sold his 55,000 shares of Lionel stock to his great-nephew Roy Cohn and retired to Palm Springs, Florida. When Cowen died in 1965, his headstone read simply "Joshua L. Cohen," with no mention of his legacy to the history of toys.

Cecil B. Day, cofounder of Days Inns of America, Inc., the son of a Baptist minister, was born in a small town near Savannah, Georgia. His cofounder of Days Inn, Richard Kessler, and Kessler's family lived in the same small community. Kessler joined Day in 1970, just as Days Inns of America, Inc., began.

Cecil Day had seen an opportunity to grab a significant portion of the hotel/motel market by offering accommodations that looked like Holiday Inn but that cost 30 percent less. He sold an apartment building in Atlanta to get the $350,000 he needed to finance the venture. Days Inns offered no meeting rooms, no lavish lobbies, and no bars, and they all looked the same. Day targeted retired people, families, and business and government travelers who traveled on small expense accounts.

After the first Days Inn opened in Savannah, Day sent Kessler to Florida to identify a second location. Kessler's trip occurred during the exciting early days of Disney World, and he returned to Atlanta convinced that Orlando was the perfect location for Days Inn's next site. Day sent Kessler back to Orlando with an agreement to give him 30 percent equity in each motel he built.

Kessler concentrated on the East Coast while Day started opening motels in Texas, but the recession of 1974 endangered the fledgling company. Days Inns had $20 million in assets, $19 million in debts, and only $100,000 in cash. In response, Day and Kessler put up all of their motels as collateral and personally guaranteed loans to buy $18 million worth of motels, including two Holiday Inns and a Sheraton, doubling Days Inns' assets. The chain became one of the most profitable of its type in the country, with a pretax margin per site 50 percent greater than for Holiday Inns and Sheratons.

Michael Dell, founder of Dell Computer Corporation (established as PCs Ltd. in 1984), was born in 1965 in Houston, Texas. Dell told *Fortune* magazine, "I always knew I wanted to run a business someday."[18] "When I was in second grade I was selling candy at school. My teacher told me then I was going to be an entrepreneur."[19] At the age of 12, he worked as a dishwasher at a Chinese restaurant and earned enough money to start a stamp collection. He later sold that collection by mail order, making a $2,000 profit. By the age of 16, he had saved enough to buy his first computer, which he used to support his next entrepreneurial venture—selling newspaper subscriptions. He bought his first BMW with the $17,000 he made.

In 1983 Dell entered the University of Texas in Austin where, to please his parents, he enrolled in premed courses. His real interest, however, was in selling computers, so he set up shop in his dorm room and sold them door-to-door and through the mail. When his parents came to visit, he would hide the computers in his roommate's bathtub so they wouldn't find out what he was doing. When they discovered his sideline business, they insisted he quit, but when he sold $180,000 worth of PCs during the next summer's break, there was no stopping Michael Dell. He set up PCs Ltd. (later to be renamed Dell Computer Corporation) in Austin and by the end of 1984 had sales of $6 million. Sales skyrocketed to $34 million in 1985, $546 million in 1990, and $2 billion in 1992, at which time Dell became the youngest CEO to make the Fortune 500.

Dell is now a multibillionaire and the richest man in Texas. He could retire comfortably but chooses to stay actively involved in his company. "I don't really think of it as working," he says.[20]

Anthony Desio, cofounder of Mail Boxes Etc., was born in 1930. He grew up in the Bronx section of New York City and worked his way through the University of Connecticut, graduating in 1958 with a degree in electrical engineering. For the next 25 years, he had a successful engineering management career with Lockheed, Western Union, and General Electric, and he served two years as a member of a presidential executive exchange program. It was only when he reached the age of 50 that he acted upon his entrepreneurial impulses.

Approaching retirement, Desio decided to "do something for myself before it was too late. . . . I had often considered starting a business of my own, but I was always too busy to do it," Desio says. "As I approached my 50th birthday, I figured that I had better do it then, or I wasn't going to do it at all."[21] His search for a business opportunity ended with the identification of a major irritant to busy Americans—the U.S. Postal Service: "I saw that companies like Federal Express and DHL had become successful by offering alternatives to the post office, and I thought the same alternatives could work for retail postal services."[22]

Desio and four partners each invested $100,000 to open a store they called "U.S. Mailboxes" in 1979. They provided many of the same services available at the post office—rented post-office boxes, shipping packages, and stamps—but they also offered 24-hour access to the boxes, suite-number addresses for customers, and a call-in service to check on mail or packages. They soon expanded these services to include printing, copying, messaging, telegrams, and faxes. "The public liked the idea from the beginning,"[23] says Desio.

With their business booming, the partners started looking for venture capital that would allow them to expand, but banks and venture capitalists weren't interested. So the partners decided to go public in order to raise the money they needed. In November 1980, the first Mail Boxes Etc. franchise opened in Solana Beach, California, followed by three stores in the San Diego area.

In 1983 Desio and one partner bought out the remaining partners. Desio describes the buyout as "one of the scariest decisions I've ever made. By 1983, we had about 100 units but we were still just breaking even. There were months we took little or no salary and some of the partners got discouraged and wanted out."[24] To raise the money he needed for the buyout, Desio collateralized everything he owned—even his wife's jewelry.

The company's 1984 profits on sales reached $1.1 million, and in 1985 revenues hit $2.2 million. A 1986 public offering raised $5.1 million and increased the company's assets to $10.25 million. Both revenues and the number of locations continued to grow steadily until, in 1997 when Desio sold out, retail sales hit $1 billion at some 3,500 stores in more than fifty countries.

Desio was named Entrepreneur of the Year first by *Inc.* (1989) and then by the International Franchise Association (1996). He started a company called Memories on Canvas, which was acquired in June 1998 by IDTec. He was made chairman of IDTec's Advisory Committee and subsequently CEO and chairman of the board.

Roy Oliver Disney, cofounder of Disney Brothers Studio (later Walt Disney Productions, Ltd.), was born in Chicago in 1893, the third son of Flora and Elias Disney. When he was 12 years old, his family moved to a small farm in Missouri where Roy and his younger brother, Walt, enjoyed the pleasures and rigors of farm life. It was during this period that the two brothers formed the bond that would only strengthen with time.

Older brothers Herb and Ray "escaped" the farm when Roy was 16, leaving him with the responsibility of its maintenance. Elias, who had been ill for some time, and Flora decided that it was more responsibility than the boy could handle if he was to continue his education, so the family regretfully put their farm up for auction and relocated to Kansas City.

Roy enrolled at the Manual Training High School, at which he excelled in academics and athletics and participated in after-school activities, including acting with the school's drama group. Elias had purchased a distribution list for the *Kansas City Star,* and Roy delivered papers for an allowance of $3 per week.

Like many of his contemporaries, Roy enlisted in the navy during World War I. His service included three hazardous Atlantic crossings on the USS *Adonis* and the USS *Houston* and ended with his discharge in February 1919. He returned to Kansas City only long enough to learn that he had contracted tuberculosis—probably while in service—and that he was being assigned to a hospital in Santa Fe, New Mexico, for treatment. Unhappy with Santa Fe's weather and the austerity of the hospital, he transferred himself, without permission, to a hospital in Tucson, Arizona. After suffering Tucson's heat and desolation, Roy decided that he was well enough to leave the hospital and headed for California.

The post–World War I years were difficult ones for returning servicemen, and Roy had to take a job selling vacuum cleaners door-to-door to survive. After experiencing angry housewives and slamming doors, Roy decided to give up his new-found career. As he recalled, "One day I got fed up. I left the sample vacuum cleaner on the curb and caught a bus home. I called the company and told them where their vacuum was. When they went to get it, it was still there."[25]

To make matters worse, Roy suffered a relapse of his tuberculosis and had to enter the veterans' hospital at Sawtelle, near Los Angeles. Roy remembered:

That was when Walt came to Hollywood. . . . I was in the hospital at Sawtelle. By correspondence he sold somebody in New York on a series of pictures. One night he found his way to my bed, which was on a row of beds on a screened porch. It was eleven or twelve o'clock at night, and he shaked me awake and showed me a telegram of acceptance of his offers. He said, 'What can I do now? Can you come out of here and help me to get this started?' So I left the hospital the next day, and I've never been back since.[26]

Walter Elias (Walt) Disney, cofounder of Disney Brothers Studio (later Walt Disney Productions, Ltd.), was born in 1901 in Chicago. Shortly after his birth, his family moved to a farm near Marceline, Missouri. It was there that Walt developed a love for animals and began drawing.

His first job as a commercial artist was probably doing weekly sketches for a barber, in exchange for which Disney received either 25 cents or a haircut. The family returned to Chicago, where Walt attended McKinley High School and studied at the Chicago Academy of Fine Arts.

Disney left high school in 1918 to enlist as a Red Cross ambulance driver in World War I. Following the war, he continued to study and to work in commercial art, and in 1923 he set out for Hollywood with $40 and sketches for an experimental film—*Alice in Cartoonland,* which combined a live girl with animated cartoon figures.

Disney and his bother Roy combined their savings of $290 and a $500 loan from an uncle to form Disney Brothers Studio—eventually to become Walt Disney Productions, Ltd. Some highlights of the next few years include the following:

- 1928: Launch of *Mickey Mouse* series.
- 1933: Release of *Three Little Pigs,* which popularized the song "Who's Afraid of the Big Bad Wolf."
- 1937: *Snow White and the Seven Dwarfs*, the first feature-length cartoon work ever filmed.
- 1940: *Fantasia* introduced visual interpretation of orchestral music.
- 1942: Release of *Bambi.*
- 1947: Release of *Song of the South.*
- 1950: Release of *Cinderella.*
- 1954: Disney enters television with the one-hour show, *Davy Crockett.*
- 1955: Disneyland opens.

Disney died from lung cancer on December 15, 1967.

Charles Ferguson, cofounder of Vermeer Technologies, Inc., received a bachelor of arts degree in mathematics from the University of California, Berkeley, in 1978. In May 1994 he joined forces with Randy Forgaard to found Vermeer Technologies, Inc., in Cambridge, Massachusetts. The pair developed FrontPage, an HTML editor and Web-page builder that would soon revolutionize Web publishing for the average computer user. The menu-driven Web authoring tool and server received raved reviews and was soon snapped up by Microsoft for the tidy price of $130 million in stock.

Debbi Fields, founder of Mrs. Fields Cookies, Inc., was born in 1956 in East Oakland, California, where she grew up as the youngest of five sisters. She learned to bake cookies at an early age and enjoyed sharing them with friends and relatives.

At the age of 13, Debbi earned her first paycheck as a ball girl for the Oakland A's baseball team, a job that she maintains prepared her to deal comfortably with large crowds. At 15 she worked part time for Mervyn's department store, where she learned the value of making the customer happy.

Soon after graduating from high school, Debbi met and married Randy Fields. Once again, she baked warm cookies—this time for Randy and his friends—but she wanted to make more of her life. She wanted to sell those warm cookies.

Despite overwhelming advice to the contrary, Fields borrowed $50,000 from her husband and opened Mrs. Fields' Chocolate Chippery in a re-vamped arcade of specialty shops in Palo Alto, California, in 1977. Customer reception was so bad she had to take her first batches of cookies out into the street and give them away. But that's all it took. People were hooked on the large, warm, high-quality cookie that was served over a napkin by smiling, friendly people.

By 1981 there were 14 Mrs. Fields Cookies stores, followed by a flurry of new store openings. But, the growth took its toll. In 1988 the company was forced to close 97 stores and posted a $19 million net loss for the year. After refocusing its strategy, the company posted a profit the next year and opened 35 stores in 1990.

Today there are more than 650 Mrs. Fields locations in the United States and over 65 international locations in 11 different countries.

William Henry (Bill) Gates, III, cofounder of Microsoft, Inc., was born in 1955 in Seattle, Washington. As a youth, he was nicknamed "Trey" because of the III following his name. Gates became engrossed with computers at a very young age—as young as 12. He and a group of students, which included future partner Paul Allen, started the Lakeside (School) Programming Group. They soon started cutting classes and hanging out at the school's computer center. They even raided the garbage cans of nearby CCC (Computer Center Corporation) in search of information on the latest technology. Gates relates, "Paul [Allen] would hoist me up on the garbage cans and I'd get the notes out with the coffee grounds on them and study the operating system."[27]

At the age of 14, Gates joined Allen once again in a venture—this time to develop a traffic-counting system. Gates was made president of Traf-O-Data, which had earned $20,000 before its customers learned that the company's employees were still in high school. At that point, Traf-O-Data's business declined. Gates graduated from high school in 1973 and enrolled at Harvard University as a prelaw major.

In 1975 Paul Allen read an article in *Popular Electronics* about the Altair 8800, the world's first commercially available microcomputer, which was manufactured by MITS. Allen immediately contacted his old friend Gates and suggested he leave Harvard and collaborate with him in developing an operating system for the 8800. Gates agreed, "We realized that the revolution might happen without us. After we saw that article, there was no question of where our life would focus."[28]

Gates joined Allen in Albuquerque, New Mexico, in June 1975, at which time they established a partnership known as Microsoft. Not only did Microsoft sell its operating system to MITS, but it also sold the program to emerging hardware companies like Apple and Commodore. In 1977 Tandy Corporation hired Microsoft to develop software for its Radio Shack computers, and in 1980 IBM contacted the company about developing an operating system for IBM's new entry into the personal computer market. The rest, as they say, is history.

Gates became a billionaire at the age of 31 and was declared the wealthiest man in America in 1999.

Earl Gilbert Graves, founder, publisher, and editor of *Black Enterprise* is also president and CEO of Earl G. Graves, Ltd., parent corporation of Earl G. Graves Publishing Company. Graves was born in New York City in 1935 and grew up in Brooklyn with his three younger siblings. Graves attended Morgan State University, where he established himself as an entrepreneur with various ventures, including selling flowers the week of homecoming. After graduating with a bachelor's degree in economics in 1957, Graves entered the army and rose to the rank of captain. He was a member of the 19th Special Forces Group, the Green Berets.

After marrying in 1960, Graves left the military and returned to Brooklyn. He was an immediate success at real estate, selling nine houses the first three months on the job. In addition, he served as commissioner for the local office of the Boy Scouts and did volunteer work for the Democratic Party in New York.

While organizing a Christmas party for underprivileged children in 1964, Graves met Senator Robert Kennedy. He later joined the senator's staff as an administrative assistant. Graves describes this experience thus: "Over the next three years, I received an education in the use of power and money in this country. . . . For the first time in my life, I was exposed to the white power elite and how it operated. . . . I saw firsthand what sort of freedom could be had with wealth and power. I became even more determined to claim at least some of it."[29]

Following Kennedy's assassination in 1968, Graves started a consulting business for black-owned businesses and began to consider the possibility of starting a magazine targeted at helping African Americans start their own business. With a $150,000 loan—made under a minority economic development program—and the support of several well-known black leaders, Graves faced the last big hurdle in starting his magazine. He knew he had to get white business owners to advertise in his magazine. His strategy for dealing with that was to emphasize "the green side of black," that is, the potential earnings from advertising to a black audience.

The first issue of *Black Enterprise* went to print in August 1970, and the magazine was showing a profit by its tenth issue. In June 1973 the first *Black Enterprise 100* listed the top 100 black-owned business in the country. The subscriber base grew to 300,000 by mid-1997, and the magazine claims to have an estimated 3.1 million readers.

In addition to his publishing interests, Graves bought and sold two radio stations and a marketing research firm. He also entered into a partnership with "Magic" Johnson to purchase the Pepsi bottling franchise in the Washington DC area. In 1997 Graves teamed with the Travelers Group to establish an $11 million fund for minority businesses.

Robert Greenberg, cofounder of L.A. Gear, was born in 1940 and raised in Boston, Massachusetts. After graduating from high school, he attended beauty school in Los Angeles and developed a fondness for the LA mystique of sun and surf. Greenberg returned to Boston and opened five hair salons, which he sold for what he described as "more money than I had ever seen in my life."[30] He sold wigs for a while and then jumped on the mid-1970s jeans bandwagon, selling his own line of jeans.

Greenberg returned to California in 1979 to pursue a new entrepreneurial venture. He saw an opportunity in the roller-skating craze of the day and opened a store that rented and sold skates. He even started building his own line of skates from sneakers. When the skating fad cooled, he saw another opportunity in the popular movie character "E.T." In 90 days, Greenberg grossed $3 million by selling shoelaces with the character's image on them.

In 1983 Greenberg opened a shop on Melrose Avenue in Los Angeles, called L.A. Gear. Since he wasn't sure which line of products—footwear, jeans, or apparel—would sell best, he sold them all and let his customers decide. "When shoes became the hottest sellers, Greenberg closed the store, sold the apparel business and declared in 1984 that he was 'officially in the shoe business.'"[31]

Greenberg decided that traditional department stores were not responding to the public's demand for the "hot" new aerobic shoes offered in athletic stores. "I saw an opportunity for department stores and women's shoe stores to sell fashion athletic shoes,"[32] he said. So he began making and marketing "shoes for show"—athletic-type shoes decorated with buckles, neon trims, fringe, and rhinestones. L.A. Gear's advertising, aimed primarily at young girls between the ages of 9 and 16 (the so-called Valley Girl niche), tied the L.A. Gear name to the image of the southern California lifestyle.

By the end of the first year of operation, L.A. Gear's sales reached $11 million. In 1986 the company went public at $11.50 per share and closed the first day at $24.75. That year also saw sales reach $36 million. Greenberg expanded his line of products in 1987 to include infant's wear, pushing sales to $70.5 million. His company was named one of the best companies in the United States by *Business Week,* an accomplishment that it repeated in 1988. The year the company began trading on the New York Stock Exchange (1989), it was named as the exchange's best-performing stock, with sales of $617 million. But this success was not to last.

In September 1991, L.A. Gear shareholders approved the sale of 34 percent of the company's stock. Shortly afterward, Greenberg stepped down as president but remained chairman and CEO. By 1998 L.A. Gear had filed Chapter 11 and Greenberg had moved on to a new venture—Skeechers U.S.A., another footwear manufacturer.

Jerry Greenfield, cofounder of Ben & Jerry's Ice Cream, was born in Brooklyn, New York, in 1951. He attended public school in Merrick, Long Island, where he met future business partner Ben Cohen.

Greenfield enrolled as a premed student at Oberlin College in Ohio. While attending Oberlin, he worked as an ice-cream scooper in the school cafeteria. After graduating from Oberlin, Greenfield applied to and was rejected by two medical schools, so he took a position as a lab technician. Following another medical school rejection in 1974, he moved to North Carolina with his girlfriend. After two years in North Carolina, Greenfield returned to New York and moved in with roommate and old friend Ben Cohen. Three years later, Ben & Jerry's was born. (For more information on the evolution of the company, see Ben Cohen's biography.)

Today, Jerry Greenfield is the chairperson of the board of Ben & Jerry's.

Bud Hadfield is the founder of Kwik Kopy.

A 1995 article in *Franchising World* sums up Bud Hadfield's life as follows: "Career-wise, Hadfield 'walked' for a good while before his franchising career took flight. He was a high school dropout labeled 'rebellious' by administrators at Cranston (Rhode Island) High. By age 24, he had roughhoused his way through the Merchant Marine and gone through myriad business projects including selling eggs, pig farming, and operating an ice cream parlor, gas station, frozen food business, fireworks stand and personnel agency."[33]

But in 1948 Hadfield followed his brother to Houston where the pair scraped together $250 of the $1,000 they needed to buy a small print shop. The balance they financed. Bud eventually bought out his brother and struggled to keep the small business going. Then in 1966 his life took a dramatic turn.

Hadfield attended a demonstration of a new camera that transferred a photographed image onto a printing plate. He recognized the potential for quick, low-cost printing and bought one of the cameras. It was the first step in starting the company he called Instant Print—changed to Kwik Kopy after threats of a lawsuit over the name. He also decided to franchise the concept.

By 1969 Hadfield had opened 12 Kwik Kopy centers and was showing a profit. By 1977 there were 500 domestic franchises and the company expanded to Britain, where they were named Kall Kwik. Today, there are Kwik Kopy centers in 20 countries.

In March 1992, Hadfield formed the International Center for Entrepreneurial Development, which is an alliance for all of his other printing operations—Cypress Publishing, American Wholesale Thermographers and Canadian Wholesale Thermographers, The Inkwell, and Copy Club. He stopped opening more Kwik Kopy centers when their numbers topped 1,000. According to Hadfield, "Our goal isn't to go on to two thousand, but to be sure that the thousand we have are strong and successful."[34]

Wilson Harrell, founder of almost one hundred companies and a columnist, was born in Georgia about 1919. During the Great Depression, he was a hobo and rode the rails. Later, he was a World War II fighter pilot and received the Purple Heart, the Air Medals with four Oak Leaves, and the Presidential Citation.

After the war Harrell started Wilson Harrell & Company, which distributed Kraft products to the huge military PX market. The company grew to $200 million in sales, but Harrell soon became bored with it. He sold the distribution company and bought the manufacturer of a household cleaner called Formula 409 for $30,000. Through some brilliant marketing maneuvers, Harrell went head-to-head with consumer-products giant Procter & Gamble and won the battle. He eventually sold the company to Clorox for $7 million and used the funds to purchase 60-food brokerage companies, with total sales exceeding $500 million.

In the mid-1960s, Harrell and two partners—David Woodstock and television personality Art Linkletter—formed Harrell, Woodstock, & Linkletter. Harrell and his partners "learned a lot and had a lot of fun"; Harrell defined "fun" as "working 80 hours a week, not sleeping, begging for money, fighting with suppliers, hating bankers."[35] He started or bought almost one hundred companies and turned around a few others. He also suffered some colossal failures, like Toasta Pizza, a pizza that baked in the toaster but melted all over everything. Then there were the giant, one-pound shrimp that died en masse just as they were supposed to go to market.

In 1995 and 1996 Harrell was named America's number-one columnist by The American Society of Business Press editors for his monthly column in *Success Magazine*. He lectured at Wharton Business School at the University of Pennsylvania, the University of North Carolina at Chapel Hill, and Emory University. He is a past publisher of *Inc. Magazine* and the founder/chairman emeritus of the Council of Growing Companies. He also wrote a regular column for the *Atlanta Business Chronicle*.

Harrell was described by *Success Magazine*'s Scott DeGarmo as "an irreverent, colorful, cigar-loving, brandy-sniffing, yarn-spinning, poker-playing, country-bred master of one-up-manship [who] has little use for piety or sanctimoniousness."[36] For example, Harrell liked to invoke "The Entrepreneur's Prayer"—"Good Lord, please let me find some way to compete with those stupid asses."[37] He also believed that entrepreneurs should have their own national anthem and that it should be the Frank Sinatra song "My Way."

Harrell died at the age of 78 in December 1997 from lung cancer.

Frank Hickingbotham, founder of TCBY (This Can't Be Yogurt), was born in McGehee, Arkansas, in 1936. He attended the University of Arkansas–Monticello, where he received a bachelor's degree in business. He then returned to McGehee to run an insurance agency.

In the late 1960s, Hickingbotham and a group of investors purchased an AQ Chicken franchise. Hickingbotham later bought the franchisor company, then sold it in 1976 and bought Dallas-based Olde Tyme Foods. When he grew tired of commuting between Dallas and Little Rock, Hickingbotham started looking for a business closer to home.

It was Hickingbotham's wife, Georgia, who found his next venture. She invited her husband to join her for lunch at Neiman Marcus in Dallas. She wanted him to taste an unusual frozen yogurt dessert, but Hickingbotham did not like yogurt and resisted the idea. Nonetheless, to satisfy his wife, he agreed to taste the dessert, and as legend has it, he exclaimed, *"This Can't Be Yogurt."*

The couple contacted the yogurt manufacturer and arranged to purchase and distribute the product through a single store, which would be manned by their son. The product proved to be so popular, however, that they soon opened two more "This Can't Be Yogurt" stores and put them in the charge of their two sons "I decided to franchise when I ran out of relatives," Hickingbotham quipped.[38] He started franchising in 1982, one store at a time, primarily to friends and customers.

In 1984, the same year the company went public, it opened its one-hundredth shop and by 1988 had 1,000 locations. During the next 10 years, the company expanded internationally, cobranded with companies like Subway, Nathan's, and Host Marriott, and expanded its product lines to include juices. In 1998 the company had approximately three thousand locations worldwide.

Soichiro Honda, cofounder of Honda Motor Company, was born in 1906 in the remote Japanese province of Hamamatsu. He was the first of nine children born to a poor blacksmith, five of whom died from malnutrition before reaching maturity. Honda showed an early aptitude for the mechanical and learned bicycle repair from his father, but he did not fare so well in his formal schooling. He managed to graduate from elementary school in 1922, completing only the tenth grade, then accepted an apprenticeship in a Tokyo auto-repair shop. After six years of apprenticeship, he borrowed the money to open a repair shop in his home town and received the first of his numerous patents—for the design of metal spokes to replace wooden ones in automobile wheels.

In 1938 Honda was working day and night to develop a cast piston ring for the Toyota Corporation. He had invested all of his money—even pawned his wife's jewelry to raise more—to finance the endeavor, but Toyota rejected the first batch of rings. It took two more years to perfect his design, by which time Japan was gearing up for war. When he was ready to build his piston-ring plant, Honda could not get access to cement, so he and his men learned how to make their own. Honda's product was in such demand in wartime Japan that Toyota advanced him $260,000 of badly needed working capital, and Honda began to train women to replace his male workers. As David Silver describes in *Entrepreneurial Megabucks,* "His factories were bombed out twice, but after each attack, Honda rushed out to pick up the extra gasoline tanks U.S. fighters threw away as they flew by. Honda called these cans 'Truman's gifts,' because they provided raw materials for his manufacturing process. When an earthquake finally leveled his factory, Honda sold his piston-ring operation to Toyota Corporation for $125,000."[39]

After the war, the gasoline shortage in Japan made it impossible to get around. Honda found it so frustrating, he attached a small motor to his bicycle, and he was soon overwhelmed by the demand for his new invention. When he ran out of gasoline-powered motors for his new motorized bicycle, he developed one that ran on pine resin. As he described, "We squeezed the resin from the pine root then mixed it with gasoline bought on the black market. The mixture gave off such a stench of turpentine that I could insist we were violating no gasoline controls by operating the motorbike."[40]

In 1948 Honda took the income from his motorbikes and, along with Takeo Fujisawa, founded the Honda Motor Company. Their initial investment of $3,200 was not adequate to get the company going, so Fujisawa decided to go directly to potential customers for funds. Five thousand dealers anted up the necessary funds, and Honda was off and running. Initially, only hard-core motorcyclists were interested in Honda's cycle, but a brilliant marketing campaign featuring the slogan "You meet the nicest people on a Honda" captured the casual, leisure-time rider. By 1965, 50 percent of the motorcycles sold in the United States were Hondas, and the company's two-year-old car business was beginning to establish itself as the producer of a superefficient, environmentally friendly automobile.

During his lifetime, Honda was responsible for some four-hundred fifty inventions and more than one-hundred fifty patents. He received honorary doctorates from Michigan Technical University and Ohio State University and he also won the Japanese Blue Ribbon in 1952. Honda died on August 5, 1991, in Japan.

H. Wayne Huizenga, founder of Waste Management, Inc., was born in 1939 in Evergreen Park, Illinois, a suburb of Chicago. He was raised in a "strict and disciplined" environment "with old-fashioned, workingman's values."[41] His family regularly attended the Dutch Christian Reformed Church and lived its rigorous precepts.

In 1953 the Huizenga family moved to Fort Lauderdale, Florida, where Wayne attended and graduated from the private Pine Crest School. After graduation he worked as a bulldozer driver, attended Calvin College in Grand Rapids, Michigan, for three semesters, served briefly in the U.S. Army, then returned to Florida to drive a garbage truck in Pompano Beach.

In 1962 Huizenga followed in the footsteps of his paternal grandfather, who owned a garbage-collection business in Chicago, and started his own company—Southern Sanitation Service—with a single truck and $500 worth of accounts. "He collected trash from 2:00 A.M. until noon and then canvassed the neighborhood door-to-door to solicit new business. 'I didn't know anything about the business. . . . I just worked hard and gave good service. If I was late picking up the garbage, the customer would call me at home to complain about the driver. *I* was the driver.'"[42]

By the late 1960s, Huizenga was operating 20 garbage trucks up and down the East Coast of Florida, as far south as Key West, and he had become a millionaire. In 1968 he established Waste Management through the merger of his company with three Chicago companies, including one that was headed by a cousin, Dean Buntrock. Buntrock brought with him the idea of creating a nationwide sanitation company, and Huizenga made it happen. They took Waste Management public in 1971 and the next year bought 90 competing companies. By the early 1980s, the company became the biggest of its kind in the world, with revenues of more than $1 billion, and Huizenga was becoming bored with his deskbound job. He retired in 1984 but remained the major stockholder in the company.

Huizenga soon tired of retirement and began using his earnings from Waste Management to buy a plethora of small businesses, hotels, and office buildings. Tagged as a "deal junkie" by an associate, Huizenga bought more than one hundred businesses, which were generating $100 million in annual revenues by the end of 1986. In 1987 a Waste Management executive introduced Huizenga to a Dallas-based chain of video-rental stores known as Blockbuster Video. Within a week, Huizenga and two partners bought almost 35 percent of Blockbuster for $18 million, and Huizenga soon took over as chairman. By the end of 1991, Blockbuster had more than two thousand locations, and in 1993 revenues reached $2.2 billion. The next year, Viacom purchased Blockbuster Entertainment Corporation for $7.6 billion.

Huizenga's interests were not restricted to garbage and videos. In 1990 he began purchasing interest in professional sports teams, starting with a 15 percent share in the Miami Dolphins. The next year, he successfully bid for a National League baseball franchise—the Florida Marlins—and in 1992 he won a franchise for a National Hockey League expansion team, the Florida Panthers.

Through it all, however, Huizenga maintained, "I'd rather build a company than manage one."[43] In May 1995, he gave up his positions at Blockbuster and assumed the responsibilities as chairman and CEO of Republic Waste Industries, Inc.

Huizenga has received many honors, including the Entrepreneur of the Year award from the Wharton School, CEO of the Year bronze award from *Financial World* magazine, and a Horatio Alger Award.

Masaru Ibuka, cofounder of Sony Corporation (originally Tokyo Tsushin Kogyo [Tokyo Telecommunications Company]), was born in 1908 in western Japan's Nikko City. He graduated from the Waseda University School of Science and Engineering in 1933 and, failing the entry exam for lifetime employment at Toshiba, joined the staff of the Naval Research Center, where he met his future partner, Akio Morita.

After the war, Ibuka found work repairing radios. Morita and he also developed and produced a line of automatic rice cookers. Unfortunately, many of the cookers burned the rice, so they were forced to look for other opportunities. They sold Morita's truck to get enough capital to form Tokyo Telecommunications Engineering Company (later renamed Sony Corporation) in 1946. (See the biography of Akio Morita for more detailed information on the evolution of the Sony Corporation.)

Ibuka served as president of Sony from 1950 to 1971 and as chairman from 1971 to 1976. He died in Tokyo on December 19, 1989, at the age of 89.

Edgar Waldo (Billy) Ingram, cofounder of White Castle, was born in Leadville, Colorado, in 1880, "in a two-room slab house roofed with tin cans."[44] His father held a variety of jobs and moved his family from Colorado to Nebraska and then to Missouri. He finally bought a hand laundry in St. Joseph, Missouri, where young Billy worked until he graduated from high school.

After high school, Billy moved to Omaha and worked for five years as a reporter and an editor for the *Omaha Bee.* Leveraging this experience, Ingram eventually moved to a job at the *Omaha Excelsior,* for which he did reporting, editing, bookkeeping, sales of advertising, and even the printing of the paper. In 1905 he found a job with R.G. Dun and Company (later Dun and Bradstreet) as a traveling agent based in Wichita. Two years later he cofounded the firm of Ingram, Yankey and Company and spent the next 13 years building successful partnerships in insurance, oil, and real estate.

No one knows exactly how Billy Ingram met Walt Anderson, but in 1921 they entered into a partnership that would change the future of fast food in America. As David Hogan describes in *Selling 'Em By the Sackful:*

> Distinguishing Walt Anderson's business [White Castle] from . . . other upstart competitors is where Billy Ingram made a profound difference. He brought to the partnership a sound understanding of the financial world and a vision for growth and expansion. As soon as Ingram entered the business in 1921, he implemented many changes in both the company's philosophy and its operation. . . . Ingram intended to repackage Anderson's existing operation completely. He first selected both a new company name and a

symbolic architecture. Accordingly, the Anderson-Ingram partnership was legally organized in March under the name of the White Castle System of Eating Houses. Ingram later explained that the rationale for this new name was to convey a more positive image of their business, with "White" signifying purity and "Castle" signifying strength, stability, and permanence.[45]

F. Kenneth (Ken) Iverson, is former president, chairman, and CEO of Nucor Corporation.

When Iverson joined Nucor Corporation (then named Nuclear Corporation) in 1962, the company did not manufacture any steel. By 1998 it was the second-largest steelmaker in the United States, second only to USX's U.S. Steel Group. Iverson, who received a master's degree in mechanical engineering from Purdue University, was hired to run Nucor's newly acquired unit, Vulcraft Corporation, which manufactured construction joists. In 1966 Iverson convinced the board of directors to invest in steelmaking, so the company could save money by producing its own steel for joist fabrication. Under Iverson's leadership, Nucor's sales went from $17.5 million in 1964 to $4.18 billion in 1997—a 23,811 percent increase.

Steven Paul Jobs, cofounder of Apple Computer, Inc., and cofounder of NeXT, was adopted in February 1955, shortly after his birth, by Paul and Clara Jobs. The youngster exhibited an early interest in electronics and while in high school attended lectures at the nearby Hewlett-Packard plant in Palo Alto, California. He attended Reed College in Portland, Oregon, for one semester, then dropped out of school and immersed himself in philosophy. According to one biographer, he "meditated, learned the I Ching, experimented with psychedelic drugs, and became a vegetarian."[46]

In 1974 Jobs took a job with Atari, Inc., where he worked on the early computer game *Breakout* just long enough to finance a trip to India. After shaving his head and backpacking through India, he returned to California where he "capped off his spiritual journey with a sojourn at a farm commune."[47]

Jobs joined a local group of computer enthusiasts, who called themselves the Homebrew Computer Club, in 1975. The acknowledged genius of this Palo Alto group was a Hewlett-Packard employee named Stephen Wozniak, whom Jobs convinced to join him in a business venture. With a total of $1,300, which they acquired by selling Jobs's Volkswagen microbus and Wozniak's Hewlett-Packard calculator, the pair set out to design and build what would become the Apple I computer—named for a summer Jobs had spent working in an apple orchard. In 1976, the partners sold 600 computers, grossing $774,000. The next year they introduced the enormously popular Apple II, a user-friendly computer that came equipped with color graphics, a keyboard, and a power supply. Within three years, the company earned $139 million, which was a 700 percent growth in revenues. When Apple went public in 1980, the stock closed after the first day at $29 per share, setting Apple's market value at $1.2 billion and making the 25-year-old Jobs a multimillionaire ($239 million to be exact).

Jobs and Wozniak's next offering, the LISA, was less successful than it predecessor, but the Apple Macintosh, released in 1984, eventually became another smash hit. At the same time, sales of Apple products began to slow and Jobs often clashed with the company's board of directors. Eventually, he was removed from the board.

Late in 1984, Jobs took part of the $100 million he earned from selling his Apple stock and started another company, NeXT. He intended to build the ultimate personal computer and poured himself and his money into the project. He and his team of developers created a new and innovative operating system, named NeXTStep, which made their computers easy to use and easy to program. Jobs hoped that NeXTStep would compete with Microsoft's MS-DOS and Windows and even convinced IBM to license his operating system for their PCs. The deal with IBM never fully materialized because, as explained by a NeXT cofounder: "[Jobs] got afraid that IBM was going to take away some of NeXT's hardware business. So he kept control over the development of NeXTStep, and that eliminated the chance that IBM would back it because IBM will not ship a product that they cannot at least shape the future of."[48]

The NeXT computer was introduced in October 1989, but despite its sleek styling, optical-disk drive, enhanced video monitor, and CD-quality music, it was a phenomenal flop. Production of the units stopped in February, 1993. NeXT changed its focus from hardware to software, and Jobs turned his attention to another company he had purchased from filmmaker George Lucas in 1986, Pixar Animation Studios. Jobs sold a three-film deal to Disney, the first of which was the 1995 blockbuster *Toy Story*, which grossed $38 million. Pixar went public on November 29, 1995, at $22 per share and closed at $39, making Jobs's personal worth almost $1.17 billion. Shortly afterward, Apple bought NeXT. They rehired Jobs as an adviser to the CEO and reappointed him to the board.

In mid-1997 Jobs agreed to "assume an expanded role as a key adviser to Apple's board and executive management team,"[49] after which the company appeared to be reinvigorated. An alliance with Microsoft provided a much-needed influx of capital to finance the production of new product lines like the Power Mac, PowerBook, and iMac. After the company posted a profit for the third consecutive quarter in mid-1998, an Apple executive proclaimed, "Apple is back."[50]

Howard Dearing Johnson, founder of Howard Johnson Company, was born in 1897. He entered his first retail business after returning from France and World War I. After Johnson's father, John Hays Johnson, died, Howard inherited both a cigar store and his father's debts. He ran the cigar store until 1924, then liquidated it—although he couldn't liquidate the $10,000 debt.

Johnson's next retail attempt was a run-down drugstore near the railroad station in Wollaston, Massachusetts. When the owner died, his heir offered the store and its $28,000 in debts to Johnson in exchange for $2,000 in working capital. So in 1924, Johnson started his first food business, complete with soda fountain, candy counter, tobacco, and newspaper stand. Initially, the newspaper stand supported the rest of the operation, grossing $30,000 per year and employing 75 delivery boys. Then Johnson bought an ice-cream recipe from a German pushcart vendor for $300. The essence of the peddler's secret was that it doubled the usual amount of butterfat in the ice cream and used only natural flavorings. Johnson began cranking out ice cream in his basement, using an old hand-cranked freezer, and by 1928 he was grossing about $240,000 from ice cream sold in the store and on nearby beaches.

Johnson began to open ice-cream stands in the Boston area and soon had a dozen stands that also offered "grilled-in-butter frankforts." He continued to expand the number of flavors of ice cream he offered, eventually topping out at 28. Then in 1929, he convinced a family friend, Reginald Sprague, to open a quality restaurant and ice-cream stand on Cape Cod—the first Howard Johnson's restaurant. Sprague agreed to sell Howard Johnson's ice cream exclusively and "to buy other foodstuffs that Johnson could produce. As long as his name and design were to be used, Johnson was to set the standard for all food products used in the restaurant. This agreement served as a precedent for franchise arrangement that Howard Johnson Company [the pioneer in restaurant franchising] has maintained with restaurant owners."[51]

By 1940 Johnson had 135 profitable restaurants scattered along the entire East Coast of the United States, and he became a millionaire. He controlled the quality of the food served in his franchises, preparing and processing it in centrally located, company-operated facilities and then shipping it to the restaurants for final preparation. His post–World War II marketing strategy targeted vacationing families by offering simple but high-quality food, insisting on immaculate cleanliness, hiring courteous staff, and providing special accommodations for children.

By 1951 the company operated or licensed 300 restaurants, with annual sales of $31,880,000. Those numbers grew to 450 restaurants and over $66 million in revenues by 1956. During the intervening years the company opened a chain of steak houses, known as Red Coach Grills, and began franchising motor lodges, the first of which opened in Savannah, Georgia, in 1954.

In 1959 Johnson decided to turn the reigns of the company over to his son, Howard Brennan Johnson. However, the elder Johnson continued to scout out new locations for restaurants and motel sites and continued to enjoy the products of his $200 million-a-year empire. "He never lost his taste for the ice cream that made him famous. It was his favorite dish. He kept at least 10 flavors in the freezer of his Manhattan penthouse. Every day of his life Howard Johnson enjoyed at least one ice cream cone."[52]

Herbert David (Herb) Kelleher, cofounder of Southwest Airlines, was born in Camden, New Jersey, in 1931. He received a bachelor of arts (cum laude) from Wesleyan University in 1953 and a law degree (cum laude) from New York University in 1956. He passed the bar in New Jersey in 1957 and in Texas in 1962, after clerking in the New Jersey Supreme Court from 1956 to 1959. He worked with a series of law partnerships before joining forces with Rollin King to start "a different kind of airline." According to the Southwest Airlines Web site, "They began with one simple notion: If you get passengers to their destinations when they want to get there, on time, at the lowest possible fares, and make darn sure they have a good time doing it, people will fly your airline."[53] And apparently that's true because since their maiden voyage in 1971, Southwest has become the fifth-largest major airline in the United States, flying some 52 million passengers per year.

Kelleher, who has served as general counsel, president, chairman, and CEO of the airline, has received a number of honors and awards over the years including CEO of the Year by *Financial World* in 1982 and 1990, Best

Chief Executive Regional Airline Industry by *Wall Street Transcript* in 1982, Texas Business Hall of Fame in 1988, and Master Entrepreneur award by *Inc. Magazine* in 1991.

Philip H. (Phil) Knight, cofounder of Nike, Inc., was born in 1938 in Oregon. "Buck," as he was nicknamed, enjoyed running as a youth, but few people at the time considered that a real sport. He continued running at the University of Oregon, where he met running coach Bill Bowerman. The coach, who was known as the "Professor of Competitive Responses," was constantly trying to make shoes lighter because, he reasoned, "carrying one extra ounce for a mile was equivalent to carrying something like an extra thousand pounds in the last 150 yards [of a race]."[54] Knight often played guinea pig for Bowerman's experiments.

Knight graduated from the University of Oregon with a degree in accounting in 1959 and then enrolled in the Stanford University business school. He is said to have had an epiphany when one professor told his students to write a term paper about something they liked. Knight, of course, thought of running, but he reconsidered his favorite sport in light of the way Japanese manufacturers had been able to produce inexpensive cars and consumer electronics. His term paper explored how high-quality, low-cost shoes could be made using cheap Asian labor.

When Knight graduated from Stanford in 1964 with an MBA, he and former coach Bowerman split the cost of a shipment of shoes manufactured by the Onitsuka Tiger Company, which also produced knock-off Adidas shoes. The new partners peddled their Blue Ribbon Sports shoes out of the trunk of Knight's car. Knight also worked as an accountant and taught at Portland State University to supplement his income from the fledgling shoe business. By 1972 shoe sales reached $3 million, and Knight decided that he was ready to design his own line. He paid an art student at Portland State $35 to create the company's logo—the swoosh symbol—and an employee supplied the brand name, Nike, the name of the Greek mythological winged goddess of victory.

The first Nikes went on sale in 1972. Over the next few years, the combination of innovative designs, athlete endorsements, and a new fitness craze skyrocketed Nike to the top. For example, when tennis player John McEnroe hurt his ankle, he started wearing Nike's three-quarter top shoe. Sales for that style went from ten thousand pairs to over a million pairs in just a few months. In fact, by 1980 Nike was producing about a hundred styles of shoes for 12 different sports and reached sales of $270 million. But Nike made one serious misstep. The company had concentrated so much on designing shoes for sports professionals that it missed the emerging market for stylish aerobic shoes. By 1986 Reebok had captured that market and taken over the position of highest-grossing shoe company. It would take Nike four years to regain its position as number one. In 1996 Nike showed net profits of $550 million on sales totaling $6.5 billion, making Knight the sixth-richest person in the United States.

C. James (Jim) Koch, founder of Boston Beer Company, is a sixth-generation brewmaster. His great-great grandfather, Louis Koch, who originally brewed beer in Germany, founded a brewery in St. Louis in 1860, brewing Louis Koch Lager. Although one of the largest breweries in St. Louis, it was eventually eclipsed by neighboring giant Anheuser-Busch. Jim Koch's great grandfather, Charles Jerome Koch, was brewmaster at several St. Louis breweries in the late nineteenth century, and his grandfather, Charles Joseph Koch, who received a diploma from America's only brewmaster's school, the Siebel Institute, in 1908, was in great demand at local breweries and later invented and patented an important malt process.

Prohibition closed the doors of all breweries by the end of 1919, but Charles Joseph Koch stayed in business by making supplies for home brewers. When prohibition ended, he was one of the few experienced brewers left in the United States. His son, and Jim's father, Charles Joseph Koch Jr., began apprenticing as a brewmaster in 1942 and received his degree from the Siebel Institute in 1948. But with the advent of lighter, less-flavorful beers produced by the large national brewers, small, specialized breweries like the Koch's began to close. Jim's father left the beer business.

To his father's dismay, Jim decided to leave his management consulting job in 1983 and continue the family's brewing tradition. Armed with Louis Koch's recipe, Jim began producing test batches. He changed the name of the family beer from Louis Koch Lager to Samuel Adams Boston Lager. In April 1985, Koch introduced his beer to Boston, the company's new home. Six weeks later Samuel Adams Boston Lager was voted the Best Beer in America.

Ray Kroc, founder of McDonald's Corporation, was born in 1902 in Chicago. "When I was a kid, I saw my dad struggling to make ends meet on a meager salary," Kroc later recalled.[55] So, at an early age, he resolved to make money—lots of it.

Kroc attended public school in Oak Park, Illinois, a Chicago suburb, until he was a high school sophomore. At 15, he falsified his age, joined the Red Cross ambulance corps, and became an ambulance driver during World War I. (He was in the same company as Walt Disney, who was only 16 years old at the time.)

After the war, Kroc returned to high school but dropped out again to become a jazz pianist. His early career as a musician, however, was cut short by the realization that marriage and a musician's hours don't mix. He took a more traditional job as a salesman for the Lily-Tulip Cup Company for a while and then became musical director for radio station WGES in Chicago. (One of his discoveries was a song-and-dance team that later became famous as Amos 'n' Andy.)

Kroc was drawn to the promise of wealth from Florida real estate during the land boom of the 1920s. He attempted to sell property in Fort Lauderdale but was caught in the 1926 collapse in the real estate market. He was so broke he had to play piano in a nightclub to send his wife and daughter back to Chicago by train. He followed them in a Model T Ford: "I will never forget that drive as long as I live. I was stone broke. I didn't have an overcoat, a topcoat, or a pair of gloves. I drove into Chicago on icy streets. When I got home, I was frozen stiff, disillusioned and broke."[56]

Kroc returned to his job at Lily-Tulip and in 1937 invented a machine that could mix five milk shakes at a time. He became the exclusive distributor for the "multimixer" and started a small company to sell it.

In 1954 Kroc's curiosity was aroused when he learned that one of his customers was operating eight multimixers in one location. He went to see for himself why Maurice (Mac) and Richard (Dick) McDonald needed so many milk-shake mixers. When he arrived at their San Bernardino, California, restaurant, he was shocked. "They had people standing in line clamoring for hamburgers. I figured that if every McDonald hamburger place had eight Multimixers, I would get rich."[57]

The McDonald brothers were not interested in expanding their operation beyond the six franchises they had sold in California, but before he left town, Kroc had a 99-year contract to represent McDonald's exclusively. He opened the first McDonald's franchise in Des Plaines, Illinois, on April 15, 1955, followed the same year by franchises in Fresno and Reseda, California. By 1960 there were 228 restaurants, with annual sales in excess of $37 million.

The partnership between Kroc and the McDonald brothers was always strained. The brothers attempted to put restrictions on the franchises that Kroc found unacceptable, so he bought them out in 1961 for $2,700,000—lock, stock, and Golden Arches. When he discovered that the brothers were not willing to give up their San Bernardino store, he built a brand-new restaurant directly across the street. They were soon out of business.

In 1972, McDonald's opened its two-thousandth restaurant, reported sales in excess of $1 billion, and sold more than 10 billion hamburgers. Kroc served as president until 1968, as chairman (1968–77), and later as senior chairman (1977–84) of McDonald's board of directors. He also owned the San Diego Padres baseball team from 1974 to 1979. Kroc died in San Diego on January 14, 1984.

Edwin Herbert Land, founder of the Polaroid Corporation, was born in 1909 in Bridgeport, Connecticut. He became interested in photography as a child and later explained, "To a child, a photograph gives a permanent thing that is both outside himself and part of himself."[58] His first photograph was of the family dog, which was always running away. The photograph, he explained, made a difference, "There [in the picture] I had him. He couldn't get away."[59]

Land attended the Norwich Academy, where he showed an aptitude for physics. After graduating in 1926, he entered Harvard University, taking an 18-month sabbatical to continue his research on the polarization phenomena. He returned to Harvard for a while but left before graduation to join George Wheelwright III, a physics professor at Harvard, in establishing the Land-Wheelwright Laboratories in 1932.

In 1934 Land-Wheelwright manufactured the first polarizer for commercial uses, the Polaroid J-sheet. The next year, Eastman Kodak began using polarized filters in its cameras, and in 1936 the American Optical Company began marketing polarized sunglasses.

Land founded the Polaroid Corporation in 1937, with financial backing by a number of Wall Street businessmen, just in time to become a major contributor to the United States' war efforts. Land, who eventually patented more than five hundred inventions, developed a number of weapons improvements, including optical elements used in infrared night-vision instruments. He consulted with the navy on guided missiles and participated in the project to create computerized thermal homing heads for large bombs. The company also produced filters for periscopes, range finders, aerial cameras, goggles, and gun sights.

With the return of peace, Land was able to pursue an idea he had while on vacation in 1943. He had taken a picture of his three-year-old daughter, who wanted to know why she couldn't see the picture "right now." During the remainder of his vacation, Land mentally designed a camera and film that would produce an immediate photograph. He later described the process as "cumulative creativity." "All that we at Polaroid had learned about making polarizers and plastics, and the properties of viscous liquids, and the preparation of microscopic crystals . . . was preparation for that day in which I suddenly knew how to make a one-step photographic process."[60]

Land demonstrated his photographic process to the American Optical Society in February 1947 and released the Model 95 camera at Christmas 1948. It weighed four pounds, made sepia-toned prints, and was an immediate commercial success, grossing $5 million in the first year. Polaroid introduced black-and-white film in 1950, followed by faster-developing film in 1955 and color film in 1963. When it released the "no-garbage" SX-70 in 1972, the Polaroid Company expected the same enthusiastic reception they had gotten for their earlier products, but they sold only 700,000 of the cameras. Land later explained that "several small problems for the customer, one of them with focusing, affected the sales and that in introducing the SX-70, the company 'did underestimate how infinitely important a small amount of instruction is.' "[61] The SX-70 eventually lived up to its potential, becoming a best-seller for the Polaroid Corporation.

Land retired as president in May 1975 and as CEO in 1980, although he remained chairman of the board and continued to support Polaroid's research program as a consulting director. He received many honors and awards, including the National Medal of Science and the Presidential Medal of Freedom. He also received honorary doctoral degrees from Columbia, Yale, Harvard, and several other colleges and universities. He was elected to the National Inventors Hall of Fame in 1977. Land died in 1991.

Chris Larsen, cofounder of E-Loan, holds a bachelor of science degree from the San Francisco State University and an MBA from Stanford University. He worked with Chevron Corporation and NASA/Ames Research before cofounding Palo Alto Funding Group, a successful mortgage brokerage, with Janina Pawlowski. In 1991 Larsen and Pawlowski developed the E-Loan interface which allows mortgage customers to search an extensive database of loan products and apply for loans.

Charles Lazarus, founder of Toys "R" Us, was born in 1923 in Washington, D.C. His father rebuilt bicycles and sold them in the family shop. When Charles asked his father why they didn't sell new bicycles, his father told him that it was because the big chain stores could sell them cheaper—an idea the young Lazarus would remember.

After his service as a cryptographer during World War II, Lazarus took over the family business but changed the merchandise from rebuilt bicycles to baby furniture. The business thrived for a while, with all the returning GIs and their brides starting families, but eventually Lazarus noticed that families didn't buy more than one crib. He needed to find a line of merchandise that would keep customers coming back for more. In 1953 he switched to selling toys and changed the company name to Children's Supermarket, with the "r"s printed backward.

Following the lead of the superstore discounters, Lazarus promised to undercut his competition by at least 20 percent and to have a bigger and better selection than any other toy store. The Children's Supermarket thrived, but Lazarus was unhappy with the new name. He wanted a name with shorter words so he could use larger letters on his signs. He decided on Toys "R" Us, retaining the backward "R."

In 1966 Lazarus sold his chain to Interstate Stores for $7.5 million but retained a seat on the board. Although Interstate failed in 1978, Toys "R" Us survived and regrouped under Lazarus's leadership.

William Powell (Bill) Lear, founder of Lear, Inc., (1939), Lear Jet Corporation (1963), and Lear Motors Corporation, was born in 1902 in Hannibal, Missouri. His parents divorced when he was six, and his mother, whom he described as "a dominating woman with a violent temper,"[62] moved him to Chicago, where she remarried. Lear attended public school and worked shining shoes and at other odd jobs. He was stymied in his early efforts at inventing by the lack of funds and by his mother's "unsympathetic attitude." "I remember working out a blueprint for my future when I was twelve years old. I resolved first to make enough money so I'd never be stopped from finishing anything; second, that to accumulate money in a hurry—and I was in a hurry—I'd have to invent something that people wanted; and third, that if I ever was going to stand on my feet, I'd have to leave home."[63]

After completing eighth grade, Lear quit school to work as a mechanic. At 16 he lied about his age and joined the navy, where he studied radio communications during World War I. After the war, he flew war-surplus planes and worked as a radio engineer. During this time, he designed one of the first nonbattery home radio receivers and the first home radio with a built-in speaker.

In the early 1920s, Lear invented the first automobile radio, but failing to get sufficient financial backing to produce it commercially, he sold the idea to the Motorola Corporation in 1924. Over the next three decades, Lear made one attempt after another at maintaining a company of his own (the Quincy Radio Laboratory [1922], Lear Radio Laboratory [1924–1928], Lear Developments Company [1931–1934], Lear Avia Corporation [1934–1949]). He also invented hundreds of electronic devices, including the first commercial radio compass for airplanes (1935) and the first light-weight autopilot for jets (1949).

In 1939 Lear founded Lear, Inc., which produced motors and other devices for the U.S. Air Force during World War II. The company's war contracts totaled $100 million. Following the war, Lear developed a miniature autopilot for smaller fighter planes and later for jets. By 1962 Lear's sales reached $90 million, and the company added stereophonic sound systems and miniature communication satellites to its product line. Lear wanted to add small, low-priced jets as well, but the board of directors refused to sign off on the investment. His response was to sell his share of the company for $14,300,000 and found Lear Jet Corporation.

The first of Lear's "baby jets" hit the market in the summer of 1963 to a cool reception. By late 1964, Lear was forced to take his company public, selling 500,000 shares of stock, in order to keep it afloat. The relatively low cost of the planes began to attract attention; by mid-1966, 120 jets had been delivered to customers.

In addition to jets, Lear Jet Corporation also manufactured gyros, autopilots, compressors, and stereotape systems for cars. Lear recalls, "When the stereo tape came along, it was a natural for cars. The trouble was size. The experts were saying you couldn't put eight tracks on a quarter-inch tape and still house the entire package including a radio in no more room than that required for the standard auto radio. Since it was 'impossible,' the industry leaders stayed out. We did it."[64]

A *Saturday Evening Post* article summarized Lear's persona as follows:

All his life Lear has regarded himself as a rebel who despises the classical approach. To the dismay of his business-minded directors, he will affirm his belief that the earth is under observation by flying saucers from other planets, or predict that it may be possible someday to transport humans by breaking them into atomic particles, transmitting the atoms over electric waves and reassembling them at the end of the circuit. . . . When rocket expresses are blue-printed, it's a good bet that somewhere in the vanguard of planners there will be a place for Bill Lear.[65]

Lear died in Reno, Nevada, on May 14, 1978.

Bernard (Bernie) Marcus, cofounder and chairman of the board of Home Depot, was born in 1929 in Newark, New Jersey. Raised in a tenement, he learned to survive in a tough neighborhood. During his teens, he started earning money for college by working as a waiter, busboy, and even an emcee.

Marcus graduated from Rutgers University in 1952 with a bachelor of science degree in pharmacy. After graduating, he opened a small pharmacy, which he later sold to the Two Guys discount chain. He took a job running the chain's cosmetic departments, where he first learned about the concept of box retailing. His success in that position led to his promotion to vice president of hard-goods merchandising and advertising for Two Guys' parent corporation, Vornado, Inc.

In 1972 Marcus left Vornado to become president and chairman of the board of Handy Dan Home Improvement Centers, a subsidiary of the Daylin Corporation. It was at Daylin that Marcus began experimenting with the concept of discounting and that he met Arthur Blank, who was the company's comptroller. Both of them were caught in a 1978 corporate buyout, after which they lost their jobs.

Rather than follow the corporate path once again, Marcus decided to try to make a go of it on his own—or at least in the company of Blank and another ousted Daylin employee, Ronald Brill. One year later, they opened their first Home Depot store in Atlanta, Georgia, followed the same year by a second. Since they took their company public in 1981, Home Depot's stock has increased more than 37,000 percent. Sales in 1999 exceeded $38 billion at more than nine hundred ninety locations. Other Home Depot companies include EXPO Design Center, Villager's Hardware, Home Depot Special Order Center, and Home Depot Maintenance Warehouse.

Konosuke Matsushita, founder of Matsushita Electric Industrial Company (makers of Panasonic, Technics, and Quasar brand products), was born in 1894 in a small Japanese farming village. He quit school at the age of nine and left home to work as an apprentice to a hibachi maker in Osaka. A nervous and sickly youth, Matsushita was only a mediocre student. In 1910 he joined the Osaka Electric Light Company as an employee and seven years later started an electrical business of his own—Matsushita Electric Industrial Company (MEI).

The first major success of MEI was a bicycle lamp with a new type of battery, followed by a diversified line of batteries, radios, and related products. The company expanded into household appliances in the 1930s, during which time Matsushita developed his philosophy of business and leadership. Following a visit to a temple of the Tenrikyo sect, Matsushita became nearly obsessed by the image of happy, hard-working people who donated their time to the temple. He concluded that if a corporation could be made meaningful like a religion, then people would be both more productive and more satisfied.

In May 1932, Matsushita addressed the workers and executives and Matsushita Electric. He reminded them of the company's accomplishments over the previous 15 years—280 registered patents, factories in 10 locations, and more than a thousand employees. Then he proclaimed: "This is what the entrepreneur and the manufacturer should aim at: to make all products as inexhaustible and as cheap as tap water. When this is realized, poverty will vanish from the earth."[66] After 1933 MEI's emphasis on service, honesty, and teamwork became a source of competitive advantage. In a 1935 directive, Matsushita urged: "No matter how large Matsushita Electric might become in the future, never forget to maintain the modest attitude of a merchant. Think of yourselves as being employed in a small store, and carry out your work with simplicity, frugality, and humility."[67]

Matsushita lost a number of factories during World War II, but he emerged with a new vision of where he wanted to take his company. He became convinced that he had much to learn from Europe and the United States, and in 1951, at the age of 56, he traveled to the United States for a three-month crash course. He subsequently built an $80 billion-a-year

(1997) home appliance and consumer electronics company, manufacturing such brands as Panasonic, Technics, and Quasar.

Matsushita died on May 8, 1989.

James W. (Jim) McLamore, cofounder of Burger King, was born in New York City in 1926 to wealth and culture, but his world changed drastically in the first three years of his life. His maternal grandfather died shortly after the stock-market crash wiped out the family fortune, and his mother was soon committed to a sanitarium, where she died in 1933. The family was forced to sell its city townhouse and suburban home and to move to the family farm (Edgehill) in Central Valley, New York. After his father lost his job with Chase National Bank, the family had to sell cherished possessions as well as 200 acres of the farm. Eventually, they began renting out their home and bungalow to vacationers and moved into the farmhouse where the farm manager had lived.

Jim started first grade at the age of five in the Central Valley Public Schools. He later claimed that, because he was always younger than his classmates, he learned to compete at an early age. He attended high school at Mount Hermon School for Boys in Massachusetts, a nondenominational school at which students performed many of the chores, from cleaning to yard work to working in the dairy. McLamore recalls having a severe case of homesickness when he arrived at Mount Hermon, but his father responded: "Jimmy, I'm not going to take you home. You are going to stay here and tough it out, so you had better prepare yourself for it."[68] McLamore poured himself into his studies and athletics and began to assume leadership roles, including being elected president of the junior and senior classes.

While a senior, McLamore took an aptitude test that advised him to pursue a business career in sales or marketing. It was no surprise to him. After all, he had been intrigued by an Edgehill neighbor, the very wealthy Edward Henry Harriman, and had enthusiastically read the Horatio Alger stories. McLamore writes: "My goal after leaving Mount Hermon and entering college was to ultimately build a successful business career. Quite candidly, I hoped to get rich in the process. I was determined to succeed."[69]

McLamore enrolled at Cornell University because, as a New York resident, he received lower tuition. The fact that Cornell offered a business program only in the School of Hotel Administration didn't faze him, but the $200 tuition was a real stumbling block. A tuition loan and a $50 scholarship from the American Hotel Association saved the day. McLamore admits: "I had no way of knowing in 1943 how big the hospitality industry would become. I happened to be standing right in the path of progress, though I didn't realize it then."[70]

After one year at Cornell, McLamore found himself eligible for the draft, so he joined the U.S. Merchant Marine, primarily because of its relatively high pay. He was assigned to the Naval Reserve Officer's Training Corps at Cornell where he could fortunately continue taking his electives at the hotel school. McLamore was still at Cornell when the war ended, and he had met his future wife, Nancy. The couple began their marriage when the postwar job market was at its bleakest, but Jim finally landed a job as the food-service director for the Wilmington, Delaware, YMCA. McLamore recalls: "It was during my tenure as director . . . at the Wilmington YMCA that I began to think in terms of organizing people and developing operating systems. This seemed to me the necessary first step in building a profit-making enterprise."[71] Little did he know that this job would lead to his association with Burger King.

McLamore had noticed the success of a 24-hour-a-day restaurant across the street from the YMCA. The Toddle House, a clone of the highly lucrative White Castle chain, was part of the trend toward short-order restaurants, and McLamore was convinced that he could ride this trend to success. In 1949 he rented a shop for $300 a month and began redesigning the interior. As McLamore described it:

I decided to make the interior of the restaurant different. . . . Instead of putting in a ten-seat, straight counter, which was standard at the time, I installed a horse-shoe-shaped counter with 14 seats. And instead of having a small space for food preparation, I designed a much larger production area. . . . I also felt that the larger area inside the restaurant could be made very attractive by using linoleum floor and wallpaper. This would give the customers a pleasant view of the food preparation processes and provide a certain amount of ambience. . . . I also installed one of the first air-conditioning units that were just coming onto the commercial market. A distinct competitive advantage: The Toddle House didn't have one![72]

The first restaurant, called The Colonial Inn, opened in Wilmington on January 4, 1950. It was an immediate success, even receiving the recommendation of restaurant critic Duncan Hines. According to McLamore,

"The Colonial Inn whetted my appetite for business growth. I was anxious to keep moving."[73] Then he met David Edgerton.

Edgerton was the sole proprietor and owner of the Insta Burger King in Miami, Florida. McLamore was impressed with Edgerton and with his restaurant's simple food-service concept—simple menu, low prices, high margins, and fast service—which could easily be expanded into a chain of restaurants. In 1954 McLamore and Edgerton cofounded Burger King of Miami, Inc., which became Burger King Corporation in 1972. The company was bought by Pillsbury Company in 1967 and today has more than 10,600 locations worldwide.

Edward Miller, cofounder of Spic and Span, Inc. was born in 1907 in Cedar Rapids, Iowa. His mother died six weeks after his birth, and his father, an immigrant tinsmith from Poland, was forced to put young Edward and his two-year-old sister in an orphanage for two years. When Miller was seven, his father remarried and moved the family to Madison, Wisconsin, where young Edward was known as a quiet and studious child who worked hard to help support his family. According to Miller, "In high school, I used to make and sell arm bands on a Saturday for Badgers games. I sold programs. Then I started selling newspapers. . . . I had enough to put myself through college from my newspaper earning."[74]

While attending the University of Wisconsin, Miller met his future business partner, Harry Plous. The two were fraternity brothers, and in 1928 Plous asked Miller if he would help out one summer in the Plous family business—the Union Dye Works of Kenosha. After graduating with a degree in marketing, Miller joined the company full time. He recalls that he had no intention of going into the dry-cleaning business—his first love was advertising—but the Great Depression had begun, and jobs were scarce. His plans were to move on one day, but then he fell in love with and married the boss's daughter, Shirley.

In 1934 Miller opened a branch in Milwaukee, which was called Spic and Span. In less than two years, his store overshadowed the Kenosha headquarters, and the entire operation was moved to Milwaukee. Miller approached the dry-cleaning business the same way he had approached other challenges in his life, learning all he could about the business and constantly innovating. He invented the "Steaming Susie," a tailor's dummy with vents through which steam is forced to smooth out wrinkles from the inside, avoiding seam impressions. He later sold the patent, but the equipment is still used worldwide. He also perfected a process called Aqua-Kleen, which uses special detergents and timed cycles to clean garments with water.

When Louis Plous died in 1950, Miller (president) and Harry Plous (vice president) expanded the operation further. By 1959 they had 43 stores, and they later expanded into Los Angeles, Atlanta, and Florida. They closed these out-of-state stores in the 1980s when Spic and Span bought out one of its largest competitors. Miller turned over the day-to-day operation of the company and the presidency to his son Robert, but he remained actively involved in the business until his death in 1999 at the age of 93.

Thomas Stephen (Tom) Monaghan, cofounder of Domino's Pizza, was born in 1937 in Ann Arbor, Michigan. His father died when he was only four years old, and his mother found it difficult to deal with Tom and his younger brother Jim. She placed them in the first of a series of foster homes, eventually placing them in St. Joseph's Home for Boys when Tom was six.

Mrs. Monaghan settled in Traverse City, Michigan, and brought her two sons home the year Tom was in sixth grade. Shortly afterward, he exhibited his early entrepreneurial skills by growing vegetables in their backyard and selling them door-to-door. He also caught and sold fish and sold newspapers on street corners. Unfortunately, young Tom and his mother did not get along very well, and she sent him to another foster home before he entered eighth grade.

While attending St. Francis High School in Traverse City, Monaghan decided that he wanted to become a priest, but the rigors of seminary proved too much for him. He was expelled in less than a year.

After another altercation with his mother that resulted in his spending a night in jail and being placed in a detention home for six months, Monaghan went to live with an aunt and uncle in Ann Arbor. His poor performance in high school kept him from realizing the dream of studying architecture at the University of Michigan. Instead, he enrolled in the architectural trade school at Ferris State College and worked a series of jobs to pay his tuition. When his improved performance still failed to get him into the University of Michigan, he enlisted in the U.S. Marine Corps to obtain its educational benefits. He was discharged from the marines in July 1959 with $2,000 that he saved for tuition, but he invested his savings in a get-rich-quick scheme and wound up broke.

Monaghan finally got his dream of attending the University of Michigan in the fall of 1958, but he floated in and out of school, working at a variety of odd jobs, for the next two years. Then in September 1960, his brother called him with a business proposition.

Jim Monaghan, who was a mailman, overheard a conversation about a pizza shop in the college town of Ypsilanti, Michigan, that was for sale. The selling price for DomiNick's was $500, plus the takeover of some debts, and Jim suggested that his brother and he buy the restaurant. Tom reasoned that he could work there at night and attend the university during the day. The brothers gave the owner, Dominick DiVarti, $75 as a down payment and borrowed the rest—about $900—from the post office credit union.

The partnership between Tom and his brother lasted less than a year, at which time he exchanged the restaurant's delivery car for Jim's share of the business. The pizzeria did well, primarily because of its student customers, so Monaghan began to look into the possibility of opening a second shop in another college town, and, with it, acquiring a new partner. Jim Gilmore took over the operation of the original restaurant, and Monaghan opened a new shop in Mount Pleasant, Michigan. He then opened a third shop in Ann Arbor in 1962, another in Ypsilanti in 1963. The partnership with Gilmore was dissolved in 1965, and Monaghan renamed his chain Domino's. The name "was Italian, it was unique, . . . and it was close to DomiNick's both in sound and in spelling, so if someone were to look up our old name in the phone book, the new name would be in the same vicinity."[75]

Monaghan believed that he could compete on the basis of quality, using only the best ingredients, freshly made dough, and whole-milk cheeses. He limited his menu to pizzas and introduced the concept of 30-minute delivery. In 1967 he sold his first franchise site—his second Ypsilanti store—and opened his first out-of-state store in Vermont in 1968. By January 1969, there were 12 stores with 12 more in development. Growth was steady at 100 stores in 1975, 200 in 1978, 500 in 1979, 2,000 by 1985, and 5,000 by 1989, with an additional 260 in other countries.

In 1989 Monaghan announced that he was handing over the presidency of Domino's so that he could devote more time to charities and to the Catholic church. He continued to act as chairman and CEO until 1998, when he sold 93 percent of the company to Bain Capital, Inc.

Robert Gerald Mondavi, founder of Robert Mondavi Winery, was born in Virginia, Minnesota, in 1913. When he was 10 years old, his family moved to the Napa Valley town of Lodi, California, where his father, Cesare, became associated with the Sunnyhill Winery in St. Helena. Mondavi recalls, "My father suggested I become a winemaker. It was a new industry, and I decided to grow with it."[76] First, however, he attended Stanford University where, in 1936, he received a bachelor's degree in economics. After graduating, he joined his father on the production staff at the Sunnyhill Winery.

In 1943 Robert recommended that his father buy the failing Charles Krug Winery. Cesare agreed on the condition that Robert and his younger brother Peter work there. Peter took over production, and Robert handled marketing and development. But the two brothers didn't agree on the way the company should be run. Robert wanted to grow the company rapidly, Peter resisted, and Cesare intervened to keep the peace. Following their father's death, the brothers clashed, and Robert left Krug in 1965. While retaining 24 percent of the Krug stock, he wanted to start his own vineyard.

Mondavi started the Robert Mondavi Winery with two partners and a total investment of $200,000. In 1969 the two partners sold their shares of the vineyard to Ranier Companies, a Seattle beer merchant that controlled the Canadian beer manufacturer Molson. While Ranier invested heavily in the vineyard, let Mondavi keep his name, and did little to interfere with the company's operation, Mondavi was unhappy with the fact that he held only a 25 percent share in the company. By 1978 he was able to orchestrate the purchase of enough shares of Ranier to control more than 60 percent of his winery.

Mondavi approached winemaking more as an art than a science. He wanted to enhance the subtleties in flavor that American wines lacked at the time. Through his research and experiments, he discovered a number of factors that effected the resulting wine, including differences in room temperature during fermentation and the use of oak barrels rather than the steel or redwood vats commonly used in American wineries. He also produced new classes of wines such as the chenin blanc (a sweeter pinot blanc) and the fume blanc (a drier version of sauvignon blanc combined with wine made from the semillon grape). Both creations became popular sellers.

In 1978 Mondavi also forged a partnership with the Baron Philippe de Rothschild, under which Mondavi provided the land and production facilities and the baron provided the expertise of his wine master. The result was a premium California cabernet, sold under the label Opus One. Mondavi later brokered similar successful deals with winemakers in Chile and Italy.

In 1990 Mondavi turned operation of the winery over to his two sons, Michael and Tim. In 1993 the company became only the third winery in this country to offer public shares (the family retained 70 percent ownership) and has performed well since.

Robert Mondavi has received numerous awards, including the Medal of Honor from L'Ordre Mondial, the Merit Award from the American Society of Enology and Viticulture, and nine Man of the Year awards.

Akio Morita, cofounder of the Sony Corporation (originally named Tokyo Tsushin Kogyo [Tokyo Telecommunications Company]), was born in 1921 in Kasugaya, Japan. His family were wealthy sake brewers who expected the eldest son to take over management of the family's brewery some day, but Morita was only interested in electronics. He eventually convinced his father to groom his younger brother for the brewery job, while he studied physics at Osaka Imperial University.

When he graduated in 1944, Morita was commissioned as a lieutenant in the Imperial Japanese Navy and was assigned as a technical engineer at the Naval Research Center, where he met his future partner Masaru Ibuka. In 1946 Morita and Ibuka founded the Tokyo Telecommunications Company with $500 in funds provided by the Morita family.

The electronic manufacturing company, renamed Sony 12 years later, first produced vacuum-tube voltmeters, amplifiers, communications devices, and a commercially unsuccessful tape recorder. When Morita read about the transistors developed by Bell Laboratories, he was convinced that he could produce a commercially successful transistorized radio. Sony subsequently released the first AM transistor radio in 1955, the first pocket-sized transistor radio in 1957, the first two-band transistor radio in 1957, and the first FM transistor radio in 1958, followed by the introduction of an all-transistor television set in 1959, a transistorized video tape recorder in 1960, and the first small-screen transistorized television set in 1961.

Morita and his family lived in Manhattan in the early 1960s while he was setting up the Sony Corporation of America. Highly sophisticated, yet low-key, ads introduced the new company to the American public without hinting at the company's foreign base. The ads also introduced the buying public to previously unknown products they would learn to want. In 1963 Sony became the first Japanese company to offer stock for sale in the United States and seven years later became the first Japanese company to be listed on the New York Stock Exchange. The company enjoyed unprecedented success over the next two decades; however, Sony's 1989 buyout of Columbia Pictures for $3.4 billion, one of Morita's last initiatives, turned sour. Morita had been convinced that if Sony had owned a studio that could produce movies in Beta format, they would not have lost the VCR war. Unfortunately, the buyout was perceived as just another in a wave of Japanese buyouts of U.S. companies and property. This backlash was accompanied by a series of management blunders that resulted in a $3.2 billion loss for Sony in 1994.

Morita suffered a cerebral hemorrhage while playing tennis in November 1993, and shortly after announcing the huge loss in 1994, he resigned as chairman. After that he spent much of his time in rehabilitation at his home in Hawaii. Morita died of pneumonia in a Tokyo hospital on October 3, 1999.

David Packard, cofounder of Hewlett-Packard, was born in 1912 in Pueblo, Colorado, where he grew up and attended public school. After graduating from Centennial High School in 1930, he enrolled in Stanford University, majoring in electrical engineering. He graduated from Stanford in 1934 with a bachelor's degree and entered graduate school at the University of Colorado. After only a few months of graduate study, he took a job with the General Electric Company in Schenectady, New York.

Packard returned to Stanford in 1939 and obtained a degree in electrical engineering. He also renewed his friendship with fellow student William R. Hewlett. The future partners set up a workshop in Packard's garage, using $538 in capital to equip it. The Hewlett-Packard Company soon invented a weight-reducing machine, a bowling alley foul-line indicator and an electronic harmonica tuner. Their first commercial sale was to Walt Disney in 1939. Disney ordered eight audio-oscillators for the sound track of the movie *Fantasia*.

Packard and Hewlett reinvested all of their profits into the company, a policy they would continue to follow. They also strategically located their plant near Stanford so they could recruit bright students and keep current with cutting-edge research. Early on, they decided to concentrate on electronic measuring and test instruments, as well as medical and chemical instruments, including heart-monitoring instruments and atomic clocks for the Apollo spacecraft. They later became leaders in the design and manufacture of computers and participated in the development of handheld calculators and ink-jet printers.

When the company was incorporated in 1947, Packard became president and remained so until 1964. He served as CEO and chairman of the board from 1964 to 1968, then took a leave of absence from 1969 to 1971 to serve as deputy secretary of defense in the Nixon administration. He returned to the position of chairman of the board of Hewlett-Packard in 1972 and resigned that position in 1993. When he resigned, Hewlett-Packard was second only to IBM among U.S. computer manufacturers. Packard died on March 26, 1996.

Ross Perot, founder of Electronic Data Systems (EDS) and Perot Systems Corporation, was born Henry Ray Perot in 1930 in Texarkana, Texas. He was the second son of Gabriel Elias ("Big Ross") Perot, whose first son, Gabriel Ross Perot, died in 1927 at the age of three. Henry Ray Perot had his name legally changed to Henry Ross Perot when he was 12 years old, "partly in an effort to assuage his father's grief over the death of his namesake."[77]

Ross attended school, first at the private Patty Hill Elementary School and then in public schools, in Texarkana. Beginning at the age of seven or eight, he always had a job—breaking horses for a dollar a horse, selling garden seeds, selling Christmas cards, and delivering newspapers. He also achieved the rank of Eagle Scout only 16 months after becoming a Boy Scout, a rank that takes most scouts three to five years to attain. He later said, "The day I made Eagle was more important to me than the day I discovered I was a billionaire."[78]

After graduating from Texarkana High School (1947), Perot attended Texarkana Junior College for two years, all the while applying for an appointment to the U.S. Naval Academy. In 1949 he received an appointment and was sworn in as a midshipman. He studied engineering and "thrived on the discipline and regimentation."[79] He was elected president of the class of 1953 and, among other positions, served as chaplain, shore-patrol officer, alcohol and narcotics officer, and first-aid officer. Due to the outbreak of the Korean War, Perot's initial two-year commitment was extended to four years, during which he served on board the destroyer USS *Sigourney* and the aircraft carrier USS *Layte*. He was honorably discharged from the navy in 1957 as a lieutenant. One biography reports that it was also during this period that Perot began pronouncing his surname in the French manner—pe-ROH—rather than the way it was pronounced in Texarkana: PEE-roh.[80]

Perot moved to Dallas after his discharge from the navy and took a job as a salesman for IBM. He was soon outselling all of his colleagues, but in

1961 IBM set quotas on how much salesmen could earn. The next year, when Perot reached his quota limit by January 19, he decided to leave IBM and start his own business.

With a $1,000 loan from his wife and his salary as a part-time consultant for Texas Blue Cross, Perot incorporated EDS on June 27, 1962—his thirty-second birthday. He planned to sell not just hardware but a package of hardware, software, and technical support. His first significant sale did not come until 1965 when he anticipated the huge market that Medicare and Medicaid would create for data-processing companies. He captured contracts with Blue Cross/Blue Shield in 11 states, computerizing their billing systems. He then expanded to service the private sector and by 1968 was showing a profit of $2.4 million.

Perot's success was partly due to his ability to anticipate a very lucrative market, but it was also due to the exacting standards he set for employees— EDS's motto was "Eagles don't flock; you find them one at a time." But, EDSers began to resemble their IBM counterparts. A strict dress code required dark suits, white shirts, conservative ties, closely cropped hair, and no facial hair (most employees were male and many were military veterans). The code of personal conduct forbade such behaviors as marital infidelity. As Perot put it: "We clearly codified what EDS is, what an EDSer is. Everything is just nailed down as succinctly as possible. I want people who are smart, tough, self-reliant, have a history of success since childhood, a history of being the best at what they've done, people who love to win."[81]

In 1984 Perot sold EDS to General Motors (GM) for $2.5 billion ($1 billion in cash and 11.3 million shares of GM stock). He remained chairman of EDS but joined the GM board of directors—a relationship that was troubled from the first day. Perot publicly criticized GM saying, "Revitalizing GM is like teaching an elephant to tap dance. You find the sensitive spots and start poking"[82] The unholy alliance between Perot and GM ended in December 1986 when GM bought Perot out for a reported $700 million.

General Motors' agreement with Perot stipulated that he could not start another for-profit computer-service company for at least three years and that he could not compete, even without compensation, for 18 months. Exactly 18 months later, on June 1, 1988, he established Perot Systems Corporation. In 1989 he invested $20 million in Steve Jobs's new venture, the NeXT Computer, but it was his decision to run for president in 1992 that thrust Perot back into the limelight. His first run for the presidency cost him

$60 million and netted only 19 percent of the popular vote, but he was back again for a run in 1996, netting only 8 percent of the vote.

Perot has received numerous awards and honors, including the Winston Churchill Award and the Raoul Wallenberg Award. He was inducted into the National Business Hall of Fame and received the Smithsonian Computerworld Award. For public service he received the Jefferson Award and the Patrick Henry Award, and he received the Horatio Alger award for succeeding in defiance of obstacles.

Ross is a noted philanthropist. He has contributed more than $100 million to various causes including the Boy Scouts, the Girl Scouts, and the Salvation Army.

Stephen M. Pollan, attorney, financial consultant, and career adviser, was born in 1929. As an attorney and career adviser, he has offered advice to clients, including such companies as AT&T, for more than thirty years. He has appeared on CNBC, the *Today Show, Good Morning America*, and *The Nightly Business Report*, and he is also a regular contributor to a variety of magazines, including *Working Woman, Personal Finance, Worth*, and *New York*. Pollan has written and edited a number of books, including *Live Rich: Everything You Need to Know to Be Your Own Boss, Die Broke: A Radical, Four-Part Financial Plan, Lifescripts for the Self-Employed, Starting Over: How to Change Careers or Start Your Own Business, Turning No into Yes*, and *The Business of Living*.

Anita Roddick, née Perella, founder of The Body Shop, was born in Littlehampton, Sussex, England, in 1942. Like other Italian immigrant families in this seaside town, Roddick's family operated a restaurant—The Clifton Café. Her mother cooked, her grandmother prepared vegetables, and the children helped after school and on weekends, taking orders, clearing tables, cleaning up. According to Roddick, "The work ethic, the idea of service, was second nature to us."[83]

When Roddick's mother married Uncle Henry, the man Roddick would later learn was her biological father, he transformed the Clifton Café into an American-style diner, complete with jukebox, ice-cream sundaes, and Coca-Cola. Roddick remembers this transformation as her first lesson in marketing aesthetics. "I remember being dazzled by the Americana, by the Vargas girls on the Coca-Cola promo cards, by the brilliant colours on the jukebox and the style of everything. I absorbed it all."[84]

Roddick attended Catholic school at St. Catherine's convent, where she learned the power of trading. Uncle Henry had brought a lot of bubble gum and comic books back with him from the United States, and she swapped these commodities for collections of cigarette cards and movie albums. She tightly controlled the flow of goodies into her market, whetting her customers' appetites.

After Uncle Henry's death, Roddick and her siblings returned to work in the family café, but this time their presence was required to make ends meet. She was enrolled in the Maude Allen Secondary Modern School for girls, where she proved to be a "deeply unpromising pupil for the first year"[85] but where she later learned the joys of learning. Both her teachers and her mother encouraged her to "Be special," to "be anything but mediocre."[86]

Roddick attended the Newton Park College of Education at Bath for three years and credits one instructor at Newton for helping her develop an appreciation for art and design. In 1962 she traveled to Israel on a scholarship to complete her thesis on "The Children of the Kibbutz" and spent time hitchhiking around the country immersing herself in history and ideology. Her travels there taught her that she could go anywhere she chose by herself. Over the next few years she returned to Littlehampton to teach in her old school, hitchhiked to Greece for a holiday and returned through Geneva where she worked for a short time for the United Nations, took her savings from the United Nations job and took a boat to Tahiti, traveled to Australia by way of the New Hebrides and New Caledonia, and wound up being thrown out of South Africa for going to a jazz club on "black night." She met her future husband—Gordon Roddick—after she returned to Littlehampton.

The Roddicks purchased and ran a small hotel in Littlehampton, later adding a restaurant. They then opened the very successful Paddington's Restaurant, where they took advantage of the British attraction to American-style hamburger restaurants. Their lives were consumed with running these businesses until one day when Gordon crawled into bed and said, "This is killing us. I can't cope with it any more. Let's pack it in."[87] And pack it in they did. Gordon decided to take a couple of years off and pursue a childhood ambition—riding a horse from Buenos Aires to New York. In the meantime, Anita was supposed to "find a little shop" to run.

The "little shop" turned out to be an idea of Anita's to sell natural cosmetic products in different sizes and in cheap containers. As Anita reasoned, if you can buy an ounce of candy or cheese, why can't you buy an ounce of lotion? She even had a name for her new venture—The Body Shop, after the garages she had seen in the United States that banged the dents out of cars. With Gordon's support, Anita opened her first Body Shop in Kensington Gardens, Brighton, on March 27, 1976. She offered 25 hand-mixed products.

Franchising allowed the company to expand rapidly to its current fifteen hundred-plus stores in 47 countries, with sales of £605.8 billion for the 52 weeks ending February 27, 1999.

Roddick has continued to pursue other passions, including pushing for a ban on animal testing in Britain, the Save the Whales campaign, the Romanian Relief Drive, the Brazilian Healthcare Project, the Children of Chernobyl charity, and support of women's rights at the Fourth World Conference of Women in Beijing, China.

William (Bill) Rosenberg, founder of Dunkin' Donuts, was born in Boston, Massachusetts, in the late 1930s, educated in public schools, and forced to leave school in the eighth grade to help support his family during the Great Depression. At the age of 17, Rosenberg started working for a company that distributed ice cream from refrigerated trucks. At 20, he was promoted to assistant manager, and by 21 he was made branch manager. Eventually, he became national sales manager.

During World War II, Rosenberg worked for Bethlehem Steel, becoming a union delegate and contract coordinator. After the war, he invested $5,000 in a mobile industrial catering business known as Industrial Luncheon and shortly thereafter had 140 catering trucks, 25 in-plant outlets, and a vending operation. When he realized that 40 percent of his revenues was coming from doughnuts and coffee, he started a retail shop—the Open Kettle—for those products. In 1950 he opened the first shop known as Dunkin' Donuts in Quincy, Massachusetts. In 1955, after opening six Dunkin' Donuts, he decided to franchise further operations, and the first franchise agreement was signed. By 1990, when Allied Comecq PLC purchased Dunkin' Donuts, there were 2,000 open shops.

Rosenberg remains chairman emeritus of the company.

Pleasant Rowland, founder of Pleasant Company and developer of the American Girl collection, describes an influential part of her childhood as follows: "I can remember discovering the books in my grandmother's second-floor bookshelf that my dad had had when he was little. I discovered the Oz books there. I remember just delving into them, barely moving for days at a time, flung across my bed. I was an avid reader. And I had three sisters. We played with our dolls. It was just a simpler time. . . . The real inspiration for The American Girl's Collection came somewhere from that childhood experience."[88]

In the intervening years, Rowland taught kindergarten through third grade, became a television news reporter in San Francisco for a short while, and developed the first reading program for kindergarten children. She spent the decade of the 1970s writing textbooks; she then married and moved to Wisconsin.

On a fateful trip to colonial Williamsburg, Virginia, with her husband, Rowland was moved by "the entire experience of walking in the footsteps of that colonial world. I realized," she says, "we have not done a good job bringing history alive for kids in schools. . . I thought, isn't there some way that I can make the magic of this historic place come alive for little girls?"[89] This idea stayed with her over the next several months, but it took one more event to set The American Girl's Collection into motion—Christmas 1983. She was searching for special gifts for her nieces, preferably the same sweet romantic types of dolls that she and her sisters had played with as girls; it was the same year that Cabbage Patch dolls hit the market. She laments, "Neither of my choices [Cabbage Patch or Barbie] were particularly pretty and I didn't think they were of a very high quality. But most important, they didn't say anything about what it meant to be a girl growing up in America. And they weren't something I thought anybody was going to treasure."[90] Thus, in 1986 the Pleasant Company was born.

Rowland combined her love for history with a commitment to educational products. "It was an idea of books and dolls that would bring history alive, that would provide girls with role models, showing that the essentials of growing up haven't changed very much, in spite of the differences in the world in the last two hundred and fifty years."[91] She took her total lack of business experience, her entire life savings, and no marketing research and within 10 years built a profitable doll, clothing, and publishing empire. Today she dominates the 7-to-12-year-old girls' market with *American Girl* magazine, American Girl Gear, and The American Girl Collection. The company has sold over 50 million books and 4 million dolls. Sales in 1998 topped $287 million.

Harland Sanders, founder of the Kentucky Fried Chicken Corporation (KFC), was born near Henryville, Indiana, in 1890. His culinary experience began at the age of six when, following the death of his father, he was left to care for his two younger siblings. A *New Yorker* profile of the Sanders indicates that by the age of seven he "was excelling in bread and vegetables and coming along nicely in meat."[92] His mother remarried when he was 12, and the young Harland was sent to work as a farmhand near Greenwood, Indiana, where he stayed until he was 15. After that, he worked at a variety of jobs, including insurance salesman, buggy painter, plowman, streetcar conductor, ferryboat operator, and eventually as an "ashdoodler" on various railroads. While working on the railroads, he took a correspondence course in law, earning a doctor of law degree from Southern University.

In 1929 Sanders opened a filling station in Corbin, Kentucky. In addition to cooking meals for his family, he began preparing meals for the occasional traveler who showed up. His meals were simple, Southern-style fare of pan-fried chicken, fresh vegetables, and homemade bread. When demand for his food outstripped demand for gasoline, Sanders closed the station and opened Sanders Café. As he related later, he even "hightailed it up to Cornell University and took an eight-week course in Restaurant and Hotel Management, learnin' all about table d'hote and things like how many potatoes to cook."[93] But, the colonel, as he could rightly call himself since receiving his honorary military title from the governor of Kentucky in 1936, had one problem that Cornell could not solve—pan-fried chicken took too long to prepare, and deep-fried chicken did not meet his standards. In 1939 Sanders found the solution to his frying dilemma—the pressure cooker. With this new gadget he could prepare perfectly cooked chicken, seasoned with his own concoction of 11 common herbs and spices, in eight or nine minutes.

Sanders's restaurant prospered until 1956, when a new interstate highway bypassed the café and he was forced to sell it at auction for only $75,000. Rather than retiring on his little bit of savings and Social Security, Sanders decided to explore another business option he had initiated in 1952 when he sold his recipe for chicken to a select number of restaurateurs. Under their arrangement, Sanders received four cents for every chicken they prepared with his process. Maybe others would be willing to do the same.

So, at the age of 66, Harland Sanders set out to establish a franchise business, adopting his now-famous attire of a white suit, white shirt, white moustache and goatee, black string tie, black shoes, and cane, all of which were suppose to create an image of old Southern gracious living. The first two years were a struggle, but by 1960 there were more than two hundred restaurants paying to use the colonel's process. By 1963 there were more than six hundred outlets, grossing Sanders $300,000 per year, but as he put it, "The popularity of Kentucky Fried Chicken was beginning to run right over me and mash me flat."[94] After several rejections, he finally agreed to sell his company to John Y. Brown Jr. and Jack Massey for $2 million and a lifetime salary of $40,000 per year (later increased to $75,000). In exchange, Sanders served as advisor, spokesman, and member of the board of directors until his resignation in 1970. Sanders died near Shelbyville, Kentucky, on December 16, 1980.

Howard Schultz, founder of Starbucks Coffee Company, was born in 1953 in Brooklyn, New York, and was raised in the city's Bay View housing project. He later cited his father's financial hardships (as a truck and cab driver and factory worker) as the source of his drive for success and his concern for his employees. "What I remember most was the way [my father] was treated in his adult life, which beat him down. He didn't have the self-esteem to feel worthy of a good job. So I try to give people hope and self-esteem through a company that respects them."[95]

Schultz became the first member of his family to graduate from college, earning a bachelor of science degree in business from Northern Michigan University in 1975. After graduating he took a job in the sales and marketing division of Xerox Corporation. After three years at Xerox, he was recruited to be the vice president and general manager of Hammerplast, U.S.A., an American subsidiary of a Swedish company that specialized in housewares. One of his clients was a Seattle-based coffee store named Starbucks Coffee Company.

Starbucks, founded in 1971, started as a single store that featured freshly roasted gourmet coffee beans and an assortment of imported teas and spices. A second store opened near the University of Washington in 1972. The owners were so impressed by Schultz's energy and marketing skills that they offered him part ownership to join the company in 1982. He became their head of marketing and retail operations.

While on vacation in Italy in 1983, Schultz had what he described as an epiphany. He realized that coffee—its selection, brewing, and consumption—was a vital part of most Italians' social life. They started and ended their days mingling with their friends and sipping their coffee. "Why not open a coffee bar in Seattle? Coffeehouses in Italy are a third place for people, after home and work. There's a relationship of trust and confidence in that environment. As Americans, there are very few things we have confidence in."[96]

When Schultz returned to Seattle, he failed to convince his two partners of the potential of his idea and left Starbucks in 1986 in frustration. He started his own chain of espresso bars, called Il Giornale, in Seattle but soon heard that the Starbucks chain was up for sale. With the financial support of Seattle investors, Schultz bought Starbucks' 11 stores for $3.8 million. He then began to overhaul the company completely, first expanding his offerings to include exotic coffees like espresso, cappuccino, café latté, iced coffee, mocha, and many others. He then tackled the atmosphere of the stores themselves, providing bright, clean interiors with tables, artwork, and classical and jazz music in the background. Finally, he turned his attention to his employees. He trained them not only to brew a good cup of coffee but also to understand the importance of customer service. "Service is a lost art in America. . . . It's not viewed as a professional job to work behind a counter. We don't believe that. We want to provide our people with dignity and self-esteem, so we offer tangible benefits. The attrition rate in retail fast food is between 200 and 400 percent a year. At Starbucks, it's 60 percent."[97]

On June 26, 1992, Starbucks went public with an opening price of $17 per share, generating $110 million in capital that funded its expansion. By 1994 the company had 470 locations, growing to 1,000 stores by early 1997. Schultz has also orchestrated strategic business alliances with companies like Barnes & Noble Bookstores, Pepsi-Cola, Dreyers Grand Ice Cream, Westin Hotels, ITT Sheraton Hotels, and United Airlines.

Schultz is a major sponsor of CARE, receiving the CARE Humanitarian Award in 1992. Starbucks received an American Business Ethics Award and the Corporate Conscience Award in 1996.

Ricardo Semler, CEO and President of Semco, S.A., was born about 1958. His Austrian-born father worked as an engineer for DuPont in Argentina until 1953, when he moved to São Paulo, Brazil, and founded Semler & Company. The company began by manufacturing centrifuges and expanded its product line to include marine pumps.

After earning his MBA from Harvard at the age of 20, Ricardo Semler returned to Brazil to work for his father. The two clashed over management styles from the very beginning. The elder Semler followed the traditional, autocratic, paternalistic approach to management, while his son was a proponent of participatory management. When Ricardo threatened to leave the company over these differences, his father retired and transferred majority ownership to him.

In 1982 Ricardo Semler took control of Semler & Company. On his first day, he fired two-thirds of the company's top management, began planning for product diversification, and changed the company name to Semco. He subsequently dismantled his father's management structure and replaced it with a more flexible organization based on three core values: employee participation, profit sharing, and the free flow of information.

Frederick W. (Fred) Smith, founder of Federal Express, was born in 1944 in the Memphis, Tennessee, suburb of Marks, Mississippi. His father, who died when Fred was four years old, was a successful entrepreneur in his own right, founding the Dixie Greyhound Bus Lines and cofounding the restaurant chain Toddle House. Young Fred inherited two important things from his father—the money he would later use to start his company and a letter urging his son to put his inheritance to work to build something great and not to become part of the idle rich.

Smith took his father's admonition to heart, and despite having to overcome a congenital bone disease that forced him to wear braces and walk with crutches as a youth, he eventually played basketball and football in prep school and was voted "Best All-Around Student." He learned to fly at the age of 15, and the next year he and two of his school friends founded a recording studio, Ardent Record Company, which is still in business.

In 1962 Smith entered Yale University, majoring in economics and political science. As a junior, he wrote a term paper analyzing the existing freight services and suggesting that there might be a market for high-priority, time-sensitive delivery of goods such as medicines and electronic components. His professor was not impressed with the idea and gave Smith a "C" on his paper, but the idea stayed with Smith throughout his two-tour career in the U.S. Marine Corps and even after he purchased controlling interest in Arkansas Aviation Sales.

Smith engaged two consulting firms to investigate the viability of creating his delivery service and learned from their reports that there was a high degree of dissatisfaction with the dependability of existing services. In addition, customers in smaller, less-accessible locations had to wait for scheduled carriers to pick up or deliver their packages. Smith was convinced that he could fill these gaps. All he had to do was find the money.

As an inducement to other investors, Smith committed more than $8 million of his family money to his project. Private investors, including Peter Wilmott, Roger Frock, Michael Fitzgerald, Arthur Bass, and Vincent Fagan, add $40 million, and several banks rounded out the total investment of $90 million, the largest single venture-capital start-up in American history at that time. Federal Express was incorporated on June 1, 1971, and began operation on April 17, 1973, with service to 22 cities.

The first three years of business were difficult ones, with heavy debts and many personal sacrifices. Company lore includes Smith's selling his private plane to raise capital, using his $27,000 gambling winnings to meet payroll, and stories of couriers leaving behind watches as collateral for gasoline to fuel the company's planes and trucks. But it all paid off in 1976 when Federal Express's revenues grew to $109 million, a net income of $8.1 million. Subsequent deregulation of the airline industry helped boost earnings to $20 million in 1977, and in the first public stock offering in 1978, 1,075,000 shares were sold at $3 per share.

Smith's personal honors include two Purple Hearts, Silver and Bronze Stars, and the Vietnamese Cross of Gallantry. Federal Express was voted one of the best-managed companies in 1981, was named one of *Fortune*'s "Top 10 Business Triumphs of the 1970s," and won the Malcolm Baldrige National Quality Award in 1990.

Thomas G. Stemberg, cofounder of Staples, Inc., was born in Orange, New Jersey, on January 18, 1949. Following the death of his father when he was 13 years old, Tom and his mother returned to his parents' native Vienna, Austria, where he attended the American International School. He returned to the United States to attend Harvard University, from which he received a bachelor's degree in 1971 and an MBA in 1973.

Stemberg began his career with the Jewel Company's Star Markets, where he became vice president for sales and merchandising. While at Jewel, he introduced the first line of generic foods sold in the United States, as well as the concept of warehouse specials. In 1982 he moved to First National Supermarkets, where he served as president of the Edwards-Finast division and established the Edwards Food Warehouse chain. It was during this period that he developed the concept of an office superstore, a chain of discount stores that would serve businesses with fewer than 100 employees by providing a broad selection of products sold at an average of 50 percent below list price.

Stemberg met his Staples cofounder, Leo Kahn, in 1980 when they participated in a televised debate on marketing concepts. Kahn "virtually invented the idea of no-frills, deep discount supermarket retailing,"[98] and he admired Stemberg's success in warehousing. Backed by a group of investors that included Bain Capital, Hambro International Ventures, Harvard Management, Bessemer Ventures, and Adler & Company, the two opened their first store in Brighton, Massachusetts, in 1986.

The company continued to grow steadily and methodically, completing its initial public offering in April 1989. A total of 3,250,000 shares were sold at $19 per share. By 1999 the company's revenues topped $7 billion through more than a thousand superstores, mail order catalogs, e-commerce outlets, and contract business.

R. David (Dave) Thomas, founder of Wendy's Old Fashioned Hamburgers, was born in Atlantic City, New Jersey, in 1932 and was adopted soon afterward by Rex and Auleva Thomas from western Michigan. Thomas's adopted mother died when he was five years old, and his father moved him from town to town over the next 10 years. Thomas estimates that he lived in a dozen places by the time he was 15 and as a result never felt that he belonged. To make matters worse, his maternal grandmother told him when he was 13 that he had been adopted. "It really hurt that nobody told me before. It is a terrible feeling to know my natural mother didn't want me."[99]

Thomas started working when he was about 12 years old to help his father make ends meet. He delivered groceries and worked behind a drugstore soda fountain. He and his father also ate many meals at cheap restaurants, resulting in Dave's decision to own his own restaurant: "I thought if I owned a restaurant, I could eat all I wanted for *free*. What could be better than that?[100]

When Thomas's family moved to Fort Wayne, Indiana, in 1947, he found a job as a busboy in a Hobby House restaurant. He dropped out of school after the tenth grade to work full-time at Hobby House and refused to leave Fort Wayne when his father decided to move again. Instead, he moved into the local YMCA and later joined the U.S. Army. Thomas was assigned to the army's Cook and Baker's School at Fort Benning, Georgia, and then as a cook and staff sergeant in Germany where he was responsible for feeding up to two thousand people.

After his discharge from the army in 1953, Thomas returned to the Hobby House in Fort Wayne as a short-order cook. When his boss bought into Kentucky Fried Chicken, he offered Thomas a proposition: If Thomas could make the four failing chicken outlets profitable, his boss would transfer to him 45 percent of the ownership of the restaurants. Thomas recalls, "The stores were practically bankrupt. I had four kids and a wife, and I was making $135 a week. But I made up my mind that I was going to be in business for myself."[101]

Thomas was so successful at turning around the Columbus restaurants, he attracted the attention of Harland Sanders, the real Colonel Sanders, who became a mentor for the young restaurateur. In 1968 Thomas sold his share of the franchises back to the corporation for more than $1 million in KFC stock and took a position in the corporate office. A conflict with the new owners, however, forced Thomas out within a year.

Thomas then took part of the money from the sale of the franchises to build his own chain of restaurants. He intended to specialize in hamburgers but to distinguish his chain from others by offering a variety of toppings, using fresh meat, and making burgers to order. He wanted a wholesome logo for his company, so he decided to use the likeness of his daughter Wendy, who was eight years old when the first Wendy's Old Fashioned Hamburgers opened on November 15, 1969. Wendy's showed a profit within six weeks of opening. By 1963 Thomas began to expand aggressively, selling citywide and regional franchises instead of single-site franchises.

An incident in the late 1970s made Thomas question his ability to continue running Wendy's. Senior officers in the company recommended installing salad bars, but Thomas resisted. He eventually gave in, and when the change proved to be enormously profitable, he thought others might be more qualified to run the company. "Here's a company I didn't want to screw up. I see a lot of entrepreneurs start something they can't finish."[102] In 1982 he resigned as CEO and took the position of senior chairman.

By the end of the 1980s, service at some of the restaurants began to decline and they were losing money. A new CEO accepted his position in 1989 only if Thomas would return as a guiding force in the company. Thomas had no management duties, but he would serve as Wendy's "spokesman, in-house cheerleader, and roaming quality-control man."[103] Thus began Dave Thomas's career in advertising.

One of the ad agency executives who produced the Wendy's commercials exclaimed, "Those first commercials, *oy gevalt!*"[104] According to a *Chicago Tribune* reporter, despite Thomas's "immense fortune," he "still talks like the grillman he was when he got his start. He mixes up his verbs and comes up with words that can't be found in any dictionary."[105] So, Thomas's lines were limited to phrases like "I sure could go for a Big Dave's Deluxe" and "If you make a grilled chicken sandwich at Wendy's, they will come." The new spots were a huge hit, and as Bob Garfield of *Advertising Age* reported, Thomas was "still playing the part of a guileless bumpkin, but now . . . it's obvious he's playing a part."[106]

Thomas also became actively involved in promoting adoption, establishing a program within the company that paid medical and legal bills for employees who adopted. He serves on the board of directors of Children's Hospital in Columbus and St. Jude Children's Research Hospital in Memphis, Tennessee. He received the Horatio Alger Award in 1979 and deciding to lead by example, earned a high school general equivalency diploma. His classmates voted him "most likely to succeed."

Robert Edward (Ted) Turner, founder of Turner Broadcasting System, Cable News Network (CNN), and Turner Network Television (TNT), who is sometimes called "the Mouth of the South," was born in 1938 in Cincinnati, Ohio. Turner had a tumultuous relationship with his father who by many accounts was verbally and physically abusive to his son. Even Ted's mother is quoted as saying that 90 percent of the arguments she had with her husband were over his beating Ted too hard. His father even charged him for his room and board, which Ted paid by working at his father's outdoor-advertising company during the summer.

Turner spent most of his early school years in boarding and military schools, including the Georgia Military Academy, outside Atlanta, and the McCallie School in Chattanooga, Tennessee. After resisting the rigid structure of these environments for several years, he grew to appreciate his life at McCallie. He became a company commander of company and won a Tennessee state high school debating contest. "Probably no single thing or institution has influenced my life more [than the McCallie School],"[107] he later related.

After high school, Turner attended Brown University, where he majored in economics. He had a reputation for partying and was eventually suspended from Brown. He spent six months in the U.S. Coast Guard, returned to Brown, and this time was expelled for good, for having a female visitor in his room.

In 1960 Ted began working as a junior salesman for his father's company, Turner Advertising Company. Then in 1963, Ed Turner shot and killed himself, six months after overextending himself financially by purchasing additional billboard operations. What triggered this act of desperation may have been stress, alcoholism, or even manic depression. Ted later said of his father's death that it left him alone, "because I had counted on him to make the judgment of whether or not I was a success."[108] At the age of 24, Ted became president and CEO of Turner Advertising, and the company thrived under his leadership.

In 1970 Turner bought a debt-ridden UHF television station in Atlanta, Channel 17, which he christened WTCG (**T**urner **C**ommunications **G**roup). Shortly afterward he bought a second station in Charlotte, North Carolina, which he named for himself—WRET (**R**obert **E**dward **T**urner). He ran relatively inexpensive reruns of sitcoms, did not try to compete with the "big three" networks in programming areas like the news, and used his own billboards to advertise his stations. Then in 1976, he bought his own professional sports teams—the last-place Atlanta Braves baseball team and the last-place Atlanta Hawks basketball team—which guaranteed sports programming for the stations.

When Turner learned about cable systems in the early 1970s, he began broadcasting to regional cable systems on land-based microwave delivery systems. Then when RCA launched its first satellite, Turner was one of the first businessmen to decide to invest in the new technology. On December 27, 1976, Channel 17 beamed a signal around the country and Superstation TBS was born.

In 1980 Turner sold WRET for $20 million to help fund the launch of a 24-hour live-news network—CNN. When ABC and Westinghouse attempted to compete with his new network by offering a news report that was updated every half hour, Turner countered by launching Headline News.

Then in 1986, Turner added another jewel to his broadcasting crown by purchasing MGM's library of films, which he used for programming on Superstation TBS. Turner later added two more networks—TNT in 1988 and TCM (Turner Classic Movies) in 1994, to capitalize on the library's wealth of films. He later purchased Hanna-Barbera's library of 8,500 cartoons and launched the Cartoon Network; and he acquired New Line Cinema and

Castle Rock production companies. Finally, he established an in-house production company, Turner Pictures.

Turner's biggest deal, however, was completed with the merger of TBS
and Time Warner in 1996. He became the vice chairman of Time Warner,
holds 2 of the 17 seats on the board, and his stock in TBS was transferred
into new Time Warner stock, which accounts for 11 percent of its shares.
His responsibilities involve overseeing Time Warner's cable networks division, which consists of Turner Broadcasting Systems, HBO, Cinemax, and
Time Warner's interests in Comedy Central and Court TV.

Turner's social and philanthropic activities include staging the Goodwill
Games and forming the Better World Society to support socially conscious
television programming. In 1997 he became one of the largest individual
donors in the United States when he pledged $1 billion to the United Na-
tions over the next 10 years. In 1998 the list of Turners awards and honors
took 32 lines in *Who's Who in America, 1998.*

Jay Van Andel, cofounder of Amway Corporation, was born in Grand Rapids, Michigan, in 1924. He attended Pratt Junior College (1945), Calvin
College (1942 and 1946), and Yale (1943–1944), and served as a first lieutenant in the U.S. Air Force from 1943 to 1946.

Van Andel met his future business partner and cofounder of Amway,
Rich DeVos, while in high school. The pair planned to start a business together as soon as their military tours ended. They first partnered in the Wol-
verine Air Service in the 1940s and then owned Western Michigan's first
drive-in restaurant, bought a boat, and set off to sail to South America.

Their personal success as independent distributors of Nutrilite vitamins
convinced the partners that this method of person-to-person selling could
make them and others wealthy. They created what they called the Amway
Sales and Marketing Plan and launched their business with one product.
By the early 1960s, Amway's sales topped $500,000 from a single prod-
uct, and by the end of the decade they topped $100 million from 200
products.

The second generation of Van Andel and DeVos families took over the
company in the 1990s. Steve Van Andel and Dick DeVos succeeded their
fathers as chairman and president, respectively. Retail sales continue to
grow, and in fiscal 1997 Amway reached a record $7 billion year.

Jay Van Andel holds numerous honorary degrees and awards, just a few
of which include being knighted as a Grand Officer of Orange-Nassau, The

Netherlands, receiving the George Washington Medal of Honor, and receiving the UN Environment Program Achievement Award.

Lillian Vernon, founder of Lillian Vernon Corporation, was born Lillian Menasche in Leipzig, Germany, in 1927. At the age of five, she fled with her family to the Netherlands to escape the Nazis, and five years later the family relocated to the United States. The family lived in Manhattan, where her father started a zipper-manufacturing business and later sold leather products like camera cases, handbags, and belts.

Vernon quickly became Americanized, perfecting her English by watching movies while working as an usher in a theater. In 1949 she married Samuel Hechberg, the owner of a small clothing store. While pregnant with her first son in 1951, she began to worry about the family's income. Her husband's earnings of $75 a week was not going to be sufficient to support a family, so she decided that she needed to earn about $50 a week to help out. But how? "It was very unfashionable for women to work in those days. So I thought mail order was a wonderful thing I could do out of the house, stay home, change diapers, do the whole thing."[109]

Vernon decided to market items that her father could produce—handbags and belts—but to personalize them with gold monograms. She named her business Vernon Specialties Company, after Mount Vernon, New York, where she lived, and spent $495 to place a five-inch ad in the September 1951 issue of *Seventeen*. Within three months of placing that first ad, she had received $32,000 worth of orders, and she expanded her offerings to combs, buttons, and cuff links. All items were delivered with free monogramming. As she explained, "Monogrammed items make such nice gifts. You simply can't rush out to a store and buy a present that's instantly monogrammed. It takes planning and thought. That makes the gift all the more special to the recipient. No one can start a mail-order business today the way I did in 1951, but if I had to start over now, I'd definitely begin with monogrammed merchandise again."[110]

By 1954 Vernon's operation filled three rented buildings in Mount Vernon, which housed a warehouse, a shipping department, and a monogramming workshop. When she grew dissatisfied with the merchandise she could buy, she set up her own manufacturing plant for items like charm bracelets and bobby-pin holders. She later produced customized containers for some of the large cosmetic companies, including Revlon, Elizabeth Arden, Avon, and Max Factor.

While pregnant with her second child in 1965, Vernon decided to change her advertising technique from magazine ads to a catalog. She later described the response to her first 16-page catalog, of which she mailed 125,000 copies, as "fabulous." She received "thousands and thousands" of orders for a one-dollar sterling silver monogrammed ring. At the same time, she managed to keep the entire enterprise a secret. "I was a closet worker. Nobody knew for years that I had a job."[111]

In 1965 Vernon renamed her business the Lillian Vernon Corporation and assumed the titles of chairman and CEO. The corporation posted sales of $1 million in 1970, a figure that grew to $112 million in 1987 when Vernon sold 35 percent of the company's stock. The sale yielded about $28 million, with $12 million of it reportedly split among Vernon and her children. The balance was used to develop a computerized national distribution center in Virginia Beach, Virginia.

The company began to move into specialty markets with the release of its "At Home" catalog in 1989, followed by "Lilly's Kids" in 1990. By 1995 the Vernon Corporation was publishing 26 editions of seven different catalogs and had a total circulation of over 179 million.

Vernon remarried in 1970 and was known as Lillian Vernon Katz until 1990, when she had her named changed legally to Lillian Vernon. She has received numerous awards and honors, including induction into the Direct Marketing Association Hall of Fame, the Ellis Island Medal of Honor, and the Big Brothers/Big Sisters National Hero Award. She has five honorary college degrees and served as chairperson of the White House National Business Women's Council.

Samuel Moore (Sam) Walton, founder of Wal-Mart Stores, Inc., was born in Kingfisher, Oklahoma, in 1918. When he was five years old, his family moved to Columbia, Missouri, where he attended Hickman High School. Walton excelled at athletics, playing quarterback on the football team, captaining the basketball team, and participating on the track team. He was class president, student council president, and star of the senior play. He graduated in 1936 and enrolled at the University of Missouri, where he studied economics and served as senior class president. After receiving his bachelor of arts degree in 1940, Walton took his first retailing job at a JC Penney store in Des Moines, Iowa.

Walton was drafted in 1942 and served as a communications officer in the army intelligence corps at a stateside assignment. He was released from the military in 1945 and intended to pursue an MBA at the University of Pennsylvania, but a lack of funds forced him to return to his trainee's job at JC Penney. The same year, Walton bought a Ben Franklin variety store in Newport, Arkansas. He built the store into a success, but because he lost his lease, he was forced to start over—this time in Bentonville, Arkansas. Sam and younger brother James bought into the Ben Franklin franchise, eventually controlling 15 stores in Arkansas and Missouri.

During his travels for Ben Franklin, Walton developed the theory that large retailers should locate in smaller towns. "There was a lot more business in those towns than people ever thought."[112] When Ben Franklin's management nixed his idea, Walton went out on his own in 1962 and opened the first Wal-Mart Discount City, in Rogers, Arkansas. By 1970 there were 25 stores, and by 1983 the chain had become the eighth-largest retailer in the United States. At the time of his death, April 5, 1992, Walton was proclaimed to be the richest man in the United States by *Forbes* magazine.

An Wang, founder of Wang Laboratories, was born in Shanghai, China, in 1920. When he was six years old, his family moved to Kun San, where his father taught English in a private elementary school. The school did not offer a kindergarten or first or second grades, so Wang began his formal education in the third grade. He later commented that this experience was "a little like being thrown in the water when you don't know how to swim. You either learn how to swim—and fast—or you sink."[113] His parents recommended that he take a year off between elementary and junior high school to get his age and grade back in sync, but he insisted on taking the entrance exam, scoring the highest of any of the applicants. His performance in junior high school was mixed. He was gifted in mathematics but did poorly in the humanities.

At 13, Wang entered Shanghai Provincial High School, where he was first exposed to English through many of his textbooks. Because he was much younger and therefore smaller than his peers, he did not participate in many of the team sports, but he learned that he could play individual sports like table tennis. Upon graduation from high school, he entered Chiao Tung University in Shanghai, a school that Wang called the MIT of China, where he studied electrical engineering with an emphasis on communications. His experience at Chiao Tung was greatly effected by the Japanese seizure of Beijing and the coming of World War II. To protect students, the Chinese government moved the university to buildings within the International Settlement. Wang recalled that "there was war all around me, but not in the nine square miles within which I spent the next three years."[114]

After graduating from Chiao Tung in 1940, Wang worked for a short time as a teaching assistant, then took a job with Central Radio Corporation, designing and building transmitters and radios for government troops. As the end of World War II approached, he heard about a program to send Chinese engineers to apprentice in American industry. He jumped at the chance and arrived in the United States in June 1945, along with several of his colleagues. Wang described what happened next as a "piece of luck."

As his fellow Chinese engineers began to find positions in various in industries, Wang decided that he would prefer spending his two-year appointment at Harvard University. He applied to Harvard in the summer of 1945, and as luck would have it, there were openings at the school because of the war. He completed the work for his master's degree in 1946 and, after a short assignment in Canada, completed his doctorate at Harvard in 1948.

After receiving his doctorate, Wang began working at the Harvard Computation Laboratory along with such computer pioneers as Howard Aiken and Jay Forrester. While there, Wang invented the magnetic pulse controlling device—the principle on which magnetic core memory is based—which he licensed to IBM. Using the funds from this transaction, he set up his first factory over a garage, and in 1951 Wang Laboratories was born.

An Wang died on March 24, 1990.

Notes

Chapter I

[1] Wilson Harrell, *For Entrepreneurs Only* (Hawthorne, NJ: Career Press, 1994), p. 18.

[2] Ibid.

[3] Ibid., p. 19.

[4] Ibid.

[5] Ibid.

[6] Mary Kay Ash, *Mary Kay on People Management* (New York: Warner Books, 1984), p. 123.

[7] Diane Jennings, *Self-Made Women: Twelve of America's Leading Entrepreneurs Talk about Success, Self-Image, and the Superwoman* (Dallas: Taylor Publishing, 1987), p. 41.

[8] Ibid., p. 41.

[9] Ray Kroc and Robert Anderson, *Grinding It Out: The Making of McDonald's* (Chicago: Contemporary Books, 1977), p. 192.

[10] Brian O'Reilly, "What It Takes to Start a Startup," *Fortune,* June 7, 1999, p. 140.

[11] Jennings, *Self-Made Women,* p. 127.

[12] Bob Thomas, *Building a Company: Roy O. Disney and the Creation of an Entertainment Empire* (New York: Hyperion, 1998), p. 190.

[13] Bud Hadfield, *Wealth within Reach* (Dallas: Word Publishing, 1988), p. 37.

[14] Ibid., pp. 40–41.

[15] An Wang, with Eugene Linder, *Lessons: An Autobiography* (Reading, MA: Addison-Wesley, 1986), p. 109.

[16] Debbi Fields, *One Smart Cookie,* (New York: Simon & Schuster, 1987), p. 137.

[17] Victor K. McElheny, *Insisting on the Impossible: The Life of Edwin Land* (Reading, MA: Perseus Books, 1998), p. 45.

[18] Ash, *Mary Kay on People Management*, pp. 124–125.

[19] Sam Walton and John Huey, *Sam Walton: Made in America—My Story* (New York: Bantam Books, 1993), pp. 38–39.

[20] Wilson Harrell, "Swapping Principle for Profit Will Not Pay Off in the Long Run," *Atlanta Business Chronicle*, January 31, 1997, p. 1D.

[21] David Carnoy, "Richard Branson," *Success,* April 1998, pp. 62–63.

[22] Steve Hamm, "The Education of Marc Andreessen," *Business Week, Industrial/Technology Edition,* April 13, 1998, p. 92.

[23] Randall E. Stross, *The Microsoft Way: The Real Story of How the Company Outsmarts Its Competition* (Reading, MA: Addison-Wesley, 1996), pp. 233–234.

[24] Christian Williams, *Lead, Follow, or Get Out of the Way* (New York: Times Books, 1981), p. 111.

[25] Howard Schultz and Dori Jones Yang, *Pour Your Heart into It: How Starbucks Built a Company One Cup at a Time,* (New York: Hyperion 1997), p. 332.

[26] Richard Branson, *Losing My Virginity: How I've Survived, Had Fun, and Made a Fortune Doing Business My Way* (New York: Times Books, 1998), p. 343.

[27] Tom Monaghan, *Pizza Tiger* (New York: Random House, 1986), p. 7.

[28] *Forbes: Great Minds of Business* (New York: John Wiley & Sons, 1997), p. 155.

[29] Earl G. Graves and Robert L. Crandall, *How to Succeed in Business without Being White: Straight Talk on Making It in America* (New York: HarperBusiness, 1997), p. 123.

[30] Timothy Patrick Cahill, *Profiles in the American Dream: The Real-Life Stories of the Struggles of American Entrepreneurs* (Hanover, MA: Christopher Publishing House, 1994), p. 37.

[31] Porter Bibb, *Ted Turner: It Ain't as Easy as It Looks* (New York: Crown, 1993), p. 106.

[32] Gene N. Landrum, *Profiles of Genius: Thirteen Creative Men Who Changed the World* (Buffalo, NY: Prometheus Books, 1993), p. 222.

[33] Vincent Alonzo, "Cutting Loose," *Incentive,* May 1995, p. 35.

[34] James W. McLamore, *The Burger King: Jim McLamore and the Building of an Empire* (New York: McGraw-Hill, 1998), p. 43.

[35] Gail Degeorge, *The Making of a Blockbuster: How Wayne Huizenga Built a Sports and Entertainment Empire from Trash, Grit, and Videotape* (New York: John Wiley & Sons, 1996), p. 102.

[36] Jennings, *Self-Made Women,* p. 133.

[37] Landrum, *Profiles of Genius,* p. 223.

[38] Jay Van Andel, *An Enterprising Life: An Autobiography* (New York: HarperBusiness, 1998), pp. 16–18.

[39] Landrum, *Profiles of Genius,* p. 169.

[40] Cahill, *Profiles in the American Dream,* p. viii.

[41] Landrum, *Profiles of Genius,* p. 127.

[42] Lloyd E. Shefsky, *Entrepreneurs Are Made Not Born* (New York: McGraw-Hill, 1994), p. 97.

[43] Anita Roddick and Irene Prokop, *Body and Soul: Profits with Principles—The Amazing Success Story of Anita Roddick and the Body Shop* (New York: Crown, 1991), p. 87.

[44] Fred Lager, *Ben & Jerry's: The Inside Scoop—How Two Real Guys Built a Business with a Social Conscience and a Sense of Humor* (New York: Crown, 1994), pp. 20–29.

[45] Ben Cohen, Jerry Greenfield, and Meredith Maran, *Ben & Jerry's Double-Dip: How to Run a Values-Led Business and Make Money Too* (New York: Simon & Schuster, 1997), pp. 24–25.

[46] Monaghan, *Pizza Tiger,* pp. 62–64.

[47] Degeorge, *The Making of a Blockbuster*, pp. 45–46.

[48] *Forbes: Great Minds of Business*, p. 49.

[49] Fields, *One Smart Cookie,* pp. 56–59.

[50] Schultz and Yang, *Pour Your Heart into It,* p. 65.

[51] Ibid.

[52] Robert Mondavi and Paul Chutkow, *Harvests of Joy: My Passion for Excellence; How the Good Life Became Great Business* (New York: Harcourt Brace, 1998), pp. 24–25.

[53] Landrum, *Profiles of Genius,* p. 221.

[54] Satoru Otsuki, *Good Mileage: The High-Performance Business Philosophy of Soichiro Honda* (Japan: NHK Publishing, 1996), pp. 169–171.

[55] Thomas Stemberg, *Staples for Success* (Santa Monica, CA: Knowledge Exchange, 1996), p. 150.

[56] Jennings, *Self-Made Women,* p. 42.

[57] Ron Lieber, *Upstart Start-Ups* (New York: Broadway Books, 1998), p. 15.

[58] A. David Silver, *Entrepreneurial Megabucks: The 100 Greatest Entrepreneurs of the Last 25 Years* (New York: John Wiley & Sons, 1985), p. 17.

Chapter 2

[1] Lillian Vernon, *An Eye for Winners: How I Built One of America's Greatest Direct-Mail Businesses* (New York: HarperCollins, 1996), p. 63.

[2] Warren Buffett, "Track Record Is Everything," *Across the Board,* October 1991, p. 59.

[3] Ibid.

[4] Walton and Huey, *Sam Walton,* pp. 258–259.

[5] Stemberg, *Staples for Success,* pp. 72–73.

[6] Ibid.

[7] Ibid., pp. 70–71.

[8] Ibid., p. 71.

[9] Michael Dell and Catherine Fredman, *Direct from Dell: Strategies That Revolutionized an Industry* (New York: HarperBusiness, 1999), pp. 201–202.

[10] Ibid., 82.

[11] Wilson Harrell, "Hog Hunt," *Success,* August 1997, p. 96.

[12] Ibid.

[13] Roddick and Prokop, *Body and Soul,* p. 68.

[14] Ibid.

[15] Ibid.

[16] Landrum, *Profiles of Genius,* p. 88.

[17] Stemberg, *Staples for Success,* p. 28.

[18] Craig E. Aronogg and John L. Ward, *Contemporary Entrepreneurs: Profiles of Entrepreneurs and the Businesses They Started, Representing 74 Companies in 30 Industries* (Detroit, MI: Omnigraphics, 1992), p. 127.

[19] Bernie Marcus and Arthur Blank, *Built from Scratch: How a Couple of Regular Guys Grew the Home Depot from Nothing to $30 Million* (New York: Random House, 1999), p. xvi.

[20] Mary Kay Ash, *Mary Kay,* (New York: Harper & Row, 1981), p. 29.

[21] Mondavi and Chutkow, *Harvests of Joy,* p. 24.

[22] Stemberg, *Staples for Success,* p. 148.

[23] Williams, *Lead, Follow, or Get Out of the Way*, p. 14.

[24] Tom Chappell, *The Soul of a Business,* (New York: Bantam Trade Paperbook, 1994), p. 113.

[25] *Forbes: Great Minds of Business*, p. xx.

[26] Aronogg and Ward, *Contemporary Entrepreneurs*, p. 227.

[27] Shefsky, *Entrepreneurs Are Made Not Born*, pp. 126–127.

[28] Schultz and Yang, *Pour Your Heart into It,* p. 77.

[29] Mondavi and Chutkow, *Harvests of Joy,* p. 77.

[30] McElheny, *Insisting on the Impossible*, p. 403.

[31] Ash, *Mary Kay,* pp. 119–120.

[32] "Hall of Fame Inductees: Phineas Taylor (P.T.) Barnum," <http://www.ltbn.com/tribbarnum.html>, (May 13, 1999).

[33] David Packard, *The HP Way,* (New York: HarperBusiness, 1995), pp. 97–98.

[34] Chris Roush, *Inside Home Depot: How One Company Revolutionized an Industry through the Relentless Pursuit of Growth* (New York: McGraw-Hill, 1999), p. 14.

[35] Aronogg and Ward, *Contemporary Entrepreneurs*, p. 111.

[36] Ibid., p. 182.

[37] Joseph J. Fucini and Suzy Fucini, *Entrepreneurs: The Men and Women behind Famous Brand Names and How They Made It* (Boston: G.K. Hill, 1985), p. 4.

[38] Ibid., pp. 6–7.

[39] Dell and Fredman, *Direct from Dell,* p. 200.

[40] Vernon, *An Eye for Winners*, p. 206.

[41] David G. Hogan, *Selling 'Em by the Sack: White Castle and the Creation of American Food* (New York: New York University Press, 1997), p. 131.

[42] *Forbes: Great Minds of Business*, p. 154.

[43] Vernon, *An Eye for Winners,* p. 212.

[44] "Hall of Fame Inductees: Phineas Taylor (P.T.) Barnum."

[45] Branson, *Losing My Virginity,* pp. 352–353.

[46] Williams, *Lead, Follow, or Get Out of the Way*, p. 55.

[47] Richard Branson, "Risk Taking," *Journal of General Management,* Winter 1985, p. 8.

[48] Ibid., p. 10.

[49] Bill Gates, with Collins Hemingway, *Business @ the Speed of Thought: Using a Digital Nervous System* (New York: Warner Brothers, 1999), p. 162.

[50] Echo Montgomery Garrett, "Branson the Bold," *Success,* November 1992, p. 25.

[51] Branson, "Risk Taking," p. 7.

[52] Schultz and Yang, *Pour Your Heart into It,* p. 76.

[53] Gregory K. Ericksen, *What's Luck Got to Do with It? Twelve Entrepreneurs Reveal the Secrets behind Their Success* (New York: John Wiley & Sons, 1997), pp. 50–51.

[54] Walter Guzzardi, "Wisdom from the Giants of Business: A Directory of the Laureates," *Fortune,* July 3, 1989, p. 80.

[55] Dell and Fredman, *Direct from Dell,* p. 206.

[56] Ibid., pp. 206–207.

[57] Lesley Hazleton, "Profile: Jeff Bezos," *Success,* July 1998, p. 60.

[58] Dell and Fredman, *Direct from Dell,* p. 208.

[59] Landrum, *Profiles of Genius,* p. 221.

[60] Mondavi and Chutkow, *Harvests of Joy,* p. 53.

[61] Ibid.

[62] Degeorge, *The Making of a Blockbuster,* p. 17.

[63] Schultz and Yang, *Pour Your Heart into It,* p. 35.

[64] "A Fable concerning Ambition," *Economist,* June 21, 1997, p. 69.

[65] Dell and Fredman, *Direct from Dell,* p. 109.

[66] Jaclyn Fierman, "Winning Ideas from Maverick Managers," *Fortune,* February 6, 1995, p. 80.

[67] Michael A. Cusumano, *Competing on Internet Time: Lessons from Netscape and Its Battle with Microsoft* (New York: Free Press, 1998), pp. 93–95.

[68] Williams, *Lead, Follow, or Get Out of the Way,* p. 13.

[69] Cusumano, *Competing on Internet Time,* p. 94.

[70] Walton and Huey, *Sam Walton,* pp. 229–230.

[71] Dell and Fredman, *Direct from Dell,* pp. 203–205.

[72] John P. Kotter, *Matsushita Leadership: Lessons from the Twentieth Century's Most Remarkable Entrepreneur* (New York: Free Press, 1997), p. 6.

[73] Ash, *Mary Kay on People Management,* p. 91.

[74] Mary Kay Ash, *Mary Kay You Can Have It All: Lifetime Wisdom from America's Foremost Woman Entrepreneur* (Rocklin, CA: Prima, 1995), p. 4.

[75] Ibid., p. 92.

[76] Ash, *Mary Kay You Can Have It All,* p. 4.

[77] Schultz and Yang, *Pour Your Heart into It,* p. 200.

[78] Cohen, Greenfield, and Maran, *Ben & Jerry's Double-Dip,* p. 48.

[79] Ibid., pp. 49–50.

[80] Roddick and Prokop, *Body and Soul,* p. 16.

[81] Graves and Crandall, *How to Succeed in Business without Being White,* pp. 136–138.

[82] R. David Thomas, *Dave's Way* (New York: Berkeley Books, 1992), pp. 105–111.

[83] Warren Buffett, "Warren Buffett: How I Goofed," *Fortune,* April 9, 1990, pp. 95–96.

[84] Ibid., p. 95.

[85] Branson, *Losing My Virginity,* p. 343.

[86] Roush, *Inside Home Depot,* p. 213.

Chapter 3

[1] Cohen, Greenfield, and Maran, *Ben & Jerry's Double-Dip,* pp. 90–93.

[2] This discussion is adapted from Stephen M. Pollan and Mark Levine, *The Field Guide to Starting a Business* (New York: Fireside, 1990), pp. 121–131, 183–186.

[3] Marcus and Blank, *Built from Scratch,* p. 78.

[4] Pollan and Levine, *The Field Guide to Starting a Business,* p. 135.

[5] Roddick and Prokop, *Body and Soul,* p. 73.

[6] Schultz and Yang, *Pour Your Heart into It,* p. 73.

[7] Ibid., pp. 73–74.

[8] Harrell, *For Entrepreneurs Only,* pp. 134–135.

[9] Graves and Crandall, *How to Succeed in Business without Being White*, p. 164.

[10] Ibid., p. 165.

[11] Ibid., pp. 164–165.

[12] Thomas, *Dave's Way,* pp. 102–103.

[13] Monaghan, *Pizza Tiger,* pp. 251–252.

[14] Ibid., p. 249.

[15] Marcus and Blank, *Built from Scratch,* p. 186.

[16] Ibid., p. 188.

[17] Ibid., p. 187.

[18] Fields, *One Smart Cookie,* pp. 63–64.

[19] Cohen, Greenfield, and Maran, *Ben & Jerry's Double-Dip,* pp. 91–92.

[20] Graves and Crandall, *How to Succeed in Business without Being White*, p. 164.

[21] Ibid.

[22] Cahill, *Profiles in the American Dream,* p. 40.

[23] Roddick and Prokop, *Body and Soul,* pp. 71–72.

[24] Ibid., 72.

[25] Harrell, *For Entrepreneurs Only,* p. 135.

[26] Monaghan, *Pizza Tiger,* pp. 252–254.

[27] Graves and Crandall, *How to Succeed in Business without Being White,* p. 163.

[28] Based on a story in Cecil B. Day Jr., *Day by Day,* (Middle Village, NY: Jonathan David Publishers, 1990), p. 154.

[29] Charles H. Ferguson, *High Stakes, No Prisoners: A Winner's Tale of Greed and Glory in the Internet Wars* (New York: Times Books, 1999).

[30] Charles H. Ferguson, "True Finance: The Education of an Internet Entrepreneur," *Fast Company,* October 1999, p. 286.

[31] Ibid., p. 294.

[32] Ibid., p. 296.

[33] Stemberg, *Staples for Success*, p. 38.

[34] Harrell, *For Entrepreneurs Only*, p. 94.

[35] Marcus and Blank, *Built from Scratch,* pp. 49–50.

[36] Ibid., pp. 50–51.

[37] Ibid., p. 70.

[38] Ibid., pp. 70–73.

[39] Schultz and Yang, *Pour Your Heart into It,* p. 68.

[40] Mondavi and Chutkow, *Harvests of Joy,* p. 153.

[41] Harrell, *For Entrepreneurs Only*, p. 98.

[42] Ibid.

[43] Lager, *Ben & Jerry's: The Inside Scoop*, p. 28.

[44] Vernon, *An Eye for Winners*, p. 208.

[45] Ibid., p. 51.

[46] Ibid.

[47] Gates, with Hemingway, *Business @ the Speed of Thought,* p. 205.

[48] Fields, *One Smart Cookie*, pp. 9–10.

[49] Gates, with Hemingway, *Business @ the Speed of Thought,* p. 214.

[50] Vernon, *An Eye for Winners*, p. 66.

[51] Hadfield, *Wealth within Reach*, p. 53.

[52] Bibb, *Ted Turner*, pp. 83–84.

[53] Vance H. Trimble, *Overnight Success: Federal Express and Fredrick Smith, Its Renegade Creator* (New York: Crown, 1993), pp. 161–162.

[54] Lager, *Ben & Jerry's: The Inside Scoop*, p. 18.

[55] Ibid., pp. 19–20.

[56] Stemberg, *Staples for Success,* p. 105.

[57] Schultz and Yang, *Pour Your Heart into It,* p. 186.

[58] Ibid., pp. 186–189.

[59] Stemberg, *Staples for Success*, p. 108.

[60] Marcus and Blank, *Built from Scratch,* p. 93.

[61] Robert D. Hof, "Inside an Internet IPO," *Business Week,* September 6, 1999, pp. 60–73.

[62] Ibid., p. 68.

[63] Schultz and Yang, *Pour Your Heart into It,* p. 188.

[64] Ibid.

[65] Lager, *Ben & Jerry's: The Inside Scoop*, pp. 124–125.

Chapter 4

[1] Roush, *Inside Home Depot,* p. 13; Marcus and Blank, *Built from Scratch,* p. 80. According to Roush, the kids had $250, but Marcus recalls that they were given $700. We use Marcus's figure.

[2] Aronogg and Ward, *Contemporary Entrepreneurs*, p. 460.

[3] Fields, *One Smart Cookie,* pp. 80–81.

[4] Ibid., p. 81.

[5] Ibid.

[6] Walton and Huey, *Sam Walton,* pp. 205–206.

[7] Ibid., pp. 207–208.

[8] Ibid., p. 208.

[9] Lager, *Ben & Jerry's,* p. 29.

[10] Joe Vitale, *There's a Customer Born Every Minute: P.T. Barnum's Secrets to Business Success* (New York: AMACON, 1998), pp. 33–34.

[11] Roddick and Prokop, *Body and Soul,* p. 79.

[12] Harrell, *For Entrepreneurs Only*, p. 109.

[13] Ibid., pp. 110–111.

[14] Cusumano, *Competing on Internet Time*, p. 72.

[15] Carnoy, "Richard Branson," p. 63.

[16] Tim Jackson, *Richard Branson, Virgin King: Inside Richard Branson's Business Empire* (London: HarperCollins, 1995), pp. 248, 305–306.

[17] Des Dearlove and Stuart Crainer, *Business the Richard Branson Way: Ten Secrets of the World's Greatest Brand Builder* (New York: AMACOM, 1999), p. 99.

[18] Katherine Callan and Michael Warshaw, "Secrets of the Empire Builders," *Success,* September 1996, p. 29.

[19] Michael Adams, "Fly Boy," *Successful Meetings,* August 1992, p. 36.

[20] Callan and Warshaw, "Secrets of the Empire Builders," p. 29.

[21] Thomas, *Dave's Way,* pp. 61–62.

[22] Lager, *Ben & Jerry's,* pp. 31–33.

[23] Graves and Crandall, *How to Succeed in Business without Being White*, pp. 151–153.

[24] Ibid., p. 151.

[25] Ibid., p. 153.

[26] Ash, *Mary Kay You Can Have It All,* pp. 192–193.

[27] Williams, *Lead, Follow, or Get Out of the Way*, p. 120.

[28] *Forbes: Great Minds of Business*, pp. 133–134.

[29] Landrum, *Profiles of Genius*, p. 195.

[30] Akio Morita, with Edwin M. Reingold and Mitsuko Shimomura, *Made in Japan: Akio Morita and Sony* (New York: E.P. Dutton, 1986), p. 79.

[31] McElheny, *Insisting on the Impossible*, p. 459.

[32] Packard, *The HP Way,* p. 120.

[33] Morita, with Reingold and Shimomura, *Made in Japan,* p. 58.

[34] Ibid., pp. 58–60.

[35] Ibid., pp. 59–60.

[36] Ibid.

[37] Akio Morita, *From a 500-Dollar Company to a Global Corporation* (Pittsburgh, PA: Carnegie Mellon University Press, 1985), p. 20.

[38] Gerandine Willigan, "High-Performance Marketing: An Interview with Nike's Phil Knight," *Harvard Business Review,* July 1992, p. 92.

[39] This discussion of White Castle is based on Hogan, *Selling 'Em by the Sack,* pp. 74–77.

[40] Mondavi and Chutkow, *Harvests of Joy,* pp. 159–160.

[41] Bibb, *Ted Turner: It Ain't as Easy as It Looks*, p. 79.

[42] Kroc and Anderson, *Grinding It Out,* pp. 106–107.

[43] Harrell, *For Entrepreneurs Only*, p. 104.

[44] Ibid., pp. 104–105.

[45] Ibid., p. 105.

[46] Ibid., p. 106.

[47] Ibid.

[48] Roddick and Prokop, *Body and Soul,* pp. 113–114.

[49] Lager, *Ben & Jerry's,* p. 31.

[50] *Current Biography Yearbook 1995* (New York: H.W. Wilson, 1996), p. 564.

[51] Ibid.

[52] Ibid., p. 565.

[53] Harrell, *For Entrepreneurs Only*, p. 107.

[54] Ibid., p. 106.

[55] Cohen, Greenfield, and Maran, *Ben & Jerry's Double-Dip,* p. 130.

[56] Donald Katz, *Just Do It: The Nike Spirit in the Corporate World* (New York: Random House, 1994), p. 150.

Chapter 5

[1] Kevin Freiberg, Jackie Freiberg, and Tom Peters, *Nuts! Southwest Airlines' Crazy Recipe for Business and Personal Success* (New York: Broadway Books, 1996), pp. 121–122.

[2] Monaghan, *Pizza Tiger,* p. 246.

[3] Ibid.

[4] "Hall of Fame Inductees: Bud Hadfield," <http://www.ltbn.com/tribhadfield.html>, (May 13, 1999).

[5] Cahill, *Profiles in the American Dream*, pp. iv–v.

[6] Ibid., p. iii.

[7] Fields, *One Smart Cookie,* p. 132.

[8] Ibid., p. 89.

[9] Ibid., pp. 89–90.

[10] Maxwell Boas and Steve Chase, *Big Mac: The Unauthorized Story of McDonald's* (New York: Dutton, 1976), pp. 26–27.

[11] Cahill, *Profiles in the American Dream*, p. iv.

[12] "Spic and Span Follows a Clean Philosophy," *Milwaukee Journal-Sentinel,* August 3, 1997. Also found at <http://www.onwis.com/business/news/0804cleaners.stm>, (August 4, 1997).

[13] Ibid.

[14] Schultz and Yang, *Pour Your Heart into It,* pp. 5–6.

[15] *Blueprints for Service Quality: The Federal Express Approach—AMA Management Briefing* (New York: AMACOM, 1997), p. 14.

[16] Monaghan, *Pizza Tiger,* p. 9.

[17] Kotter, *Matsushita Leadership*, p. 5.

[18] Graves and Crandall, *How to Succeed in Business without Being White*, pp. 35–36.

[19] Fields, *One Smart Cookie,* pp. 74–76.

[20] Roush, *Inside Home Depot*, pp. 10–12.

[21] Marcus and Blank, *Built from Scratch*, pp. 135–136.

[22] Ibid., p. 135.

[23] Dell and Fredman, *Direct from Dell,* pp. 163–166.

[24] Ibid., p. 165.

[25] Ibid., p. 169.

[26] Marcus and Blank, *Built from Scratch,* p. 135.

[27] Hadfield, *Wealth within Reach*, p. 115.

[28] Ibid.

[29] Ibid., pp. 145–146.

[30] Ash, *Mary Kay You Can Have It All*, pp. 213–214.

[31] Freiberg, Freiberg, and Peters, *Nuts!* pp. 209–210.

[32] Dell and Fredman, *Direct from Dell,* pp. 139–140.

[33] Gates, with Hemingway, *Business @ the Speed of Thought*, pp. 187–188.

[34] Ibid., p. 188.

[35] Ibid., p. 187.

[36] Marcus and Blank, *Built from Scratch,* pp. 140–141.

[37] Ash, *Mary Kay on People Management*, p. 104.

[38] Roush, *Inside Home Depot*, p. 82.

[39] Dell and Fredman, *Direct from Dell,* pp. 167–168.

[40] Marcus and Blank, *Built from Scratch,* pp. 133–134.

[41] Jackson, *Richard Branson, Virgin King*, pp. 247–248.

[42] Dell and Fredman, *Direct from Dell,* p. 144.

[43] Herb Kelleher, "Customer Service: It Starts at Home," *Secured Lender,* May–June 1998, p. 69.

[44] Dell and Fredman, *Direct from Dell,* pp. 158–159.

[45] Ibid., p. 140.

[46] Marcus and Blank, *Built from Scratch,* p. 142–143.

[47] Kelleher, "Customer Service," p. 70.

[48] Dell and Fredman, *Direct from Dell,* p. 130.

[49] Degeorge, *The Making of a Blockbuster*, p. 136.

[50] Gates, with Hemingway, *Business @ the Speed of Thought,* pp. 159–160.

[51] Ibid., pp. 192–193.

[52] Dell and Fredman, *Direct from Dell,* pp. 144–145.

[53] Gates, with Hemingway, *Business @ the Speed of Thought,* pp. 197–198.

[54] Dell and Fredman, *Direct from Dell,* p. 151.

[55] Ibid., pp. 151–152.

[56] Gates, with Hemingway, *Business @ the Speed of Thought,* pp. 193–194.

[57] Michael Dell, "Service Sells," *Executive Excellence,* August 1993, p. 8.

[58] Gates, with Hemingway, *Business @ the Speed of Thought,* p. 4.

[59] Kelleher, "Customer Service," p. 68.

[58] Freiberg, Freiberg, and Peters, *Nuts!* pp. 269–270.

[59] Nora Wood, "Still Crazy after All These Years," *Incentive,* February 1997, p. 30.

Chapter 6

[1] Cohen, Greenfield, and Maran, *Ben & Jerry's Double-Dip,* p. 165.

[2] Ken Iverson and Tom Varian, *Plain Talk: Lessons from a Business Maverick* (New York: John Wiley & Sons, 1998), p. 21.

[3] Ash, *Mary Kay You Can Have It All,* p. 221.

[4] Manfred F.R. Kets de Vries, "Charisma in Action: The Transformational Abilities of Virgin's Richard Branson and ABB's Percy Barnevik," *Organizational Dynamics,* Winter 1998, p. 8.

[5] Kotter, *Matsushita Leadership*, p. 216.

[6] Walton and Huey, *Sam Walton*, pp. 161–162.

[7] Marcus and Blank, *Built from Scratch,* p. 104.

[8] Dell and Fredman. *Direct from Dell,* p. 110.

[9] Ibid., p. 109.

[10] Ibid., p. 110.

[11] Ibid.

[12] Michael A. Cusumano and Richard W. Selby, *Microsoft Secrets: How the World's Most Powerful Software Company Creates Technology, Shapes Markets, and Manages People* (New York: Free Press, 1995), p. 58.

[13] Dell and Fredman, *Direct from Dell,* p. 111.

[14] Ibid.

[15] Stross, *The Microsoft Way,* p. 37.

[16] Ibid.

[17] Ibid.

[18] Michael A. Verespej, "Flying His Own Course," *Industry Week,* November 20, 1995, pp. 22–23.

[19] William G. Lee, "A Conversation with Herb Kelleher," *Organizational Dynamics,* Autumn 1994, p. 72.

[20] Ross Perot, "Change Is Fun," *Executive Excellence,* September 1996, pp. 10–11.

[21] Harrell, *For Entrepreneurs Only*, p. 79.

[22] Dell and Fredman, *Direct from Dell,* p. 121.

[23] Ricardo Semler, *Maverick: The Success Story behind the World's Most Unusual Workplace* (London: Century Press, 1993), p. 42.

[24] Roddick and Prokop, *Body and Soul,* pp. 22–23.

[25] Robert L. Shook, *The Entrepreneurs: Twelve Who Took Risks and Succeeded* (New York: Harper & Row, 1980), p. 106.

[26] Liz Harman, "Starbuck's Schultz Reveals How Firm Keeps Perking," *San Diego Business Journal,* September 29, 1997, p. 4.

[27] Cohen, Greenfield, and Maran, *Ben & Jerry's Double-Dip,* p. 165.

[28] Ibid., pp. 165–166.

[29] Schultz and Yang, *Pour Your Heart into It,* pp. 80–81.

[30] G. Gendron and B. Burlingham, "The Entrepreneur of the Decade," *Inc.,* April 1989, p. 119.

[31] Daniel Ichbiah and Susan L. Knepper, *The Making of Microsoft: How Bill Gates and His Team Created the World's Most Successful Software Company* (Rocklin, CA: Prima, 1991), p. 226.

[32] Thomas, *Dave's Way,* p. 64.

[33] Otsuki, *Good Mileage,* p. 39.

[34] Ibid., p. 40.

[35] Ibid., pp. 39–40.

[36] Ibid., p. 175.

[37] Ash, *Mary Kay on People Management*, p. 17.

[38] Ronald B. Lieber, "Why Employees Love These Companies," *Fortune,* January 12, 1998, p. 72.

[39] Freiberg, Freiberg, and Peters, *Nuts!* p. 285.

[40] Ricardo Semler, "Managing without Managers," *Harvard Business Review,* September–October 1989, p. 81.

[41] Walton and Huey, *Sam Walton,* p. 177.

[42] Iverson and Varian, *Plain Talk,* p. 67.

[43] Ibid., pp. 58–59.

[44] Ibid., p. 59.

[45] Semler, *Maverick,* p. 58.

[46] Ross Perot, "Caring Leaders," *Executive Excellence,* April 1996, p. 6.

[47] Semler, *Maverick,* p. 114.

[48] Ibid.

[49] Morita, with Reingold and Shimomura, *Made in Japan,* p. 154.

[50] Freiberg, Freiberg, and Peters, *Nuts!* pp. 118–119.

[51] Jackson, *Richard Branson, Virgin King*, p. 51.

[52] Marcus and Blank, *Built from Scratch,* p. 126.

[53] Ibid., p. 130.

[54] Ash, *Mary Kay,* p. 40.

[55] Walton and Huey, *Sam Walton*, p. 200.

[56] Schultz and Yang, *Pour Your Heart into It,* pp. 337–338.

[57] Ash, *Mary Kay on People Management*, p. 30.

[58] Perot, "Caring Leaders," p. 6.

[59] Dell and Fredman, *Direct from Dell,* pp. 117–118.

[60] Marcus and Blank, *Built from Scratch,* pp. 242–243.

[61] Lee, "A Conversation with Herb Kelleher," 74.

[62] Marcus and Blank, *Built from Scratch,* p. 107.

[63] Packard, *The HP Way,* pp. 135–136.

[64] Ibid., p. 137.

[65] Semler, *Maverick,* p. 5.

[66] Jane Applegate, "Acting Like an Entrepreneur," *Denver Business Journal,* November 8, 1996, p. 3B.

[67] Semler, *Maverick*, p. 100.

[68] Garrett, "Branson the Bold," p. 26.

[69] Ichbiah and Knepper, *The Making of Microsoft,* p. 227.

[70] David Sheff, "The Interview: Richard Branson," *Forbes,* February 24, 1997, p. 100.

[71] Garrett, "Branson the Bold," p. 26.

[72] Ash, *Mary Kay on People Management*, p. 23.

[73] Ibid., p. 27.

[74] Ash, *Mary Kay You Can Have It All*, pp. 200–201.

[75] Ibid., p. 201.

[76] Walton and Huey, *Sam Walton,* pp. 162–163.

[77] Stross, *The Microsoft Way*, pp. 24–26.

[78] Cohen, Greenfield, and Maran, *Ben & Jerry's Double-Dip,* p. 164.

[79] Ibid.

[80] Mondavi and Chutkow, *Harvests of Joy,* p. 142.

[81] Thomas, *Building a Company,* pp. 142–143.

[82] Ibid., p. 143.

[83] Marcus and Blank, *Built from Scratch,* pp. 244–245.

Appendix

[1] Henry Goldblatt, "Billionaires," *Fortune,* October 2, 1995, p. 68.

[2] Ibid.

3 Alison L. Sprout and Kimberly Beals McDonald, "The Rise of Netscape," *Fortune,* July 10, 1995, p. 140.

4 *Current Biography Yearbook 1997* (New York: H.W. Wilson, 1998), pp. 10–13.

5 F. Goodman, "The Virgin King," *Vanity Fair,* May 1992, p. 172.

6 Ibid.

7 Ben Brown, "The Man behind MindSpring," *Southern Living,* February 1999, pp. 30GL–37GL.

8 *Current Biography Yearbook 1987* (New York: H.W. Wilson, 1988), p. 74.

9 "Outsmarting Smart Money Men," *New York,* April 22, 1985, p. 52.

10 Fucini and Fucini, *Entrepreneurs,* pp. 5–6.

11 L. Jereski, "Heart, Minds, and Market Share," *Forbes,* April 3, 1989, p. 80.

12 Amy Cartese, "Win 95, Lose '96?" *Business Week,* December 18, 1995, p. 34.

13 K. Hubbard, "For Ice Cream Moguls Ben and Jerry, Making 'Cherry Garcia' and 'Chunky Monkey' Is a Labor of Love," *People,* September 10, 1990, p. 73.

14 Ibid.

15 Ibid.

16 Aronogg and Ward, *Contemporary Entrepreneurs*, p. 107.

17 Ibid.

18 David Kirkpatrick and Patty De Llosa, "PC Competition: Now Everyone in PCs Wants to Be like Michael Dell," *Fortune,* September 8, 1997, p. 76.

19 Aronogg and Ward, *Contemporary Entrepreneurs,* p. 119.

20 *Current Biography Yearbook 1998* (New York: H.W. Wilson, 1999), p. 156.

21 Aronogg and Ward, p. 126.

22 Ibid., p. 127.

23 Ibid.

24 Ibid., p. 129.

25 Thomas, *Building a Company,* p. 41.

26 Ibid., p. 44.

27 E. Zuckerman, "William Gates III," *People,* August 20, 1990, p. 91.

28 *Current Biography Yearbook 1991,* p. 239.

29 *Current Biography Yearbook 1997,* p. 202.

30 Aronogg and Ward, *Contemporary Entrepreneurs,* p. 182.

31 Ibid., p. 183.

32 Ibid.

33 Cindy Murphy, "Karing, Kan-do Kopy King," *Franchising World,* January–February 1995, p. 48.

34 Ibid., p. 52.

35 Scott DeGarmo, "Wilson Harrell: He Did It His Way," <http://www.ltbn.com/Articles/Harrelltrib.html>, (October 21, 1999).

36 Ibid.

37 Ibid.

[38] Aronogg and Ward, *Contemporary Entrepreneurs,* p. 226.

[39] Silver, *Entrepreneurial Megabucks*, p. 232.

[40] Ibid.

[41] *Current Biography Yearbook 1995,* p. 261.

[42] Ibid.

[43] Diane Mermigas, "A Blockbuster Change," *Advertising Age,* October 3, 1994, p. 1.

[44] Hogan, *Selling 'Em by the Sack*, p. 28.

[45] Ibid., p. 30.

[46] *Current Biography Yearbook 1998*, p. 319.

[47] Ibid.

[48] *Current Biography Yearbook 1998*, p. 320.

[49] Ibid., p. 321.

[50] Ibid.

[51] *Current Biography Yearbook 1996* (New York: H.W. Wilson), p. 201.

[52] Gelbert, Doug, *So Who the Heck Was Oscar Mayer: The Real People behind Those Brand Names*, (New York: Barricade Books, 1996), p. 336.

[53] "We Weren't Just Airborne Yesterday," (Southwest Airlines Web site), <http://www.southwest.com/about_swa/airborne.html>, (November 10, 1999).

[54] *Current Biography Yearbook 1997*, p. 271.

[55] *Current Biography Yearbook 1973* (New York: H.W. Wilson), p. 230.

[56] Ibid.

[57] Gelbert, *So Who the Heck Was Oscar Mayer*, p. 339.

[58] *Current Biography Yearbook 1981* (New York: H.W. Wilson), p. 262.

[59] Ibid.

[60] Ibid.

[61] Ibid.

[62] *Current Biography Yearbook 1996*, p. 238.

[63] Ibid.

[64] *Current Biography Yearbook 1966* (New York: H.W. Wilson), p. 239.

[65] Ibid., p. 238.

[66] John P. Kotter, "Business as a Moral Undertaking: The Matsushita Story," *American Enterprise,* July 1997, p. 56.

[67] Ibid.

[68] McLamore, *The Burger King*, p. xviii.

[69] Ibid., p. xx.

[70] Ibid., p. xxi.

[71] Ibid., p. xxix.

[72] Ibid., pp. xxxi–xxxii.

[73] Ibid., p. xxxiii.

[74] Kathleen Gallagher and Avrum D. Lank, "Spic and Span Follows a Clean Philosophy," *Milwaukee Journal Sentinel,* August 3, 1997, p. 3.

[75] *Current Biography Yearbook 1990* (New York: H.W. Wilson), p. 452.

[76] J.D. Reed and Vicki Sheff, "The Patriarch," *People,* October 10, 1998, p. 151.

[77] *Current Biography Yearbook 1996,* p. 429.

[78] Ibid., 430.

[79] Ibid.

[80] Ibid.

[81] Ibid, p. 431.

[82] "Ross Perot's Crusade," *Business Week,* October 6, 1986, p. 60.

[83] Roddick and Prokop, *Body and Soul,* p. 34.

[84] Ibid., p. 35.

[85] Ibid., p. 39.

[86] Ibid., p. 43.

[87] Ibid., p. 66.

[88] *Forbes: Great Minds of Business,* p. 126.

[89] Ibid., p. 128.

[90] Ibid., p. 124.

[91] Ibid.

[92] *Current Biography Yearbook 1973,* p. 374.

[93] Ibid.

[94] Ibid., p. 375.

[95] *Current Biography Yearbook 1997,* p. 497.

[96] Ibid.

[97] Ibid.

[98] Aronogg and Ward, *Contemporary Entrepreneurs,* p. 459.

[99] Marilyn Achiron, "Dave Thomas," *People,* August 2, 1993, p. 86.

[100] Ibid.

[101] *Current Biography Yearbook 1995,* p. 563.

[102] L. Killian, "Hamburger Helper," *Forbes,* August 5, 1991, p. 106.

[103] *Current Biography Yearbook 1995,* p. 564.

[104] Ibid., 563.

[105] Ibid., 564.

[106] B. Garfield, "Dave's Way Is Right Way for New Wendy's Ads," *Advertising Age,* September 30, 1991, p. 52.

[107] *Current Biography Yearbook 1998,* p. 575.

[108] P. Painton, "The Taming of Ted Turner," *Time,* January 6, 1992, p. 22.

[109] Lisa Coleman, "I Went Out and Did It," *Forbes,* August 17, 1992, p. 102.

[110] *Current Biography Yearbook 1996,* p. 607.

[111] "CEO of Catalog Business: Lillian Vernon," *Working Woman,* June 1986, p. 62.

[112] *Current Biography Yearbook 1992* (New York: H.W. Wilson, 1993), p. 590.

[113] Wang, with Linder, *Lessons: An Autobiography,* p. 17.

[114] Ibid., p. 25.

Select Bibliography

"About 'TCBY'." <http://www.tcby.com/smoothie/about/newhistory.html>, (September 21, 1999).

"About 'TCBY': The TCBY Timeline." <http://www.tcby./smoothie/about/newtimeline.html> (September 21, 1999).

Achiron, Marilyn. "Dave Thomas," *People,* August 2, 1993, p. 86.

Adams, Michael. "Fly Boy." *Successful Meetings,* August 1992, pp. 32–41.

Adler, Carlye. "What Do Modern Girls Really Want?" *Fortune,* June 21, 1999, pp. 186[H], 186[J].

Akasie, Jay. "Learning from Mistakes." *Forbes,* April 7, 1997, pp. 20–22.

Alioto, Maryann. "Lawrence Ellison." *Directors and Boards,* Fall 1997, pp. 79–80.

Allen, Jamie. "Netscape Co-Founder Relives the Internet Revolution." <http://www.cnn.com/books/news/9906/18/netscape/>, (June 19, 1999).

Allen, Margaret. "Oh Nuts!" *Dallas Business Journal,* April 11, 1997, p. 18.

Allen, Robin Lee. "Kroc, Monaghan Exemplify Industry's Charity as Season of Good Will Nears." *Nation's Restaurant News,* October 12, 1998, p. 33.

Allerton, Haidee. "Mind over Matter." *Training and Development,* March 1996, p. 9.

Allman, W.F. "Power to the People, Etched in Silicon." *U.S. News and World Report,* June 18, 1990, p. 8.

Alonzo, Vincent. "Cutting Loose." *Incentive,* May 1995, pp. 35–36.

Alsop, Stewart. "Stewart Alsop Industry Achievement Award: Marc Andreessen." *InfoWorld,* January 29, 1996, p. 59.

"Amazon vs. Everybody." *Fortune*, November 8, 1999, pp. 120–128.

"America's Smart Young Entrepreneurs." *Fortune,* March 21, 1994, pp. 34–48.

"An Wang," <http://www.invent.org/book/book-text/106.html> (November 16, 1999).

Anderson, Duncan Maxwell. "Freedom Fighter." *Success,* June 1998, pp. 26–27.

Anderson, Duncan Maxwell, and Michael Warshaw. "The Number One Entrepreneur in America." *Success,* March 1995, pp. 32–43.

Angrist, Stanley W. "Entrepreneur in Short Pants." *Forbes,* March 7, 1988, pp. 84–85.

"Anthony Desio, Founder and Former Head of Mail Boxes, Etc., Takes Over Helm at IDTec in Vista." <http://www.newswire.cal/releases/November1998/10/c3210.html> (September 21, 1999).

Applegate, Jane. "Acting Like an Entrepreneur." *Denver Business Journal,* November 8, 1996, p. 3B.

———. "Quirky CEO: Think Like an Entrepreneur." *Triangle Business Journal,* November 15, 1996, p. 13.

Aronogg, Craig E., and John L. Ward. *Contemporary Entrepreneurs: Profiles of Entrepreneurs and the Businesses They Started, Representing 74 Companies in 30 Industries.* Detroit, MI: Omnigraphics, 1992.

"Arthur Blank." *Atlanta Business Chronicle,* July 28, 1995, p. 49.

Ash, Mary Kay. *Mary Kay.* New York: Harper & Row, 1981.

———. *Mary Kay on People Management.* New York: Warner Books, 1984.

———. *Mary Kay You Can Have It All: Lifetime Wisdom from America's Foremost Woman Entrepreneur.* Rocklin, CA: Prima, 1995.

"Bagehot: Richard Branson, MP." *Economist,* May 28, 1994, p. 59.

Banks, Howard. "When the Going Gets Tough. . . . " *Forbes,* January 2, 1995, p. 16.

Bartholomew, Doug. "Successful? Try, Try Again." *Industry Week,* February 2, 1998, p. 56–62.

Bartlett, Richard C. "Mary Kay's Foundation." *Journal of Business Strategy,* July–August 1995, pp. 16–19.

Bartz, Carol, Kenneth Iverson, Bridget Macaskill, Ann Richards, Bill Gates, George Bush, Charlotte Beers, Joan Lappin, Lynn St. James, and Ross Perot. "A New Agenda." *Working Woman,* November 1992, pp. 55–65.

Becklund, Laurie, and J.B. Strasser. *Swoosh: The Unauthorized Story of Nike and the Men Who Played There.* New York: Harcourt Brace Javonovich, 1991.

Bedi, Hari. "Right Attitude Is the Key to Success." *Asian Business,* January 1996, p. 9.

Bell, Christopher, and Jeremy Dann. "The Man Who Can Say 'No': Views on Japanese–U.S. Relations." *Harvard International Review,* Fall 1990, p. 23.

"Berkeley's Entrepreneur Forum." <http://www.haas.berkeley.edu/alumni> (March 18, 1999).

"Bernard Marcus." <http://sbe.nova.edu/alumni/bios/bernard.htm> (May 5, 1999).

Berss, Marcia. "The Next Pizza—Pasta?" *Forbes,* November 8, 1993, p. 200.

"The Best Advice I Ever Got." *Working Woman,* September 1994, p. 31.

"The Best Entrepreneurs." *Business Week,* January 13, 1997, p. 74.

"The Best Entrepreneurs." *Business Week*, January 12, 1998, p. 56.

Bibb, Porter. "I'll Be the Most Powerful Man in America." *Success,* December 1993, pp. 46–49.

———. *Ted Turner: It Ain't as Easy as It Looks.* New York: Crown, 1993.

Bing, Jonathan, Maria Simson, and Jeff Zaleski. "An Enterprising Life." *Publishers Weekly,* August 3, 1998, pp. 68–69.

Blank, Arthur. "They Sweat the Small Stuff." *Canadian Business,* May 28, 1999, pp. 51–55.

Blueprints for Service Quality: The Federal Express Approach—AMA Management Briefing. New York: AMACOM, 1997.

Boas, Maxwell, and Steve Chase. *Big Mac: The Unauthorized Story of McDonald's.* New York: Dutton, 1976.

Bose, Mihir. "High Flyer." *Director,* April 1995, p. 82.

"Boston Beer History." <http://www.samadams.com/company/background> (October 11, 1999).

Branch, Shelly. "The Brand Builders." *Fortune,* May 10, 1999, p. 132.

Brandt, Richard L. "Dell Computer Corp.'s Michael Dell." *Upside,* April 1998, pp. 98–102.

———. "Internet Kamikazes: Yahoo's Tim Koogle." *Upside,* January 1998, pp. 100, 102.

———. "Interview: Netscape's Marc Andreessen." *Upside,* March 1998, pp. 76–79.

———. "Larry Ellison." *Upside,* September 1997, pp. 86–97.

"Branson Builds with Open Mind." *Marketing,* September 22, 1994, p. 3.

Branson, Richard. *Losing My Virginity: How I've Survived, Had Fun, and Made a Fortune Doing Business My Way.* New York: Times Books, 1998.

—-. "Risk Taking." *Journal of General Management,* Winter 1985, pp. 5–11.

Brewer, Charles. "Pulp Fiction." *Inc.* (Technology Supplement), 1995, p. 79.

Brock, Pope. "Anita Roddick." *People Weekly,* May 10, 1993, pp. 101–106.

Brokaw, Leslie, and David Whitford. "Then and Now." *Inc.,* September 1994, pp. 69–77.

Brown, Ben. "The Man behind MindSpring." *Southern Living,* February 1999, pp. 30GL–37GL.

Brown, Bob. "Marc Andreessen Gets a Real Job." *Network World,* September 15, 1997, pp. 31, 36.

Brown, Thomas L. "Lessons from CNN." *Industry Week,* April 1, 1991, p. 23.

Brownstein, Mark. "Conner's Back: Finis Conner Does What He Knows Best." *Computer Technology Review,* Fourth quarter 1998, pp. 52–55.

Buckley, J. "The Pizza Man Chooses God." *U.S. News and World Report,* July 29, 1991) p. 43.

Buffett, Warren. "Warren Buffett: How I Goofed." *Fortune,* April 9, 1990, pp. 95–96.

Burlingham, Bo. "This Woman Has Changed Business Forever." *Inc.,* June 1990, pp. 34–47.

"Business: Behind Branson." *Economist,* February 21, 1998, pp. 63–66.

Butcher, Lee. *Accidental Millionaire: The Rise and Fall of Steve Jobs at Apple Computer.* New York: Paragon House, 1988.

Butler, Charles. "The Magnificent Seven." *Sales and Marketing Management,* November 1994, pp. 41–50.

Button, Graham. "Sam and Libby Try Again." *Forbes,* March 15, 1993, p. 19.

Button, Kate. "Larry Ellison." *Chief Executive,* July–August 1993, p. 22.

Byfield, Ted, and Virginia Byfield. "Sometimes the Wealthy Actually Do Sell Everything and Give to the Poor." *Alberta Report/Western Report,* October 26, 1998, p. 38.

Byman, Jeremy. *Ted Turner, Cable Television Tycoon.* Greensboro, NC: M. Reynolds, 1998.

Byrd, Alan. "Former Days Inn CEO Now Developing Orlando Hotels." *Atlanta Business Chronicle,* June 2, 1995, p. 6B.

Cahill, Timothy Patrick. *Profiles in the American Dream: The Real-Life Stories of the Struggles of American Entrepreneurs.* Hanover, MA: Christopher Publishing House, 1994.

Calderbank, Alison. "Robert Noyce." *Computer Reseller News,* June 1, 1997, p. 116.

Callan, Katherine, and Michael Warshaw. "Secrets of the Empire Builders." *Success,* September 1996, pp. 29–33.

Carlino, Bill. "Ray Kroc." *Nation's Restaurant News,* February 1996, pp. 96–105.

Carlton, Jim. *Apple: The Inside Story of Intrigue, Egomania, and Business Blunders.* New York: Times Books, 1997.

Carney, Karen E. "Kwik Kopy Printing Corp., Cypress, Texas." *Inc.,* November 1995, p. 53.

Carnoy, David. "Richard Branson." *Success,* April 1998, pp. 62–63.

Carter, John Mack, and Joan Feeney. *Starting at the Top: America's New Achievers: Twenty-Three Success Stories Told by Men and Women Whose Dreams of Being Boss Came True.* New York: Wm. Morrow, 1985.

Cartese, Amy. "Win 95, Lose '96?" *Business Week,* December 18, 1995, p. 34.

Case, Steve. "Ten Commandments for Building the Medium: Setting Priorities." *Vital Speeches of the Day,* May 1, 1998, pp. 431–435.

"CEO Interview: Michael Dell." *Sales and Marketing Management,* October 1997, p. 52.

"CEO of Catalog Business: Lillian Vernon." *Working Woman,* June 1986, p. 62.

Chakravarty, Subrata N. "The Vindication of Edwin Land." *Forbes,* May 4, 1987, pp. 83–84.

Chappel, Tom. "The Soul of a Business." *Executive Female,* January-February 1994, p. 38.

———. *The Soul of a Business.* New York: Bantam Trade Paperbook, 1994.

Charan, Ram. "Managing to Be Best." *Time,* December 7, 1998, p. 145.

"Charles Schwab: The Cut-Rate Cowboy Ups the Internet Ante." *Journal of Business Strategy,* September–October 1996, p. 38.

Chouinard, Yvon. "Coming of Age: Yvon Chouinard." *Inc.,* April 1989, p. 54.

Chowdhury, Neel. "Matsushita's Legacy Lives On." *Fortune,* March 31, 1997, p. 111.

"Chris Larsen." <http://www.econference.org/content/bios/larsen.html> (November 10, 1999).

Clancy, Heather. "Dynamic Duos: Andrew Grove and Gordon Moore." *Computer Reseller News,* June 1, 1997, pp. 13–18.

Cohen, Andy. "The 80 Most Influential People in Sales and Marketing History." *Sales and Marketing Management,* October 1998, p. 70.

Cohen, Ben, Jerry Greenfield, and Meredith Maran. *Ben & Jerry's Double-Dip: How to Run a Values-Led Business and Make Money Too.* New York: Simon & Schuster, 1997.

Coleman, Lisa. "I Went Out and Did It." *Forbes,* August 17, 1992, p. 102.

Colvin, Geoffrey. "How to Be a Great eCEO." *Fortune,* May 24, 1999, pp. 104–110.

"Company History." <http://www.dominos.com/Press/CompanyHistory.cfm> (April 25, 1999).

"Company History." <http://www.lillianvernon.com/lv/about/abt12com.html> (April 25, 1999).

Cone, Edward. "Beyond Business." *Informationweek,* July 21, 1997, pp. 46–54.

"Conner Peripherals." <http://www.conner.com> (September 21, 1999).

Conlon, Ginger. "Mark Andreessen." *Sales and Marketing Management,* July 1996, p. 53.

Coolidge, Carrie. "A Promise Kept." *Forbes,* August 10, 1998, pp. 92–93.

Corry, John. "The Amway Way: Seeking the Profit of Many." *American Spectator,* October 1998, pp. 82–83.

Coursey, David. "Egad! Larry Ellison Just Might Be Right!" *Computerworld,* September 23, 1996, p. 133.

Cullis, Michael D. "Advice from the Experts." *Franchising World,* January–February 1996, p. 45.

Current Biography Yearbook 1940 (New York: H.W. Wilson, 1941).

Current Biography Yearbook 1952, pp. 590–591. New York: H.W. Wilson, 1953.

Current Biography Yearbook 1966, pp. 238–240. New York: H.W. Wilson, 1967.

Current Biography Yearbook 1967 (New York: H.W. Wilson, 1968).

Current Biography Yearbook 1969 (New York: H.W. Wilson, 1970).

Current Biography Yearbook 1973, pp. 230–232, 374–376. New York: H.W. Wilson, 1974.

Current Biography Yearbook 1981, pp. 262–265. New York: H.W. Wilson, 1982.

Current Biography Yearbook 1987, pp. 74–76. New York: H.W. Wilson, 1988.

Current Biography Yearbook 1990, pp. 452–454. New York: H.W. Wilson, 1991.

Current Biography Yearbook 1991 (New York: H.W. Wilson, 1992).

Current Biography Yearbook 1994 (New York: H.W. Wilson, 1995).

Current Biography Yearbook 1995, pp. 261–263, 562–565. New York: H.W. Wilson, 1996.

Current Biography Yearbook 1996, pp. 201–203. New York: H.W. Wilson, 1997.

Current Biography Yearbook 1997, pp. 10–13, 496–498. New York: H.W. Wilson, 1998.

Current Biography Yearbook 1998, pp. 575–577. New York: H.W. Wilson, 1999.

Current Biography, April 1999. New York: H.W. Wilson, 1999.

Curtis, Carol E. "All Pleasure, No Guilt." *Forbes,* March 25, 1985, pp. 194–198.

Cusumano, Michael A. *Competing on Internet Time: Lessons from Netscape and Its Battle with Microsoft.* New York: Free Press, 1998.

Cusumano, Michael A., and Richard W. Selby. *Microsoft Secrets: How the World's Most Powerful Software Company Creates Technology, Shapes Markets, and Manages People.* New York: Free Press, 1995.

Daniels, Linda. "Twelve Years and 12 Winners: Where Are They Now?" *Atlanta Business Chronicle,* April 24–30, 1998, p. 2B.

Darrow, Barbara. "Michael Dell." *Computer Reseller News,* November 16, 1998, pp. 126–127.

Davey, Tom. "One-Hit Wonders: Tech Stars Here Today, Gone Tomorrow." *San Francisco Business Times,* March 17, 1995, p. 4A.

Davidson, Andrew. "The Davidson Interview: Anita Roddick." *Management Today,* March 1996, pp. 42–46.

Davidson, Charles. "Brewer Is Building MindSpring on Core Values." *Atlanta Business Chronicle,* February 7, 1997, p. 10A.

Day, Cecil B., Jr. *Day by Day.* Middle Village, NY: Jonathan David Publishers, 1990.

Dearlove, Des, and Stuart Crainer. *Business the Richard Branson Way: Ten Secrets of the World's Greatest Brand Builder.* New York: AMACOM, 1999.

DeGarmo, Scott. "Why He's Number One." *Success,* March 1995, p. 4.

Degeorge, Gail. *The Making of a Blockbuster: How Wayne Huizenga Built a Sports and Entertainment Empire from Trash, Grit, and Videotape.* New York: John Wiley & Sons, 1996.

Dell, Michael. "Making the Right Choices for the New Consumer." *Managing Service Quality,* 1994, pp. 22–25.

———. "Maximum Speed." *Executive Excellence,* January 1999, pp. 15–16.

———. "Service Sells." *Executive Excellence,* August 1993, pp. 6–8.

———. "Where House." *Forbes,* November 30, 1998, p. 217, 236.

Dell, Michael, and Catherine Fredman. *Direct from Dell: Strategies That Revolutionized an Industry.* New York: HarperBusiness, 1999.

Dennehy, Robert F. "The Executive as Storyteller." *Management Review,* March 1999, pp. 40–43.

Denton, D. Keith. "Keeping Employees: The Federal Express Approach." *SAM Advanced Management Journal,* Summer 1992, pp. 10–13.

DeTar, Jim. "A Disk Drive Company for Basic PCs." *Electronic News,* September 21, 1998, pp. 16–18.

Doescher, William F. "Short-Changing Black Capitalists." *D&B Reports,* May–June 1993, pp. 10–11.

Doler, Kathleen. "Interview: Jeff Bezos, Founder and CEO of Amazon.com Inc." *Upside,* September 1998, pp. 76–80.

Downer, Lesley. "Branson's American Invasion." *Fortune,* December 9, 1996, pp. 32–36.

"Dunkin' Donuts." <http://dunkindonuts.com/corpinfo/> (November 9, 1999).

Dunlap, Charlotte. "Top 25 Executives: Marc Andreessen." *Computer Reseller News,* November 13, 1995, p. 135.

Edstrom, Jennifer, and Martin Eller. *Barbarians Led by Bill Gates: Microsoft from the Inside.* New York: Henry Holt, 1998.

Edwards, David. "Honda at 50." *Cycle World,* December 1997, p. 10.

Edwards, Owen. "Gordon Moore." *Forbes* (ASAP Supplement), December 5, 1995, p. 158.

"E-Loan at a Glance." <http://www.eloan.com/s/show/corpsummary/> (October 11, 1999).

Ericksen, Gregory K. *What's Luck Got to Do with It? Twelve Entrepreneurs Reveal the Secrets behind Their Success.* New York: John Wiley & Sons, 1997.

Ewing, Terzah. "Eight Revolutionaries." *Forbes,* September 11, 1995, p. 166.

"Executive Profile: Robert Mondavi." *San Francisco Business Times,* February 28, 1997, p. 9.

"A Fable concerning Ambition." *Economist,* June 21, 1997, p. 69.

Faltermayer, Edmund. "Does Japan Play Fair?" *Fortune,* September 7, 1992, pp. 38–52.

Farnham, Alan. "Mary Kay's Lessons in Leadership." *Fortune,* September 20, 1993, pp. 68–77.

Ferguson, Charles H. "True Finance: The Education of an Internet Entrepreneur." *Fast Company,* October 1999, pp. 282–296.

Ferguson, Tim W. "Mondavi Bucks the Tide." *Forbes,* October 23, 1995, pp. 203–206.

Fernandes, Lorna. "Mr. Nice Guy." *San Francisco Business Times,* June 26, 1998, p. 17.

Fields, Debbi. *One Smart Cookie.* New York: Simon & Schuster, 1987.

Fierman, Jaclyn. "Winning Ideas from Maverick Managers." *Fortune,* February 6, 1995, pp. 66–80.

"Fifty for the Future." *Newsweek,* February 27, 1995, p. 42.

Fisher, Anne. "Excuse Me, Please, Do You Mind If I Sell You Something?" *Fortune,* June 21, 1999, p. 190.

Fisher, Maxine P. *Walt Disney.* New York: Franklin Watts, 1988.

"For the Two Biggest Failures of All Time, Life Couldn't Be Better." *Inc.,* May 1998, p. 78.

Forbes: Great Minds of Business. New York: John Wiley & Sons, 1997.

Freiberg, Kevin, Jackie Freiberg, and Tom Peters. *Nuts! Southwest Airlines' Crazy Recipe for Business and Personal Success.* New York: Broadway Books, 1996.

Frumkin, Paul. "Alan Stillman." *Nation's Restaurant News* (Special Issue), February 1996, p. 157.

Fucini, Joseph, and Suzy Fucini. *Entrepreneurs: The Men and Women behind Famous Brand Names and How They Made It.* Boston: G.K. Hall, 1985.

———. *Experience, Inc.: Men and Women Who Founded Companies after the Age of 40.* New York: Free Press, 1987.

Gage, Deborah. "Scott McNealy." *Computer Reseller News,* (Special Fall Comdex Issue Supplement), November 18, 1996, p. 159.

Gallagher, Kathleen, and Avrum D. Lank. "Spic and Span Follows a Clean Philosophy." *Milwaukee Journal Sentinel,* August 3, 1997, p. 3.

Garfield, B. "Dave's Way Is Right Way for New Wendy's Ads." *Advertising Age,* September 30, 1991, p. 52.

Garrett, Echo Montgomery. "Branson the Bold." *Success,* November 1992, pp. 21–26.

Garvey, Martin J. "Sun's McNealy Stumps Again." *Information Week,* September 14, 1998, p. 499.

Gates, Bill. *The Road Ahead.* New York: Viking, 1995.

Gates, Bill, with Collins Hemingway. *Business @ the Speed of Thought: Using a Digital Nervous System.* New York: Warner Brothers, 1999.

"The Gateway Story." <http://www.gateway.com/about/info/index.shtml> (June 1, 1999).

Gaudin, Sharon. "Scott McNealy: Q&A." *Computerworld,* November 4, 1996, p. 30.

Geer, C.T., and J. Zweig. "Paulson's Pride." *Forbes,* October 29, 1990, p. 156.

Gelbert, Doug. *So Who the Heck Was Oscar Mayer: The Real People behind Those Brand Names.* New York: Barricade Books, 1996.

Gendron, G., and B. Burlingham. "The Entrepreneur of the Decade." *Inc.,* April 1989, p. 114.

Gibbs, Edwina. "Sony Marketing Master Morita Dies." *USA Today,* October 4, 1999.

Gillin, Paul. "Monticello Memoirs." *Computerworld,* August 5, 1996, pp. 67–70.

———. "Net Essentials: Larry Ellison." *Computerworld,* January 4, 1999, p. S45.

Girishankar, Saroja. "InternetWeek Interview: Michael Dell." *InternetWeek,* April 13, 1998, p. 8.

———. "Interview." *Internetweek,* October 6, 1997, p. 177.

Gitomer, Jeffrey. "Debbi Fields Proves Success Is Oh-So Sweet in the Cookie Business." *Business Press,* March 6, 1998, p. 161.

———. "Mrs. Fields' Sales Success with Cookies: How Sweet It Is." *Business Journal Serving Charlotte and the Metropolitan Area,* May 20, 1996, p. 19.

———. "Passion Is the Secret Ingredient to Sweet Success." *Atlanta Business Chronicle,* April 18, 1997, p. 4C.

Gof, Janet. "Matsushita Leadership: Lessons from the Twentieth Century's Most Remarkable Entrepreneur." *Japan Quarterly,* July 1998, pp. 101–102.

Goff, Leslie. "Inside Intel." *Computerworld,* May 17, 1999, p. 99.

Goldblatt, Henry. "Billionaires." *Fortune,* October 2, 1995, p. 68.

Goodman, F. "The Virgin King." *Vanity Fair,* May 1992, p. 172.

Graves, Earl. "The Entrepreneur in You." *Black Enterprise,* September 1998, p. 11.

———. "Higher Learning, Higher Earning." *Black Enterprise,* January 1999, p. 9.

———. "LWB: Living While Black." *Black Enterprise,* May 1999, p. 15.

———. "Memoirs of a Serious Player." *Directors and Boards,* Spring 1997, pp. 16–21.

———. "Serious Advice for All for Success." *Directors and Boards,* Spring 1997, p. 19.

Graves, Earl, and Robert L. Crandall. *How to Succeed in Business without Being White: Straight Talk on Making It in America.* New York: HarperBusiness, 1997.

Greco, Susan, and Alessandra Bianchi. "What Am I in For?" *Inc.,* July 1992, p. 66.

Grimes, Brad. "Lessons from MindSpring." *Fortune,* June 21, 1999, pp. 186[C]–186[H].

Gross, Thomas, and John L. Neuman. "Picking the Best Strategists' Brains." *Marketing News,* October 10, 1988, p. 16.

Grube, Lorri. "Lillian Vernon." *Chief Executive,* March 1994, p. 23.

Guthey, Eric. "Of Business Biography, Media Romance, and Corporate Family Drama." *Business and Economic History,* Winter 1997, pp. 290–297.

Guzzardi, Walter. "Wisdom from the Giants of Business: A Directory of the Laureates." *Fortune,* July 3, 1989, pp. 78–91.

"H. Wayne Huizenga." <http://www.sbe.nova.edu/alumni/bios/huizenga.htm> (June 1, 1999).

Hadfield, Bud. "Creative Management." *Success,* November 1993, pp. 95–100.

———. *Wealth within Reach.* Dallas: Word Publishing, 1988.

Hafner, Katie. "Fred Smith: The Entrepreneur Redux." *Inc.,* June 1984, pp. 38, 40.

Hagendorf, Jennifer." Ted Waitt: Gateway." *Computer Reseller News,* November 9, 1998, p. 131.

Haight, Timothy. "James Clark and Marc Andreessen." *Network Computing,* September 15, 1995, p. 76.

"Hall of Fame Alumni: Bernard Marcus." <http://www.sbe.nova.edu/alumni/bios/bernard.htm> (May 5, 1999).

"Hall of Fame Alumni: H. Wayne Huizenga." <http://www.sbe.nova.edu/alumni/bios/huizenga.htm> (June 1, 1999).

"Hall of Fame Alumni: Jack A. Smith." <http://www.sbe.nova.edu/alumni/bios/jack.htm> (June 1, 1999).

"Hall of Fame Alumni: R. David Thomas." <http://www.sbe.nova.edu/alumni/bios/thomas.htm> (June 1, 1999).

"Hall of Fame Inductees: Anita Roddick." <http://www.ltbn.com/tribroddick.html> (June 1, 1999).

"Hall of Fame Inductees: Bill Gates." <http://www.ltbn.com/tribgates.html> (May 13, 1999).

"Hall of Fame Inductees: Bill Rosenberg." <http://www.ltbn.com/tribrosenberg.html> (June 1, 1999).

"Hall of Fame Inductees: Bud Hadfield." <http://www.ltbn.com/tribhadfield.html> (May 13, 1999).

"Hall of Fame Inductees: Debbi Fields." <http://www.ltbn.com/tribfields.html> (May 13, 1999).

"Hall of Fame Inductees: Earl Graves." <http://www.ltbn.com/tribgraves.html> (May 13, 1999).

"Hall of Fame Inductees: Edward Lowe." <http://www.ltbn.com/triblowe.html> (June 1, 1999).

"Hall of Fame Inductees: Edwin Land." <http://www.ltbn.com/tribland.html> (June 1, 1999).

"Hall of Fame Inductees: Fred Deluca." <http://www.ltbn.com/tribdeluca.html> (May 13, 1999).

"Hall of Fame Inductees: Mary Kay Ash." <http://www.ltbn.com/tribash.html> (May 13, 1999).

"Hall of Fame Inductees: Phineas Taylor (P.T.) Barnum." <http://www.ltbn.com/tribbarnum.html> (May 13, 1999).

"Hall of Fame Inductees: Richard Branson." <http://www.ltbn.com/tribbranson.html> (May 13, 1999).

"Hall of Fame Inductees: Ted Turner." <http://www.ltbn.com/tribturner.html> (June 1, 1999).

"Hall of Fame Inductees: Warren Buffett." <http://www.ltbn.com/tribBuffett.html> (May 13, 1999).

"Hall of Fame Inductees: Wayne Huizenga." <http://www.ltbn.com/tribhuizenga.html> (May 13, 1999).

"Hall of Fame Inductees: Wilson Harrell." <http://www.ltbn.com/tribharrell.html> (October 21, 1999).

Hallett, Anthony, and Diane Hallett. *Encyclopedia of Entrepreneurs.* New York: John Wiley & Sons, 1997.

Halper, Mark, and Rich Karlgaard. "Larry Ellison: Samurai Interview." *Forbes* (ASAP Supplement), April 8, 1996, pp. 54–55.

Hamblen, Matt. "A Search for New Heroes: IT Innovators Lauded." *Computerworld,* June 15, 1998, p. 28.

Hamm, Steve. "The Education of Marc Andreessen." *Business Week (Industrial/ Technology Edition),* April 13, 1998, pp. 84–92.

———. "Jim Barksdale, Internet Angel." *Business Week,* May 10, 1999, pp. 60–61, 64–65.

Harari, Oren. "Turner and Gates: An Essay on Paradigms." *Management Review,* April 1996, pp. 49–52.

Harman, Liz. "Starbuck's Schultz Reveals How Firm Keeps Perking." *San Diego Business Journal,* September 29, 1997, p. 4.

Harrell, Wilson. "Creative Courage." *Success,* June 1997, p. 98.

———. "Decision Power." *Success,* April 1996, p. 96.

———. "Do You Venture Forth as Buccaneer or Farmer?" *Atlanta Business Chronicle,* January 17, 1997, p. 1C.

———. "Entrepreneurial Personalities from Start-Up to Fortune 500." *Atlanta Business Chronicle,* November 29, 1996, p. 1B.

———. "Entrepreneur's Insurance." *Success,* March 1997, p. 88.

———. "Entrepreneurs Minimize Risk with Creativity and Aggression." *Atlanta Business Chronicle,* October 4, 1996, p. 1C.

———. *For Entrepreneurs Only.* Hawthorne, NJ: Career Press, 1994.

———. "The Good Fight." *Success,* February 1996, p. 102.

———. "Hire a Financial Translator Who Speaks the Language of Bankers." *Atlanta Business Chronicle,* August 15, 1997, p. 1C.

———. "Hog Hunt." *Success,* August 1997, p. 96.

———. "A Leader Like You." *Success,* February 1997, p. 102.

———. "The Measure of a Man." *Success,* October 1997, p. 108.

———. "Move to the Future." *Success,* October 1996, p. 104.

———. "Outside Boards Help Owners to Vault Clear of Their Egos." *Atlanta Business Chronicle,* August 23, 1996, p. 1C.

———. "A Piece of the Action." *Success,* December 1995, p. 104.

———. "Scotland Could Teach the U.S. How to Support Entrepreneurs." *Atlanta Business Chronicle,* September 6, 1996, p. 1C.

———. "Shrink to Fit." *Success,* November 1997, p. 124.

———. "The Soul of Selling." *Success,* May 1997, p. 100.

———. "Start a Business, Win Inclusion in Club of Terror." *Atlanta Business Chronicle,* June 20, 1997, p. 5C.

———. "A Start-Up with a Jump-Start Will Not Stay Small for Long." *Atlanta Business Chronicle,* February 14, 1997, p. 1C.

———. "Swapping Principle for Profit Will Not Pay Off in the Long Run." *Atlanta Business Chronicle,* January 31, 1997, p. 1D.

———. "A Tale of Two Cities." *Success,* November 1995, p. 128.

———. "Terror Straps Risk Takers in for Long Roller-Coaster Ride." *Atlanta Business Chronicle,* July 4, 1997, p. 1C.

———. "This Is Your Future." *Success,* September 1996, p. 100.

———. "Time to Step Outside." *Success,* October 1995, p. 98.

———. "Winning the Future." *Success,* April 1997, p. 98.

———. "Without a Contingency Plan, You're Flying without a Net." *Atlanta Business Chronicle,* November 1, 1996, p. 1C.

———. "Your Biggest Mistake." *Success,* March 1996, p. 88.

Haynes, P. "Where East Meets West." *Economist,* March 2, 1991, p. 20.

Hazleton, Lesley. "Profile: Jeff Bezos." *Success,* July 1998, pp. 58–61.

Hein, Kenneth. "Kwik Kopy Printing." *Incentive,* June 1996, pp. 36–37.

Henderson, Danna K. "American West Airlines: Making Reorganization Work." *Air Transport World,* February 1995, pp. 26–34.

Hewitt, Bill, and Gail Cameron Wescott. "Crunch Time." *People Weekly,* October 28, 1996, pp. 117–118.

Hickman, Angela. "Wilson Harrell Column Debuts in Small Business Strategies in June." *Atlanta Business Chronicle,* May 31, 1996, p. 11B.

Hof, Robert D. "Inside an Internet IPO." *Business Week,* September 6, 1999, pp. 60–74.

Hof, Robert D., and Linda Himelstein. "eBay vs. Amazon.com." *Business Week,* May 31, 1999, pp. 128–132.

Hogan, David G. *Selling 'Em by the Sack: White Castle and the Creation of American Food.* New York: New York University Press, 1997.

"Hold the Flamboyance." *Time,* February 4, 1991, p. 60.

Holzinger, Albert G. "Netscape Founder Points, and It Clicks." *Nation's Business,* January 1996, p. 32.

"Home Depot: History." <http://www.homedepot.com/> (October 7, 1999).

Howard, Theresa. "Frank Carney." *Nation's Restaurant News,* (Special Issue), February 1996, p. 48.

————. "Robert Rosenberg." *Nation's Restaurant News,* January 1995, pp. 177–178.

Hubbard, K. "For Ice Cream Moguls Ben and Jerry, Making 'Cherry Garcia' and 'Chunky Monkey' Is a Labor of Love." *People,* September 10, 1990, p. 73.

Huey, John, and Geoffrey Colvin. "The Jack and Herb Show." *Fortune,* January 11, 1999, pp. 163–166.

Hughes, Jonathan R.T. *The Vital Few: The Entrepreneur and American Economic Progress.* New York: Oxford University Press, 1986.

Hwang, Diana. "Chapter Two: Pen Pioneer Surfs Internet." *Computer Reseller News,* May 15, 1995, pp. 51–52.

Hyatt, Joshua. "Betting the Farm." *Inc.,* December 1991, p. 36.

————. "What Business Would You Start?" *Inc.,* November 1994, p. 40.

Hyten, Todd. "Thomas Stemberg." *Boston Business Journal,* September 16, 1994, p. 21.

Ichbiah, Daniel, and Susan L. Knepper. *The Making of Microsoft: How Bill Gates and His Team Created the World's Most Successful Software Company.* Rocklin, CA: Prima, 1991.

Iida, Osamu. "Accept New Challenges." *Executive Excellence,* December 1996, pp. 11–12.

Inamori, Kazuo. *A Passion for Success: Practical, Inspirational, and Spiritual Insight from Japan's Leading Entrepreneur.* New York: McGraw-Hill, 1995.

Inamori, Kazuo, and T.R. Reid. *For People—and for Profit: A Business Philosophy for the Twenty-first Century.* New York: Kodansha International, 1997.

Ingram, Edgar Waldo. *All This from a Five-Cent Hamburger! The Story of the White Castle System.* New York: Newcomen Society in North America, 1964.

"Inside an Internet IPO." *Business Week,* September 6, 1999, pp. 60–73.

"An Interview with Herb Kelleher." *Directorship,* April 1996, pp. 1–3.

"An Interview with Scott McNealy." *Manufacturing Systems* (Supplement), October 1992, pp. 2–3.

Iverson, Ken. "How Nucor Works." *Iron Age Steel,* November 1997, pp. 56–57.

————. "My Biggest Mistake." *Inc.,* October 1998, p. 119.

————. "The Virtues of Smallness." *Across the Board,* February 1998, pp. 11–12.

Iverson, Ken, and Tom Varian. *Plain Talk: Lessons from a Business Maverick.* New York: John Wiley & Sons, 1998.

Jackson, David S. "Andrew Grove." *Time,* March 3, 1997, p. GB3.

Jackson, Tim. *Inside Intel: Andy Grove and the Rise of the World's Most Powerful Chip Company.* New York: Plume, 1998.

———. *Richard Branson, Virgin King: Inside Richard Branson's Business Empire.* London: HarperCollins, 1995.

Jakubovics, Jerry. "Domino's Pizza Founder Really Delivers." *Management Review,* July 1989, pp. 11–13.

"Japan's Other Maverick." *Chief Executive,* January–February 1993, pp. 38–41.

"Jeff Bezos." *Forbes* (Supplement ASAP), April 6, 1998, p. 56.

"Jeff Bezos: Selling Books, Running Hard!" *Forbes,* April 6, 1998, pp. 56–57.

Jennings, Diane. *Self-Made Women: Twelve of America's Leading Entrepreneurs Talk about Success, Self-Image, and the Superwoman.* Dallas: Taylor Publishing, 1987.

Jennings, Reg, Charles Cox, and Cary L. Cooper. *Business Elites: The Psychology of Entrepreneurs and Intrapreneurs.* New York: Routledge, 1994.

Jereski, L. "Heart, Minds, and Market Share." *Forbes,* April 3, 1989, p. 80.

Joachim, David, Julie Anderson, and Mitch Wagner. "InternetWeek Interview: Michael Dell." *InternetWeek,* November 9, 1998, p. 10.

Johnson, Jay L. "Top 10 Retailers: Thomas Stemberg." *Discount Merchandiser,* March 1997, p. 28.

Johnson, Maryfran. "'I'm Not a Visionary': Scott McNealy." *Computerworld,* January 4, 1999, pp. S18–S20.

"Just One Question: Larry Ellison." *Computerworld,* December 26, 1995, p. 41.

Kaelble, Steve. "It Could Have Been Indiana Fried Chicken." *Indiana Business Magazine,* November 1996, p. 7.

Kahn, Joseph P., et al. "Steven Jobs of Apple Computer: The Missionary of Micros." *Inc.,* April 1984, pp. 81–91.

Kaplan, Jerry. "The Start Up." *Fortune,* May 29, 1995, pp. 110–120.

———. *Startup: A Silicon Valley Adventure.* Boston: Houghton Mifflin, 1995.

———. "You're Not Wrong, You Know." *Inc.,* May 19, 1998, pp. 119–121.

Kapner, Suzanne. "Robert Mondavi." *Nation's Restaurant News,* January 1995, pp. 148–149.

Kapner, Suzanne, and Peter O. Keegan. "Fred DeLuca." *Nation's Restaurant News,* January 1995, pp. 49–52.

Karlgaard, Rich. "ASAP Interview: Larry Ellison." *Forbes* (ASAP Supplement), June 7, 1993, pp. 71–74.

Katz, Donald. *Just Do It: The Nike Spirit in the Corporate World.* New York: Random House, 1994.

Kelleher, Herb. "Customer Service: It Starts at Home." *Secured Lender,* May–June 1998, pp. 68–73.

Kelly, Jason. "Core Values Eclipse Technology at MindSpring." *Atlanta Business Chronicle,* April 25, 1997, p. 2B.

Kets de Vries, Manfred F.R. "Charisma in Action: The Transformational Abilities of Virgin's Richard Branson and ABB's Percy Barnevik." *Organizational Dynamics,* Winter 1998, pp. 6–21.

———. "The Virgin Iconoclast." *Across the Board,* February 1996, pp. 36–41.

Killian, Kelly, and Francisco Perez. "Ricardo Semler and Semco S.A." *Thunderbird, the American Graduate School of International Management,* 1998, pp. 1–2.

Killian, L. "Hamburger Helper." *Forbes,* August 5, 1991, p. 106.

Kirkpatrick, David, and Patty De Llosa. "PC Competition: Now Everyone in PCs Wants to Be like Michael Dell." *Fortune,* September 8, 1997, p. 76.

Klein, Calvin, Catherine Crier, and Ruth Westheimer. "How to Do Everything Better. . . ." *Self,* January 1994, pp. 63–71.

"Koch Family History." <http://www.samadams.com/company/background/kochhist.html> (October 11, 1999).

Koprowski, Gene. "AOL CEO Steve Case." *Forbes* (ASAP Supplement), October 7, 1996, pp. 94–96.

Korczynski, Ed. "Moore's Law Extended: The Return of Cleverness." *Solid State Technology,* July 1997, p. 364.

Kotter, John P. "Business as a Moral Undertaking: The Matsushita Story." *American Enterprise,* July 1997, pp. 56–59.

———. *Matsushita Leadership: Lessons from the Twentieth Century's Most Remarkable Entrepreneur.* New York: Free Press, 1997.

———. "Matsushita: The World's Greatest Entrepreneur?" *Fortune,* March 31, 1997, p. 104.

Kramer, Louise. "Col. Harland Sanders." *Nation's Restaurant News,* (Special Issue), February 1996, p. 138.

Kroc, Ray, and Robert Anderson. *Grinding It Out: The Making of McDonald's.* Chicago: Contemporary Books, 1977.

Kupfer, A. "America's Fastest-Growing Company." *Fortune,* August 13, 1990, p. 48.

LaBarre, Polly. "Patagonia Comes of Age." *Industry Week,* April 3, 1995, pp. 42–48.

Labich, Kenneth. "Is Herb Kelleher America's Best CEO?" *Fortune,* May 2, 1994, pp. 4–52.

Lager, Fred C. *Ben & Jerry's: The Inside Scoop–How Two Real Guys Built a Business with a Social Conscience and a Sense of Humor.* New York: Crown, 1994.

Landrum, Gene N. *Profiles of Genius: Thirteen Creative Men Who Changed the World.* Buffalo, NY: Prometheus Books, 1993.

"Larry Ellison." *Network World,* December 26, 1994, p. 43.

Lazarus, Charles. "Perspectives on Discount Retailing: Worldwide Strategic Planning." *Discount Merchandiser,* April 1987, pp. 48–50.

"Leadership Lessons from Matsushita." *Executive Edge Newsletter,* April 1997, p. 1.

Lee, Jeanne. "Why eBay Is Flying." *Fortune,* December 7, 1998, p. 255.

Lee, William G. "A Conversation with Herb Kelleher." *Organizational Dynamics,* Autumn 1994, pp. 64–74.

Lenzner, Robert. "The Reluctant Entrepreneur." *Forbes,* September 11, 1995, pp. 162–166.

———. "Whither Moore's Law?" *Forbes,* September 11, 1995, pp. 167–168.

Lesczynski, Jim. "Allen E. Paulson." *Chief Executive,* July–August 1991, p. 22.

Leuchter, Miriam. "Steve Case." *Journal of Business Strategy,* September-October 1996, p. 39.

Levine, Daniel S. "Help for the Novice Entrepreneur." *PC World,* November 1997, p. 80.

Lewis, Reginald, and Blair S. Walker. *Why Should White Guys Have All the Fun? How Reginald Lewis Created a Billion-Dollar Business Empire.* New York: John Wiley & Sons, 1995.

Liddle, Alan. "Howard Schultz." *Nation's Restaurant News,* January 1995, p. 183.

———. "Leon W. Pete Harman." *Nation's Restaurant News,* October 14, 1996, p. 145.

Lieber, Ron. *Upstart Start-Ups.* New York: Broadway Books, 1998.

———. "Why Employees Love These Companies." *Fortune,* January 12, 1998, p. 72.

Linden, Eugene. "Frederick W. Smith of Federal Express." *Inc.,* April 1984, p. 89.

Lorge, Sarah, and Michele Marchetti. "The Brand That Case Built." *Sales and Marketing Management,* August 1998, p. 86.

Lowe, Janet C. *Bill Gates Speaks: Insight from the World's Greatest Entrepreneur.* New York: John Wiley & Sons, 1998.

———. *Warren Buffett Speaks.* New York: John Wiley & Sons, 1997.

Lubove, Seth. "American Gothic." *Forbes,* November 21, 1994, pp. 120–121.

———. "The Growing Gets Tough." *Forbes,* April 13, 1992, pp. 68–70.

Magretta, Joan. "Power of Virtual Integration: An Interview with Dell Computer's Michael Dell." *Harvard Business Review,* March–April 1998, pp. 72–84.

Maloney, Janice. "Larry Ellison Is Captain Ahab and Bill Gates Is Moby Dick." *Fortune,* October 28, 1996, pp. 75–78.

Maloney, Jeffrey. "Legends of the Valley." *Information Week,* October 23, 1995, p. 54.

Manes, Stephen, and Paul Andrews. *Gates: How Microsoft's Mogul Reinvented an Industry—and Made Himself the Richest Man in America.* New York: Doubleday, 1993.

Mangelsdorf, Martha E. "Entrepreneur of the Year." *Inc.,* December 1992, pp. 71, 73.

———. "Entrepreneurial Traits by Nationality." *Inc.,* April 1994, p. 33.

———. "How Entrepreneurs Stay Motivated." *Inc.,* March 1998, p. 94.

Mangelsdorf, Martha E., and Alessandra Bianchi. "The Hottest Entrepreneurs in America." *Inc.,* December 1992, p. 88.

"Marcel Bich." *U.S. News and World Report,* June 13, 1994, p. 26.

Marchetti, Michele. "Mary Kay." *Sales and Marketing Management,* November 1996, p. 68.

Marcus, Bernie, and Arthur Blank. *Built from Scratch: How a Couple of Regular Guys Grew the Home Depot from Nothing to $30 Million.* New York: Random House, 1999.

Mardenfeld, Sandra. "Mary Kay Ash." *Incentive,* January 1996, pp. 54–55.

Maren, Michael, and Dan Wallace. "Masters of the Impossible." *Success,* February 1992, pp. 22–32.

Marrier, Michael. "Entrepreneurs Who Excel." *Nation's Business,* August 1996, pp. 18–28.

Martin, Michael H. "The Next Big Thing: A Bookstore?" *Fortune,* December 9, 1996, pp. 168–170.

Martin, Reed. "Recipes of the Rich and Famous." *Forbes,* October 17, 1994, p. 64.

Martin, Scott. "Is There an Ultra Marathoner in the House?" *Bicycling,* October 1996, pp. 25–26.

"Mary Kay: A Retrospective." <http://www.marykay.com/marykay/about/company /retro.html> (September 9, 1999).

"Masaru Ibuka." *Compton's Encyclopedia Online.* <http://optonline.com/comptons /ceo/20059_Q.html> (November 10, 1999).

Mason, Julie Cohen. "On Target: Lillian Vernon Focuses on Customers." *Management Review,* May 1993, pp. 22–24.

Maynard, Roberta. "Building a Winner from Scratch." *Nation's Business,* October 1997, pp. 65–70.

Mazur, Laura. "Follow the Leader." *Marketing,* February 29, 1996, pp. 20–21.

McCarthy, Terry. "Akio Morita's Voice of Reason." *World Press Review,* April 1992, p. 12.

McCune, Jenny C. "Consensus Builder." *Success,* October 1990, pp. 42–45.

———. "The Entrepreneurial Revolution." *Success,* November 1991, pp. 7–10, 62–63, 66, 70–71, 74–75.

———. "In the Beginning. . . ." *Management Review,* September 1996, p. 47.

McElheny, Victor K. *Insisting on the Impossible: The Life of Edwin Land.* Reading, MA: Perseus Books, 1998.

McInerney, Tom. "Double Trouble: Combining Business and Ethics." *Business Ethics Quarterly,* January 1998, pp. 187–189.

McLamore, James W. *The Burger King: Jim McLamore and the Building of an Empire.* New York: McGraw-Hill, 1998.

McLaughlin, Rachel, and Hallie Mummert. "The Great Mentors." *Target Marketing,* October 1998, pp. 74–81.

McNealy, Scott. "A Winning Business Model for the '90s." *Directors and Boards,* Fall 1995, pp. 4–8.

Meeks, Fleming. "The Man Is the Message." *Forbes,* April 17, 1989, pp. 148–152.

Melymuka, Kathleen. "Sky King." *Computerworld,* September 28, 1998, pp. 68–70.

Mercer, Joye. "Packard's Legacy." *Chronicle of Higher Education,* April 5, 1996, p. A31.

Mermigas, Diane. "A Blockbuster Change." *Advertising Age,* October 3, 1994, p. 1.
———. "Still a Cyber-Pioneer." *Electronic Media,* November 9, 1998, p. 32.
Mescon, Michael H., and Timothy S. Mescon. "MindSpring Provides Lesson in Basics." *Atlanta Business Chronicle,* January 22, 1999, p. 47A.
Metzger, Mark K. "F. Kenneth Iverson of Nucor: Man of Steel." *Inc.,* April 1984, p. 85.
"Michael Dell's Plan for the Rest of the Decade." *Fortune,* June 9, 1997, p. 138.
"Microsoft Timeline: Pre-Computer Timeline." <http://www.microsoft.com/MSCorp /Museum/timelines/microsoft/timeline.asp> (September 9, 1999).
Miller, Matthew. "Cookie Dough." *New Republic,* July 29, 1996, pp. 11–12.
Milliot, Jim. "Bezos, Milken, Rubin Address AAP Annual Meeting." *Publishers Weekly,* March 29, 1999, pp. 16–17.
Millman, Joel. "Zen and the Art of Fresh Produce." *Forbes,* February 15, 1993, p. 220.
Min, Janice, and Vicki Sheff-Cahan. "Wizard of Woz." *People Weekly,* February 14, 1994, pp. 61–62.
Mitchell, Russ. "Why AOL Really Clicks." *U.S. News and World Report,* December 7, 1998, p. 52.
Moeller, Michael, Steve Hamm, and Timothy J. Mullaney. "Remaking Microsoft: Why America's Most Successful Company Needed an Overhaul." *Business Week,* May 17, 1999, pp. 106–116.
Monaghan, Tom. *Pizza Tiger.* New York: Random House, 1986.
Mondavi, Robert, and Paul Chutkow. *Harvests of Joy: My Passion for Excellence; How the Good Life Became Great Business.* New York: Harcourt Brace, 1998.
Moore, Gordon E. "Intel: Memories and the Microprocessor." *Daedalus,* Spring 1996, pp. 55–80.
Moreau, D., and S. Buri. "Change Agents." *Changing Times,* November 1990, p. 112.
Morita, Akio. "Changing Trade Winds: A New Look on U.S.-Japan Trade Relations." *Executive Speeches,* June–July 1994, pp. 33–35.
———. *From a 500-Dollar Company to a Global Corporation.* Pittsburgh, PA: Carnegie Mellon University Press, 1985.
Morita, Akio, with Edwin M. Reingold and Mitsuko Shimomura. *Made in Japan: Akio Morita and Sony.* New York: E.P. Dutton, 1986.
Moscow, Alvin. *Building a Business: The Jim Walter Story.* Sarasota, FL: Pineapple Press, 1998.
Murdoch, Rupert. "Reinventing Socialism." *National Review,* September 1, 1997, pp. 38–40.
———. "Remarks on the News Corporation and the Median Industry." *Executive Speeches,* August-September 1996, p. 16.
Murphy, Cindy. "Karing, Kan-Do Kopy King." *Franchising World,* January–February 1995, pp. 48–52.
———. "A Surprise Package: Entrepreneur of the Year Anthony Desio, Founder and CEO Mail Boxes Etc." *Franchising World,* January–February 1997, pp. 25, 27.

Nee, Eric. "Larry Ellison." *Upside,* September 1994, pp. 16–33.

———. "Scott McNealy." *Upside,* May 1997, pp. 112–124.

"A New Electronic Messiah." *Economist,* August 5, 1995, p. 62.

Newsmakers 92. Detroit, MI: Gale Research Institute, 1993.

"No Cookie Monster, She." *Business News New Jersey,* May 12, 1997, p. 2.

Noack, David. "I Can't Believe It's Not the Times." *Editor and Publisher,* April 10, 1999, p. 27.

Nocera, Joseph. "Do You Believe? How Yahoo! Became a Blue Chip." *Fortune,* June 7, 1999, pp. 76–80, 84, 86, 88, 92.

Norman, James R. "A New Teledyne." *Forbes,* September 27, 1993, pp. 44–45.

Ohmae, Kenichi. "Guru of Gadgets: Akio Morita." *Time,* December 7, 1998, pp. 193–195.

"One-on-One with Scott McNealy." *VARBusiness,* February 1, 1999, p. 46.

Oppenheimer, Jerry. *Martha Stewart—Just Desserts: The Unauthorized Biography.* New York: William Morrow, 1997.

O'Reilly, Brian. "From Intel to Amazon: Gordon Moore's Incredible Journey." *Fortune,* April 26, 1999, pp. 166–190.

———. "What It Takes to Start a Startup." *Fortune,* June 7, 1999, pp. 135–136, 138, 140.

Ortega, Bob. *In Sam We Trust: The Untold Story of Sam Walton and How Wal-Mart Is Devouring America.* New York: Times Books, 1998.

Otsuki, Satoru. *Good Mileage: The High-Performance Business Philosophy of Soichiro Honda.* Japan: NHK Publishing, 1996.

"Outsmarting Smart Money Men," *New York,* April 22, 1985 p. 52.

Owen, Ted. "Habits Often a Double-Edged Sword." *San Diego Business Journal,* April 12, 1999, p. 42.

Packard, David. "Birth of a Giant: The Incredible Journey of Hewlett-Packard." *Success,* June 1995, pp. 44A–44H.

———. *The HP Way.* New York: HarperBusiness, 1995.

———. "Trust in People." *Research-Technology Management,* July-August 1996, pp. 10–11.

Painton, P. "The Taming of Ted Turner." *Time*, January 6, 1992. p. 22

Paquet, Laura Byrne. "Risking It All." *Home-Office Computing,* June 1995, pp. 54–58.

Paris, Ellen. "Rhinestone Hightops, Anyone?" *Forbes,* March 7, 1988, pp. 78–84.

Pender, Lee. "The Big Giveaway." *Computer Reseller News,* May 11, 1998, p. 103.

Pepin, Jacques. "Ray Kroc." *Time,* December 7, 1998, p. 176.

Perot, Ross. "Caring Leaders." *Executive Excellence,* April 1996, pp. 6–7.

———. "Change Is Fun." *Executive Excellence,* September 1996, pp. 10–11.

Phillips, Debra, G. David Doran, Elaine W. Teague, and Laura Tiffany. "Young Millionaires: Thirty Entrepreneurial Superstars under 40 Reveal How They Made It to the Million-Dollar Club." *Entrepreneur,* November 1998, pp. 118–126.

Picarille, Lisa. "Steve Jobs." *Computer Reseller News,* November 16, 1997, pp. 51–52.

———. "Steve Wozniak." *Computer Reseller News,* November 15, 1998, p. 53.

"Pick a Fast Horse." *Success,* September 1990, p. 12.

Pile, Robert B. *Top Entrepreneurs and Their Businesses.* Minneapolis, MN: Oliver Press, 1993.

"Pioneers." *Life,* Fall 1988, pp. 99–102.

"Pleasant Company: Company Profile." <http://www.americangirl.com/corporate /aboutpc.html> (October 11, 1999).

Pochna, Marie-France. *Christian Dior: The Man Who Made the World Look New.* Translated by Joanna Savill. New York: Arcade Publishers, 1996.

Pogrebin, Robin. "What Went Wrong with Mrs. Fields?" *Working Woman,* July 1993, p. 9.

Pollack, Andrew. "Akio Morita, Co-Founder of Sony and Japanese Business Leader, Dies at 78." *New York Times,* October 4, 1999.

Pollan, Stephen M., and Mark Levine. *The Field Guide to Starting a Business.* New York: Fireside, 1990.

Posner, Gerald. *Citizen Perot: His Life and Times.* New York: Random House, 1996.

Prendergast, Alan. "Learning to Let Go: Holding On Too Tight Almost Made the Cookie Crumble at Mrs. Fields." *Working Woman,* January 1992, pp. 42–45.

Prenon, Mary T. "The Earl of Enterprise." *Westchester County Business Journal,* November 20, 1995, p. 31.

Price, Courtney, and Kathleen Allen. *Tips and Traps for Entrepreneurs.* New York: McGraw-Hill, 1998.

"Professional Resources—Maverick: The Success Story behind the World's Most Unusual Workplace." *HR Focus,* October 1995, p. 21.

"Profile: Boston Beer Co." <http://biz.yahoo.com/p/s/sam/html> (October 11, 1999).

"P.T. Barnum." <http://www.ringling.com/history/barnum/> (October 21, 1999).

"P.T. Barnum: The Original Master of Hype." <http://www.yk.psu.edu/~jmj3 /sna_chu1.html> (October 21, 1999).

"Q&A with Jeff Bezos." *Catalog Age,* June 1996, pp. 59–60.

Quittner, Joshua, and Michelle Slatalla. *Speeding the Net: The Inside Story of Netscape and How It Challenged Microsoft.* New York: Atlantic Monthly Press, 1998.

"R. David Thomas." <http://www.sbe.nova.edu/alumni/bios/thomas.htm> (June 1, 1999).

Ramo, Joshua Cooper, with Daniel Eisenberg. "Man of the Year: A Survivor's Tale." *Time,* December 29, 1997, p. 54.

Reed, J.D., and Vicki Sheff. "The Patriarch." *People,* October 10, 1998, p. 151.

Reese, Jennifer. "PeopleSoft, Pleasanton, California." *Fortune,* July 10, 1995, p. 156.

Reid, Calvin. "Amazon.com's Jeff Bezos." *Publishers Weekly,* January 5, 1998, p. 12.

Reitman, Janet. "Computer Entrepreneur: Marc Andreessen." *Scholastic Update* (Teacher's Edition), May 11, 1998, p. 6.

"Repealing Moore's Law." *OEM Magazine,* December 1996, p. 82.

Ressner, Jeffrey. "Online Flea Markets." *Time,* October 5, 1998, p. 48.

"Rich Man, Poor Man." *Forbes* (ASAP Supplement), October 9, 1995, pp. 100–101.

Richman, Tom. "Mrs. Fields' Secret Ingredient." *Inc.*, October 1987, pp. 65–72.

Roddick, Anita. "Corporate Responsibility." *Executive Excellence,* September 1997, p. 9.

———. "Corporate Responsibility: Good Works Not Good Words." *Competitiveness Review,* 1996, pp. 1–7.

———. "Four-Letter Words!" *Executive Excellence,* February 1998, p. 19.

———. "Not Free Trade but Fair Trade." *Across the Board,* June 1994, p. 58.

———. "Resolving International Conflict: What Role for Business?" *Vital Speeches of the Day,* September 15, 1996, pp. 724–728.

Roddick, Anita, Lord Hanson, Robert Ayling, and Martin Sorrell. "Beat the Clock." *Director,* March 1997, p. 34.

Roddick, Anita and Irene Prokop. *Body and Soul: Profits with Principles—The Amazing Success Story of Anita Roddick and the Body Shop.* New York: Crown, 1991.

Rogers, Amy. "CRN Business Close-Up: An Interview with Marc Andreessen, AOL." *Computer Reseller News,* March 29, 1999, p. 208.

Rohm, Wendy Goldman. *The Microsoft File: The Secret Case against Bill Gates.* New York: Times Business Books, 1998.

Rosner, Hillary. "Lance Weatherby." *MC Technology Marketing Intelligence,* January 1999, pp. 28–29.

"Ross Perot's Crusade," *Business Week,* October 6, 1986, p. 60.

Rotenier, Nancy. "Fancy Footwork." *Forbes,* September 27, 1993, pp. 154–156.

Rouse, David. "Burger King: Jim McLamore and the Building of an Empire." *Booklist,* November 1, 1997, p. 441.

Roush, Chris. *Inside Home Depot: How One Company Revolutionized an Industry through the Relentless Pursuit of Growth.* New York: McGraw-Hill, 1999.

Salva-Ramirez, Mary-Angie. "McDonalds: A Prime Example of Corporate Culture." *Public Relations Quarterly,* Winter 1995/1996, pp. 30–32.

Schaaf, Dick. "Inside Hamburger University." *Training,* December 1994, pp. 18–24.

Schickel, Richard. *The Disney Version: The Life, Times, Art, and Commerce of Walt Disney.* New York: Touchstone, 1985.

Schlender, Brenton R. "How Sony Keeps the Magic Going." *Fortune,* February 24, 1992, pp. 76–84.

———. "Larry Ellison: Oracle at Web Speed." *Fortune,* May 24, 1999, pp. 128–136.

Schmerken, Ivy, and Karen Corcella. "Exclusive Interview with Scott McNealy." *Wall Street and Technology,* June 1994, pp. 10–16.

Schrader, Michael. "Stories of Success, Inspiration for the Entrepreneur." *Nation's Restaurant News,* February 2, 1998, p. 26.

Schuller, Robert, Ross Perot, et. al. "For Achievers Only." *Manager's Intelligence Report,* August 1995, p. 5.

Schultz, Howard, and Dori Jones Yang. *Pour Your Heart into It: How Starbucks Built a Company One Cup at a Time.* New York: Hyperion, 1997.

"Science and Technology Almanac 1999: 1998 Obituaries." <http://www.science-almanac.com/ibuka.html> (November 10, 1999).

Sellers, Patricia, and Andrew Erdman. "Companies That Serve You Best." *Fortune,* May 31, 1993, p. 74.

Semler, Ricardo. "Managing without Managers." *Harvard Business Review,* September–October 1989, pp. 76–84.

———. *Maverick: The Success Story behind the World's Most Unusual Workplace.* London: Century Press, 1993.

———. "Who Needs Bosses?" *Across the Board,* February 1994, pp. 23–25.

———. "Why My Former Employees Still Work for Me." *Harvard Business Review,* January–February 1994, pp. 64–74.

Seremet, Patricia. "The Queen of the Catalog: Lillian Vernon, Entrepreneur." *Marketing News,* June 8, 1998, p. 17.

Shawcross, William. *Murdoch: The Making of a Media Empire.* New York: Touchstone Books, 1997.

Sheff, David. "The Interview: Richard Branson." *Forbes,* February 24, 1997, pp. 94–102.

Shefsky, Lloyd E. *Entrepreneurs Are Made Not Born.* New York: McGraw-Hill, 1994.

Sheridan, John H. "Tale of a 'Maverick.'" *Industry Week,* June 8, 1998, pp. 22–28.

Shook, Carrie. "Subway Owners, Beware: CEO May Be Coming." *Baltimore Business Journal,* May 26, 1995, p. 35.

Shook, Robert L. *The Entrepreneurs: Twelve Who Took Risks and Succeeded.* New York: Harper & Row, 1980.

Silver, A. David. *Entrepreneurial Megabucks: The 100 Greatest Entrepreneurs of the Last 25 Years.* New York: John Wiley & Sons, 1985.

Simpson, Roderick. "Redmond's Front Page." <http://www.wired.com/wired/4.04/eword_pr.html> (March 18, 1999).

Sischy, Ingrid. *Donna Karan: New York.* New York: Universe Publishers, 1998.

"Sketchers U.S.A., Inc." *Industry Standard.* <http://thestandard.net/companies/company_display/0%2C1591%2C57738%2C00.html> (September 21, 1999).

Slovan, Margie. "Bound for the Internet." *Nation's Business,* March 1997, pp. 34–35.

Smith, Maura. "Crash Landing." *Forbes,* May 18, 1998, pp. 16–17.

Smith, Scott S. "Dell On. . . . " *Entrepreneur Online.* <http://zeus.flashpoint.com/page.hts?N=7704&Ad=S> (April 25, 1999).

Sobel, Robert, and David B. Sicilia. *The Entrepreneurs: An American Adventure.* Boston: Houghton Mifflin, 1986.

"Soichiro Honda." *U.S. News and World Report,* August 19, 1991, p. 16.

"Sony Chairman Says Burden Is on Tokyo to Improve." *Japan Times Weekly International Edition,* February 1–7, 1993, p. 7.

Southwick, Karen. "An Interview: Jeff Bezos, Amazon.com." *Upside,* October 1996, pp. 29–34.

"Spic and Span Follows a Clean Philosophy." *Milwaukee Journal-Sentinel*, August 3, 1997.

Sprout, Alison L., and Kimberly Beals McDonald. "The Rise of Netscape." *Fortune,* July 10, 1995, p. 140.

Stapinski, Helene. "Entrepreneurs with Clout." *Success,* June 1997, p. 41.

"Staples, Inc." *Boston Business Journal,* October 13, 1995, p. 16.

Stedman, Craig. "Computer Industry: David Packard 1912–1996." *Computerworld,* April 1, 1996, p. 32.

Stein, Tom. "Masters of the Web." *Success,* December 1996, pp. 31–35.

Stemberg, Thomas. *Staples for Success.* Santa Monica, CA: Knowledge Exchange, 1996.

"Steve Case." *Washington Business Journal,* November 6, 1998, p. 16.

"Steven M. Pollan." <http://geocities.com/Hollywood/7000/stephen.htm> (November 30, 1999).

Stevens, Tim. "Father of the American Minimill." *Industry Week,* November 20, 1995, pp. 25–26.

———. "Service with Soul." *Industry Week,* February 5, 1996, pp. 29–30.

Stodghill, Ron, II. "A Tale of Pizza, Pride, and Piety." *Time,* October 26, 1998, p. 66.

Stross, Randall E. *The Microsoft Way: The Real Story of How the Company Outsmarts Its Competition.* Reading, MA: Addison-Wesley, 1996.

———. "Millionaire High." *U.S. News and World Report,* April 21, 1997, p. 62.

Suarez, Ruth. *Superstar Entrepreneurs of Small and Large Businesses Reveal Their Secrets.* Piscataway, NJ: Research and Education Association, 1998.

Sullivan, Michael, and Lorri Grube. "Michael Dell." *Chief Executive,* June 1993, p. 20.

Surowiecki, James. "Steven Jobs' Imperial Ambition." *Across the Board,* February 1998, pp. 40–41.

Swisher, Kara. *AOL.com: How Steve Case Beat Bill Gates, Nailed the Netheads, and Made Millions in the War for the Web.* New York: Times Books, 1998.

Taft, Darryl. "Larry Ellison." *Computer Reseller News,* November 14, 1994, p. 127.

Taninecz, George. "Kazuo Inamori: 'Respect the Divine and Love People.' " *Industry Week,* June 5, 1995, pp. 47–51.

Taylor, Alex, III. "Kings of the Road." *Fortune,* June 7, 1999, pp. 150–154.

Taylor, Alex, III, and Shaifali Puri. "The Man Who Put Honda Back on Track." *Fortune,* September 9, 1996, p. 92.

Taylor, Russell R. *Exceptional Entrepreneurial Women.* New York: Praeger Publishers, 1988.

Tetzeli, Rick. "What It's Really Like to Be Marc Andreessen." *Fortune,* December 9, 1996, pp. 136–156.

"Think Globally, Bake Locally." *Fortune,* October 14, 1996, p. 205.

Thomas, Bob. *Building a Company: Roy O. Disney and the Creation of an Entertainment Empire.* New York: Hyperion, 1998.

Thomas, R. David. *Dave's Way*. New York: Berkeley Books, 1992.

———. "My Biggest Mistake." *Inc.*, September 1998, p. 129.

———. "Treat People Right." *Executive Excellence*, February 1996, p. 91.

———. "What Makes for Success? ACHIEVING Excellence." *Speeches of the Day*, September 15, 1996, pp. 720–724.

Thurm, Scott. "How an Entrepreneur Sparked 11—Yes, 11—High-Tech Start-Ups." *Wall Street Journal*, June 3, 1999, pp. A1, A10.

Tiazkun, Scott. "Larry Ellison." *Computer Reseller News*, November 16, 1998, p. 155.

Toll, Erich E. "Hands Off." *World Trade*, May 1995, pp. 66–70.

Trachtenberg, Jeffrey A. *Ralph Lauren: The Man behind the Mystique*. Boston: Little, Brown, 1988.

"Tribute to Wilson Harrell." <http://www.ltbn.com/Articles/Harrelltrib.html> (October 21, 1999).

Trillin, Calvin. "American Chronicles: Competitors." *New Yorker*, July 8, 1985, pp. 31–45.

Trimble, Vance H. *Overnight Success: Federal Express and Fredrick Smith, Its Renegade Creator*. New York: Crown, 1993.

Tucker, Robert B. "Federal Express's Fred Smith." *Inc.*, October 1986, pp. 34–50.

Tweney, Dylan. "Who Should Be Named Netpreneur of the Year?" *InfoWorld*, December 14, 1998, p. 54.

Upbin, Bruce. "Have Fun, Kill the Enemy." *Forbes*, January 27, 1997, p. 68.

Useem, Jerry. "The New Buzzword in Disk Drives: Cheap." *Fortune*, May 10, 1999, p. 140.

"User-Friendly Wins the Race." *Business Week*, November 2, 1998, p. 114.

Van Andel, Jay. "Enduring Legacy." *Saturday Evening Post*, January 1999, pp. 46–51.

———. *An Enterprising Life: An Autobiography*. New York: HarperBusiness, 1998.

———. "The Home Team." *Saturday Evening Post*, November 1998, pp. 54–57.

———. "The Trials of Being Very Rich." *Across the Board*, November-December 1998, p. 10.

Verespej, Michael A. "Flying His Own Course." *Industry Week*, November 20, 1995, pp. 22–24.

Vernon, Lillian. "Entrepreneurs and Professional Managers." *Management Review*, February 1999, p. 13.

———. "An Eye for Winners." *Success*, November 1996, pp. 45–52.

———. *An Eye for Winners: How I Built One of America's Greatest Direct-Mail Businesses*. New York: HarperCollins, 1996.

———. "How I Created One of America's Greatest Direct Mail Businesses." *Direct Marketing*, October 1996, p. 24.

Vitale, Joe. *There's a Customer Born Every Minute: P.T. Barnum's Secrets to Business Success*. New York: AMACON, 1998.

Vizard, Michael, and Katherine Bull. "Oracle's Mission." *InfoWorld,* September 14, 1998, pp. 1, 22.

Vizard, Michael, and Katherine Bull. "Piloting PeopleSoft." *InfoWorld,* August 24, 1998, pp. 1, 57.

Wallace, James. *Overdrive: Bill Gates and the Race to Control Cyberspace.* New York: John Wiley & Sons, 1997.

Walton, Sam, and John Huey. *Sam Walton: Made in America–My Story.* New York: Bantam Books, 1993.

Wang, An, with Eugene Linder. *Lessons: An Autobiography.* Reading, MA: Addison-Wesley, 1986.

"We Weren't Just Airborne Yesterday." <http://www.southwest.com/about_swa /airborne.html> (November 10, 1999).

Weil, Nancy. "Netscape's Andreessen Sees Freewaring Coming of Age." *InfoWorld,* May 4, 1998, p. 68.

Weiner, Adam J. "Internet Innovators Searching for 'Morethandollars.com.' " *Boston Business Journal,* February 26, 1999, p. 43.

Weisman, K. "Succeeding by Failing," *Forbes,* June 25, 1990, p. 160.

Welles, Edward O. "Captain Marvel." *Inc.,* January 1992, pp. 44–47.

Wetherbe, James C. *The World on Time: The 11 Management Principles That Made FedEx an Overnight Sensation.* Santa Monica, CA: Knowledge Exchange, 1996.

Wheeler, David, Maria Sillanpaa, and Anita Roddick. *The Stakeholder Corporation: The Body Shop: Blueprint for Maximizing Stakeholder Value.* London: Pitman Publishing, 1997.

"Who's Who: A Look at the Backgrounds of the Most Influential Executives in the PC Industry." *Computer Reseller News,* November 13, 1995, p. 171.

Who's Who in America, 1998, Chicago: A. N. Marquis, 1997.

Who's Who in America, 1999, Chicago: A. N. Marquis, 1998.

Wiesendanger, Betsy. "Labors of Love." *Working Woman,* May 1999, pp. 43–44, 47–48, 50, 52, 54, 56, 59.

Wilcox, Joe. "Scott McNealy." *Computer Reseller News,* November 16, 1998, p. 149.

Willett, Shawn. "Database Dynamo: Larry Ellison." *Computer Reseller News,* November 15, 1998, pp. 35–36.

———. "Larry Ellison." *Computer Reseller News,* November 17, 1997, p. 131.

Williams, Christian. *Lead, Follow, or Get out of the Way.* New York: Times Books, 1981.

Williams, Tish. "Larry Ellison and the No-Good, Very Bad Day." *Upside,* September 1997, pp. 36–37.

Williford, Steve. "Speaking from Experience, Author Welcomes First-Time Entrepreneurs to Club of Terror." *Memphis Business Journal,* September 11, 1995, p. 47.

Willigan, Gerandine. "High-Performance Marketing: An Interview with Nike's Phil Knight." *Harvard Business Review,* July 1992, pp. 90–101.

Wilson, Steve. "Busy Year for Black Enterprise." *Folio,* October 1, 1995, p. 22.

Wingfield, Nick. "Web Opens IS." *InfoWorld,* October 23, 1995, pp. 57–59.

"The Wit and Wisdom of Ted Turner." *Across the Board,* July–August 1997, pp. 13–14.

Wolfe, Tom. "Robert Noyce and His Congregation." *Forbes* (ASAP Supplement), August 25, 1997, pp. 102–106.

Wolff, Carlo. "Creativity Is His Theme Song." *Lodging Hospitality,* October 1998, pp. 27–28.

Wood, Nora. "Still Crazy after All These Years." *Incentive,* February 1997, p. 30.

Yamada, Ken. "Andrew Grove." *Computer Reseller News,* November 18, 1996, p. 142.

Yang, Catherine, Heather Green, and Andy Reinhardt. "AOL Has to Do Something Quickly." *Business Week,* May 17, 1999, p. 38.

Yochum, David. "Six Tips from a Lady Who Started Empire in Kitchen, in Spare Time." *Washington Business Journal,* November 22, 1996, p. 50.

Yosi, Umberto. "Best of Breed: Yahoo!'s Tim Koogle." *Forbes* (ASAP Supplement), October 7, 1996, p. 80.

Yu, Albert. *Creating the Digital Future: The Secrets of Consistent Innovation at Intel.* New York: Free Press, 1998.

Zuckerman, E. "William Gates III" *People,* August 20, 1990, p. 91.

Index